Trading Classic Chart Patterns

WILEY TRADING

Trading Classic Chart Patterns

Thomas N. Bulkowski

John Wiley & Sons, Inc.

For general information on our other products and services, or technical support, please contact our Customer Care Department within the United States at 800-762-2974, outside the United States at 317-572-3993 or fax 317-572-4002.

Wiley also publishes its books in a variety of electronic formats. Some content that appears in print may not be available in electronic books.

Library of Congress Cataloging-in-Publication Data:

Bulkowski, Thomas N., 1957–
    Trading classic chart patterns / Thomas N. Bulkowski.
        p.   cm.— (Wiley trading)
    Includes index.
    ISBN 0-471-43575-9
    1. Stocks. 2. Stocks—Mathematical models. 3. Stock price indexes—Mathematical models. I. Title. II. Series.
    HG4661.B85   2002
    332.63'222—dc21   2001006299

10 9 8 7 6 5 4 3 2 1

*History measures the wealth of one's existence by the essence
of what remains, so I want it to have mattered that I lived.
Therefore, I dedicate this book to the Bulkowski brothers:
Dave, Rich, Tom, and Jim. Four explorers charting
different paths through unknown territory.*

Wish us luck.

*And to the innocent bystanders, the firemen, the policemen who died in the
terrorist attacks of September 11, 2001. You gave
your lives so that others may live. May I be fortunate enough
to have my life end with such style, such heroism.*

Preface

I am under attack. Every time I call engineering, they promise the same thing: "The shields will be up soon, Captain," yet the port side continues taking hits.

When I wrote *Encyclopedia of Chart Patterns* (Wiley, 2000), I knew the reference—with its chart pattern performance statistics—could change the shape of the financial world, but I did not know how upset those still believing the earth was flat would be. I fear this book is pushing deeper into enemy territory. You see, this book also uses performance statistics to illustrate my claims, but it goes further.

Have you ever wondered how much influence the general market has on performance? How about market capitalization? Should you really get excited when a gap occurs during the breakout? How important is high breakout volume anyway? This book details the answers to those questions and many more, but—and this is important—it presents an easy-to-use system that separates the chart pattern mongrels from the purebreds, the slackers from the overachievers. It gives you the knowledge to trade chart patterns, *and stocks*, successfully.

For the most popular and common chart patterns, review the chapter tables for a score, then total the scores. Scores above zero mean performance is likely to beat the median; scores below zero mean you should probably look elsewhere. Do not consider the scoring system as a robust, mechanical trading system, but more as an investment checklist. The method is not foolproof to be sure, but I am very pleased with out-of-sample tests and actual trades I have made using the system. I detail several in this book.

Now that my little ship has encountered customer reviews, news groups, chat rooms, and other violent anomalies, I am hoping the shield modifications this time around will do better. To those who quibble with the statistics, I ask that you show me a better way, as David Ipperciel did when he told me about his horizon failure rate. To those who say the writing is too wordy, I say that I write for the novice investor—explaining concepts thoroughly—but also present challengingly new ideas for the professional. To those who scoff at chart patterns themselves, I suggest they continue searching until they find a trading style that works for them. It may include fundamental analysis, it may include technical indicators, or it may use chart patterns, but if it works, keep it and keep using it.

Chart patterns work for me. I began trading stocks more than 20 years ago, and now that is all I do—that is, except for the odd book, magazine article, puttering in the garden, playing my guitar, bird watching, and, well, you get the idea.

If you are new to chart patterns, technical analysis, or to stock market investing itself, have no fear. The first part of this book presents new research on trendlines, support and resistance, placing stops, selling considerations, and common trading mistakes. Part Two is where you find the warp engines that propel the book deeper into uncharted territory. I discuss the most common and popular chart patterns, provide the scoring system details for each pattern, and showcase the results. Consider Part Two as a reference section: alphabetically arranged chapters with plenty of easy-to-understand and easy-to-use tables with lots of pictures!

Think of this book not as advocating a trading system, but as a system to *select* better performing chart patterns. Do additional research as necessary, because how you trade your selections is up to you.

Thomas N. Bulkowski
February 2002

Acknowledgments

I wish to thank David Ipperciel for giving me lessons on his *horizon failure rate*. I use it throughout the book. Thanks, David.

Thanks also to Bernice Pettinato of Beehive Production Services. If you ever write a book, her company is the best at shepherding it through production. Added bonus: She returns your manuscript bound with really long rubber bands. Think of the terror you can inflict!

Last, but just as important, are the editors responsible for this book, Pamela van Giessen and Claudio Campuzano. They have to put up with endless questions breeding numerous complaints from cranky writers. Fortunately, I was not one of them!

T.N.B.

Contents

Trading Classic
Chart Patterns

Introduction

A ringing phone; the first indication that something was wrong. Very wrong. Especially when the person on the other end was Mary. "I own Cisco Systems," she gloated, and instantly I knew I was in trouble. I also owned the stock, and I knew that whatever Mary bought went down as sure as the sun sets in the west.

Mary is new to the world of stock market investing. She believes in fundamental analysis, but does not have the time or inclination to do it properly. Technical analysis? Forget it. If she looks at a stock chart at all, it only shows closing prices—like watching television using only a quarter of the screen.

To her, the small stake in a self-directed IRA—where she trades—is play money as her other, professionally managed retirement accounts hold the bulk of her savings. Make no mistake; she is a very talented, well-respected, senior vice president making big bucks at a growing company. She is not an early adopter—one who buys the latest cell phone because it is smaller than the dozens she already owns—but one who is willing to pay up for the good life: the in-ground swimming pool, the vacation time-share, dance and piano lessons for the kids, the BMW, the SUV, the frequent vacations to exotic locales. In other words, she lives well.

I am jealous.

THE NOVICE EXPERIENCE

Enough about Mary. Let us turn to the trade she made in Cisco Systems, shown in Figure I.1. When she called, I asked her why she bought 85 shares of the stock at 65. Her answer was as you would expect from a believer of fundamental analysis. She said Cisco was a good company with good earnings and market momentum.

1

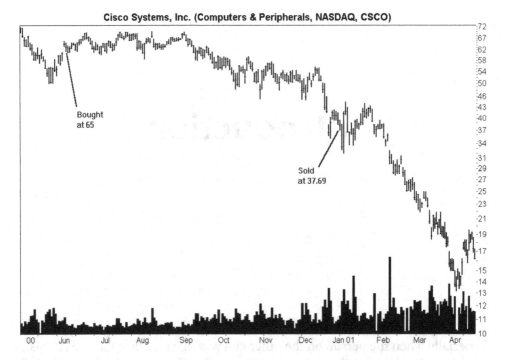

Cisco Systems, Inc. (Computers & Peripherals, NASDAQ, CSCO)

Figure I.1   Mary made a bullish bet on this trade, but failed to cut her losses. How could technical analysis have helped?

For about 2 weeks, it looked as if she was right. Prices climbed from 65 to a high of 69.56, then bounced between 58 and 70 until September. After that, prices started sliding, slowly at first, but the new trend was clearly down. As Cisco dropped, it followed the Standard & Poor's 500 Index lower, almost in lockstep. Like a drain, the declining market acted as a siphon sucking Cisco lower. The Nasdaq Composite meanwhile, formed a double top—peaks in July and September—with prices confirming the chart pattern in early October. A bearish signal; it was time to pull the trigger.

Mary knew none of this; all she cared about was the falling stock price. Why not sell? Good question. Listening to Mary discuss her trades, you can imagine the mental trading blocks building like ants reconstructing a mound after a rain storm. Phrases such as, "As soon as I sell, prices will rise," and "It has been dropping for so long that it must be near bottom," and "As soon as I break even, I will sell," and, my personal favorite, "I have decided to hold it for the long term," became part of the lexicon, the justification for holding onto a losing position.

On December 29, Mary sold the stock. Her reason? "I was sick of taking losses." She received a fill at 37.69, for a tidy 42% loss. The good news, if you can call it that, is that she got out when she did. She could have ridden the stock to its low of 13.19, a massive 80% decline. Still, a 42% loss is not what most would call "cutting your losses short."

A BETTER WAY

What about my trade? Those who know me understand that I like chart patterns and trade them often. For me, they make it easy to time the market—something the experts claim is impossible to do profitably for any length of time. You should get used to it, though, because every time you trade, you *are* timing the market whether you want to admit it or not.

During bear markets, bullish chart patterns are like budding flowers in winter: a rare sight. As soon as the market turns, it is as if spring arrives and the head-and-shoulders bottoms, the double bottoms, and other bullish patterns sprout forth and start blooming. The trick is that some of the patterns are weeds and some are orchids; distinguishing them is the subject of this book. I get to that later.

In the meantime, let us return to the Cisco situation. Figure I.2 shows what I saw when I looked at the same chart Mary did (but the time scale is shifted somewhat—the June to December periods overlap). The precise name for this chart pattern is a broadening formation, right-angled and descending. It sports a flat top, a down-sloping trend along the minor lows, and a volume pattern that can best be described as irregular. This pattern is as rare as finding water in a desert.

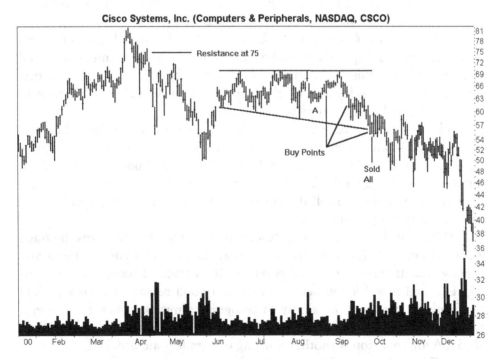

Figure I.2   A right-angled, descending, broadening formation with a partial decline (point A). Prices failed to break out upward, as predicted, dooming the trade.

A computerized notebook chronicles my trading experience, so I can watch for bad habits forming and learn from past mistakes. Here is what I wrote for the first purchase: "8/23/00. I bought 300 shares at the market and received a fill at 65.97. I expect the last hour rush to push this up even more [I was right. The stock closed at 67.19, which was 6 cents below the daily high]. Why buy? Partial decline in a broadening formation, right-angled and descending. The stock will pause briefly at 70 then zoom up to 75 and on to 80. I expect help from the Nasdaq Composite that broke out downward from an ascending broadening wedge, pulled back, and should continue higher. Downside is 61.88, where I must sell."

The key is the mention of a partial decline, and it appears at point A in Figure I.2. Prices touch the top trendline then head lower—but do not touch the lower trendline—curl around, and, usually stage an immediate, upward breakout. If things worked out as expected, the stock would have climbed to the resistance area at 75, burned its way through, then paused near the old high of 82. My guess is that it would stop at the round number 80, a common resistance point, then retrace some of its gains, curve around, and form a second top (for a double-top pattern). The trick would be to sell near the top.

None of that happened. After tagging the top trendline, prices moved lower in a stair-step decline.

Here is the next notebook entry: "Saturday 9/9/00. Trend channels suggest the stock should drop to about 62 (from the current 64) then rise. Prices touch an up trendline drawn from the June 30 low to the present, ignoring the two down spikes on August 2–3, suggesting a rebound Monday. Stop is still 61.88. The Nasdaq Composite looks as if it double topped, pierced an up trendline, and now appears to be heading down. With September here and October to follow, this might not be a good time to buy. For this stock, the best days to buy are Tuesday and Wednesday [based on linking price changes to days of the week], so I'm going to delay buying."

The general market was now declining—never a good sign when you own a stock. As with many trades, the technical evidence was mixed, but there were warning signs of trouble ahead. Instead: "9/11/00. I bought 200 at 61.25, shooting from the hip. I think that the stock will stop here, and it is a good buy-in price. Tomorrow will tell if I am right. Downside is 56–57, upside is 70, pause at 75 then upward to 80."

Whenever I write the words "shooting from the hip," it means the trade is about to go bad. These are the trades that *feel good, feel right*, but never are. Having recently reviewed my 20 years' worth of trades, I recognize this trading flaw, and now I know better (which is a good reason to keep a trading notebook: It gives you the ability to recognize a mistake when you make it again!). Notice how the stop-loss price magically changed from 61.88 to 56–57. A lowered stop is another warning of a trade gone bad.

"9/26/00. I bought 300 at the market open and received a fill at 58.16. Indicators were almost uniformly negative. Outside day [a chart pattern] with the close near the lower end implies a lower low today. Right-angled broadening formation meant that I couldn't tell the breakout direction. Measured move down chart pattern from 69.63 to 58 then 63.63 to . . . 52. But did I listen? No. I bought anyway and the stock moved below the formation with bid/ask of 54.75–54.88, well below the stop price of 56."

Averaging down in a falling market is never a good idea, but it is a common mistake for novice investors and turkeys like me—ones who know better. After I bought, the stock closed outside the chart pattern, signaling a downward breakout. Even though I made a host of mistakes in this trade, at least I got one thing right: "9/27/00. I sold all 800 shares this morning as the stock had breached the lower trendline boundary of a descending right-angled broadening formation. Lessons on this trade: If an upside breakout from a partial decline does not appear immediately, sell. Do not buy more as the stock moves to the other side of the formation. I received a fill at 56.13, about a point higher than yesterday's close."

THE CHART PATTERN SCORING SYSTEM

Mary lost 42% and I lost 9%. Which investor would you rather be? The answer is, of course, neither.

In this book I describe a chart pattern scoring system—not a trading system—one that helps you pick better performing chart patterns to trade. How you trade the chart pattern is up to you. Use technical indicators, use fundamental analysis, use whatever method floats your boat. Just keep an eye out for the shoals.

How does the system work? Imagine that you are a farmer growing cucumbers. One day you discover that dark green plants yield the most cukes, so you keep the seeds from those plants. The next year, you plant again and find that production doubles. More research tells you how much fertilizer to use and how often to water, and that prickly cukes make good dills but lousy slicers. Through research you find the traits that make your farm more productive, more successful, magically growing cucumbers into watermelon-sized treats.

That analogy is what the scoring system does for chart patterns. I looked at the most popular and common chart patterns and found the traits that make them tick. Take double bottoms. There are four distinct varieties and each performs differently, but they all share common traits. Begin with the trend start. Where does the price trend leading to the chart pattern begin? I show you how to find the answer to that question. From the trend start, measure the time to the chart pattern then score your results with those shown in the appropriate table. Quickly run through other tables in the chapter and total the scores. Scores above zero mean the chart pattern is likely to beat the median. Scores below zero mean you are probably looking at a weed, a dog, a nonperformer.

I use this method in my stock trading and it works. Make no mistake, you are dealing with probabilities here, so even a chart pattern with the highest positive score can turn out to be a loser. Toss in some trading mistakes and anyone can turn a 50% gain into a losing situation by holding too long. That possibility is why the first part of this book covers the basics: trendlines, support and resistance, beta-adjusted trailing stops (and other stops), and common trading mistakes. Then follows the good stuff: A reference section on the most popular and commonly occurring chart patterns with a scoring system that helps separate promising chart patterns from the also-rans—all backed up by statistical research in easy-to-understand and easy-to-use tables.

So, if you invest in stocks, you can benefit from this book. Even if you do not believe in chart patterns, that will not make them go away, that will not cause them to stop working. There are many sharpshooters out there taking positions opposite your trade. Sometimes having an edge is all you need to keep from being hit. This book gives you that edge.

PART ONE
Getting Started

If you are an investor new to technical analysis, the following pages discuss critically important topics, ones you need to understand before spending any money trading securities. Become familiar with trendlines, stop-loss orders, and common trading mistakes and learn how to identify support and resistance levels before you trade.

For the experienced trader, statistics and ideas are presented that will be new to you. Incorporate them into your trading style as you see fit.

1

Down Trendlines

"If I've told you once, I've told you a thousand times. Don't exaggerate!" Is that an old saying I just made up? No, but it makes a good point. Much has been written about trendlines, all spreading the same gossip but no proof. This chapter examines common trendline traits and provides performance proof.

There are two types of trendlines that investors really care about: those that trend upward and those that trend downward (the last being horizontal, a sign of a trading range). This chapter considers down trendlines. Before discussing trendlines, I must first discuss the tools I use to construct a trendline.

TOOLS: ARITHMETIC AND LOGARITHMIC SCALES

Figures 1.1 and 1.2 show the same data series plotted over the same price and time limits with a down trendline drawn along the same end points. Why does the first trendline appear straight and the second curved? At first you might think of easing up on your medication, but your eyes are not deceiving you. Look at the scale on the right side of the figures. Figure 1.1 uses a logarithmic scale, whereas Figure 1.2 uses an arithmetic scale. The log scale plots points on a percentage basis. A 10-point move from 10 to 20 is a 100% gain, but a 10-point rise from 20 to 30 is a 50% gain. On a log scale, the rise from 10 to 20 appears larger than the rise from 20 to 30. On the arithmetic scale, the distance between 10, 20, and 30 remains the same.

What this means is that a straight line drawn on a log scale appears curved on an arithmetic scale. The reverse is also true: A straight line drawn on an arithmetic scale appears curved on a log scale.

Which scale should you use? Many serious investors use the log scale, and I include myself in this group. When you view an Internet stock in which the

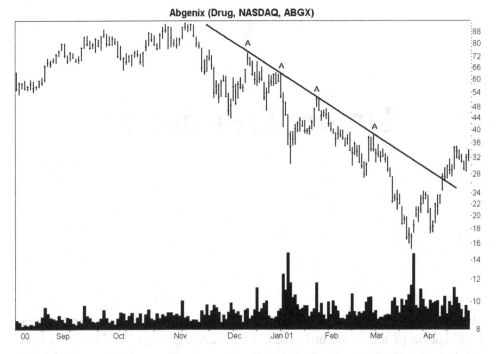

Figure 1.1 A down trendline on a semilogarithmic chart. The line is straight. Points labeled A show a few, but not all, of the minor highs.

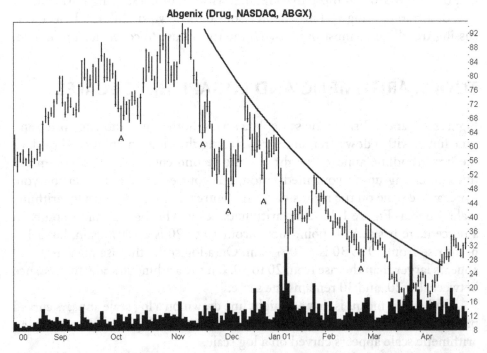

Figure 1.2 The same line on an arithmetic scale. The line is now curved. The label A shows some of the many minor lows.

price has zoomed from 2 to 200, or more recently from 200 to 2, any chart patterns in the low ranges on the arithmetic scale appear squished—flat lines—as if the stock has lost its pulse. On the log scale, the chart patterns are clearly visible, which is the major reason I switched from arithmetic to semilog charts (semilog means one axis uses the log scale, the other uses arithmetic).

MINOR HIGHS AND MINOR LOWS

Figure 1.1 also shows a few minor highs marked with the label A. A minor high is a small price peak where prices decline on either side of the peak for several days or even weeks. Minor highs are small turning points in the price trend. You can think of a minor high as the top of a foothill in a mountain range. When I mention finding the lowest minor high, think of standing in a valley looking for the top of the closest hill.

Figure 1.2 shows what minor lows look like. A minor low is just like a minor high only upside down. Prices decline, reach bottom, then climb, leaving a trough or depression on the price chart. Minor lows are also small turning points in the price trend. Think of minor lows as the small valleys between mountains. When I tell you to find the highest minor low, think of standing on the tallest peak looking for the closest valley.

THE TYPICAL PATTERN

Consider Figure 1.1 as a typical down trendline. I generally begin drawing a trendline from the highest high on the chart to the point of interest, making sure that the line skirts, but does not pierce, as many minor highs as possible. In this chapter I used only those trendlines with at least three touches (minor highs).

You can use any time scale you wish and either arithmetic or log scales. I often switch to the weekly scale and draw a long-term trendline along the peaks, looking to see where rising prices may intersect the trendline.

The trendline pictured in Figure 1.1 shows four touches, all minor highs, with prices staging a breakout in April when prices close above the trendline. Notice that I did not include the highest high in the figure. Some will complain about that, but I think the trendline looks fine. Later I discuss the 1–2–3 trend change method that relies on the highest high as the starting point.

INTERNAL TRENDLINES AND TAILS

Figure 1.3 shows an internal trendline. An internal trendline connects the price clusters—the flat tops of the consolidation regions—not the highest price in the minor highs. Look at point A. The trendline nears or touches the tops of

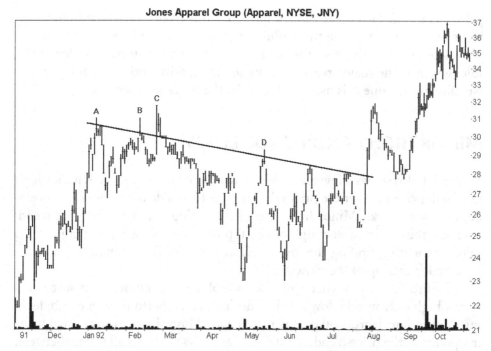

Figure 1.3   Internal trendline and tails A, B, C, and D. This trendline connects the congestion areas, not the minor highs, to show the trend.

prices surrounding the point, while the point itself is the highest high in the minor high.

Why use internal trendlines? Some chartists argue that internal trendlines better represent the trading behavior of the masses. The tails—those 1-day price spikes that look like one-day reversals; points A, B, C, and D in the figure—represent turning points and short-term trading opportunities. Most of the price action takes place at the congestion area, not at the top of the tail.

Sometimes it is necessary to draw internal trendlines because the minor highs do not quite line up. The trendline may pierce the price spikes but skirt the remainder of the tops. When necessary, that is how I draw my trendlines. I usually avoid drawing internal trendlines, but that is just a personal preference. I did not include internal trendlines for the statistics in this chapter.

POINTS AND TOUCHES

If you read the available literature about point spacing and trendline touches, the authors say that point spacing is important and the more touches a trendline has the more *significant* it becomes. I have no idea what that means. Does *significant* mean that a breakout from a trendline with three touches declines less than a five-touch trendline? The authors do not say.

Before I review the statistics, let me say that there is no right or wrong point spacing or touch count. You may find a high number of touches in a short trendline but a small number in a long trendline. The touches may be clustered in the first 3 months, then another touch will occur 6 months later with a breakout soon following. With point spacing and touch count, there are no set rules, so practice drawing trendlines and use the examples in this chapter for guidance.

Table 1.1 shows the results when I evaluated trendlines for point spacing and trendline touches. I went through 82 stocks and drew 210 trendlines sloping downward (I wanted to have at least 200 to work with, but any more than that and carpal tunnel syndrome would be a real possibility).

First, point spacing: Do trendline touches spaced close together work better than those spaced farther apart? No. Wide spacing works better. To answer the question, I found the average spacing from the first trendline touch to the last and looked at the resulting price performance after the breakout. I separated narrow spacing from wide spacing by using the median value. That is, I sorted the database and chose the midrange value, 29 days, such that half the samples were below the median and half were above it.

For those trendlines with point spacing less than 29 days, prices showed gains averaging 36%. When the point spacing was more than 29 days, the gains averaged 41%. That difference is substantial. Let me give you an example. Figure 1.1 shows a trendline with four minor high touch points and a trendline length of 79 days, measured from the first touch, 12/11/2000, to the last, 2/28/2001. I did not use the entire trendline length (that is, I did not include the breakout point), just the length from the first touch to the last minor high touch. Thus, the trendline has an average point spacing of 79/4 or 20 days.

Table 1.1
Performance Sorted by Trendline Spacing and Touches

Trendline Description	Result	Score
Narrow spacing (less than 29 days)	36% (105)	−1
Wide spacing (more than 29 days)	41% (105)	+1
Three touches	33% (85)	
Four touches	38% (63)	
Five touches	57% (40)	
Six touches	23% (10)	
Seven touches	42% (10)	
Eight touches	42% (2)	
Four touches or less	35% (148)	−1
More than four touches	48% (62)	+1

Note: The number of samples appears in parentheses.

Are trendlines with a gazillion touches more significant than those with just three? Yes. I evaluated the price performance after an upward breakout, sorted by the number of touches, and the results appear in Table 1.1. For example, there were 85 trendlines with exactly three minor high touches. The average gain from those trendlines was 33%. For the 40 stocks with five touches, the gains averaged 57%. Trendlines with six or more touches had sample sizes too small to be worth considering (below 30), so do not be alarmed with the paltry 23% gain.

Finally, the average number of touches was just over four, so I separated the trendlines into those having more than four touches and those equal to four or less. Again, the more touches there are, the better the performance after the breakout. Those trendlines with four or fewer touches showed gains averaging 35%; trendlines with more than four touches showed gains of 48%.

Before I discuss trendline length, let me mention scores. Many of the tables in this chapter list score values associated with trendline behavior. For now, ignore them. I discuss trendline scoring later in this chapter.

TRENDLINE LENGTH

Have you heard the saying, "The longer the trendline, the more significant it is"? It turns out to be true. I sorted the trendline length, measured from the first point to the breakout, then chose the median value as the separator between short and long. For the down-sloping trendlines I looked at, the median was 139 days, very close to the 137 days I found for *up* trendlines.

As shown in Table 1.2, those trendlines shorter than 139 days had gains, after the breakout, averaging 33%; this compares to a 43% gain for trendlines longer than 139 days. Not only is that result a significant difference, it is also statistically significant, meaning that it is not likely due to chance.

Separating the trendline lengths into more common categories—short term (up to 3 months), intermediate term (3 to 6 months), and long term (over 6

Table 1.2
Performance Sorted by Trendline Length

Trendline Description	Result	Score
Short trendlines (less than 139 days)	33% (104)	−1
Long trendlines (more than 139 days)	43% (104)	+1
Short-term trendlines (0 to 3 months)	34% (56)	
Intermediate-term trendlines (3 to 6 months)	35% (82)	
Long-term trendlines (more than 6 months)	46% (72)	
Really long trendlines (more than 1 year)	52% (23)	

Note: The number of samples appears in parentheses.

months)—finds that performance improves as the trendline lengthens. Short-term trendlines have gains after the upward breakout of 34%, whereas prices after long-term trendlines show a 46% improvement. I added a *really long* category, just for fun, just to see how the old timers performed. The 23 trendlines with durations over 1 year showed gains averaging 52%. To put all these numbers in perspective, the average gain from all 210 down-sloping trendlines was 38%.

ASPECT RATIOS AND ANGLES

Are trendline angles significant to performance? Yes, and Table 1.3 shows the results. Before I discuss the table, I need to warn you about the aspect ratio. The aspect ratio is the ratio of a chart's width to its height. Optimally, the ratio would be one to one; for every one unit change in width, there would be a one unit change in height. The pages that show the charts in this book are probably not one to one, nor is the computer screen I am looking at as I type this in. What appears as a diagonal 45-degree angle in this book may look like a 30-degree angle on my screen.

I suppose if you are blind in one eye and cannot see out of the other, it may make no difference to you, but the rest of us probably care about the aspect ratio. Let me make this clear so there is no confusion: The angles I measured are not the angles you see in this book nor the angles you will likely see on your computer screen. Even on my own screen, I can move the vertical or horizontal axis and make a trendline angle appear nearly flat or dangerously steep.

Table 1.3 shows that as the angle made between the horizontal and the trendline increases, performance suffers. One trendline with a 54-degree angle

Table 1.3
Performance Sorted by Trendline Angles

Degree Measure	Result	Score
60 to 90	None	−1
54	20% (1)	−1
48	37% (1)	−1
42	58% (4)	−1
36	22% (6)	0
30	25% (16)	0
24	31% (32)	0
18	28% (44)	0
12	41% (61)	+1
6	45% (33)	+1
0	75% (12)	+1

Note: The number of samples appears in parentheses.

showed a 20% rise, but the 12 trendlines that were nearly flat showed gains of 75%. Of course the sample size is too small in both cases to make that a perfect example, but the 33 samples at 6 degrees and the resulting 45% rise handily beats the 31% rise from trendlines with a 24-degree angle.

Individual degree readings are not as important as the trend. The trend shows that the steeper the angle, the worse the performance. Instead of relying on degree measures, ask yourself if the trendline is steep (–1 score) or shallow (+1 score). If you cannot decide, then the trendline is probably midrange (0 score).

TRENDLINE VOLUME

Does the volume trend have any influence on the price performance after the breakout? Yes. I used linear regression to determine whether volume was trending upward or downward over various parts of the trendline. Linear regression is commonly called the *trend function* in some spreadsheets, so it is easy to do. If you are like me and do not have a spreadsheet that supports the trend function, then you will have to resort to mathematics. I am not going to put you through that. Suffice it to say that linear regression is a way to best fit a line to the volume points. The slope of the line gives you the trend.

Performing linear regression over the entire trendline, from the first touch to the day before the breakout, shows that performance improves if volume trends downward. Table 1.4 shows that a downward volume trend results in a 45% price rise after the breakout, whereas the rise averages just 30% for those trendlines with an upward volume trend.

Does high volume near the breakout result in better performance? To answer that question, I split the trendline into thirds. The first and last third of the trendline, when volume trended upward, outperforms the same segment in the downward volume trend. Only the center third of a downward volume trend shows better performance, by 44% to 33%, for downward and upward volume trends, respectively.

Table 1.4
Performance Sorted by Volume Trend

Description	Upward Volume Trend	Up Trend Score	Downward Volume Trend	Down Trend Score
Entire trendline	30% (94)	–1	45% (116)	+1
First third	42% (71)		36% (139)	
Middle third	33% (107)		44% (103)	
Last third	43% (114)		34% (96)	

Note: The number of samples appears in parentheses.

What does all this mean? The score in Table 1.4 probably gives you a clue. I suggest you use the volume trend over the entire trendline instead of the parts. It is easier to do and is probably more meaningful. It is my belief that, for the best performance from downward trendlines, volume should also trend downward.

BREAKOUT VOLUME

Does high breakout volume propel stocks farther? Not in the trendlines I looked at. In case you are nodding off, it is time to pay attention. I averaged the volume over the 3 months leading to the breakout and spread the volume over five categories: very high, high, average, low, and very low. Then I compared the breakout day volume with the five categories.

As Table 1.5 shows, when the breakout volume was high or very high, the trendlines meeting those categories showed rises averaging 36%. When the volume was average or below—that is, average, low, or very low—prices climbed 39%. The differences are not statistically significant.

Many technical analysts swear by volume and some of the research I have done confirms that volume plays an important role in how chart patterns perform. A trendline is, after all, just another chart pattern. My guess, and it is only a guess, is that with an average trendline length of 194 days and a climb to the ultimate high averaging 174 days (combined, that is more than a year), one day's volume is insignificant.

PLUNGE, MEANDER, AND THE MEASURE RULE

I thought there would be some difference between prices that rise slowly to the breakout compared with those that shoot past. The first action I call a *meander* and Figure 1.4 shows an example. Prices *leading to* the breakout show a large overlap in their daily price range. Sometimes, prices move horizontally and seem to slide through the breakout.

Figure 1.5 shows what a price *plunge* looks like. I know you may think of a plunge as a downward price movement, and I agree, but I wrote the chapter

Table 1.5
Performance Sorted by Breakout Volume

Description	Result
Average rise on above-average breakout volume	36% (52)
Average rise on average or below-average breakout volume	39% (158)

Note: The number of samples appears in parentheses.

Figure 1.4 Price meander and the measure rule. A meander to the breakout is characterized by a large price overlap or horizontal price travel. The measure rule predicts the minimum price move. Use the largest distance (B–A) between the last trendline touch (D) and the breakout (C), measured vertically, and project the result from the breakout price (C) upward, to get the minimum target price. Prices reach the target 80% of the time. A measured move up formation follows the line CFFG.

on upward trendlines before this one, and it made sense there. Here, I am being consistent as the definition does not change from up to down trendlines. I define a price plunge as when prices zip upward, with little or no price overlap, *leading to* the breakout. Instead of moving horizontally as does the meander, prices plunge upward, as if standing on the bottom of a shallow pond and thrusting through the surface.

In both the meander and plunge, I did not include the day prices closed above the trendline, that is, the breakout day. Perhaps all this explaining has been a waste of time, because the results are disappointing. Table 1.6 shows that when prices plunge upward to the breakout, the average rise to the ultimate high measures 36%. This compares with a 40% average rise when prices meander to the breakout. The results are not statistically significant, meaning the differences may be due to chance. Never mind.

The measure rule, however, works. Before I explain that, look back at Figure 1.4. The measure rule says that the distance from the low point to the trendline projected upward from the breakout price becomes the minimum expected move. By way of example, scan the trendline from the last trendline

Figure 1.5 Price plunge. A quick price rise plunging upward to the breakout appears here.

touch (point D in the figure) to the breakout (C). The widest distance is between A and B, measured vertically. Add the price difference between A and B to the breakout price to get the target price.

The low at point A is 27.57 and the trendline directly above point A (that is, point B) is at 30.11. Add the difference, 2.54, to the breakout price, 29.29, to get the target price, 31.83. Prices reached the target price within 2 weeks after the breakout then moved horizontally as part of the corrective phase in a measured move up formation.

Table 1.6 shows that prices reach the predicted target 80% of the time. I consider values 80% or above to be reliable. Unfortunately, I believe the results are misleading. On my computer screen, point E nearly touches the trendline, so that replaces point D as the last touch closest to the breakout.

Table 1.6
Price Performance After Plunge or Meander

Description	Result
Price plunge	36% (100)
Price meander	40% (110)
Measure rule success rate	80%

Note: The number of samples appears in parentheses.

Finding the widest distance between point E and the breakout means the new price target is 30.19, which prices surpassed the day after the breakout. This is not an isolated incident, and since the measure rule success rate is an average, do not bet the farm that it will hold true.

YEARLY PRICE RANGE

Where the breakout occurs in the yearly price range can be a telling clue to eventual performance. To test this theory for trendlines, I determined if the breakout price was in the highest third, middle third, or lowest third of the 12-month price range.

As Table 1.7 shows, the best performance occurred when the breakout happened near the yearly high, with an average rise of 46%. The worst performance came from the middle third of the range, with rises averaging 33%.

What is happening, I think, is that the downward trendline appears as part of a corrective phase in a measured move up (MMU). Figure 1.4 shows what an MMU looks like. Prices begin their rise at point C, enter the corrective phase between the two Fs, then continue rising to point G in a stair-step formation. A small trendline drawn along the tops from the first F downward (as shown) might place the breakout near the yearly high. Breakouts near the yearly high have price rises that tend to soar like eagles, not fly like turkeys.

GAPS

Many technical analysts will tell you that a price gap on the breakout day improves performance. At least one hedge fund manager has been quoted saying that he uses gaps to improve performance, but do they really? Yes, at least for down trendlines.

On the day prices close above a trendline (the breakout day), a gap occurs when today's low is above yesterday's high. That leaves a gap on the price chart. As Table 1.8 indicates, those trendlines that show a gap on the break-

Table 1.7
Average Performance Sorted by Breakout Price
According to Prior 12-Month Range

Yearly Price Range	Result	Score
Highest third	46% (38)	+1
Middle third	33% (74)	−1
Lowest third	41% (72)	+1

Note: The number of samples appears in parentheses.

Table 1.8
Gaps and Performance

Description	Result	Score
Average rise after price gap on breakout	44% (30)	+1
Average rise with no price gap on breakout	38% (180)	−1

Note: The number of samples appears in parentheses.

out day have rises averaging 44%. This compares to a rise of just 38% when no gap appears. That is a statistically significant difference, so it may pay to play the gaps.

MARKET TREND

What can be learned by studying the general market trend before investing? Table 1.9 provides one answer by looking at the Standard & Poor's 500 Index as a proxy for the general market. I measured the S&P on the day the trendline started, on the day the trendline ended, and on the day prices reached the ultimate high.

The best performance after the trendline ended occurred when the market was falling during construction of the trendline (that is, from TS to TE). Prices climbed 43% compared to a 36% gain when the market was rising. I base the table scores on those results, not on the results for the ultimate high (TE to UH).

After the trendline ended, the best performance occurred during a rising market, with gains measuring 40% compared to a 16% gain during a falling market on the way to the ultimate high. I think the 16% value is too low, and the small sample size supports that belief (usually 30 samples produce statistically valid results).

The conclusion I draw from Table 1.9 is the same as I see for many other chart patterns. That is, the best performance comes during a falling market as the trendline forms, then a rising market on the way to the ultimate high.

Table 1.9
Average Price Performance of Trendlines
During a Rising and Falling Market

Market Trend	TS to TE	Score	TE to UH
Rising S&P 500	36% (138)	−1	40% (195)
Falling S&P 500	43% (72)	+1	16% (15)

Note: TS = trendline start, TE = trendline end, UH = ultimate high. The number of samples appears in parentheses.

Table 1.10
Average Price Performance of
Trendlines by Market Capitalization

Capitalization	Result	Score
Small cap (up to $1 billion)	45% (117)	+1
Mid cap ($1 to $5 billion)	26% (55)	−1
Large cap (over $5 billion)	43% (35)	+1

Note: The number of samples appears in parentheses.

MARKET CAPITALIZATION

Table 1.10 shows the performance after the breakout from a down-sloping trendline, sorted by market capitalization. Market capitalization is the number of shares outstanding multiplied by the breakout price.

Small cap stocks perform best, with rises averaging 45%, closely followed by large caps (43% rise), but the mid caps were well behind (26% gain). For other chart pattern types, the best performance comes from small caps then mid caps, and, finally, large caps, not a mix as shown in the table. Perhaps more samples would change the order.

1–2–3 TREND CHANGE

There is a method to determine whether a trend change has occurred, and Victor Sperandeo discusses it in his book, *Trader Vic—Methods of a Wall Street Master* (Wiley, 1991). Most chartists agree that piercing a trendline is not enough, as that is only the first hint of a trend change. Before I discuss the method, let us learn to draw trendlines according to the Sperandeo method.

For a down trendline, draw a line from the highest high to the lowest minor high so that the line does not intersect prices. Confused? Let us take it step by step and refer to Figure 1.6. Select the time scale that interests you. Since I use the daily scale most often, that is the one I use in this example. Find the highest high and lowest low. Point A is clearly the highest high and C is the lowest low after the highest high. Imagine you are standing in the valley above point C. Look to your left (backward in time), upward, and find the closest hilltop (not ridge but top). That would be point B, the lowest minor high before the lowest low. Draw a trendline from the highest high (A) to the lowest hilltop (B), and extend the line downward making sure that it does not pierce any prices until *after the date* of the lowest low.

Figure 1.7 shows another example of a down trendline, but this one is somewhat more difficult. Again, find the highest high and lowest low, look backward and find the nearest hilltop (either point A or B works). Connect a line between the highest high and the hilltop making sure that it does not

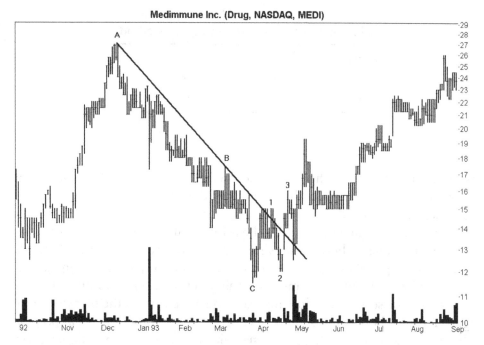

Figure 1.6 The 1–2–3 trend change method. Draw a trendline from the highest high to the lowest minor high so that the line does not intersect prices between the two points. A trend change occurs when (1) prices close above the trendline, (2) a test of the lowest low occurs, and (3) prices close above the prior minor high.

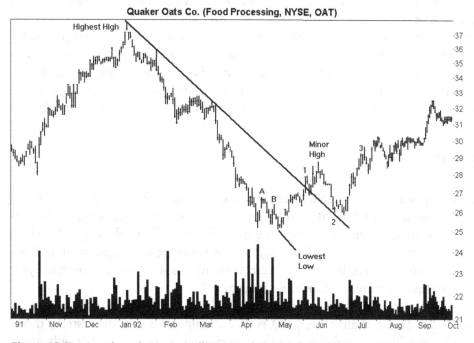

Figure 1.7 Another down trendline. Find the highest high and the lowest minor high before the lowest low. Draw a down trendline between the two such that it does not intersect prices.

Table 1.11
Performance of 1–2–3 Trend Change Method

Description	Result
Average rise	35%
Rises above 20%	74/101 or 73%

intersect prices until after the date of the lowest low. Your line should look like the one in Figure 1.7. Do not be alarmed by the wide vertical space between the trendline and the hilltop.

The 1–2–3 trend change method has three rules. First, prices must close above the trendline. In both Figures 1.6 and 1.7, this occurs at point 1. Second, prices must stop making lower lows and retest the low, which means prices often look like a double bottom—twin valleys close in price to one another. Many times, the second low does not meet the price level of the first low, as in Figure 1.7, but the attempt should be clear. The retest low appears as point 2 in both figures. Occasionally, prices may dip slightly below the first low, but that, too, is fine. The third rule is that prices should climb above the prior minor high. I use the minor high formed between the lowest low and the low retest (point 2). When prices close above the minor high, point 3 in both figures, the price trend has changed from down to up.

Does the 1–2–3 trend change method really signify a trend change? Yes, and Table 1.11 shows the results. The average rise after the 1–2–3 trend change signal completes measures 35%. This is below the 38% rise posted by all trendlines, excluding those used in the 1–2–3 trend change method. However, since I define a trend change as a price rise of at least 20% after a down-trend, 74 trendlines—or 73%—showed prices rising by at least 20% after the 1–2–3 signal. This result compares with a rate of 69% for all other trendlines.

SCORES

Scores appear in many of the tables in this chapter. Evaluate your trendline according to each table with a score and assign the associated score. Total the scores. A total above zero means the trendline is likely to show good performance (better than the median rise); scores below zero suggest weak performance (below the median rise). A zero score means it is your call whether you want to take a chance and make an investment.

The average decline for all down trendlines (excluding trendlines used in the 1–2–3 trend change method) is 38%. Using the scoring system, those trendlines with scores above zero showed rises averaging 56%, but only averaging 27% when the total score was less than zero (see Table 1.12).

Table 1.12
Trendline Performance by Score

Score	Result
Average rise of trendlines with scores above zero	56%
Average rise of trendlines with scores below zero	27%
Median rise used	30.5%
Number with scores above zero beating median rise	50/84 or 60%
Number with scores below zero doing worse than median rise	48/80 or 60%

Although such a result may sound like a significant improvement, and it is, it does not show the complete picture. I used the median rise of 30.5% to gauge whether the scoring system adds value. To add value, a score above zero (a buy signal) must be accompanied by a rise above the median rise; a score below zero (an avoid signal) must be accompanied by a rise below the median rise.

Table 1.12 shows that 60% of the scores above zero had rises over 30.5%. Avoid signals were also correct 60% of the time, that is, a score below zero correctly predicted a rise below the median rise. This result is quite good considering the median rise, at 30.5%, is not chicken feed. With that kind of an annual rise, I could buy my own country someday. Any value above the midrange score of 50% means that the scoring system adds value—which it does for both buy and avoid buying signals.

However, the scoring system is far from perfect, so use it carefully. You might try using the 1–2–3 trend change method first and then score the trendline for predicted performance. That way, there is a good chance the upward breakout will hold for a good gain.

CASE STUDY 1

Figure 1.8 shows the stock I use in this study of a trendline scoring above zero. As you look at the figure, notice that it is on the weekly chart using semilog scales. Prices reached their high on the cusp of the new year, 1994, then trended downward but bounded on the top by a down-sloping trendline. In mid-February 1996, prices closed above the trendline, marking an upward breakout. Prices rose in a stair-step climb until the end of the study.

How do you use the scoring system to rate this trendline? Start with the first table showing a score, Table 1.1. The table shows the performance of spacing and touches. Look at Figure 1.8 and count the number of times a minor high comes close to or touches the trendline. I have labeled them 1 through 5 in the figure. Wide spacing means a touch about every month (29 days apart, on average). For a trendline with five touches, that means the trend-

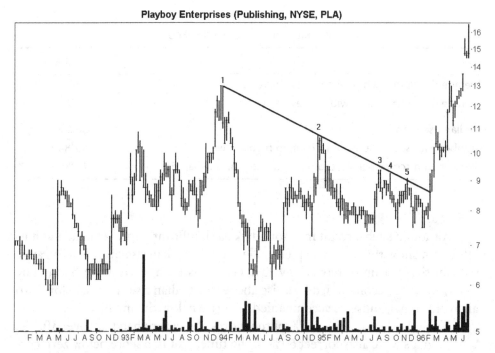

Playboy Enterprises (Publishing, NYSE, PLA)

Figure 1.8   Down trendline on the weekly scale. This trendline has a score of five, suggesting performance above the 30.5% median, and prices climbed 86% above the breakout.

line must be nearly 5 months long or else the spacing is narrow. I only measure from point 1 to point 5 and do not include the time after point 5. Since we are on the weekly scale, it is easy to see that the points appear less frequently than once a month. The actual days between touches averages 136. Wide spacing scores +1 according to Table 1.1.

Table 1.1 also shows a score for more than four touches. Since this trendline has five touches, that scores +1 for a running total of +2.

Table 1.2 discusses trendline length. Clearly this is a long trendline, measuring 767 days, well above the 139 day cutoff between short and long. Score: +1. Running total: +3.

Table 1.3 shows the performance of trendlines sorted by the angle they make with the horizontal. Split your chart into thirds: steep trendlines score –1, shallow trendlines score +1, and everything in between is neutral for a zero score. On my computer screen, the line looks shallow for a +1 score (but looks to be about 45 degrees on the printed page. Remember the aspect ratio?). Running total: +4.

Is the volume trending upward or downward from the trendline start to its end? I think you will agree that volume is higher in the first half of the trendline than in the second. Table 1.4 says that a downward volume trend scores +1. Running total: +5.

Where in the yearly price range is the breakout? Recall that a breakout occurs when prices *close* above the trendline and that occurred during the week of February 16, 1996. Looking at the weekly chart, the 12-month high occurred at a price of 9.38 at point 3 and the yearly low at 7.38, reached in both June and July. So, that places the breakout very close to the yearly high. Table 1.7 scores that condition as +1. Running total: +6.

Does a price gap occur the day prices close above the trendline? No, but check the daily scale to be sure. Prices push through the trendline in one easy motion but do not gap upward. Table 1.8 scores the absence of a gap as –1. Running total: +5.

What is the general market doing over this span? At the start of the trendline, the S&P 500 closed at 466.45. At the end of the trendline, the S&P closed at 646.32—a hefty rise. A rising market trend while the trendline is under construction (that is, from TS to TE) rates a –1 score according to Table 1.9. Running total: +4.

Market capitalization is the final table with a score. Multiply the number of shares outstanding (which you can usually get from financial reports, the Internet, or your broker) by the breakout price. With a breakout price of 8.88, the stock is a small cap. Small caps score +1 according to Table 1.10, for a final total of +5.

Scores above zero suggest performance that may beat the median 30.5% rise. Even though the end of the study cuts off prices, the stock climbed 86% above the breakout point. Obviously I chose this stock because of its score and the resulting performance. Your results may vary and even though a stock may rise by 86%, that does not mean your results will be that good. You have to buy at the breakout price, sell at the exact high, and have no trading costs. That, of course, is impossible—even for gifted traders.

CASE STUDY 2

What happens when the score totals less than zero? Figure 1.9 illustrates this case study. Prices form a valid trend after the third minor high touch. Extending the trendline into September shows where the breakout occurs.

How do you score this trendline? Since you are already familiar with scoring, we can quickly run through the tables.

Table 1.1: Spacing and touches. Three touches in just over a month qualifies the trendline as having narrow spacing. The actual spacing averages 12 days, less than the 29-day cutoff. Score: –1. Since there are four or fewer touches, that also scores –1. Running total: –2.

Table 1.2: Trendline length. The trendline length measures 109 days, below the 139 day cutoff, placing it in the short category. Score: –1. Running total: –3.

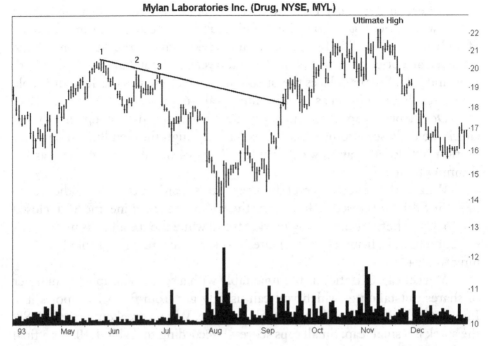

Figure 1.9 A below-zero scoring trendline. The stock climbed 22% above the breakout.

Table 1.3: Trendline angle. On my computer screen, the angle appears shallow for a +1 score. Running total: –2.

Table 1.4: Volume trend. Clearly, volume is higher in the second half of the trendline than in the first half. An upward volume trend scores –1. Running total: –3.

Table 1.7: Yearly price range. The breakout occurs in the center third of the yearly price range for a –1 score. Running total: –4.

Table 1.8: Gaps. There is no breakout day price gap for a –1 score. Running total: –5.

Table 1.9: Market trend. From the trendline start to its end, the S&P 500 climbed between those two days. A rising market scores –1. Running total: –6.

Table 1.10: Market capitalization. Lastly, the stock is a mid cap for a –1 score. Final score: –7.

From the breakout price of 18.17, the stock climbed to a high of 22.25, or 22%, before prices tumbled more than 20%, signaling a trend change. A 22% gain is below the 30.5% median rise, just as the negative score predicted.

2

Up Trendlines

Ever since I first picked up a chart and looked at it, I have wondered why stock prices follow trends. What explains the brisk upward push in a straight-line advance, and what explains the plodding stair-step rise—both scenarios touching an imaginary line of trend? The obvious answer is buying demand exceeds selling pressure for weeks or even months on end. Sometimes the demand is constant as in the straight-line advance, and sometimes it gets throttled, like the gas pedal in a car during heavy traffic, forming the stair-step advance. All I can say is that since trendlines happen, I guess they must be possible.

THE TYPICAL PATTERN

Figure 2.1 shows two upward-sloping trendlines. Ignore them. Look at the minor highs and minor lows. If you connect all the minor highs with one line and all the minor lows with another, which will give you a straighter line? For a while, the minor highs show promise from August through October. Not all peaks touch the line, but they come close. The December peak is well below the trendline, and peaks in January and February are almost flat. In April, the trend picks up again, but a line joining the peaks does not quite match up.

Look at the minor lows. I have drawn two up trendlines connecting them. Look at how points 1 through 4 match up. Perfect. Line ABCD does not do as well, but still prices stop near the trendline.

Which is best, a line drawn along the minor highs or one along the minor lows? Here is my answer: *If you draw an up trendline, draw it along the minor lows.* You will find that prices touch the trendline more often than one drawn along the minor highs, but there is a better reason. Do you know what it is?

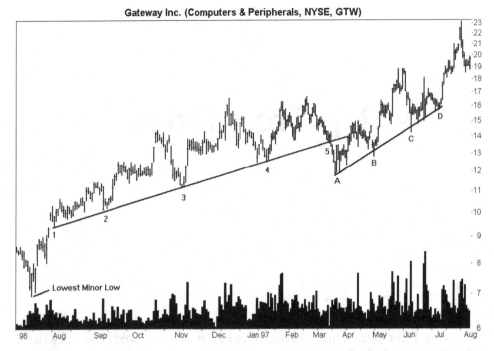

Figure 2.1 Draw up trendlines along the minor lows. Line ABCD is an example of an internal trendline that ignores downward price spikes.

Here is a hint: Pretend that you bought the stock shown in Figure 2.1 somewhere between points 3 and 4. You know that one day the up trend will change; prices will move horizontally or even plunge. Which trendline—one drawn connecting the minor highs or one drawn along the minor lows—will alert you to the potential trend change?

Point 5 shows the answer, as that point marks the location where prices close below the trendline. A line drawn along the minor lows will signal a potential trend change; one drawn along the minor highs will not.

When drawing an up trendline, connect the *significant* minor lows, not every low that comes your way. What does the word *significant* mean? My advice is to use your best judgment for the time scale you are using. Consult the figures in this chapter and throughout the book as a guide. If you still need a better definition, try searching for minor lows on the daily scale that appear at least a week apart.

If you are still awake at this point and sharp as a tack, you might recall that down trendlines connect the minor highs. The reasons mentioned for up trendlines also apply to down trendlines: Down trendlines drawn along the minor highs are invariably straighter and trend changes are easier to identify.

INTERNAL TRENDLINES AND TAILS

If you are a trendline expert, you may quibble with the drawing of both trend-lines shown in Figure 2.1. Later in this chapter, I tell you about a method I call 1–2–3 trend change, which uses the lowest minor low on the chart as the starting point for the trendline. Clearly, line 12345 does not use it.

Line ABCD shows the trendline piercing prices at B and C, and some will argue that the trendline is incorrectly drawn for that reason. Others will tell you that the line is an *internal trendline*, and it is drawn just fine. Thank you, very much.

The thinking behind internal trendlines is that the trendline should be drawn along the price clusters, ignoring the *tails*—the downward 1-day price spikes at points B and C—so that as many points as possible appear connected. Backers will speak in loud voices about the majority of traders buying at the bottom of the cluster and a few outliers trading at the extremes. "You want to make your trading decisions on crowd behavior, not the individuals," they insist.

Good point. I would argue that I am looking for a trend change, and one clue to that is waiting for prices to pierce the trendline. If trendline punctures happen every few weeks, what good are internal trendlines?

Which do I use? "I'm not prejudiced, I hate everybody!" the saying goes, and I draw my trendlines whichever way works best, but I usually avoid internal trendlines. For the statistics in this chapter, unless noted otherwise, I ignored both the 1–2–3 trend change method (which uses the lowest minor low) and internal trendlines. In other words, many trendlines looked like line 12345 in Figure 2.1.

POINTS AND TOUCHES

How many points are necessary for a valid trendline, and how far apart should the points be? By definition, it takes two points to make a straight line, but three to form a valid trendline. I often draw trendlines along two minor lows in a forming price trend just to see where, in the future, the third point may be. When the point spacing appears as regular as line 12345 in Figure 2.1, you can almost guess to the day when the next trendline touch will occur (at least for a while).

Consider Figure 2.2 that zooms in on Figure 2.1. A trendline appears beginning at point A and joins lows 1 and 2. All three points look like minor lows, but you might argue that point 1 is not a *significant* minor low as it is too close to point A and is only 1 day wide. The trendline piercing at point 3 ends the trendline. So, we really have a trendline composed of two distinct minor lows (A and 2) before the line ends.

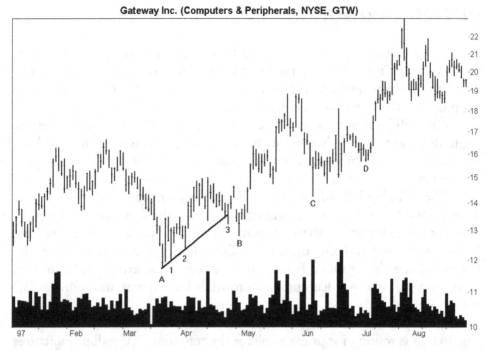

Figure 2.2 Trendline touches and spacing. How many touches make a valid trendline and how far apart should the touches appear?

Basing a trendline on two points close together reminds me of nonlinear systems and chaos theory. A small perturbation can send a system spinning out of control. A trendline starting with two close touches may not hold up in the longer term. Since trendlines also show support and resistance (covered in Chapter 3), two points spaced too far apart may not have much value either. Thus, point spacing is a judgment call, and it depends on how near or far you zoom in. The trendline in Figure 2.2 looks reasonable and projected into the future, point 3 comes close to the trendline before rebounding, almost as expected. If you zoom out and look back at Figure 2.1, a longer trendline works better for the wider scale. On the weekly or monthly scales, other trendlines may become the preferred choice.

This discussion creates two questions: How important is point spacing, and does a trendline showing more touches become more *significant*?

Table 2.1 provides the answers. I looked at 48 unique stocks and drew 199 trendlines using the daily and weekly time scales, with no duplicates between them. The number of stocks may sound small, but those stocks yielded a comparatively large number of trendlines, enough to be sure that the results would be statistically valid.

For each trendline, I counted the number of minor lows that came very near to or touched the trendline. Once prices closed below the trendline, I

Table 2.1
Performance Sorted by Trendline Spacing and Touches

Trendline Description	Result	Score
Narrow spacing (less than 28 days)	−14% (99)	−1
Wide spacing (more than 28 days)	−19% (97)	+1
Three touches	−17% (62)	
Four touches	−16% (79)	
Five touches	−17% (40)	
Six touches	−17% (10)	
Seven touches	−20% (8)	
Four touches or less	−16% (141)	
More than four touches	−18% (58)	

Note: The number of samples appears in parentheses.

made note of how far prices descended as measured from the breakout price to the lowest low (called the ultimate low) before a 20% price rise.

All trendlines had at least three touches with an average of four touches per trendline. After sorting the average time between touches, I chose the median value as the separator between narrow and wide touch spacing. For those trendlines with touches averaging less than the median 28 days, the resulting decline averaged 14%. This compares to a 19% decline for those trendlines with touches spaced more than 28 days apart. *On average, trendlines with touches spaced widely apart perform better than those spaced close together.*

Is the number of touches significant? I checked the Internet, magazines, and books when researching trendlines, and every reference I looked at said the same thing: The more touches a trendline has, the more *significant* it becomes. Does that mean a trendline with three touches will decline less than one with four or six touches?

To find out, I separated the performance of up trendlines according to the maximum number of minor lows coming very close to or touching the trendline. Figure 2.1, for reference, shows trendline 12345 having five touches, but not the ones you would expect: point 4 has two touches, and I exclude point 5 because it is not a minor low. I discarded internal trendlines, such as line ABCD.

Table 2.1 says that trendlines having only three minor low touches showed declines averaging 17%, but those with seven touches showed an average 20% decline. In between those two, the results appear pegged at or near 17%. I consider sample counts above 30 to be a good sample size to work with, so the results for touches 6 and 7 are suspect.

Since the results may be inconclusive, I found the median touch count, 4, and used that as the separator between a small number of touches, 3 or 4, from touches 5 through 7. The declines resulting from trendlines with touches of 3 or 4 was 16%, but an 18% average decline appeared for those trendlines with 5, 6, or 7 touches. *Thus, the more touches a trendline has, the greater its significance.* However, more samples may lead to a different conclusion.

I use the scores listed in Table 2.1 to evaluate the strength of the trendline breakout. For now, just ignore the scores in the tables. We cross that bridge when we come back to it later.

TRENDLINE LENGTH

When prices pierce a long trendline, is that more significant than when prices puncture a short trendline? All the references I checked said the answer was yes, but none proved it. Table 2.2 shows what I found after doing my own research.

I sorted trendline length using two methods. The first method uses the median trendline length as the cutoff between short and long. After sorting the trendline lengths, the median is the midrange value such that half the samples are shorter than the median and the other half are longer. I excluded any ties. The median trendline length was 137 days or 4.5 months. Those trendlines shorter than 137 days showed declines averaging 14%, but a 19% decline results from longer trendlines. The differences are statistically significant, meaning they are probably not due to chance.

It seemed like a good idea at the time, so I sorted the trendline length into more traditional categories: short term (up to 3 months long), intermediate term (3 to 6 months), and long term (over 6 months). Long-term trendlines worked best, having declines after the breakout averaging 20%, whereas the worst performance came from short- and intermediate-term trendlines, tied at 15%.

The average decline for all trendlines was 17% and 27 trendlines with duration's over a year had declines averaging 19%. *On average, long trendlines perform better than short ones.*

Table 2.2
Performance Sorted by Trendline Length

Trendline Description	Result	Score
Short trendlines (less than 137 days)	−14% (98)	−1
Long trendlines (more than 137 days)	−19% (99)	+1
Short-term trendlines (0 to 3 months)	−15% (54)	
Intermediate-term trendlines (3 to 6 months)	−15% (72)	
Long-term trendlines (over 6 months)	−20% (73)	
Really long trendlines (more than 1 year)	−19% (27)	

Note: The number of samples appears in parentheses.

ASPECT RATIOS AND ANGLES

Is the angle that the trendline makes with the horizontal significant? Do steep trendlines perform worse than shallow ones? Before I answer those questions, I discuss the aspect ratio. The aspect ratio is the ratio of the chart's width to its height. If you were to slide the right axis of Figure 2.2 to the left, the angle of trendline A123 would grow steeper. Stretch the bottom axis downward and the trendline angle also increases. What this means is that your chart and my chart may look different; the trendline angles may measure differently.

There is a method of making the aspect ratio one to one, so that a one-unit change in height corresponds to a one-unit change in width, but I would have to spend a day searching my files for it, and you would probably ignore it anyway. Suffice it to say that I ignored it, too, and left the aspect ratio of my computer screen alone. For reference, I am using 1,024 × 768 resolution, which allows me to pack 15 months of daily prices onto one screen. That fact does not mean anything because printing and resizing the artwork for publication changes the aspect ratio. Take any angles I describe with a grain of salt.

Table 2.3 shows the performance results for various trendline angles. If you find a stock with a trendline angle above 70 degrees, you had better pack oxygen tanks because the trend is nearly vertical!

As you scan down the table, you see that most of the samples associate with shallow angles, 6, 12, or 18 degrees, probably due to my computer screen format. Most chartists will tell you that their trendlines appear in the 30 to 45

Table 2.3
Performance Sorted by Trendline Angles

Degree Measure	Result	Score
66 to 90	None	−1
60	−35% (1)	−1
54	−15% (2)	−1
48	−9% (3)	−1
42	−16% (14)	0
36	−12% (8)	0
30	−14% (18)	0
24	−18% (15)	+1
18	−19% (42)	+1
12	−14% (46)	+1
6	−20% (44)	+1
0	−22% (6)	+1

Note: The number of samples appears in parentheses.

degree range, so shift the degree scale appropriately to your situation. You might consider breaking the scale into three ranges: shallow (+1 score), midrange (0 score), and steep (–1 score). That would save you the trouble of converting the trendline angle into a degree measure but still preserve the scoring mechanism intent.

Let me emphasize that the angle is less important than the trend. What does that mean? According to the results in the table, trendlines generally show inferior performance as the angle increases (ignoring the smaller sample sizes at 54 and 60 degrees).

TRENDLINE VOLUME

If you ask many technical analysts about the importance of volume, they will probably tell you that it is paramount. If you own a stock, high volume when prices are trending upward is a good thing. Are they pulling your leg?

I examined the slope of the line found using linear regression on the volume data to determine whether the volume was trending upward or downward. Linear regression is a complicated way of saying that I mathematically plotted a line so that it *best fit* between the volume points. Some spreadsheets call linear regression the *trend function*, so it is usually easy to do.

Table 2.4 shows the results of the study. Using linear regression on the volume data from the day the trendline began to its end, volume readings trending upward associated with price declines of 19%. That is, after the trendline ended, prices dropped 19%. This compares with a 14% decline for downward volume trends. The differences are statistically significant, meaning that they are not likely due to chance.

Splitting the trendline length into thirds and running linear regression on the volume trend over each section produced consistent results. When the volume was trending upward, the resulting decline exceeded the declines shown when the volume was trending downward. For example, when the volume pat-

Table 2.4
Performance Sorted by Volume Trend

Description	Upward Volume Trend	Up Trend Score	Downward Volume Trend	Down Trend Score
Entire trendline	–19% (105)	+1	–14% (94)	–1
First third	–17% (81)		–16% (118)	
Middle third	–19% (105)		–14% (94)	
Last third	–17% (95)		–16% (104)	

Note: The number of samples appears in parentheses.

Table 2.5
Performance Sorted by Breakout Volume

Description	Result	Score
Average decline on above-average breakout volume	19% (46)	+1
Average decline on average or below-average breakout volume	16% (153)	−1

Note: The number of samples appears in parentheses.

tern in the middle third of the trendline was rising, the resulting decline after the trendline ended was 19%. This compares with a 14% decline for a receding volume trend over the same period. Thus, *increasing volume as the trend continues is a good sign.*

BREAKOUT VOLUME

Some analysts say that a breakout occurring on high volume suggests an added push in the breakout direction, but does it really? Yes, and Table 2.5 shows the results for trendline breakouts. A breakout occurs when prices *close* below the trendline. I compared volume on the breakout day with the average volume over the preceding 3 months after splitting the average volume reading into five categories: very high, high, average, low, and very low.

When the breakout volume was high or very high, prices declined an average of 19%. This compares with a decline of 16% when the volume fell into the average or below average categories. In short, *a high volume downward breakout propels prices further.*

PLUNGE, MEANDER, AND THE MEASURE RULE

"Plunge, meander, and the measure rule" reminds me of rape, pillage, and plunder from the Middle Ages. Perhaps it is a guy thing. Anyway, I wanted to know if prices declined further when prices plunged through the trendline than if they just meandered across. The first stumbling block was the definition of plunge and meander.

Figure 2.3 shows prices plunging through the trendline. I define a plunge as a price trend that shows little price overlap from day to day leading to, but not including, the breakout day. Gaps and large 1-day downward price spikes usually associate with a plunge and not a meander.

Figure 2.4 shows a price meander. There is a large price overlap leading to the breakout, in part by a thinly traded stock, but also because prices simply flat-lined.

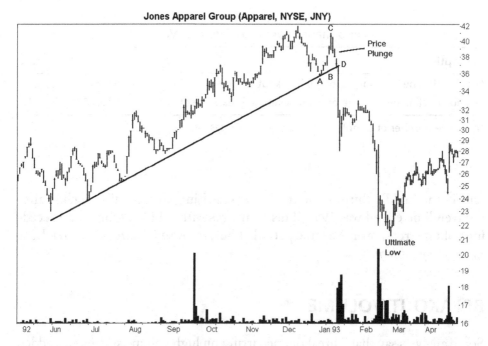

Figure 2.3   Price plunge. With little daily price range overlap, prices plunge through the trendline. Use the measure rule to predict the price decline by computing the height from the trendline (C–B) after the last minor low (A), projecting the result downward from breakout price point D.

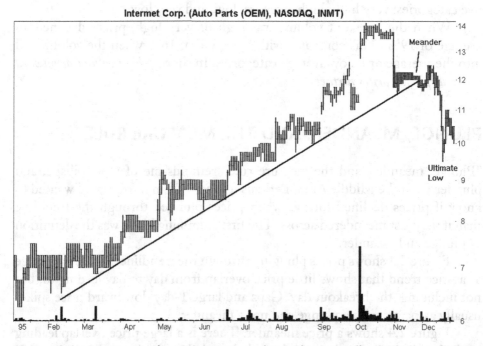

Figure 2.4   Price meander. Prices move almost horizontally, with lots of daily price range overlap before closing below the trendline.

Table 2.6
Price Performance after Plunge or Meander

Description	Result
Price plunge	–16.5% (98)
Price meander	–16.7% (103)
Measure rule success rate	63%

Note: The number of samples appears in parentheses.

Comparing the two figures and the price behavior after the breakout, you might conclude that a price plunge is usually more devastating than a meander. Wrong. Table 2.6 shows little performance difference between the two.

When prices plunge through the trendline, the resulting decline averages 16.5%. When they meander past the trendline, the decline is 16.7% or almost the same as a plunge. Statistically, the differences are not significant, meaning the results may—or may not—be due to chance. My feeling about this is simple: Do not worry about whether prices are plunging or meandering through the trendline; it probably does not make any difference.

Measure Rule Success Rate

The measure rule is a tool used to help predict how far prices will decline after a breakout. Refer to Figure 2.3 as I discuss how to use the rule. From the last minor low (before the breakout) where prices touch the trendline (point A) to the breakout point (D), locate the highest high (C). Compute the difference between that point (C) and the trendline (B), measured vertically, and project the difference from the breakout point (D) downward.

As an example, the highest high is at 41, and the trendline price directly below the peak is 36.38, for a difference of 4.62. Projecting the result below the breakout price of 36.63, gives a *minimum* target price of 32.01. Prices closed below that on the breakout day, fulfilling the measure rule.

How often does the measure rule work? Just 63% of the time (see Table 2.6). I consider values above 80% to be reliable, so the rule for up trendlines falls flat. It is perhaps even worse because of my stipulation on finding the highest high *after the most recent minor low*. For example, if you use instead the *widest distance* from a minor high to the trendline, you would use the early December peak, with a height of 8 above the trendline, giving a harder-to-reach target of 28.63.

Instead of relying on the measure rule, I would use a congestion area or other support feature as a price target. I discuss how to do that in Chapter 3 on support and resistance.

Table 2.7
Average Performance Sorted by Breakout Price
According to Prior 12-Month Range

Yearly Price Range	Result	Score
Highest third	−15% (75)	−1
Middle third	−17% (59)	+1
Lowest third	−20% (27)	+1

Note: The number of samples appears in parentheses.

YEARLY PRICE RANGE

Where a chart pattern breakout occurs in the yearly price range may influence the resulting price performance. Trendlines are no different as they are only a chart pattern with a different name. In this book, for example, you will discover that shorting a stock making new lows is often less risky and more profitable than shorting stocks making new highs, but the result depends on the chart pattern.

Table 2.7 shows the price performance after a breakout, sorted by the breakout price over the prior 12-month trading range. Since up trendlines break out downward, you might logically expect that a breakout occurring near the yearly high would have farther to fall. They do, but that is not what happens. Perhaps it is just a mathematical oddity: A 10-point decline from 100 to 90 is a 10% change, but a 10-point decline from 20 to 10 is a 50% change.

What happens is that those trendlines showing breakouts within a third of the yearly high show declines averaging 15%—the worst performance of the three ranges. Trendlines with breakouts in the center third of the yearly price range decline 17%, on average, and those near the yearly low decline by 20%. If you are looking for a stock to short after a downward breakout from a rising trendline, select those with breakout prices near the yearly low.

GAPS

If a gap occurs the day prices break out, that occurrence is supposed to be good for performance, but is it? Table 2.8 shows no statistically significant performance difference. A price gap, in case you are wondering, occurs when today's high price is below yesterday's low, leaving a blank space on the chart.

I measured all gaps on the breakout day and looked at the resulting decline to the ultimate low. When a gap occurred, prices dropped 16.8%. This

Table 2.8
Gaps and Performance

Description	Result
Average decline after price gap on breakout	16.8% (35)
Average decline with no price gap on breakout	16.5% (164)

Note: The number of samples appears in parentheses.

compares with a drop of 16.5% when no gap occurs. Performance after a gap does show a larger decline, but not so you would notice.

MARKET TREND

Does the general market trend affect the performance of stocks? Table 2.9 shows the price performance after a trendline breakout. I examined the change in value of the Standard & Poor's 500 Index on the days the trendline started and ended, then used the rising or falling reading to sort the performance of the trendlines after a breakout.

A rising general market while the trendline was under construction (from TS to TE) resulted in a price decline after the breakout measuring 17%. This statistic compares to a 13% loss when the market was declining over the same period. Using the same method but from the trendline end to the ultimate low gives similar but unusual results. A downward breakout from a trendline in a rising market showed a 19% loss, but the loss was just 15% in a falling market. The belief is that a rising tide lifts all boats; a rising market would tend to limit the decline of a stock, and a declining market would tend to depress a stock further. For the stocks and trendlines I looked at, the opposite seems to occur. Apparently a rising tide tends to swamp a sinking boat quicker.

Incidentally, I base the scores in the table on the TS to TE period, that is, when the formation is under construction.

Table 2.9
Average Price Performance of Trendlines
During a Rising and Falling Market

Market Trend	TS to TE	Score	TE to UL
Rising S&P 500	–17% (173)	+1	–19% (71)
Falling S&P 500	–13% (26)	–1	–15% (128)

Note: TS = trendline start, TE = trendline end, UL = ultimate low. The number of samples appears in parentheses.

Table 2.10
Average Price Performance of Trendlines
by Market Capitalization

Capitalization	Result	Score
Small cap (up to $1 billion)	–22% (94)	+1
Mid cap ($1 to $5 billion)	–17% (60)	0
Large cap (over $5 billion)	–12% (45)	–1

Note: The number of samples appears in parentheses.

MARKET CAPITALIZATION

Market capitalization is the number of shares outstanding times the breakout price. After sorting the stocks showing trendlines by their market capitalization, I found that small cap stocks declined farthest, averaging 22%. Large caps, however, declined only 12%. Table 2.10 lists the results.

The trading implications of this table are clear: Consider shorting small cap stocks after a trendline breakout, but avoid shorting mid cap and large cap stocks. If you own shares in a large cap and it breaks out downward, consider whether an average 12% loss is worth weathering. However, just because the table shows a 12% decline does not mean your high-tech large cap will be trouble free. One of its subsidiaries could get involved in asbestos litigation and the entire company could declare bankruptcy.

1–2–3 TREND CHANGE

The discussion by now may lead you to believe that once prices close below an up-sloping trendline, a trend change occurs from up to down. If you research the issue, you will find that chartists claim that a piercing of the trendline is only an *indication* of a trend change. Is this correct?

I suppose the answer rests on how you define a trend change. Throughout this book, I consider a trend change to be a 20% change in prices. For up trendlines, that means prices must fall by 20%. Why 20%? It is an arbitrary limit, but one I base on the definition of bull and bear markets. Most investors regard the start of a bear market as when prices decline by 20%; a bull market occurs when prices rise by 20%. My definitions of the ultimate low, ultimate high, and the trend start also use the 20% figure.

Victor Sperandeo, author of *Trader Vic—Methods of a Wall Street Master* (Wiley, 1991), used a different approach. Consider Figure 2.5, which shows his technique. To determine whether a trend change has occurred, there are three

Figure 2.5 1–2–3 trend change method. A trend change occurs when prices (1) pierce a trendline, (2) retest the old high, and (3) close below the minor low.

tests. First, prices must pierce the trendline. Second, a test of the high must occur. Third, prices must drop below a prior minor low. I call this the 1–2–3 trend change approach.

1. Draw the trendline. This is tricky so pay attention. Imagine that you printed Figure 2.5 without the trendline. Find the highest high on the chart. That high occurs in early February and I show it as point A. Next, find the lowest price *before* the highest high. That price occurs in October and it appears as point B. Take a ruler and place it between those two points. Notice that if you were to draw a line connecting the low at point B with the high at point A, it would overwrite many price bars. Instead, hold the ruler down at the lowest low (point B) and swivel the ruler clockwise until prices no longer intersect the ruler until *after* the date of the highest high. Draw the line and it should look like the figure; prices should touch the trendline at point C, but not pierce the line until days after reaching the highest high.

    To briefly summarize step 1, find the highest price, then the lowest price *before* the high, anchor your trendline at the low, and swivel it clockwise until prices no longer intersect the trendline *between* the dates of the low and the high. The figure shows the trendline breakout at point 1.

2. Prices must retest the high. After prices pierce the trendline, they should drop, round about, and attempt a new high again. Prices can either fall short, draw even, or rise *slightly* above the old high, but should not start making new highs big time! What you are looking for are prices attempting to rise above the highest high but failing to do so. In short, look for a double top. Figure 2.5 shows the retest of the high at point 2, a minor high below the highest high.

3. Finally, prices must decline below a prior minor low. Find the lowest price between points A and 2. Prices must close below that point, shown as point 3. In the figure, you can see that prices gapped down and closed below point 3 on February 26. That day completed the 1–2–3 trend change signal.

How well does the 1–2–3 trend change work? Table 2.11 provides one answer. For the 67 trendlines obeying all three conditions of the 1–2–3 method, prices declined an average of 21% after the breakout, exceeding the 17% average decline for all trendlines that ignored the 1–2–3 approach.

How many times did the 1–2–3 trend change signal accurately predict a decline of 20% or more (that is, a trend change)? Answer: 29 or 43% of the time. To put it another way, the method has a 57% failure rate. That failure rate is above the scoring system (51%) but below the 62% failure rate for generic up trendlines without scoring.

Before you conclude that Sperandeo's method does not work as well as expected, let me issue these caveats. First, my interpretation and implementation of his method may be flawed. Everyone makes mistakes, including me. To improve performance, Sperandeo mentions a 2B method that I did not test. The 2B method may improve performance because it seeks to short a stock more quickly.

From my understanding, Sperandeo's method is like waiting for confirmation of a double top. Throw in a trendline kicker, which sometimes delays the sell-short signal, and you are done. However, there is a difference between a double top (which has identification requirements) and a retest of the high.

Table 2.11
Performance of 1–2–3 Trend Change Method

Description	Result
Average decline	21%
Declines above 20%	29/67 or 43%

Consider reading Sperandeo's book and experimenting with the method yourself before drawing any conclusions.

SCORES

Several times in this chapter I mention the scoring system. To use the system, evaluate your trendline according to the tables that show scores, and add the scores together. Total scores above zero suggest performance that may beat the median decline; scores below zero suggest underperformance. A zero score is a toss-up. The case studies in the next sections apply the scoring system.

How does the scoring system perform? Table 2.12 shows the results. When you average the performance of prices after a downward breakout from all trendlines, you find that prices decline 17% before encountering a 20% price rise (a trend change). If you use the scoring system, those trendlines with scores above zero show losses averaging 20%. Those with scores below zero show losses of just 12%.

Using the median (midrange) decline as the benchmark to beat, I counted the number of trendlines with scores above zero that also beat the median. These represent the sell-short signals and they were correct 62% of the time. When the scores were less than zero and the percentage decline fell short of the median, these represented the avoid-selling-short signals. They were correct 71% of the time. Anything above 50% means the system adds value, but the results suggest the system is far from perfect.

If you expect the breaking of a trendline to represent a trend change (predicting a 20% trend change), and you sell a holding or short a stock, you will be wrong 62% of the time. Only about one in three trades will decline more than 20%. If you use the scoring system, the chances of success improve to one in two trades: The failure rate drops from 62% to 51%. Even if you use the scoring system, you still have to trade the stocks perfectly to achieve an average 20% decline. Keep that in mind. This is not a perfect system, but it does improve results.

Table 2.12
Trendline Performance by Score

Score	Result
Average decline of trendlines with scores above zero	20%
Average decline of trendlines with scores below zero	12%
Median decline used	16.92%
Number with scores above zero beating median decline	55/89 or 62%
Number with scores below zero doing worse than median decline	34/48 or 71%

CASE STUDY 1

How do you use the scoring system to help predict price performance after the breakout? This case study shows you how to score a trendline, one that results in a score above zero.

Figure 2.6 shows the trendline to be evaluated. Let us begin with Table 2.1, which reviews trendline touch spacing. The trendline started on March 26, 1993, and the last minor low, point 5, was on October 26, 1993. The number of days between those two dates is 214, according to my spreadsheet. Thus, the five touches—shown by numbers in the figure—are an average of 43 days apart. Notice that I did not include the end of the trendline in either the point count or the date. According to Table 2.1, a spacing above 28 days gives a +1 score.

Is the trendline short or long? This time, we measure from the first time prices touch the trendline to the day prices close below the trendline, that is, from March 26 to December 1. The trendline measures 250 days. According to Table 2.2, the trendline is above the median 137 days, so it scores +1 for a running total of +2.

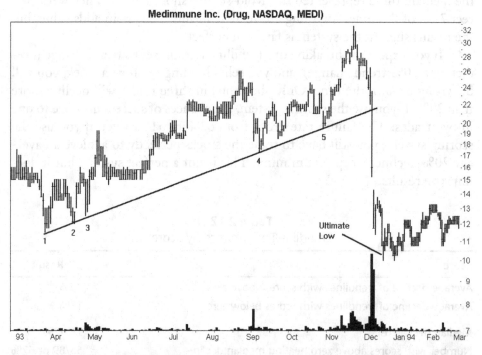

Figure 2.6 This trendline has an above-zero score. Prices dropped 55% before rebounding by at least 20%. A year later, prices reached a low of 3.38, a decline of 85%.

What angle does the trendline make with the horizontal? When trying to determine the trendline angle, try asking yourself whether the trendline is steep or not. If it is steep, score it a –1; shallow ones score +1. Anything in between would score zero. On my computer screen, it appears shallow. Table 2.3 scores a shallow angle as +1, for a +3 running total.

Is the volume trend over the course of the trendline increasing or decreasing? I used linear regression on the volume data from the day the trendline started to the day before the breakout to determine the slope of the volume trend. Over that time, volume was trending upward (which you may have guessed from looking at the figure). An upward volume trend, according to Table 2.4, scores +1. Running total: +4.

Is the breakout volume above average? Yes. Volume spikes upward as prices plunge. Table 2.5 rates heavy breakout volume +1, for a running total of +5.

Skipping to the next table with scores, Table 2.7, we compare the breakout point with the yearly price range. Over the 12 months before the breakout, prices ranged from a high of 32.63 (the high to the right of point 5) to a low of 11.50, at point 1. The breakout occurs at a price of 22. Just by looking at the figure, you can probably guess that the breakout price is in the center third of the yearly price range. To be more precise, divide the yearly price range into thirds, (32.63 – 11.50)/3, giving 7.04. If you add 7.04 onto the low price and subtract 7.04 from the high, you get a middle price range of 18.54 to 25.59. The breakout price of 22 is in that range. Table 2.7 rates the middle range as a +1 score, so the running total is +6.

What is the general market doing while the trendline is under construction (from trendline start to end)? On the date the trendline began, the S&P 500 closed at 447.78. The day the trendline ended, the S&P closed at 461.89, so the general market climbed between those two days. Table 2.9 says a rising market gives a +1 score. Running total: +7.

Finally, for market capitalization, multiply the number of shares outstanding (Web sites usually have this information) by the breakout price of 22, which places the stock in the small cap category. Table 2.10 scores small caps as +1. Final total: +8.

Scores above zero stand a better chance of performing above the 16.92% median and this one does. From the breakout, prices dropped to the ultimate low of 10 in just over a week. A 20% climb from this price would be a rise above 12 and that happened on January 4 (measured low to close), signaling a trend change. From the breakout point to the ultimate low, prices tumbled 55%.

CASE STUDY 2

Figure 2.7 shows a steep trendline drawn across the minor lows in an uptrend. Since you know the thinking behind the various tables by now, I run through them quickly to determine a score.

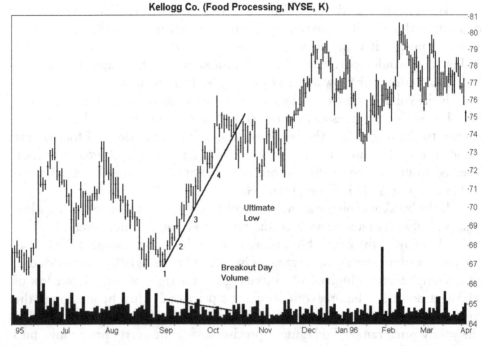

Figure 2.7   A trendline with a negative score. Performance is usually worse than the median decline when the score totals less than zero. Here, prices decline by 5%, then climb substantially.

Table 2.1: Touch spacing. There are four touches in 32 days, measured from point 1 to point 4 (not the trendline end). That gives a touch spacing of 8 days, well below the 28-day median. Table 2.1 scores narrow spacing as –1.

Table 2.2: Trendline length. The entire trendline measures 43 days, well below the median 137, for a –1 score. Running total: –2.

Table 2.3: Trendline angle. Looking at Figure 2.7, you can see that the angle is quite steep (you can score it –1 if you prefer). On my computer screen, however, the angle appears more shallow, at 42 degrees, for a zero score. Running total: unchanged at –2.

Table 2.4: Volume trend. Figure 2.7 shows clearly that volume is trending downward for a –1 score. Running total: –3.

Table 2.5: Breakout volume. On the breakout day—the day prices closed below the trendline—volume declined from the day before, and it certainly did not reach the level of the December or January peaks. The volume level is average, scoring –1. Running total: –4.

Table 2.7: Yearly price range. Where does the breakout fall in the yearly price range? The yearly high occurred at a price of 76.25, the low at 52.50, and the breakout at 74.13. Thus, the breakout occurs near the yearly high, scoring –1. Running total: –5.

Table 2.9: Market trend. From the day the trendline started to the day it ended, the general market climbed. A rising market from the trendline start to end scores +1 for a running total of –4.

Table 2.10: Market capitalization. The stock is a large cap for a –1 score. Final total: –5.

Trendlines with scores below zero tend to do less well than the median 16.92% decline, but nothing is guaranteed. Your trading skills, trading costs, the industry trend, and other factors will influence how your trade performs. From the breakout price of 74.13, the stock dropped to a low of 70.50 before moving up substantially. The decline measured just 5%, a wimpy performance as predicted.

3

Support and Resistance

As I was researching support and resistance, one thing struck me more than anything else: The topic is seldom mentioned. There are oodles of articles on trendlines, for example, but few dedicated to support and resistance. That lack is a shame, because support and resistance are the single most important concepts in trading stocks. If you know where support and resistance levels are, you can tell how much money you stand to gain and how much you risk losing—before you place a trade. That scenario is like sitting down to play poker with your buddies and knowing not only what they hold in their hands, but what cards will be dealt.

Defining support and resistance is not as easy as I thought. You might say that support occurs when buying demand halts a price decline; resistance is when selling pressure overwhelms buying demand and stops a price rise. Those definitions are certainly true, but you could just be describing a minor low or minor high. Perhaps a better definition would include several minor lows or minor highs stopping near the same price multiple times.

Technical analysts speak of support *levels* and resistance *levels*. Support and resistance are not individual price points, but rather thick bands of molasses that slow or even stop price movement. Prices do pierce support or resistance areas, and sometimes it occurs quite quickly; at other times, numerous attempts must be made by enthusiastic buyers trying to overwhelm just as enthusiastic sellers. Eventually, one of the two warring parties wins. If buyers win, prices burst through the resistance level and may even gap upward. If sellers win, prices tumble. For investors, the trick is to anticipate where prices will stall and to trade accordingly.

Support and resistance (SAR) come in a variety of flavors that all revolve around the stalling price theme. I begin with what I consider to be the weakest and move to the most important support and resistance types.

ROUND NUMBER SAR

Figure 3.1 shows weekly prices on a semilog chart with horizontal lines at 20, 30, and 40. Notice that prices approach 10 three times and rebound. At 20, there are even more points where prices touch or overshoot by a dollar or two. SAR zones are just that—zones, not specific price levels—so overshoot or undershoot commonly occurs. At 30, SAR becomes even more defined beginning on the far left of the chart in September 1996 and moving into 1998. At 40, the air is thin and only a few areas are able to live in the rarefied atmosphere, notably in late 1996 to early 1997 and again in mid-2000.

Why does round number support or resistance happen? Suppose you bought a stock at 21. Are you more likely to sell at 29.63, 30, or 31.38? Chances are, your first answer is the round number 30, just as it is for everyone else.

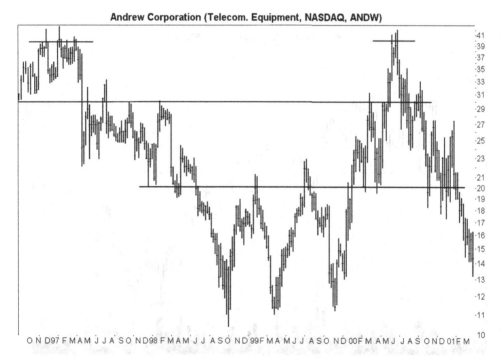

Figure 3.1   Round number support and resistance. Prices bump up against a resistance level or find support, near round numbers.

When everyone dumps shares at 30, what happens? Even though there is a buyer for every seller, the stock heads down because selling pressure is greater than buying demand.

I used round number SAR to my advantage recently. Here is my notebook entry for the first part of the trade shown in Figure 3.2. "4/16/01. I bought 500 shares, filled at $20.10. This has confirmed an Adam & Eve double bottom. All, or almost all, of the other drug stocks I follow have hit lows, then double bottomed, most more uneven than this one. Small resistance at 22, but expect a rise to 26. Downside could be as low as the old double bottom low of 11.75. That would be a too-far-away loss of 42%. Beta-adjusted trailing stop says 17.89 for a loss of 11%, a more reasonable number. The formation scores a +4. This stock does not have a good stop-loss point yet. General market is down, but could be at or near a bottom."

You can see that after I bought, the stock climbed to 24 in short order, threw back to the price level of the breakout, 17.75, then climbed. Prices struggled to rise above 24 before finally punching through and zipping up to 30.

Here is my notebook entry for the sale. "5/23/01. I sold 500 shares this morning at the open. The stock has nearly tripled from 11 to 30 in less than 2 months, too quick for my taste. I have made almost 50% and I think the stock is bumping up against a resistance level. It is time to leave."

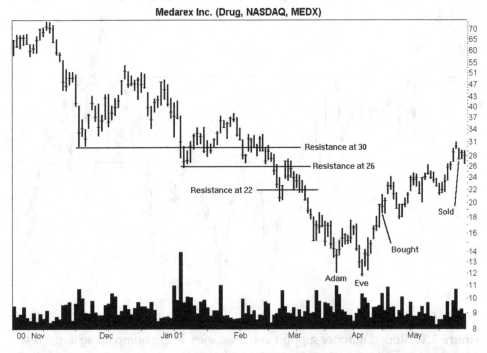

Figure 3.2   A round number trade. I bought the Adam & Eve double bottom and sold the stock the day after it reached 30, pocketing a 45% gain in less than 2 months.

I placed a market order to sell at the next day's open and received a fill at 29.26, less than the prior close of 30.02. Apparently, other traders had the same idea and the stock gapped lower on the open. By the end of the day, the stock tumbled to close at 27.36, a decline of 2.66 points and just a penny above the daily low. Even though the gap down was alarming, I certainly felt pleased to get out well above the daily low. The stock peaked at a high of 32.25 then tumbled to 11.91.

Table 3.1 shows some statistics for round number SAR. I looked at over 2,100 horizontal consolidation regions and checked how often a round number was between the region's high and low. In 22% of the cases, a round number was involved in the support or resistance zone. I explain what a horizontal consolidation region is later in this chapter. For the moment, think of it as an area where prices move horizontally—a support or resistance zone with flat tops, flat bottoms, or both.

Table 3.1
Round Number SAR Statistics

Description	Result
Number of times horizontal consolidation region includes round number: up breakouts	201/900 or 22%
Number of times horizontal consolidation region includes round number: down breakouts	265/1222 or 22%
Ultimate high stops near round number ± $0.50	57/900 or 6%
Ultimate high stops near round number ± $1.00	94/900 or 10%
Ultimate high stops near round number ± $1.50	125/900 or 14%
Ultimate low stops near round number ± $0.50	99/1222 or 8%
Ultimate low stops near round number ± $1.00	162/1222 or 13%
Ultimate low stops near round number ± $1.50	226/1222 or 18%
Number of times ultimate high stopped above horizontal consolidation region with round number SAR	101/201 or 50%
Number of times ultimate high stopped between horizontal consolidation region with round number SAR	62/201 or 31%
Number of times ultimate high stopped below horizontal consolidation region with round number SAR	38/201 or 19%
Number of times ultimate low stopped above horizontal consolidation region with round number SAR	36/265 or 14%
Number of times ultimate low stopped between horizontal consolidation region with round number SAR	105/265 or 40%
Number of times ultimate low stopped below horizontal consolidation region with round number SAR	124/265 or 47%

The next two sets of lines (ultimate high stops and ultimate low stops) in the table show how often prices, after a chart pattern breakout, stop near a round number. In other words, prices reach the ultimate high or ultimate low, then the price trend reverses. For upward breakouts, prices stop within 50 cents of a whole number 6% of the time. This compares to an 8% rate for downward breakouts. I added the $0.50, $1.00, or $1.50 buffers to capture ending prices *near* the round number (only 2% of the time does the ultimate high or ultimate low stop exactly at a round number).

The remainder of the table shows an analysis of where the ultimate high or low stops in those stocks having a horizontal consolidation region showing round number support or resistance. For upward breakouts, half the time (50%), prices pushed through the round number resistance zone. Almost a third of the time (31%), prices stopped somewhere within the price range of the consolidation zone. The remainder of the time, 19%, prices did not climb to the horizontal consolidation region.

For downward breakouts, prices remained above the support region 14% of the time. Over a third of the time, 40%, prices stopped declining within the horizontal consolidation region, and the remainder of the time, 47%, prices pushed through the support zone and continued lower.

What do all the numbers mean? About one in five horizontal consolidation regions will form around a round number. When that happens, prices will stop within the price levels bounded by the top and bottom of the region about a third of the time. Half the time, prices will push on through the region.

MOVING AVERAGE SAR

Moving averages sometimes highlight support or resistance areas, but what is a moving average? The first time I was asked that was by a co-op student when I was a senior software engineer. My jaw dropped in surprise because he had never heard of moving averages, despite the many college math courses he had taken.

I explained that a moving average is just an average in which the oldest number is dropped in favor of a more recent number. For example, the sum of 1, 2, 3, 4, and 5 is 15, and the average is the sum divided by the number of elements. Since there are five numbers involved, the average is 15/5 or 3. In a moving average, the oldest element (1 in this case) gets dropped off and the new number (6, for example) is added in. The sum then becomes 2 + 3 + 4 + 5 + 6, or 20, and the new average is 20/5 or 4. A plot of the moving average would show a point at 3 and another at 4.

For stocks, the method is just the same only the numbers represent prices. A 200-day moving average would sum 200 days worth of prices, and each day the oldest price would be dropped in favor of the most recent quote. In this way, the average would move, hence the name, moving average.

Airgas, Inc (Chemical (Specialty), NYSE, ARG)

Figure 3.3 Moving average SAR. Sometimes a moving average offers clues to SAR when the average nears or touches prices. A 40-week moving average appears here.

Figure 3.3 shows a 40-week moving average, a commonly chosen value. I add the closing prices each week for 40 weeks then plot the first point, drop off a week, and add in the new week, continuing the process until finished.

Notice how prices sometimes bump against the moving average and bounce off, as in June through September 1997. The moving average seems to repel prices, supporting them sometimes and resisting a price advance at other times. This price movement is not unusual and is a key trait of SAR. What is a support level later becomes a resistance level, and vice versa.

CHART PATTERN SAR

Many of the larger chart patterns show support or resistance. As an example, look at the Eve & Adam double top shown in Figure 3.4. Imagine that you thought highly of the stock and bought it at 39, as shown.

For a while, you felt good as prices climbed above your purchase price but within a week, things started going bad. Prices dropped. Since it was only a retrace in an uptrend—a stair-step pattern upward—there was nothing to worry about. You knew enough to hold on until the brief retrace finished. "Maybe you

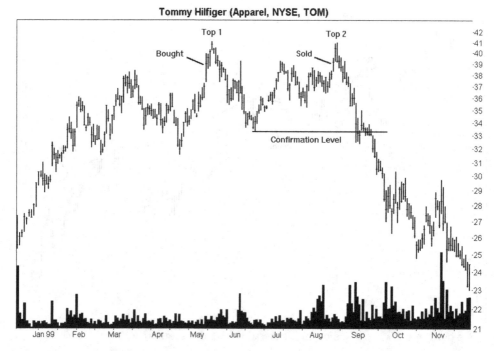

Figure 3.4 An Eve & Adam double top. People tend to sell a losing position as soon as they get their money back, forming a double-top chart pattern.

should buy more," your conscience asked innocently, even as the pros on the other side of the trade snickered.

As prices tumbled each day, you grew more concerned. Your stock had morphed from a prize winner into a dog that even an animal shelter would not accept. The brilliant management team running the company suddenly did not know squat; your dead mother could run the company better. Then you announced those fateful words: "As soon as I get my money back, I'm selling." The stock continued down, and that only hardened your resolve. What started as an angry sputter turned into a solemn promise: break even then sell.

Eventually, prices found support at the 33–34 level—the bottom of prior minor lows—leveled off, then climbed. When the stock reached 39, you were as good as your word. You sold.

You were not alone. Many other investors did the same thing. They bought high, rode the stock lower, then vowed to sell at the break-even point. They did, and all the selling pressure stopped the rise cold for 2 days near 41. Investors started panicking as prices tumbled; volume spiked upward. Months later, with selling pressure abating and buying demand catching up, the stock stabilized at a much lower level.

Crowd psychology: That is why a double top forms. When I see a top forming like Top 1, I often think that there may be another top forming across the valley. When it might occur is a mystery, but I keep an eye out for it. Sometimes, I even buy in the valley low, expecting a rebound, and sell near the second top.

Whenever you see a chart pattern, trendlines drawn along the pattern's edge mark the SAR boundary. Sometimes, if the chart pattern is tall enough, you can trade it: buy at the lower trendline and sell at the upper one. This takes nimble trading and a bit of luck, so it is not for most investors. Most would do better to limit their trading to sure things, if there is such a thing.

Figure 3.5 shows another example of SAR. The symmetrical triangle contains prices using resistance along the chart pattern's top and support along the bottom, following the trendlines. Eventually, buying demand burns through resistance, but prices do not climb very far. The rise collapses and throws back to the formation top. For a week or so, the top trendline supports prices but they eventually push through the support zone and find support at a prior minor low.

In September, the rally falters as prices bump against a resistance zone set up by the lower formation trendline extended into the future. The resistance does not end there but continues well into the future, posing a problem for prices almost a year later.

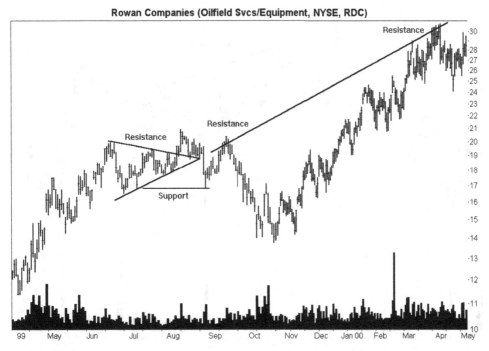

Figure 3.5 A symmetrical triangle. The bottom trendline projected into the future identifies resistance zones that prices struggle to pierce.

The trading lesson for chart pattern SAR is simple: find all the chart patterns you can in the recent past, and extend their trendlines into the future. Prices may struggle when they meet those trendlines, so be prepared. Before you place a trade, ask yourself how profitable the trade will be should prices stall at the trendline.

TRENDLINE SAR

Trendlines, by definition, highlight SAR. Take a look at Figure 3.6. Beginning in July and running through December, prices run up against an imaginary, down-sloping, ceiling. Drawing a trendline connecting the minor highs shows the trend—a line of resistance.

How is this useful? I looked at the chart and saw a rounding top. Beginning at point B (far left), rounding up to the July high, then down to the early October low, the rounded shape was unmistakable (maybe not to you, but on my computer screen, it appears more rounded, and no, I do not wear glasses). According to the chapter on rounding tops from my previous book, *Encyclopedia of Chart Patterns* (Wiley, 2000), a rounding top fails 19% of the time. I con-

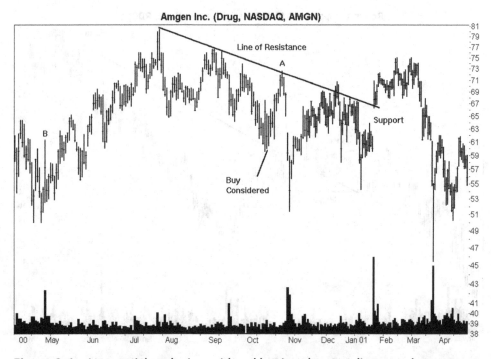

Figure 3.6   A potential trade. I considered buying the rounding top chart pattern (point B, through the July high to the early October low) until I noticed the downward trendline that imposed an upward limit to the price rise.

sider chart patterns with failure rates less than 20% to be reliable, so this one just squeaks by.

Waiting for prices to close above the dome high, the breakout point, results in a 6% failure rate. Instead of waiting for the breakout, the book mentions an early entry point, described as one-third up the dome from the right low. With a dome low of 59.50 and a top of 80.44, the buy price would be 66.48, that is, 59.50 + (80.44 – 59.50)/3. The book says that the early entry price is usually high enough to exceed any overhead resistance posed by a down-sloping trendline. Time to buy?

The obvious thing to do was draw in the trendline, starting with the highest high on the chart, sloping downward, as the figure shows. The trendline, at about 73, rests above the 66.48 entry point. If things went wrong, the stock would rise from 66.48 to 73 then collapse. If I traded the stock perfectly, I would make just 9%—not even worth considering. The worst case downside would be a drop to the twin lows of April, to 50, a round number support zone. I decided to avoid the stock.

What happened? The stock climbed to the trendline, point A, then dropped like a stone. Had I owned the stock, I probably would have waited for a slight retrace that never came. In short, I would have been caught in the down draft and perhaps sold the stock in the low 50s. Instead of a 9% gain, I would be looking at a loss perhaps as high as 25%.

Before you make a trade, ask yourself where prices should meet resistance in their climb, and where support should be if price's tank. Some analysts say that a four-to-one ratio of gain to loss for a trade is worth considering. Trying to find a trade with that kind of ratio is difficult.

OLD HIGH, OLD LOW SAR

Prices stall at old highs and lows and Figure 3.7 shows examples of such stalling. The horizontal line illustrates support in mid-1997 and late 1998, then flips to resistance in November and December 1999.

The numbers on the figure represent some of the common support or resistance areas. Notice how area 3 changes from support in late 1997–1998 to resistance in August 1998. Numbers 5 and 6 show the same situation; what was once support changes to resistance.

When you look at a price chart, scan for major turning points. Sometimes, prices will attempt to reach those levels and fail. Prices may rise slightly above an old high or drop below an old low—this is clear in Figure 3.7 (numbers 2, 5, and 6, for example)—but do not be fooled. If prices stall after reaching a major turning point, it *may* mean the trend is in the process of changing. There are no guarantees, as the horizontal line below point 2 shows. The downtrend begun at the chart's high, stalled at 2, but eventually continued down to 6.

Figure 3.7 Old highs and old lows on the weekly scale. Major turning point's set up support or resistance areas that pose problems for continued price movement. The numbers represent common SAR areas.

HORIZONTAL CONSOLIDATION REGION SAR

You might think of congestion as something that happens during allergy season, but as it applies to stocks, I feel there is one type you should be looking for. I call it the horizontal consolidation region (HCR).

Figure 3.8 shows an example of congestion SAR. Above the ascending triangle rests a resistance area just waiting to trap advancing prices, which is exactly what happened in early February. Those investors buying the triangle breakout probably took a loss if they did not sell quickly enough. Prices climbed to the bottom of the consolidation region, stalled, then backtracked to the triangle apex—a support region highlighted by the horizontal trendline. A week later, prices tumbled. It was not until late October that prices finally climbed back above 11. Another storm front waited at 14, showing a stronger horizontal consolidation pattern. Part of it appears in the figure, but it extends backward until December 1996.

An HCR is an important factor to consider when trading stocks, whether you use chart patterns or not. In Part Two of this book, I spend a fair amount of time describing HCRs, how to locate them, and what they mean to performance. For now though, let me describe the key elements, then provide some statistics.

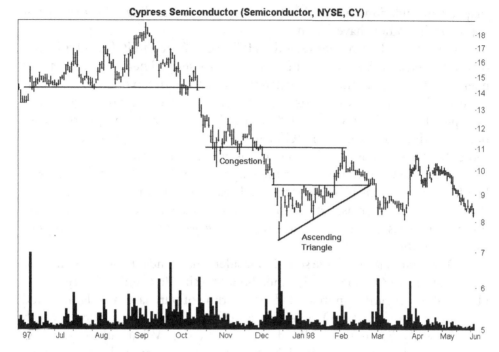

Figure 3.8 Congestion SAR. Seeing the congestion area above the ascending triangle allows you to estimate how far prices are likely to climb.

For upward breakouts from a chart pattern, the HCR must be located above the chart pattern and on or after the trend start leading to the pattern; for downward breakouts, it will be hiding below but also on or after the trend start. In Part Two, I show you how to find the trend start, but that is not important now.

Like the two horizontal consolidation areas shown in Figure 3.8 (marked by the two horizontal trendlines before the ascending triangle), the most potent regions tend to have flat tops, flat bottoms, or both, and to be several weeks long. Ignore any outlier spikes. In essence, you are looking for a region where prices move horizontally, bounded by a common price.

HCR STOPPING POWER

Now to the statistics. Do HCRs close to the chart pattern show more support or resistance than those farther away? If you read most books about technical analysis, the authors state—in no uncertain terms—that the farther a support or resistance area is from the current price, the weaker or less significant it becomes. That makes sense, but my research says it is wrong. Let me explain. I only looked at HCRs between the trend start and the formation, not just any shaped consolidation region. What I am saying is my findings may or may not apply to what others have found.

I measured the days between the HCR's end (since a HCR always comes before the chart pattern) and the chart pattern start. Then, I created a frequency distribution to show how often the ultimate high (up breakouts) or ultimate low (down breakouts) stopped within the consolidation region. For example, Table 3.2 shows that 38% of the chart patterns with upward breakouts had prices stop within an HCR (surrounded by a 5% price buffer to catch those that fall short or overshoot) that was within 7 days away.

What the table shows is that the stopping power of the HCR starts out low for those regions nearby (because a breakout can usually power through the nearby SAR), increases strength up to 28 days away, then oscillates up and down, regardless of the breakout direction. *Support or resistance does not grow weaker over time.*

Does that make intuitive sense? Consider what Linda did with her mutual fund. Just before October 1987, Linda bought a sizable chunk of a large, popular, and well-regarded mutual fund. At the time of purchase, a dollar invested was worth a buck. After October 19, a dollar invested was suddenly worth something like 77 cents—a 23% decline in one day. What did she say? "As soon as I break even, I'm selling." Notice that she did not qualify it with how long she was willing to wait. In fact, it took about a year and a half for the fund to get back to break-even, and when it did, she sold.

Now, imagine that others did the same thing. On the chart you would see resistance to upward price movement as those investors reached break-even and sold. Prices would flat line, matching an event that happened 1.5 years ago. Does time matter? Not to Linda.

Speaking of time, I did not limit the HCRs to just 70 days before a chart pattern, but did a frequency distribution that encompassed up to 530 prior days. The trend remained the same as that shown in the table, that is, a consolidation region occurring nearly 1.5 years ago showed as much stopping power as one occurring a month ago. Also note that the table shows that HCRs below a chart pattern are slightly more effective in stopping a decline than those above the chart pattern. By that I mean the percentages in the down breakout row are higher than the up breakout row.

Table 3.2
Time Between HCR and Chart Pattern,
by How Often Prices Stop Within the HCR

Description	Time Between HCR and Chart Pattern (days)									
	7	14	21	28	35	42	49	56	63	70
Up breakouts	38%	43%	45%	47%	41%	48%	50%	34%	43%	47%
Down breakouts	44%	55%	60%	67%	51%	56%	63%	51%	59%	60%

Table 3.3
Dollar Distance Between HCR and Chart Pattern,
by How Often Prices Stop Within the HCR

Description	Percentage above Breakout Price							
	5	**10**	**15**	**20**	**25**	**30**	**35**	**40**
Up breakouts	48%	51%	53%	38%	42%	27%	32%	15%
Down breakouts	64%	60%	52%	64%	41%	55%	20%	29%

One last note about downward breakouts: *An HCR a month or so before the chart pattern poses the highest risk to a declining price trend.* It stops the decline 67% of the time.

Table 3.3 shows the stopping power of HCRs as the distance from the HCR to the chart pattern grows. For example, with upward breakouts, those chart patterns with an HCR within 5% above the breakout price (using the percentage difference between the bottom of the region and the breakout price) showed prices that stopped within the HCR 48% of the time. This strength peaked for those HCRs up to 15% away, then the stopping power generally decreased as the distance increased.

For downward breakouts, the stopping power was usually more robust than those for upward breakouts but the trend was similar. Prices stopped within the HCR 64% of the time when the top of the HCR was less than 5% below the breakout price. The stopping power generally decreased as the distance increased. In essence, we can say that *the farther away an HCR is (vertically, on a price basis, not horizontally, on a time basis), the weaker it is.*

Does the length of the HCR make a difference in its stopping power? Table 3.4 provides the answer. Although it is difficult to see the trend among a bunch of numbers, up breakouts show a rising trend as the HCR length increases from 7 days wide to 70. For example, 40% of the time prices stop within the HCR when the length of the region is a week wide. At the other end of the chart, 58% of the time prices stop within the HCR price range when the region is 70 days wide. For upward breakouts, length is important. Downward

Table 3.4
HCR Length, by How Often Prices Stop Within the HCR

Description	HCR Length (days)									
	7	**14**	**21**	**28**	**35**	**42**	**49**	**56**	**63**	**70**
Up breakouts	40%	44%	34%	45%	46%	41%	51%	46%	47%	58%
Down breakouts	61%	51%	60%	55%	62%	61%	49%	55%	53%	66%

Table 3.5
HCR Volume, by How Often Prices Stop Within the HCR

Low Volume Multiplier	High Volume Multiplier	Below Average Volume (%)	Average Volume (%)	Above Average Volume (%)
0.5	2.0	22	19	6
0.75	1.25	18	20	19
0.75	1.2	18	20	19
0.75	1.1	18	20	20
0.9	1.1	18	22	20

breakouts, however, are essentially flat, suggesting that the length of the support region has little effect on its stopping power.

For both upward and downward breakouts, let me say that the regions may have been based on prior regions of support or resistance at the same price level, but not included in the HCR dates. For example, picture a double top, each peak of which appears flat. The most recent peak might be an HCR of a week long and one where the trend starts, but it also may assume the prior peak at the same price level would also lend a hand in stopping a price trend. However, since the earlier peak is before the trend start, statistically, it is not included as part of the HCR.

Table 3.5 shows volume measurements and their effect on HCRs. I computed the average volume from the HCR start to its end and compared it to the average of the prior 90 days. When the HCR volume was one-half (0.5) the 90-day average, 22% of the chart patterns showing HCRs had prices stop within the HCR. For high volume, HCRs with twice the average volume or higher, prices stop within the HCR just 6% of the time.

You can see in the table that as the low volume multiplier approaches the average of the prior 90 days, the effectiveness drops from 22% to 18%—not much of a change. High volume, as it approaches the 90-day average, shows effectiveness rises from 6% to 20%, a substantial change, but one not far above the 18% shown by low volume, and below the 22% effectiveness of the average volume HCR.

The question is, does high volume within an HCR suggest greater stopping power? No. This answer differs from the commonly held belief that volume is important. The higher the volume within the consolidation region, technical analysts say, the more support or resistance the area will show. The table suggests otherwise, that *average* volume in a consolidation region shows the best stopping power.

Tables 3.6 and 3.7 show where prices stop in relation to the HCR. For example, in Table 3.6, a broadening top has prices stop within the HCR (sur-

Table 3.6
HCR Effectiveness by Chart Pattern, Up Breakouts

Chart Pattern	Within Region ±5% (%)	Push Through Region (%)	Do Not Reach Region (%)
Broadening top	38	57	5
Double bottom, Adam & Adam	51	39	10
Double bottom, Adam & Eve	42	47	11
Double bottom, Eve & Adam	45	48	7
Double bottom, Eve & Eve	39	52	9
Head-and-shoulders bottom	42	50	8
Scallops, descending	52	38	10
Triangles, ascending	35	59	6
Triangles, descending	26	59	16
Triangles, symmetrical	40	53	7
Triple bottoms	44	47	10
Average	41	50	9

Table 3.7
HCR Effectiveness by Chart Pattern, Down Breakouts

Chart Pattern	Within Region ±5% (%)	Push Through Region (%)	Do Not Reach Region (%)
Broadening top	58	31	11
Diamonds	55	36	9
Double top, Adam & Adam	59	34	7
Double top, Adam & Eve	65	29	6
Double top, Eve & Adam	64	28	8
Double top, Eve & Eve	57	34	10
Head-and-shoulders top	56	35	9
Scallops ascending	53	32	14
Triangles, ascending	24	52	24
Triangles, descending	53	40	7
Triangles, symmetrical	57	28	15
Triple tops	56	37	7
Average	55	35	11

rounded by a 5% buffer) 38% of the time. Another 57% of the time, prices eventually push through the overhead resistance and continue higher, whereas the remainder, 5%, never make it up to the resistance area at all.

Looking at the averages, up breakouts have HCRs that work about 41% of the time. Downward breakouts have HCRs that stop prices more often, 55% of the time, on average. If you add the "do not reach region" numbers to the within region values, you find that prices either never make it to the region or stop within it 50% to 66% of the time. If making money in the stock market is important to you, pay attention to HCRs before you invest.

PRICE PREDICTION

Before trading, look for HCRs. Compute the likely advance from the breakout price to the base of the consolidation region. If prices stop at the consolidation region, would the trade still be worth taking? If the answer is no, do not be an idiot. Look elsewhere.

Check the downside, too. If prices drop, where will they stop? If the support zone is too far away, select a closer stop point and place a stop-loss order there.

Table 3.8 summarizes the various SAR features described in this chapter. How do you make use of this information? The best way is to scan your chart looking for the SAR areas before you trade.

Figure 3.9 illustrates a trade I made and here is my notebook entry. "12/4/98. Instead of buying 1,000 shares, I bought 500 at 7.75 today. Looks like a head-and-shoulders bottom with prices moving up. Limited shares to 500 because price of oil is predicted to move down into single digits from 11.18 yesterday. Still, this lowers my average purchase price. Stock is up 0.25 on the day."

Table 3.8
Summary of SAR Areas

SAR Description	Explanation
Round number	Prices sometimes pause near round numbers, such as 10, 20, and 30
Moving average	Prices find SAR near popular moving averages, such as the 200-day (40-week) moving average
Chart pattern	Extend the trendlines outlining chart patterns to anticipate where prices may stall
Trendline	A trendline shows likely SAR areas
Old high or low	Prices commonly stop near old highs and lows
HCR	Prices pause during stair-step trends. When prices return to the horizontal step, they tend to pause.

Figure 3.9 A stock trade. I bought an unconfirmed head-and-shoulders bottom and sold near the top of an unconfirmed double top for a 46% profit.

Suspecting a head-and-shoulders bottom gave me confidence to place the trade. I believed that the right shoulder low had completed because it approached the depth of the left shoulder low. In other words, prices found a support zone. The downside would be a drop to the head low, at 5.44, quite a decline from the 7.75 purchase price, but marginally below the 6.31 right shoulder low. With a gap thrusting prices higher the day before, the trade seemed like a safe bet.

When prices curled around and dropped below my purchase price to a low of 6.63, I was not that concerned because the low (point A in Figure 3.9) rested on an up-sloping trendline connecting the head and right shoulder lows.

Prices quickly recovered and started a straight-line uphill run beginning in March. As they approached the price of the old high, I became nervous. The old high, at 13.50, represented the confirmation point of the head-and-shoulders bottom. If prices did not close above this price, then the head-and-shoulders was just another three-bump squiggle, not a valid chart pattern.

To me, the stock looked as if it was making a double top—a twin peak formation in which prices run up against resistance, then tumble. The right shoulder low, at 6.31, was the confirmation point, the point at which a twin peak pattern turns into a valid double top. I was not willing to watch my gains decline from 13.50 to 6.31 before selling. The flip side of this meant that there was a 65% chance that prices would not make it down to the confirmation price, but post a new high instead. I am not making up the 65% figure, that is the failure rate for unconfirmed double tops I found when researching my previous book, *Encyclopedia of Chart Patterns* (Wiley, 2000).

When it became clear to me that prices had peaked, I sold 1,100 shares. Recall that I bought just 500 shares. No, I did not short the stock; I just sold some stock I had purchased earlier. On the trade, I bought at 7.75 and sold at 11.38. After commissions, I made a net profit of 46% in about 4 months.

The point of this trade is not to show how to trade unconfirmed chart patterns, which I do not recommend, but to see how SAR levels play a key role in determining how far prices will rise and fall. Hoping that prices will rise to the old high at 13.50 sets an upper limit, a target in which to take profits. A predicted low of 5.44 suggests how far prices might fall. With a purchase price of 7.75, the maximum decline would be an absurd 30%, and the rise would represent a 74% gain, or a win/loss ratio of about 2.5 to 1. That represents the best and worst cases for the high and low, respectively. With a closer stop-loss point, say, the right shoulder low at 6.31, the potential loss would shrink to 19%, still too large (best is below 10%), but more manageable.

Make an objective analysis of the likely price rise and fall before you trade. Those figures will set you up with price targets, warning areas where getting out of the trade may cut your losses short or allow you to retain more profit.

Incidentally, not shown in Figure 3.9 is that prices never confirmed the double top. Instead, they dropped to a low of 8.69 and reached a new high of 14.25. What did I do? I did the same maneuver again and bought at 9.38 and sold at 12, after the stock peaked, netting 28% in 4 months.

4

Stops, Bats, and Selling

When I was a software engineer, it was my good fortune to be assigned the task of developing software for an elaborate office telephone system. My boss and I sat down in a conference room to talk about the design and we soon had a bunch of circles drawn on a white board. After an hour, he looked at his watch and announced that he had a meeting to attend, handed me the marker pen, and told me to finish up. I sat for several minutes looking at the scribblings, pondering different ideas, different solutions, before the ultimate solution occurred to me. I smiled, erased the scribblings, and went back to my office, knowing that I had found the answer to life, the universe, and everything.

The next day, my boss asked to see my design. I walked to the marker board, drew two circles with lines connecting them and replied, "The entire design consists of two states: on hook or off hook."

He did not swat me upside the head and call me an idiot; he did not jump up and yell, "Eureka!" Instead, he asked a simple question. I paused, knowing that my simplified solution would fail, that my idea had crumbled under the weight of a question. I spent several days fleshing out the various states a complex phone system could find itself in, eventually developing a beautiful system, an elegant system, one that was the envy of the industry.

Management killed the project.

There is a point to this story, and I call it Bulkowski's Law: *If a stock declines, sell it.* That simple law is all you need to know about making money in the stock market. You might squeal like a pig and claim that, as with the phone system, I have oversimplified life as we know it, but I would reply that the stock market is a game with just one rule: If a stock declines, sell it. What else is there to know?

Plenty, it turns out. In the stock market, it is easy to make money, but even easier to lose it. How, then, do you know when it is time to sell? This chapter focuses on money management techniques to answer that question.

STOP-LOSS SELL ORDERS

There are many types of stops, but the most popular is the stop-loss order. A stop-loss order to sell is a command you give to your broker to sell shares of a stock should it decline to a certain price. A stop-loss order does not mean that you are selling a stock at a loss, nor does it guarantee a price at which your order will be filled.

For example, say you own a stock that you bought at 3, and it is now trading at 21. You place a stop-loss order with your broker to sell the shares should the price drop to 20. If the stock trades at 20, the stop-loss order becomes a market order, and you will likely receive $20 per share, but you could also receive some other price, depending on market conditions. That is all there is to it. A stop-loss order tries to protect a profit or minimize a loss.

Figure 4.1 shows a trade I made where a stop-loss order came in handy. I saw the small Adam & Eve double bottom form and waited for confirmation,

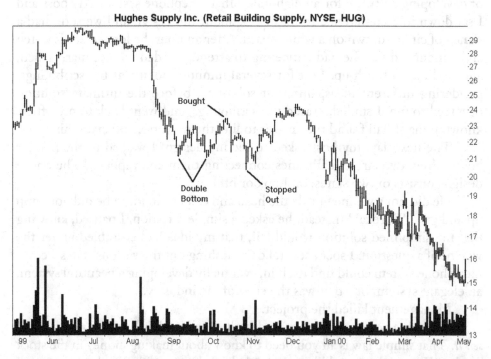

Figure 4.1   Stop-loss order. When the Adam & Eve double bottom failed to carry through, the stock tumbled and I was stopped out at 20.88, limiting my loss to 11% instead of a potential 36%.

that is, prices to close above the high between the two lows. The day after confirmation occurred, I bought. Here is my trading notebook entry. "10/12/99. Resistance at 26, support at 22. I bought 300 at 23.38 and expect this to continue rising due to hurricane season boosting sales without impacting outlets. That's the hope. Lowes and Home Depot are doing well, but others are not, such as Fastenal and Building Materials Holding. They are probably not a distributor like this company. I bought because of the double bottom and higher low when compared to the March 1999 low. There is a bunch of resistance at 26, so I anticipate a stall at 25.50 to 25.88. If it punches through, it's up, up, and away. Downside is the twin lows at about 21. Sell at 20.88. That's a downside of 10%."

I placed a stop-loss order with my broker and it was a good thing I did, too. After I bought, the stock fell into a pit. When prices reached 20.88, my stop point, the stock sold and I received a fill at that price. Including commissions, the loss was about 11%. If I had held onto the stock, you can see that it recovered somewhat but soon tumbled to a new low of 14.88, a decline of 36% from the purchase price.

PROFIT-OBJECTIVE STOP

Suppose you have been following your favorite Internet stock closely without taking action. For months, it has been trending down but touched bottom recently, bounced up, and hit the floor a second time: a potential double bottom. A month later, the stock closed above the confirmation point, the highest high between the two bottoms, indicating a valid double bottom and a buy signal. You step up to the plate and buy 1,000 shares at 10 but promise yourself that if you make $2,000, you will sell. That is a profit-objective stop. You set in advance how much money you are willing to make before selling.

You could also do this on the losing side. If your Internet stock releases an earnings report that is worse than expected, and the stock tumbles to 8, you have lost $2,000. That is your loss objective, and you decide to sell.

I have used this type of stop, but infrequently. Many times I feel like a miser counting my coins, watching my net worth, scanning my holdings. When a stock climbs and profit rises into four figures, the word *sell* crosses my mind. I do not, usually, but I watch the stock more closely for signs of topping out. If I feel the stock has peaked, or if the fundamentals have changed, then I sell.

Figure 4.2 shows a short-term trade I made trying to take advantage of an earnings surprise. As if expecting a good earnings report, the stock formed an ascending triangle, portending an upside breakout. The release of quarterly earnings on January 18 showed them well above the consensus estimate. On that day, the stock jumped 17%, from 9.06 to 10.63, closing near the daily high of 10.75, and handily bursting through the top of the ascending triangle on huge volume.

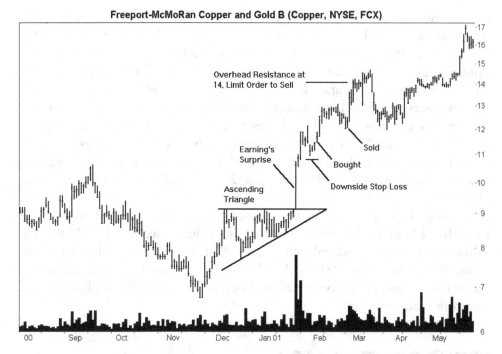

Figure 4.2 A short-term trade around an earnings report. After surprisingly good earnings, prices shot up, paused for a week, then continued their rise. This trade tried to take advantage of that behavior.

I have traded stocks long enough to know not to try to snag stocks with large 1-day price moves, so I waited (I should have used a stop order to buy just above the ascending triangle top). From my research, I discovered that a good earnings report sends a stock higher, but after a few days, the stock gives back some of its gains. Then, after an additional week, the stock will resume its rise. If you do not already own the stock, that is the time to buy.

Here is my notebook entry for the trade. "1/31/01. I bought 1,000 shares at the market. After shooting higher on better than expected earnings, the stock moved lower for several days and is now showing signs of climbing again. Think of this as an anti-DCB [dead-cat bounce chart pattern] trade: a large rise, followed by a 1-week pause, then a resumption of the climb. Fundamentally, Phelps Dodge says it is going to close some production due to high energy costs. This will help FCX as its operations are not in the Midwest or West, but in Indonesia. Downside is 10.75, upside is 14, maybe 18 if it clears resistance at those points. Copper prices have trended down recently, after peaking in September and a lower peak in December 2000."

Three days after reaching a retrace low, I bought the stock. Prices climbed above the prior minor high of 12.13 in short order, as predicted. That point is when I decided to use a profit-objective stop.

"2/5/01. I placed a limit order to sell 1,000 shares at 14. This is the top of the measure rule for a measured move up chart pattern, and it also ties with the top of prior resistance in March 2000." The stock's enthusiastic climb weakened, and prices meandered higher instead of continuing their burst upward. It looked as if momentum was turning.

"2/20/01. I canceled the limit order and watched the stock climb this morning. When prices crested, I sold 1,000 shares and it filled at 12.46, just below the 12.50 high. Reasons for sale include Indonesia unrest and a report of potential pollution problems at a mine in Indonesia, but it's not known whether FCX is the owner. This gives me a profit of over $650 even as the market has tanked big time. Now, it will probably zoom to 14. Another reason to sell is that I looked back and found a day when prices closed near the daily low. The following day, prices climbed but tied the prior day's high. In following days, the price continued down.

"For this trade, hold time was 3 weeks. The price of copper has broken out downward from a symmetrical triangle and is now resting at the bottom of an unconfirmed triple bottom. The likelihood is for copper prices to continue down. Indeed, prices dropped below the triple bottom support level yesterday."

You can see from the figure that I sold 1 day short of another up-leg. The stock reached my initial target of 14 and approached 18, another target I mentioned in my notebook entry. If I had held on, that would have meant a rise of about 50%.

Profit-objective stops can be useful to get you out at what you consider a good profit, or when you expect the stock to peak. Many times, I use the measure rule for chart patterns—usually the formation height added to the breakout price—to estimate how far prices will climb. Coupled with resistance levels and other factors, it is sometimes best to predict the upside limit. However, profit-objective stops do just that: They limit how much money you can make. Call it greed; how greedy are you?

TIME STOP

A time stop is when you make a trade, and know that if the stock does not move in, say, a week, you will sell. The thinking behind this stop type is to maximize your use of capital.

Some analysts argue that the longer you are in a trade, the less likely it is that the trade will work; the best trades are those that work immediately. Therefore, you want to have quick inventory turns, grabbing a few points then selling, buying again, and selling after another quick move. If a stock stays flat, sell it and buy a more promising situation. Do not tie up your trading capital for too long waiting for a move to occur. This method is useful for traders that have a limited capital base—a small portfolio.

I have not used this stop much except when I was moving my account from one brokerage to another. I suspected that a stock I owned was going to move soon, so I wanted to time the exit, but I had to move fast before the account transferred.

You may want to sell your holdings before going on vacation, for example, or just after the holidays to pay bills.

I am not too keen on time stops, but they do have their uses. It has been my experience that the less trading I do, the better my return. Time stops are contrary to that thinking, but if it works for you, great!

VOLATILITY STOP

When I think of a volatility stop, I first think of options. Buy when the volatility is low and sell when the volatility is high, or the reverse if you like the short side. There are times when you might consider closing out your position. Triple witching days, when contracts on stock options, stock index options, and stock index futures all expire on the same day, are notorious for high volatility. The trading day before holidays is usually thinly traded, so a stock may be more susceptible to large price swings. Anniversaries of stock market crashes also cause butterflies in the stomachs of investors. Finally, earnings announcements or earnings warnings can cause huge price movements.

For me, I only worry about earnings announcements when I am considering buying a stock. If I know that a stock is going to announce earnings in a few weeks, I will usually pass on the trade until after the announcement, then reevaluate.

TRAILING OR PROGRESSIVE STOP

A trailing stop, sometimes called a progressive stop, is perhaps the most useful of the stop types. It is nothing more than raising a stop-loss order as the stock climbs. There is no mechanism that I am aware of to do this automatically; you must cancel the old stop and place a new one at the new price.

Suppose the stock pictured in Figure 4.3 intrigued you. From December through April, you watched as the complex head-and-shoulders bottom formed. As an end-of-day trader, when prices closed above the neckline, you decided to buy the stock the next day and received a fill at 13.50, the closing price for the day. Immediately after buying, you considered stop placement.

You know from experience that the lowest shoulder represents a good area to place a stop-loss order, shown in the figure as point 1. At 0.15 below the shoulder low, or 10.11, that would mean a 25% decline before being stopped out. That is too much of a loss, so you look for a closer stop point.

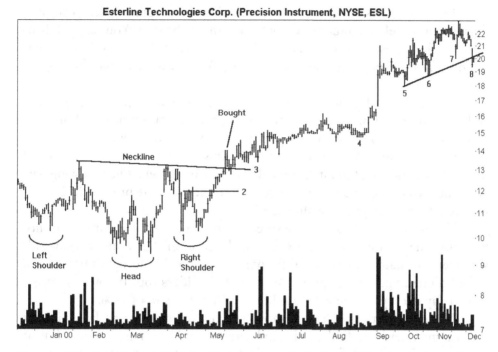

Figure 4.3 A trailing stop. Raise the stop as prices rise, but be sure to cancel the old stop. The flat shelf at point 2 marks a promising buy point once prices close above it.

Point 2, which marks the top of a flat shelf, still represents a too-large loss of 18%, but it appears to be a safe bet, so you place the stop-loss order at that price.

The next 2 days, the stock declines and you wonder whether the stock will continue declining and stop you out. Instead, the stock recovers. When it begins moving horizontally during July, you worry about a rounding-top chart pattern forming, so you move the stop to just below the neckline price, at 12.88 (point 3). With the stock trading at 15, the stop is 14% below, but there are no appealing points closer.

Instead of rounding over, the stock was only gathering strength for the next move up. It shoots out the top of the horizontal consolidation region formed during July and August, and climbs to 19, where it again moves horizontally (during September). You decide it is time to move the stop up to point 4, just below the consolidation region. From 19 where the stock is trading to 0.15 below point 4, 14.61, the stock must decline 23% to be stopped out. Normally, you like to limit any give backs to 10%, but there is not another good place to put the stop. If the stock gets sold at 14.61, that would represent a gain of just 8%, not including commissions.

The stock eases down to point 5, then climbs and rounds over to point 6. Finally, a well-defined minor low in which to move the stop! You call your broker, cancel the existing stop, and raise it to 17.85, 0.15 below point 5. That represents a much more tolerable stop loss of 5% as measured from the current price of 18.75.

Again, the stock moves up in a stair-step fashion from point 6 to point 7, and you raise the stop to 0.15 below point 6, the closest minor low. You draw a trendline connecting the lows at points 5 and 6 and extend it forward in time as the figure shows. When prices close below the trendline at point 8 and below the minor low at point 7, you believe it is time to sell. The following day, you cancel your stop and sell the shares. From the purchase price of 13.50, you receive a fill at 20, a profit of almost 50%.

Months later, you look at the stock and discover that if you drew a trendline from the lowest low on the chart, at the head of the complex head-and-shoulders formation, it would skirt point 4, point 8, and continue upward before piercing prices just after a head-and-shoulders top. If you sold at the close a day later, you would have sold at 24.60, for a gain of 82%.

The point of this trade is to show how trailing stops work, how difficult it can sometimes be to find good stop locations, and how hard it is to sell near the top. Selling a stock for a profit is like an airplane crash landing: Anytime you can walk away, it was a good landing.

BREAK-EVEN STOP

When you have made enough money in a trade, raise the stop to the break-even point. That sounds like good advice, but how much money do you need to make before raising the stop? Suppose you bought a stock at 20, and 18 was the stop price. The risk in this trade is $2 a share (20 − 18). When the profit rises to double the risk, raise the stop to break even. In this example, cancel the stop at 18 and raise it to 20 when the stock closes above 24.

Of course, you will want to place the stop below a support level, so arbitrarily raising it to 20 may not be the best course. Look for a nearby support zone and place the stop just below it, and be sure to raise the stop as prices rise.

MENTAL STOP

A mental stop is arguably used the most, but few investors have heard the term. This stop is not called in to your broker, but is held in your head. "I'll sell when the stock drops to 10," you might say. Novice investors—when the price reaches 10—will usually find an excuse to ignore the stop and hold on, riding the stock down. The pros use mental stops to prevent what is called running or gunning the stops. That is when floor traders force the price down to a support level where they expect stops to reside, sometimes causing stops to trigger in cascade fashion. They buy when the selling pressure abates and the stock rises. The same is true on the upside, where stops are hiding just above a resistance level. After the buying pressure diminishes, the stock moves lower.

Mental stops are what I use most often. Before placing a trade, I consider how far prices could fall and how far I expect them to rise. I calculate the stop-loss amount and try to hold potential losses to 10% of the trade cost, or less. If I feel the stock is topping out or if it declines to my sell point, I issue a market order and sell. I have broken 1,000 share orders into smaller lots, hoping for a better price later in the day, only to be disappointed. Now, I just sell the whole kit and caboodle.

If you use mental stops, be sure to act on them. Do not lower a mental stop or find some other excuse to hold a position. Remember Bulkowski's law: If a stock declines, sell it. That is all you need to know to make money in the stock market.

BETA-ADJUSTED TRAILING STOP

Many times a prior minor low marks the location for a stop-loss order. Other investors may want to sell at a fixed percentage down, say 10%, from the price at the high-water mark. Still others may prefer to lose a fixed-dollar amount, such as 1% or 2% of total trading capital, before being forced to sell. What if you base the stop-loss point not on the price, but on stock volatility?

That concept is behind what I call a beta-adjusted trailing stop (BATS). Beta is a number that compares the volatility of an individual stock with the general market. Stocks with a beta of 1 tend to be as volatile as the market. A stock with a beta of 1.5 means that if the market moves by 1%, the stock will move 1.5%. The idea behind BATS is to place a stop far enough away so that normal intraday volatility does not hit the stop.

The results of my research appear in Table 4.1. Creating the table is somewhat complicated so you might want to skip this paragraph. I did a frequency distribution of the stocks in my database, sorted by their beta value. This gave me the total number of stocks in each beta range. Then, for each stock, I substituted the average percentage down—as measured from the prior day's low to the next day's low (for declining prices only)—into the frequency distribution table. The result was a sum of the average percentage decline for stocks in a given beta range. I divided the sum by the frequency totals found in the prior step then multiplied the results by five. Five was found by performance testing. Since stocks at low prices are more volatile than those at higher prices, I adjusted the table entries appropriately.

Table 4.1
Beta-Adjusted Trailing Stops

					Beta				
Stock Daily High Price	0.4 or Less (%)	0.41 to 0.6 (%)	0.61 to 0.8 (%)	0.81 to 1.0 (%)	1.01 to 1.2 (%)	1.21 to 1.4 (%)	1.41 to 1.6 (%)	1.61 to 1.8 (%)	More Than 1.8 (%)
10 or less	10	10	11	11	13	14	16	17	18
10.01 to 20	9	10	11	11	13	14	15	16	17
20.01 to 30	9	9	10	11	12	13	14	15	16
30.01 to 40	9	9	10	10	11	13	14	15	16
40.01 to 50	8	9	10	10	11	12	13	15	16
More than 50	8	8	9	10	11	12	13	14	15

How do you use Table 4.1? Use the Internet, your broker, or other source to find a stock's beta. It is a readily available number. When you buy a stock, use the daily *high* price—not the price at which you bought—and the beta to find the appropriate stop-loss percentage in the table. Calculate the stop price using the percentage as applied to *the daily high price*. Sell the stock if it *closes below* the stop price.

Let me give you an example. Say Tom's Clam Cove has a beta of 1.3 and a *daily high price* of 39 on the day of purchase. Using Table 4.1, you can see that the price resides in the 30.01 to 40 price range and in the 1.21 to 1.4 beta range. The intersection of the row and column gives a stop loss of 13%. Sell the stock when it *closes below* 33.93, or 13% down from the day's high price. If the stock then climbs to a new high, say, 41, make the calculation again and place a stop 12% below 41, or 36.08.

As the stock makes new highs, recalculate the stop-loss percentage and move the stop price upward as necessary. *You should never lower the stop.* In the previous example, should the stock decline from 41 back to 39, the stop must remain at 36.08 even though the table indicates it should be lower.

Look again at the table. Notice how the stop percentage climbs as beta rises, and how the percentage falls as the price climbs. That is as it should be. Also consider how large the stop values are. For a $9 stock with a 2.0 beta, the stop loss is a massive 18%. To me, taking an 18% hit is twice as high as I like. Therefore, you might consider BATS as being a worst-case scenario. If you get a BATS sell signal, it is time to exit because the trend has changed. Sell immediately.

If you own a highly volatile issue, adjust the table accordingly, including expanding the price or beta ranges. Make adjustments in the stop-loss percentages if you feel they are either too small or too large. Then place the stop.

STOP PLACEMENT AND SELL SIGNALS

Through the examples in this chapter and in the first three chapters of this book, you can make some educated guesses about stop placement. Simply put, place a stop below a support level (for trades from the long side) or above a resistance level for short sales. A support level such as a nearby minor low, trendline, consolidation, or other technical feature all qualify. Read the chapters on support and resistance and trendlines for additional ideas.

Let us assume that you trade from the long side, that is, you are not selling short. Figure 4.4 shows a variety of technical features. Let us run through each individually.

Old high resistance. Whenever prices climb to an old high, usually one that marked a new yearly high but perhaps it is just one of significant proportions, prices usually pause. From the chart, it is not clear that the peak in February 2000 qualifies, but prices approached the 45 level multiple times before finally pushing through in June.

Sometimes, as in the case of a double top, prices not only stop at the second high, but tumble much lower. If you want to keep a large portion of your profit, or if it is a quick trade, set a stop (that is, a limit order to sell) just below

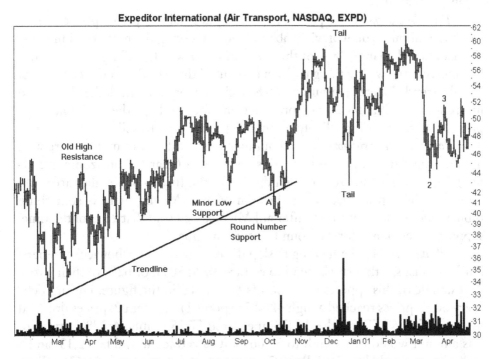

Figure 4.4 Potential sell signals. Old highs, trendline pierces, tails, and minor low breech, all issue trading signals if you are tuned in to the right channel.

the price of the old high. *Recognize that in 65% of the cases, prices will not fall below the confirmation price* (the lowest low between the two peaks), *but will make a new high.* The 65% number is the failure rate for unconfirmed double tops I found by research.

Minor low support. When prices return to the level of a recent minor low, there is a good chance that they will rebound because a minor low represents a support area, which is why minor lows are so popular as stop points. Since everyone knows this, I can imagine it as a site for stop running.

Tails. Perhaps this is the visual representation of stop running. One thing is clear: a tail represents a short-term trend reversal. I highlight two of the more significant ones in the figure, both in December and both showing a short-term trend change.

I almost had to change my underwear when this happened to a stock I owned. I looked at the chart from the prior day and saw a large, multipoint downward tail. When the market opened, I got a quote and relaxed. Prices had already rebounded and the downward spike was actually good news. It meant that the sellers had been flushed out of the market, and only buying demand remained to push prices up, which is what happened.

Sometimes a tail is really a one-day reversal chart pattern with significant investment implications. There are qualifications for a one-day reversal, so refer to my previous book, *Encyclopedia of Chart Patterns* (Wiley, 2000), for a complete analysis.

Trendline support. At point A in the figure, falling prices pierce the up trendline. Should you worry? Probably not. A piercing of an up trendline only signals a trend change 38% of the time. In other words, selling after a trendline pierce is the wrong thing to do in two out of three trades. A pierce does not signal a trend change, a minimum 20% decline in prices. Check the chapter on up trendlines (Chapter 2) to score the trendline. Perhaps the trendline has a positive score, meaning a likely trend change and time to sell.

Round number support. Round number support does not quite square with me, but the figure highlights the 40 support area (near the horizontal trendline). You can see that 50 bounded the top of the July to September area, and 60 called the top in December through March. Maybe there is something tubular about round numbers after all! My research says that 22% of the time, support or resistance forms around a round number.

Fibonacci retrace. I am going to skip the explanation of Fibonacci numbers, but let us just say that stocks tend to retrace 38%, 50%, or 62% of their gains. An example of this appears using points 1, 2, and 3 in the figure. During February 2001, prices reached a high of 60.75 (point 1). At point 2, prices dropped to a low of 43.50. Thus, the decline measured 17.25 points. A 38% retrace of this amount would be a climb to 50.06, a 50% retrace would be 52.13, and a 62% retrace would be 54.20. Point 3, the top of the retrace, is at 51.63, a climb of 47%, or very close to the 50% mark. The retracement numbers need not be dead on: Some call for a third, half, or two-thirds retracement. Anything higher than two-thirds probably signals a trend change.

Measured move. Since I have mentioned a measured move up (MMU) in this book, I might as well show you what one looks like. Figure 4.5 shows an MMU, beginning from point 1, to the corrective phase between points 2 and 3, and completing the final up leg at 4. The thinking regarding an MMU is that the first leg, 1 to 2, will approximate the length or percentage gain in the second leg, 3 to 4. After the MMU, prices often correct to the price level of the corrective phase (the consolidation between points 2 and 3).

Sometimes, an MMU will follow another MMU, in cascading fashion. At other times, MMUs appear nested, with a large MMU encompassing a smaller one. If you buy a stock and it stair steps higher, then falters, it might return to the corrective phase. Consider selling immediately (near point 4) instead of riding the stock back down (to 5). You can always buy back in at a lower price.

Straight-line run or quick rise. Prices skyrocket, usually for a few days in a straight move up, pausing only at the end of the move. There, prices consolidate, sometimes forming a diamond top pattern, before crashing back down to the origin of the move. It is as if the stock cannot tolerate the rarefied

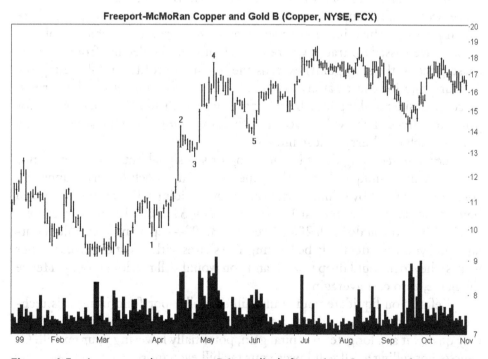

Figure 4.5 A measured move up. Prices climb from 1 to 2, correct from 2 to 3, then resume their rise to 4, completing the measured move up. Point 5 shows a retrace to the corrective phase (2 to 3).

atmosphere of high altitude. If you ever ride one of these elevators, consider stepping off near the top. Do not wait for the cable to snap before trying to claw your way out as prices plummet.

When a stock does not do what you expect, sell it. I learned this lesson the hard way when I bought a partial decline from a broadening top. The probabilities suggested that prices would flip around and stage an immediate upward breakout. They did not. Prices returned to the top trendline, then tumbled. I sold at a lower price. If a chart pattern does not behave as you expect, sell your position and look for a more promising opportunity.

Renewed rallies show shrinking volume—a topping pattern. Head-and-shoulders tops, for example, typically show the highest volume on the left shoulder, lower volume during formation of the head, and diminished volume on the right shoulder. After prices close below the neckline, it is time to turn out the lights. The stock is going lower.

If you believe a stop is going to be hit, why not sell immediately? I faced this situation with an investment in Southwest Airlines, which you can read about in Chapter 11 on head-and-shoulders tops. After the stock failed to perform as expected, I believed that the stock would tumble, so I sold immediately instead of waiting for prices to hit the stop. It was a good call, as I made a small profit instead of a larger loss.

If a stop cannot be placed nearby, then the stock is too expensive. This occurrence occasionally happens with a stock I want to buy. At the buy price, there may not be a nearby minor low or some other support area in which to place a stop. I have passed up trades where the risk of loss (the decline from the purchase price to the stop point) exceeds the potential profit (typically using the measure rule for chart patterns coupled with the location of overhead resistance). Consider looking for a better opportunity with another stock or wait for prices to retrace. That will get you in with a closer stop. After all, are you really in that much of a hurry to lose money?

Zero cost averaging. This is not a stop or sell signal but more of a money management technique. When the paper profit in a stock has risen above its cost, cover the cost by selling a portion of your holdings. For example, say you bought 300 shares of a stock at 10, so your cost is $3,000. The stock price rises to 15. What do you do? Sell 200 shares for $3,000—replacing your initial outlay—and you will effectively be holding 100 shares with a cost of zero. In other words, the stock could drop to zero and you would still not lose money. Hence the name, zero cost averaging.

Before you liquidate your multimillion dollar portfolio using this technique, remember to consider taxes. Holding a short-term investment longer may qualify it as a long-term capital gain, potentially lowering your tax bill. Of course, not selling at all will lower your tax bill even more!

Tax selling. Speaking of taxes, when August comes around, I think ahead to the turbulent months of September and October, and my thoughts inevitably turn to end-of-year tax selling. If I own a stock that has a loss, I usu-

Table 4.2
Chart Pattern Stop Locations to Prevent a Massive Loss

Chart Pattern	Stop Location
Broadening top, up or down breakout	$0.15 beyond opposite trendline boundary
Diamond top, up or down breakout	$0.15 beyond opposite trendline boundary
Double bottom, up breakout	$0.15 below lower of two bottoms
Double top, down breakout	$0.15 above the higher of the two tops
Head-and-shoulders bottom, up breakout	$0.15 below lower of two shoulders
Head-and-shoulders top, down breakout	Just above the lower of the two shoulder troughs or just above the neckline, whichever is higher
Rectangle, up or down breakout	$0.15 beyond opposite trendline boundary
Scallop, ascending, up breakout	$0.15 below bowl low
Scallop, descending, down breakout	$0.15 above right bowl lip
Triangles, ascending, up breakout	$0.15 below sloping trendline or nearest minor low
Triangles, descending, down breakout	$0.15 above horizontal trendline
Triangles, symmetrical	For upward breakouts: $0.15 below formation low. Downward breakouts: $0.15 above formation high
Triple bottoms, up breakout	$0.15 below lowest low
Triple tops, down breakout	$0.15 above highest high

ally sell it before the end of the year to help offset any gains. That way, I am selling my losers and keeping my winners. Remember that everyone else is trying to sell their shares too, including mutual funds and other institutions, so consider selling earlier when you may get a better price.

Chart pattern stops. Table 4.2 shows the location of stop-loss orders that will help prevent a massive loss. However, many times you will want to place a stop closer to the buy point. A nearby minor low or congestion area will usually do the job.

SELLING HINTS

As an investor and author, I have used a few techniques to ease buying or selling anxieties. For the buy side, I ask myself if the trade is worth writing about. If it is not, then perhaps it would be best to skip the trade. Another trick is to pretend that you are teaching a class on investing. What would you advise the class to do, sell or hold the stock? If the answer is sell, then do it.

If teaching is not a good example, then use your mother. If a stock is declining, would you advise her to hold, buy more, or dump the turkey? Before you answer, remember that she is retired, on a fixed income, and needs the money to buy luxuries—like food.

I am sure you can invent situations that are appropriate to you. Pretend you are the chief financial officer of a company that owns shares of a stock moving lower. When a subordinate asks what to do, what is your answer? Follow your own advice.

Some suggest that you ask if a stock is worth buying again. If the answer is no, then sell your holdings. In my opinion, that technique is too drastic as it causes you to sell your winners.

5

Common Trading Mistakes

What mistakes do investors commonly make that you can avoid? The list is shorter than I imagined, but investors are creative people, so I am sure that if we put our minds to work, we can come up with new ways to lose money.

Inability to Cut Losses. This mistake has to top the list. When a stock declines, investors just cannot seem to sell. They always believe that the stock will come back, that it will recover. It probably will, if the company does not declare bankruptcy first.

Figure 5.1 shows an example of investors' unwillingness to sell. Those investors who bought at the 1995 top of 47.38 had to wait until March 2000 just to break even. During that time, the stock dropped to a low of 8.31, a decline of 82%. I am sure many of you have such a trade in your past. For example, I bought a pile of Michaels Stores between March 1989 and September 1990, at prices ranging from 3.50 to 5.13 (pre-split). The stock bottomed at 2.88 after I bought the last batch in October 1990, then went up. A lot. The stock peaked at 46 in May 1994. From there, it was water torture time as the stock drifted lower to 8.06, recovered to nearly 40, tumbled to 15.50, climbed to nearly 50, sank to 18, and clawed its way back into the 40s again. The monthly chart looks like a wicked roller coaster.

Did I sell? Sure. I sold several times in the 30s, twice in the 40s, and several times within spitting distance of 40, but also bought additional shares, some at much higher prices than where I sold. I traded the stock 35 times over the years handing my broker fees of more than $1,500. I consider this to be both my best trade, because it was a 10 bagger, and perhaps my worst trade, because I rode the stock back down.

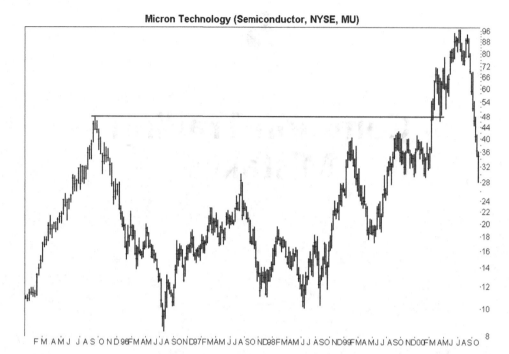

Figure 5.1 A large rise then fall in 1995. Investors that bought near the top of the 1995 bull market in semiconductor stocks had to wait until 2000 to get their money back.

The cutting-losses category must also include selling the winners and keeping the losers. I think I had this disease early in my trading career. I would keep a loser hoping that it was just about to turn around, and I sold the winners because I felt they had peaked. That, of course, was just the opposite of what should have been done.

Cutting Your Losses and Letting Your Profits Run. To cut your losses and let your profits run sounds like good advice—and it is—but it can end like the 1995–1996 decline in Figure 5.1. The problem is that you tend to hold onto a stock—letting your profits run—believing that the decline is just a retrace in an uptrend. You might even decide to ride out the decline, hoping that it will rise from the ashes and form a second top, even with the first. When it does not, it looks like Figure 5.1, a mountain surrounded by a moat filled with tears from investors crying over their losses.

Stops: Failing to Set Price Targets. How many times have you bought a stock and not set a stop-loss point, or not thought about how far you expected the stock to climb? I frequently speak with a friend that never thinks about his stop price or profit objective. To me, it is no wonder that his losses are eight times as high as his profits!

Setting price targets is not hard to do. Just look for support and resistance (SAR) zones before you buy. Expect that prices will stall at those locations and trade with those targets in mind.

Some other stop problems include stops that are too far away, failure to raise stops as the price climbs, lowering stops, or ignoring mental stops. If you take the time to think of a stop price, place the order. Place stops close enough so that you will not take a large loss, but not too close that you risk being stopped out. As the price moves in your favor, cancel the old stop and place a new stop at a higher price. Never lower your stop, as you will only create a larger loss. If you want to pretend that you are a serious trader, act on your mental stops, just as the pros do.

Averaging Down: Buying More When a Stock Drops. As a stock declines, you add to your holdings, thereby lowering your average cost. I have done it, hoping that the stock will soon recover. Many times, though, the stock continues down, so what you thought was a bargain was really throwing good money after bad.

Buying a declining stock is like trying to catch a falling knife: It is very dangerous indeed. Consider the fate of one investor. He bought Applied Materials at 86 then again at 65.75. "I'm going to ride this one out," he wrote. He was taken for a ride, all right. The stock reached a low of 26.59, and has yet to climb to his buy price.

Before you average down, be sure you understand why the stock is going down and why you think it will recover. Then wait. Wait to see if the stock continues dropping. If the reason is a bad quarterly report or an earnings warning, you should not add to your holdings until after the *next* quarter, at the earliest. Chances are, the next quarter will be a bad one too. It is like rebuilding a house after a fire: things take time.

Putting All Your Eggs in One Basket. I have some of my IRA money in nondiversified mutual funds, which means the funds own 25 or 30 stocks instead of 150. They concentrate their buying in a few issues that they know very well, instead of dabbling in a multitude of mediocre ones. The good news is that during a rising market—when their trading style is in favor—they act like rockets (no, they do not explode, they go up). The bad news is that in a bear market they fall just as fast, just as far.

Take a look at your own portfolio. Do you own just a few issues? Are they all in the same industry? If the answer is yes, then you may be taking excessive risk. Who am I to talk? As I write this, I own only two stocks with the majority of my portfolio in cash. For well over a year now, the market has been tumbling, so cash is king. As the market averages have posted negative gains, I have been racking up positive ones. My two stocks are up over 25% each while my IRA mutt funds are down 10%.

The point I am making is that sometimes it can pay to hold a concentrated portfolio. Most of the time, though, you should probably own about 10 stocks, most in different industries. Hold many more than that, and your trading may suffer. Should you put all your eggs in one basket, do not drop the basket. Watch it closely because you can never tell what is going to hatch.

Overdiversifying. I remember sitting in the library doing investment research when I overheard two men talking. One said to the other, "I own 42 companies. I can't keep track of them all." No kidding! He went on to say that many were in the oil business. Let me say this: Buy as many issues, in different industries, as you can comfortably track and successfully trade. Try this test: Close your eyes and name each stock in your portfolio and its closing price. If you miss a few names or your prices are way off, either you have a short-term memory as bad as mine, or you own too many stocks.

Buying Too Early. If you trade chart patterns, your losses will sooner or later force you to wait for confirmation before buying a stock. What is confirmation? It is a price at which any squiggle becomes a valid chart pattern. Many times, it is the highest high or lowest low in the pattern. Consider double bottoms. If you see a twin bottom forming and decide to buy the stock, the chances are 64% that prices will resume their downward trek. Only one in three trades will rise above the high posted between the twin bottoms and confirm the pattern as a valid double bottom. After confirmation, the chances are 97% that prices will continue rising at least 5%.

Chasing the Action; Buying Too Late. I keep my trading skills sharp by trading on paper even as I put real money into the market. Stocks I would not think of investing in, I buy with abandon on paper. The problem I found was that when prices quickly rise after an upside breakout, they just as quickly fall. Clearly the best technique is to place a stop order to buy at or just above the breakout price. That way, should the stock make a fast up move, you will automatically be along for the ride. Buying near the breakout price increases the odds of a profitable trade and lowers your risk. Otherwise, wait for a retrace or a throwback and for prices to resume climbing before buying.

Overtrading. As I trade, I log my completed trades into a spreadsheet so I can track my progress. One thing I have noticed is that the more trading I do, the worse my results. This may be the law of averages kicking in, but more likely is that I am cutting my profits short.

The charting program I wrote displays the buy and sell points (for both paper and real trades), and it usually shows that I would have done better by holding longer. My timing is good; I usually exit near the minor high, but about 2 months before the absolute high or a trend change. Even as the market has grown more volatile, I am working on staying in the trade longer, trying to climb the step ladder to a higher rung.

Another problem is that I like to trade. Soon after placing a trade, I will find another stock worth buying. Sometimes chart patterns are like termites, if you see one, there are probably others lurking nearby if you look close enough. At market turns, chart patterns make their appearance and it is time to jump in with both feet. At other times, it is my imagination—the thrill of placing a trade—that is the motive force. Now, I question my motives before I trade, trying to weed out the impulsive need for an adrenaline rush from the level-headed trading style I seek to maintain.

Undertrading. When I pick on my brother for a bad trade he has made despite my warnings, he replies that I am unwilling to sell Michaels Stores because of taxes. He is right, of course! I have let the stock sink instead of paying long-term capital gains taxes. Had I sold, the money saved would have paid the tax bill and then some. Instead, I sell a little each year, timing the sale, but not so much that it pushes me into a higher tax bracket.

Periodically review all your trades, and see what trading mistakes you are making. Do this when you are in a slump, but at least annually.

Stupid Trading. I have made some stupid trades in my day. I remember when I first started trading. I bought a company called Nuclear Pharmacy. Why? Because my mutt fund owned it and it had a sexy name. Yes, I did all the fundamental analysis I could on the stock and satisfied myself that the buying decision made sense. Two weeks later, the stock tanked.

More recently, I recall a fund manager who got into hot water because he publicly touted the merits of buying a stock and sold it the next week after prices rose. Another analyst issued a buy recommendation on a stock in his own portfolio that he was actively selling. The point I am making here is just because your mutual fund owns a stock is no reason to own it yourself. If you own the mutual fund, you already own the stock. Why buy it again?

I recall buying a stock because it paid a large dividend. It was not a utility, but a normal stock in the defense industry. At the time, the Cold War had ended years earlier and the Navy was cutting back on its purchase of sonobuoys, which the company made. I think I collected two quarterly dividend checks before they eliminated the dividend. If a company, including utilities, is paying a large dividend, it may be at risk or the company may be a risky investment. Or both!

Also in the dividend genre is when a company cuts its dividend. Sell immediately. A dividend cut is a clear signal that there is danger ahead. Business is not booming, they are taking a new direction, and the current is pulling them closer and closer to the rocks. Dump the turkey. If you look at the stock chart, it will have been trending downward for quite some time. You should have sold long ago. Make it up to yourself and sell it now.

Buying Risky Stocks, IPOs. If you cannot sleep because you are worrying about your latest Internet high flyer, then sell it. If your stomach is in knots or you feel glued to the quote screen instead of paying attention to your day job, then sell. Sometimes your body sends signals that your mind chooses to ignore. Pay attention. If you still want to buy stocks that are too volatile, diversify into more stable stocks. They will put balance into your portfolio and help offset the risk of your volatile selections.

Before investing in an initial public offering (IPO), look at the chart history of recent IPOs. Chances are, their stock prices are much lower a year later. Many of the once hot Internet IPOs are flaming out as I write this. One investor was able to get into a popular IPO at the offering price (that is a big clue: if Joe investor can buy at the offering price, then the IPO will be a dog). He borrowed all he could and put $26,000 into the stock. It recently was worth just $2,000.

Investing Using Margin. I was flying home to visit my parents and reading an investment magazine on the plane. The man seated next to me asked if I invested, then said he once traded commodities. He told me that he put on a position but was hospitalized for an unrelated reason. When the margin call came, he told his wife to deposit additional funds with the broker immediately. She ignored his advice and the broker liquidated the position. He lost $16,000 but it could have been worse. "If I had stayed in that position, I would have been killed," he remarked. He stopped trading after that.

Another investor I know used the teaser rates on his credit card to put $7,500 into the market. He effectively borrowed the money at 4% with the knowledge that he needed to repay the loan within 3 months or the annual rate would soar to 15%. With the money, he bought a mid cap mutual fund that he knew would recover from the high tech debacle quickly. Three months later, when it was time to repay the loan, the mutual fund was 30% lower. What did he do? He decided to keep the money in the fund and let the loan convert to the higher rate. Big mistake.

When it comes to margin, "always borrow from a pessimist," the saying goes. "He doesn't expect to be paid back." But a broker does.

Bottom Fishing and the Dead-Cat Bounce. This one gives me cold chills, flashbacks to the early days when I bought stocks because of the fundamentals and without any trace of technical analysis.

Figure 5.2 shows a stock a relative asked my opinion about. At point 1, the company beat earnings projections but forecast softer performance. At point 2, a major brokerage firm increased its price target for the stock. You can see how good a call that was. At point 3, the day I e-mailed my relative telling him to avoid the stock, the company issued an earnings warning after the market closed (and after I sent the e-mail). The news sent the stock down 32% in one session, the start of a dead-cat bounce chart pattern. The stock completed the bounce phase in early November then stair-stepped lower.

I remember warning my relative about the dead-cat bounce, how it usually signaled a declining price trend, and reminding him about the chapter in my book where he could find the gory details. What did he do? He bought the stock anyway, receiving a fill at 21.85 on October 23. "I can't see it getting any lower," he wrote. It bottomed at 5.04.

I am sure that over our investment careers, we all have bought a stock trending lower. We try to buy value, hoping the price will rise, and even add

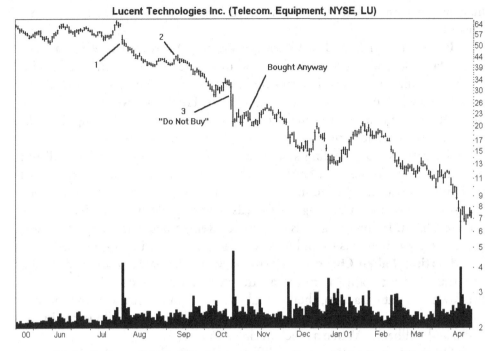

Figure 5.2 Bottom fishing. Buying a stock as it descends, believing it has bottomed even as management warns that the coming quarters will be rough, is foolish. A dead-cat bounce occurred as the stock dropped 32% on October 11, bounced slightly higher in coming weeks, then continued down.

to our position as the price drops and the value becomes more compelling. Unfortunately, hope alone will not keep a sinking stock afloat. *If a company's stock does a dead-cat bounce, stay away from the stock for at least 6 months*—longer if it is still declining—regardless of the appealing chart patterns you see or the investment hype.

While I am on the dead-cat bounce (DCB), if you own a stock that does a DCB, try to time the bounce phase, then sell. If you have trouble pulling the trigger, just look at Figure 5.2 and see how a typical DCB works. Never, never, never listen to those who talk up the stock just after the 30% to 70% 1-day decline. They are the ones causing the stock to bounce by calling it "a good value," or "if you liked it at 30, you will love it at 20." Chances are, they are the ones dumping their holdings at the top of the bounce just before it resumes its decline.

Listening to Chat Room Chatter. An investor I know listened to the chat room chatter about a promising media company. He bought 3,200 shares of the stock at $1.25 and rode it all the way down. It was delisted from Nasdaq and trades at 6 cents, if it trades at all. His $4,000 investment is now worth $192.

Stay away from the pump-and-dump chatter and do your own homework. Check reputable sources and recognize that those making a recommendation may also own the stock and have a vested interest in seeing the stock move. Buyer beware.

Failing to Stick with a Working Trading System. I received a letter from a fan in Canada who thanked me for my article in an investment magazine about ascending triangles. He said he had used the techniques outlined and made money in 9 of 10 trades. What did he do? He threw away the methodology and his profits when he bought a speculative mining stock on impulse. The stock was Bre-X, and it turned out to be a massive gold-mining scam.

Sometimes, your trading system will run into a slump and you will buy loser after loser. When that happens, why not step to the sidelines and paper trade until the losers change into winners? Maybe your losses are telling you that something in your trading style needs tweaking. Perhaps you have picked up a bad habit. In investing, it is easy to do. Remember that the quickest way to double your money is to fold it in two and put it back in your pocket!

Getting Taken Out on a Throwback or Pullback. In my paper trading, this situation happens to me all the time. I buy a stock the day after a breakout and put on a stop, then get taken out when the stock throws back to the breakout price. In actual trading, I use mental stops and allow for throwbacks and pullbacks. When a stock declines too far, I sell.

Different chart patterns have different throwback and pullbacks rates, so do not be surprised when a retrace happens to you. In a bull market, the odds favor the stock recovering and moving up; in a bear market, stocks decline (no kidding!). Follow other stocks in the same industry to see how they are behaving. Often I use them as clues. Take my investment in Home Depot, a stock I planned to be married to for years. When competitor Lowes announced that lower lumber prices and slowing sales would hurt results, Home Depot dropped too, but only marginally—5%. That drop was a warning, but I chose to ignore it because the stock was a "core holding." Sometimes core holdings are like apples: They rot if you hold them long enough. A week later, Home Depot plunged from 48.94 to 34.88 in one session on an earnings warning, and said coming quarters would be difficult. I rode the dead-cat bounce as high as I thought the stock would carry, then sold it all.

"You don't lose any money till you sell." My jaw dropped when I read that in an e-mail I received from a fellow investor. Perhaps that is his answer to poor money management: Put on blinders, stand on the tracks, and hope the approaching train will somehow miss you. When I was a novice investor, I used to justify my losses similarly. Now, I always sell before the losses become a problem. Look back at Figure 5.1 and see how long the 1995 paper loss took to change into a real profit.

WARNINGS AND SOLUTIONS

In Chapter 4 I mentioned some selling tricks. Here are three warnings:

1. If you mentally beat yourself up when taking a loss, that will make it harder to buy a stock the next time. You will do what it takes to avoid the pain; you will find yourself watching the screen instead of jumping in and trading.
2. If you jump for joy, whoop and holler for an hour about a killing you made in an investment, chances are it will be tougher to sell the next time. You will want to hold on as the stock declines, arguing that it will soon rebound and post new highs.
3. If after you sell, you follow the stock closely and punish yourself when it moves higher.

These are all mental traps waiting to snare both the novice investor and experienced trader. When I take a loss, it hurts, sure, but I do not dwell on it. I consider it a *cost of doing business*. If it is not a life or death situation, it is not worth worrying about. The same goes for the profit side. I like the chance to prove that money cannot make me happy just like everyone else, but I do not dwell on my winners.

After reading about common trading errors, the question you may be asking is what to do about them. The simplest and most banal answer is, *don't do that*. To put it another way, follow Bulkowski's law: *If a stock declines, sell it*. That law is all you need to know about investing. How you choose to interpret the law is up to you. Your interpretation can make you rich beyond your wildest dreams, or it can leave you owing so much money that your broker cannot afford to foreclose.

One of the hardest things to do in investing is to develop an investment style that works for you. Keep pounding away and the breaks will come. Failing that, it may be that your sole purpose in life is not to be Warren Buffett, but to serve as a warning to others.

PART TWO
Chart Patterns
Reference Section

In the pages that follow, you will find some startling discoveries about the behavior of chart patterns, and a scoring system to take advantage of that behavior. Use the chapters as a reference tool to read before you undertake a trade. The case studies at the end of each chapter show you how to use the scoring system and how a chart pattern is likely to perform. The system is not perfect, but chart patterns with scores above zero typically do twice as well as those with scores below zero. Add your own research to the scoring system (such as how the industry is behaving) along with other technical or fundamental factors to help shape your own trading style.

Whether you trade chart patterns or use other criteria to position your trades, I believe that the information will prove valuable to you. At the end of the book a statistics summary compares the performance of chart patterns against one another. The Glossary and Methodology discusses how I gathered the statistics and explains the concepts in an easy to understand manner.

6

Broadening Tops

The classic definition of a broadening formation is just as it sounds, a chart pattern in which prices make higher highs and lower lows over time; the price action *broadens* out, hence, the name. When I wrote *Encyclopedia of Chart Patterns* (Wiley, 2000), I separated broadening patterns into two basic types: broadening bottoms and broadening tops, believing that there might be a performance difference. There was, but it was not something to write home about, and mom does not care anyway. In this book, I recombine the patterns into the generic *broadening tops* category. This category does not include ascending or descending right-angled broadening formations or broadening wedges. They probably deserve their own chapters but are too rare to consider.

THE TYPICAL PATTERN

Figure 6.1 shows what a typical broadening top with an upward breakout looks like. Prices trend upward beginning from the trend start to the formation start, then waffle up and down, forming higher highs and lower lows. Bounding the minor highs on the top of the pattern is an up-sloping trendline while on the bottom, another trendline slopes downward. The two trendlines broaden out over time giving the broadening top its characteristic shape.

Figure 6.2 shows another broadening top, but this one has a downward breakout. Prices plunge through the lower trendline in late April and quickly reach the ultimate low before moving decidedly higher. If you had shorted this stock on the downward breakout, you would have had only a few days

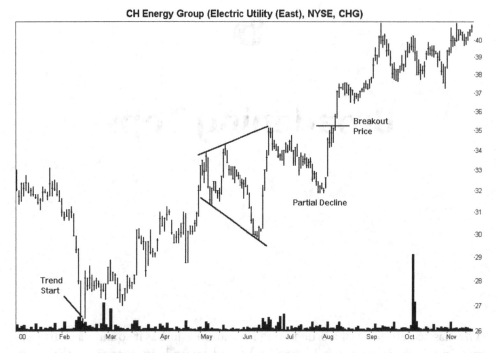

Figure 6.1 A broadening top with upward breakout. A partial decline predicts an immediate upward breakout.

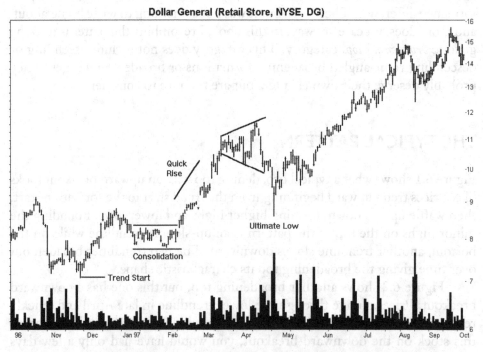

Figure 6.2 A broadening top with downward breakout. A quick, straight-line rise leading to the formation suggests that prices will retrace their gains.

to cover your short before prices climbed above your stop point, changing profits into losses. Notice the irregular volume pattern; that is characteristic of broadening tops.

TREND START

If you examine the figures accompanying this chapter, you will see that the price trend leading to a broadening top is usually of short-term duration (as the sample size in Table 6.1 shows). Prices rise, sometimes quickly in a straight-line advance, then begin waffling up and down forming the broadening pattern.

Before I discuss the statistics, let us find the trend start using Figure 6.2 as an example. Pretend you are standing on the broadening top, looking backward in time. Since prices drop away from the formation, we will mark the trend start as the point where prices change trend by rising. If prices were climbing away from the broadening top instead of dropping away from it, then we would be looking for a point where the trend changes from up to down.

To find where the trend starts, find the lowest low before prices climb by 20%, measured from the lowest low to the closing price. When the trend is climbing away from the formation, look for the highest high before prices drop by 20%, as measured from the highest high to the close. In Figure 6.2, the trend starts in late November, at a low of 7.08. A 20% rise means prices must close at 8.50 or higher, which occurs near the late October peak.

If prices overshoot or undershoot the start of the formation by a few days, just ignore it. Figure 6.8, later in this chapter, shows an example of overshoot.

Having found the trend start, we can measure the time from that point to the formation start. In this case, it measures 112 days (just over 3 months), placing it in the intermediate-term category according to Table 6.1.

For the broadening tops I looked at, I measured the trend start–formation start duration then examined the resulting rise or decline after the breakout. The table shows the results, sorted by the breakout direction and trend duration.

Table 6.1
Average Performance of Broadening Tops Sorted
by Price Trend Leading to the Pattern

Trend Start to Formation Start	Upward Breakout	Score	Downward Breakout	Score
Short term (0 to 3 months)	33% (82)	−1	−15% (85)	−1
Intermediate term (3 to 6 months)	36% (36)	+1	−17% (42)	+1
Long term (over 6 months)	41% (20)	+1	−15% (36)	−1

Note: The number of samples appears in parentheses.

The best performing broadening tops with upward breakouts associated with long-term price trends leading to the pattern. They showed rises after the breakout averaging 41%. For downward breakouts, the intermediate term associated with the best performance (17%).

I discuss how to score the chart pattern later in this chapter, so just ignore the score values for the moment.

HORIZONTAL CONSOLIDATION REGIONS

In the stock market, a horizontal consolidation region (HCR) is an area where prices move almost horizontally for weeks (even months) before staging a breakout. Without these HCRs, where the rise becomes a straight-line run, the results are spectacular providing you get out near the top. In many cases, the quick, steep advance also turns into a straight-line decline. Figure 6.2 shows an example of a straight-line run, then an even quicker decline, nearly retracing the gains back to the consolidation region.

I define an HCR as one located between the trend start and the outer edge of the broadening top. When prices rise into the pattern, for example, use the lowest low in the pattern as the price boundary; for price declines, use the top of the broadening top as the price boundary. I allow the region to span the trend start.

Look for flat tops, flat bottoms, or prices moving generally horizontally for several weeks to months. An HCR applies only when the region is in the price path. For upward breakouts, that means the region should appear above the broadening top; downward breakouts need the region below the chart pattern.

Figure 6.2 shows a good example to make selection clearer. The consolidation region appears between the trend start and the lowest low of 9.91 in the chart pattern. If the consolidation region were too close to the formation bottom, price wise, you should ignore it because prices would likely plunge through the region. In such a case, look for the next closest region. The January consolidation region has flat tops suggesting a support zone, and since the breakout is downward, the consolidation region resides below the chart pattern in the price path.

Figure 6.3 shows another example of an HCR that formed just before a broadening top. The region acts as a support zone thereby limiting the downward price movement.

Table 6.2 lists the performance when an HCR appeared before a broadening top but its effects lay in the future price path. The widest difference was with upward breakouts. When an HCR appeared above the top of the chart pattern but either spanning or after the trend start, prices climbed only 31%. This statistic compares to a 35% rise when no consolidation region existed. For downward breakouts, there was no performance difference.

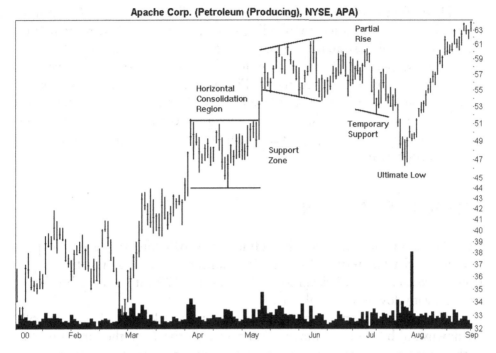

Figure 6.3 An HCR forms before a broadening top. The consolidation region often acts as a support zone, as in this case, resulting in a decline of just 14%. The lower formation trendline, extended into the future, acts as temporary support in early July.

The average length of the consolidation region was 37 days for upward breakouts and 43 days for downward breakouts. So, if you are trying to determine if there is a consolidation region between the trend start and the formation, it should be obvious.

Table 6.2
Average Performance of Broadening Tops
with and Without a Consolidation Region

Description	Upward Breakout	Score	Downward Breakout	Score
Consolidation region	31% (29)	–1	–16% (95)	0
No consolidation region	35% (116)	+1	–16% (73)	0
Average length (days)	37		43	
Prices stop within region ±5%	38% (14)		58% (57)	
Prices push through region	57% (21)		31% (30)	
Prices do not reach region	5% (2)		11% (11)	

Note: The number of samples appears in parentheses.

How often do prices stop within the consolidation region? I measured this by adding a 5% buffer surrounding the region because prices often fall a bit short or climb just above the region. For upward breakouts, 38% of the time prices stopped within the region; for downward breakouts, just over half the time (58%) prices stopped there. The table also shows how often prices eventually pushed through the region and those cases where prices reached the ultimate high or ultimate low before reaching the consolidation region. Note that the sample size is comparatively small (anything less than 30 samples) so the numbers may be inaccurate.

INSIDE THE PATTERN

Table 6.3 shows important statistical findings. Broadening tops are a comparatively rare chart pattern, so I kept looking until I found enough that I thought would give accurate statistical results. I uncovered 179 with upward breakouts and 171 with downward breakouts.

The average rise measured 34% for upward breakouts and a loss of 16% for downward breakouts. I measured the average rise from the formation top to the ultimate high and the average decline from the formation bottom to the ultimate low. See Glossary and Methodology for more details.

For both breakout directions, I measured the percentage change in the S&P 500 Index from the date the formation broke out to the date of the ultimate high or low. During the time after an upward breakout, the S&P climbed 4%. After downward breakouts, the S&P dropped 2%.

Since a small number of excessively high returns can skew the average upward, I include the median gain or loss. I like to think of the median value as the most likely rise or decline since half the returns are below the median and half are above. The median rise for upward breakouts is 25%, whereas the median loss is 14%.

Table 6.3
Important Statistical Findings

Description	Upward Breakouts	Downward Breakouts
Number of formations	179	171
Average rise or decline	34%	16%
Standard & Poor's 500 change	+4%	−2%
Median rise or decline	25%	14%
Rises or declines more than 50%	30/145 or 21%	5/168 or 3%

Table 6.4
Maximum Price Rise or Decline Versus Failure Rate

Maximum Price Rise or Decline (%)	Upward Breakout Failure Rate	Downward Breakout Failure Rate
5	12 or 8%	21 or 13%
10	27 or 19%	56 or 33%
15	41 or 28%	91 or 54%
20	63 or 43%	117 or 70%
25	74 or 51%	135 or 80%
30	84 or 58%	145 or 86%
35	93 or 64%	153 or 91%
50	115 or 79%	163 or 97%
75	127 or 88%	168 or 100%
100	133 or 92%	168 or 100%

Note: The sample count for upward breakouts is 145 and 168 for downward breakouts.

I applied a 50% benchmark to upward and downward breakouts to see how many broadening tops exceeded that value. For upward breakouts, 21% of the broadening tops had prices climb 50% or more; for downward breakouts, only 3% made the cut, before encountering a 20% trend change.

FAILURE RATES

Perhaps the most important statistic, if comments from my previous book are any gauge, is the failure rate. Tables 6.4 and 6.5 list failure rates according to

Table 6.5
Horizon Failure Rates and Average Rise or Decline

Time Since Breakout	Upward Breakout Failure Rate (%)	Upward Breakout Average Rise (%)	Downward Breakout Failure Rate (%)	Downward Breakout Average Decline (%)
1 week	23	5	34	3
2 weeks	29	5	35	3
3 weeks	28	5	36	3
1 month	28	7	44	2
2 months	37	8	55	-1
3 months	40	7	46	-2
6 months	41	6	47	-6

two different methods. Table 6.4 shows what the failure rate is for a given stock price rise, as measured from the breakout point to the ultimate high or low. For example, 12 of 145 broadening tops showed gains below 5% before topping out, and 21 of 168 formations with downward breakouts showed losses of 5% or less. The breakout price for upward breakouts is the highest high in the formation; for downward breakouts, it is the lowest low. The ultimate high and low are the highest high or lowest low after the formation but before a 20% trend change.

How is this analysis helpful? If you look at your past trades and see that, due to commissions, slippage, and other costs, the stock price must change by 10% before you begin to show a profit, then 19% of the broadening tops with upward breakouts will fail to meet your minimum profit objectives, on average, and a third with downward breakouts will fail.

Let us say that you want to find the best chart pattern with the lowest failure rate, one that is likely to give you a 50% gain. From Table 6.4, we see that 79% of the broadening tops with upward breakouts, and nearly all (97%) of the ones with downward breakouts will fail to meet your profit objectives. Obviously, you want to invest in broadening tops with upward breakouts. Even so, three of every four trades will fall short of a 50% gain. Perhaps you should skip broadening tops and look at another pattern type?

One last comment about Table 6.4. Look at how the failure rate jumps as the maximum price rises. Just 8% of the formations with upward breakouts fail to climb more than 5%, but more than double that rate (19%) will not make it to a 10% rise. The failure rates climb so rapidly that performance may be less than you hope.

Horizon failure rates appear in Table 6.5. The analysis looks at the daily closing price relative to the breakout price weekly for the first month, monthly for the first quarter, and 6 months after the breakout. The first entry under Upward Breakout Failure Rate, for example, means that of those broadening tops with upward breakouts, 23% showed closing prices below the breakout price after 1 week.

For upward breakouts, the horizon failure rate generally creeps upward over time, by climbing from 23% after 1 week to 41% after 6 months. For downward breakouts, the failure rate is higher, peaking at 55% after 2 months. I find those numbers alarming. If half the formations with downward breakouts are higher in 2 months' time, then why short the stock? Let me put this another way. By definition, the horizon failure rate is zero at the end of the first day—the breakout day. In less than a week, a third of the chart patterns will fail (downward breakouts only) and that is the good news. The longer you hold the stock short, the more likely it is that prices climb (that is, the failure rate climbs).

Table 6.5 also shows the average price change as measured from the breakout price, over time, for upward and downward breakouts. For upward breakouts, prices climb strongly, by 5% in the first week, then slowly move higher until peaking after 2 months.

For downward breakouts, the losses peak at 3% in the first 3 weeks, then momentum falters and prices rise. Sometime during the second month, prices climb enough that a short position will show a loss. By month 6, the decline is –6%, meaning a rise of 6%.

YEARLY PRICE RANGE

Table 6.6 shows the performance of broadening tops sorted by the breakout price in the yearly price range. For each chart pattern, I computed the yearly price range and split the range into thirds and matched the breakout price with the associated range. For example, those broadening tops with upward breakouts that showed a breakout price close to the yearly high had rises averaging 37%. This compares to a 22% rise when the breakout was in the center third of the yearly price range. For downward breakouts, the best performing were those with breakouts near the yearly low. They showed declines averaging 19%.

In essence, the table shows that those stocks making new highs continue rising, whereas those making new lows are the ones to short. To put it another way, do not buy a stock that is falling (hoping it will bottom) nor short a stock that is rising (expecting it to fall). In such cases, momentum is working against you.

TALL AND SHORT PATTERNS

Table 6.7 shows the performance of stocks sorted by formation height. To do this, I measured from the highest high to the lowest low in each chart pattern, then divided the result by the breakout price. After sorting the results, I split the numbers according to the median value. Half the results were above the median and half below.

Table 6.6
Average Performance Sorted by Breakout Price
According to Prior 12-Month Range

Yearly Price Range	Upward Breakouts	Score	Downward Breakouts	Score
Highest third	37% (95)	+1	–14% (27)	–1
Middle third	22% (27)	–1	–14% (70)	–1
Lowest third	33% (14)	–1	–19% (60)	+1

Note: The number of samples appears in parentheses.

Table 6.7
Performance of Short and Tall Broadening Tops

Description	Upward Breakout	Score	Downward Breakout	Score
Tall (above the median)	42% (72)	+1	−17% (84)	+1
Short (below the median)	27% (73)	−1	−15% (84)	−1
Median percentage of breakout price	17.49%		18.29%	

Note: The number of samples appears in parentheses.

What the table shows is that tall broadening tops with upward breakouts perform head and antlers above the short fellas. Downward breakouts are less impressive, although tall patterns still outperform the vertically challenged.

VOLUME TREND

Table 6.8 shows the effect of a rising or falling volume trend from the formation start to its end and the resulting price performance. For example, those broadening tops with a falling volume trend showed gains averaging 36% (upward breakouts). This statistic corresponds to a 33% gain for a rising volume trend. Downward breakouts showed no discernible performance difference.

BREAKOUT VOLUME

Continuing the volume study, it has often been said that a high-volume breakout is good for performance. Table 6.9 confirms that belief. See Glossary and Methodology for more details on how I computed the volume level, but suffice it to say that I compared the breakout volume with an average for the stock. Those broadening tops with above-average breakout volume showed rises of 38% for upward breakouts, and declines of 17% for downward breakouts. This result handily beats the 33% rise and 15% loss when the breakout volume was average or below average.

Table 6.8
Linear Regression Volume Trend and Performance

Description	Upward Breakout	Score	Downward Breakout	Score
Rising volume trend	33% (78)	−1	−16% (98)	0
Falling volume trend	36% (67)	+1	−16% (70)	0

Note: The number of samples appears in parentheses.

Table 6.9
Breakout Volume and Performance

Description	Upward Breakout	Score	Downward Breakout	Score
Average rise or decline on above-average breakout volume	38% (37)	+1	17% (41)	+1
Average rise or decline on average or below-average breakout volume	33% (108)	−1	15% (127)	−1

Note: The number of samples appears in parentheses.

PARTIAL RISES AND DECLINES

Table 6.10 shows statistics related to partial rises and declines. Figure 6.1 shows a good example of a partial decline. Prices touch the top trendline, then move lower but fail to reach the bottom trendline before heading back up and soaring out the formation top. A partial decline correctly predicts an upward breakout 77% of the time, which is the good news. The bad news is that the formation is likely to underperform. The average rise when a partial decline appears is 32% versus 36% for those broadening tops without a partial decline but an upward breakout. However, a partial decline allows a better entry point in case you were going to buy the stock anyway, so maybe you can compensate for the underperformance.

Figure 6.4 shows an intraformation partial decline. An intraformation partial decline is a partial decline that appears within a broadening top but does not result in an immediate upward breakout. Why is this important? Imagine that you were considering buying the stock shown in the figure. The price action was forming higher highs and lower lows—a broadening price pattern—that became clear after prices touched each trendline twice (shown by numbers

Table 6.10
Performance After the Formation Ends

Description	Result	Score
Partial decline correctly predicts upward breakout	68/88 or 77%	
Performance after a partial decline	32% (54)	−1
Performance without a partial decline	36% (91)	+1
Intraformation partial decline frequency	31/350 or 9%	
Partial rise correctly predicts downward breakout	91/129 or 71%	
Performance after a partial rise	−15% (89)	−1
Performance without a partial rise	−17% (79)	+1
Intraformation partial rise frequency	37/350 or 11%	

Note: The number of samples appears in parentheses.

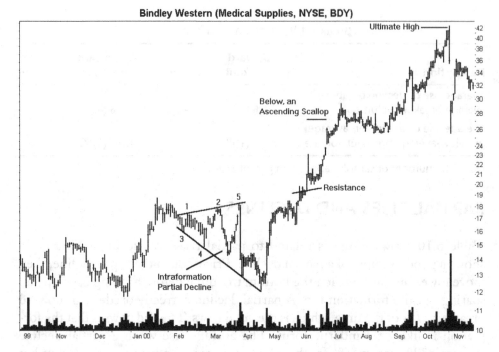

Figure 6.4 An intraformation partial decline. Prices must touch the top and bottom trendlines twice, setting up a valid broadening top, before an intraformation partial decline is valid. An ascending scallop formation appears in June. A small resistance area forms along the top formation trendline extended into the future.

1 through 4). After point 2, when prices approached the bottom trendline—without touching it—then began to climb, you decided to buy the stock. It was, after all, a partial decline in a broadening top. You hoped prices would zoom across the formation and shoot out the top, staging an upward breakout as well-behaved partial declines portend. Instead, after prices touched the top trendline (point 5), they plummeted the next day and zipped to the other side, making two successively lower lows. After that, prices recovered quickly and finally staged an upward breakout.

If you purchased the stock during the intraformation partial decline and held the stock until prices reached the ultimate high, your gain would be between 198% (if you bought at the intraformation low) and 133% (assuming you purchased at the breakout high shown at point 5). Either way, you would have doubled to nearly tripled your money, but in the interim, you would have suffered a paper loss of up to 34% (measured from the high at point 5 to the lowest low in the formation after point 5). A properly placed stop-loss order would have cashed you out long before prices reached the formation low, and you would have missed the subsequent rise.

Intraformation partial declines occurred in only 9% of the broadening tops I studied (including one chart pattern that had two). When they did occur, they had almost an even chance (52%) of seeing an eventual upward breakout. It is my belief that should you see a partial decline forming, buy the stock. If prices fail to stage an upward breakout, then sell the stock once it becomes clear that prices are heading down again; do not wait and hope that prices will eventually break out upward. They may not.

Since broadening tops with a partial decline underperform those without a partial decline (32% average gain versus 36%, respectively), if you cannot buy at a price below the formation top, then consider skipping the trade.

Figure 6.5 shows a partial rise. Prices touch the bottom trendline at point 1, then rise but do not touch the top trendline before rounding over and breaking out downward. Had you shorted this stock at the partial rise high (45.25) and covered at the low (3.91), you would have made a profit of 91% in about a year. However, shorting a stock on a partial rise is more risky than going long on a partial decline. Partial rises result in a downward breakout 71% of the time. When partial rises do work, the average price declines by 15% versus 17% for those broadening tops without partial rises (measured from the lowest formation low to the ultimate low). Since you can sell short at a higher price—during a partial rise—you should be able to improve the performance. For the example shown in Figure 6.5, that means shorting near a price of 45.25 instead of the breakout price of 39.50—a difference of 13%.

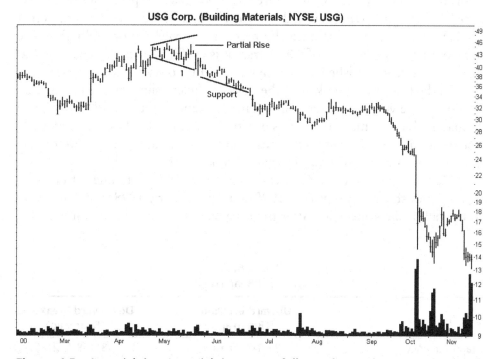

Figure 6.5 A partial rise. A partial rise successfully predicts a downward breakout 71% of the time but with a smaller loss. Prices find support along the bottom formation trendline extended into the future.

There are times when prices showing a partial rise drop to the lower trend-line boundary then recross the formation. This occurrence is called an intraformation partial rise. It is the same as an intraformation partial decline only flipped upside down. Intraformation partial rises only occur 11% of the time (including two formations in which two occurred). The likelihood of an intraformation partial rise correctly predicting a downward breakout is just 46%.

BULL AND BEAR TRAPS

If you are a lucky investor, you will never come across a bull or bear trap, but I bet you will. Table 6.11 indicates that the likelihood of stumbling across a bull trap is 14%; for bear traps, the likelihood is 29%. Figure 6.6 shows a bear trap and Figure 6.9 (later in this chapter) shows a bull trap.

A bear trap occurs after a downward breakout entices traders to short the stock (dropping less than 10%) before prices recover and move substantially higher (above the formation high). A bull trap appears after an upward breakout when prices rise by less than 10%, curve around, and drop below the formation low.

Can you predict a bull or bear trap? Yes, if you are lucky. Most of the bear traps I looked at had breakouts close to the formation end and on high or very high volume, like that shown in Figure 6.6. If you read my previous book, *Encyclopedia of Chart Patterns* (Wiley, 2000) closely, you would have discovered that a breakout on heavy volume usually predicts a throwback or pullback to the breakout price. In the case of a bear trap, it is as if investors sell their stock as a group, and when finished, allow buying demand to send prices upward.

In the bear traps I looked at, there was sufficient support to halt a further decline. Since you can locate support and resistance zones ahead of time, you should be able to remove from consideration any stock that has a meager profit potential. Just look for support or resistance zones and, if prices were to stop at that level, consider whether it would still be worth the trade.

Returning to Figure 6.6, prices declined to a support zone set up years ago (but not shown) by a peak in 1995, a trough in early 1998, and congestion in the fall of the same year. After the broadening top breakout, prices pulled

Table 6.11
Bull and Bear Traps

Description	Upward Breakouts (Bull trap)	Downward Breakouts (Bear trap)
Trap frequency	21/145 or 14%	48/168 or 29%
Score if trap predicted	−1	−1
Score if trap not predicted	+1	+1

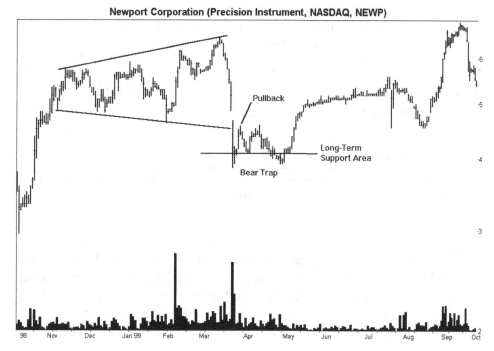

Figure 6.6 A bear trap appears as prices reverse direction after a downward breakout and encounter a long-term support area. Bear traps are twice as likely to occur as bull traps.

back to the lower trendline boundary, then moved somewhat horizontally for a month. Those traders that sold short on the downward breakout either covered their short with a meager profit or were cleaned out. A year after the breakout, the stock was at 50; then 6 months later, it was at 192. Such a rise is a world of pain if you failed to cover your short—one good reason for never shorting in the first place.

Figure 6.9 (later in the chapter) shows a bull trap, where prices zoom out the top, meet past resistance at 21, and throw back to the breakout price. Unfortunately, the throwback does not end there and prices continue moving lower, reaching a low of 6.75.

MARKET TREND

For stocks, does a rising tide lift all boats? Yes. To answer that question, I looked at two time periods: from formation start to end and from formation end to ultimate high (up breakouts) or ultimate low (downward breakouts). During those periods, I determined whether the S&P 500 Index was rising or falling—for each formation—and looked at the resulting performance of the broadening top. Table 6.12 list the results. For example, broadening tops in

Table 6.12
Average Price Performance of Broadening Tops
During a Rising and Falling Market

Market Trend	FS to FE	Score	FE to UH	FE to UL
Rising S&P 500, up breakout	36% (88)	+1	35% (121)	
Falling S&P 500, up breakout	32% (57)	−1	33% (24)	
Rising S&P 500, down breakout	−16% (96)	+1		−16% (67)
Falling S&P 500, down breakout	−15% (72)	−1		−16% (101)

Note: FS = formation start, FE = formation end, UH = ultimate high, UL = ultimate low.
The number of samples appears in parentheses.

which the market was rising during creation of the formation (FS to FE) and
that had an upward breakout, showed gains averaging 36%. This result compares to a 32% average rise when the S&P declined over the same period.

Since you cannot know ahead of time how the S&P will behave after you
buy a stock, I base the score values in Table 6.12 on the FS to FE period.

MARKET CAPITALIZATION

For broadening tops, does the market capitalization of a stock influence the
chart pattern's performance? Yes, and Table 6.13 shows the results. Market
capitalization is the number of shares outstanding multiplied by the current
market price. I used the breakout price in the calculation, that is, the highest
high in the formation for upward breakouts and the lowest low for downward
breakouts.

For upward breakouts, the best performing are those stocks with small
capitalizations—under $1 billion or large caps, over $5 billion. Large caps also

Table 6.13
Average Price Performance of Broadening
Tops by Market Capitalization

Capitalization	Up Breakouts	Score	Down Breakouts	Score
Small cap (up to $1 billion)	36% (60)	+1	−21% (62)	+1
Mid cap (1 billion to $5 billion)	31% (52)	−1	−19% (64)	+1
Large cap (over $5 billion)	36% (51)	+1	−11% (42)	−1

Note: The number of samples appears in parentheses.

held up best after a downward breakout, having losses averaging just 11%. By contrast, small cap stocks tumbled 21% after a downward breakout. This result suggests small caps are the ones to short and large caps are the ones to hold in a declining market.

SCORES

To use the scoring system, evaluate your chart pattern according to each table with a score. Add the scores together. Scores above zero suggests the chart pattern may beat the median performer; below zero suggests underperformance. Since you are dealing with probabilities, nothing is guaranteed. You could have a chart pattern with a perfect score and it might rise only 5%. You might find a chart pattern with a highly negative score, but it might perform brilliantly. As always, your trading skill also affects the outcome and there is no way the statistics can account for that.

Table 6.14 shows how broadening tops with scores above zero performed (38% average rise for upward breakouts and 23% average decline for downward breakouts) compared to scores below zero (21%, 11%, respectively). Clearly the scoring system can help weed out the weak performing chart patterns.

To assess the accuracy of the signals, I looked at each stock and compared its score and percentage change with the median rise or decline. The system correctly indicated that 58% of the chart patterns with scores above zero would climb above the median, and it correctly said avoid a stock 69% of the time because it would climb less than the median rise. For downward breakouts, the system correctly predicted selling short 79% of the time and avoid shorting 74% of the time. Anything above 50% means the system adds value.

Table 6.14
Formation Performance by Score

Score	Up Breakouts	Down Breakouts
Average rise or decline of chart patterns with scores above zero	38%	23%
Average rise or decline of chart patterns with scores below zero	21%	11%
Median rise or decline used	22.81%	12.79%
Percentage with scores above zero beating median rise or decline	48/83 or 58%	41/52 or 79%
Percentage with scores below zero doing worse than median rise or decline	24/35 or 69%	45/61 or 74%

CASE STUDY 1

Figure 6.7 shows a broadening top that provides a good opportunity to apply the tips from the tables showing scores. First, where does the trend start? Since prices drop away from the chart pattern looking backward in time, we will be searching for the lowest low before a 20% price rise. The trend start occurred on February 25, 1999, just off the figure, at a low price of 7.25. A 20% rise from the low would be 8.70, and prices closed above that level on February 8, verifying that the February 25 low was the trend start. The elapsed time from the trend start to the formation start is 132 days, or into the intermediate term (3 to 6 months) category. Table 6.1 says the score for intermediate term price trends is +1.

Does an HCR exist in the price path? No. Since prices enter the broadening top from the bottom, prices would have to break out downward to pose a threat but they break out upward instead. According to Table 6.2, no consolidation region scores +1. Running total: +2.

Skipping to Table 6.6, the next table with scores, we need to find where the breakout occurs within the yearly price range. The breakout price occurs at

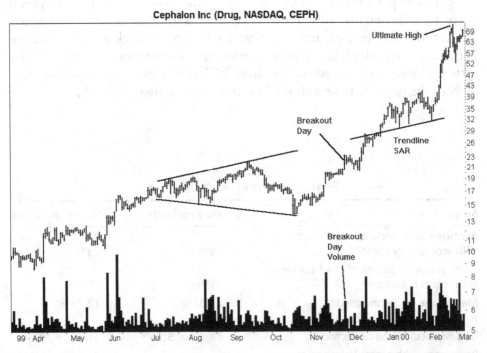

Figure 6.7 A broadening top with a high score. After the breakout, the stock soared 234%.

22.13, the top of the formation. The yearly high, within 1 year of the breakout, occurs at a price of 22.13 and the yearly low at 6.63. Since the breakout price is also the yearly high, the search ends there. Table 6.6 says that upward breakouts in the highest third of the yearly price range score +1. Running total: +3.

How tall is the pattern? The high is at 22.13 and the low is at 14 for a height of 8.13. As a percentage of the 22.13 breakout price, the height measures 37% (or 8.13/22.13). This result is well above the median 17.49% shown in Table 6.7, so the formation is a tall broadening top. That scores +1 for a running total of +4.

Is volume trending upward or downward from the formation start to its end? If you look at Figure 6.7, you can see that volume is very high during August then tapers off toward the October low. Thus, you can probably guess that volume was falling over the entire formation length and you would be right. However, I used linear regression to verify the results and the volume trend is, indeed, downward. Table 6.8 rates a falling volume trend +1. Running total: +5.

What about the breakout volume? As you can see in Figure 6.7, breakout volume is just average, certainly not meeting any of the higher peaks. Average breakout volume according to Table 6.9 rates –1, for a running total of +4.

Since we are dealing with an upward breakout, is there a partial decline just before the breakout? No. Prices touch the bottom trendline then advance at a steady clip. A partial decline would touch the top trendline, move lower, but not come close to or touch the lower trendline. Clearly that does not happen in this example. Table 6.10 says no partial decline rates +1 for a running total of +5.

What about a bull trap? Since the breakout occurred at the yearly high, there was no overhead resistance to block a price advance. Table 6.11 says bull traps only occur 14% of the time, so they are not much of a threat anyway. Score: +1. Running total: +6.

On July 7, 1999, the S&P 500 Index closed at 1395.86, and on October 19, it closed at 1261.32. Thus, the index fell during creation of the formation. Table 6.12 indicates that during FS to FE, a falling S&P scores –1. Running total: +5.

Finally, using the breakout price of 22.13 multiplied by the number of shares outstanding places the stock in the small cap category, scoring +1 in Table 6.13. Final score: +6.

Anything above zero means consider the stock for purchase. The higher the score, the stronger the signal suggesting more has to go wrong before the stock runs into trouble. This result is not always the case, so use your own tools to verify that the stock is worth trading. In this case, the stock climbed to a high of 73.81 before encountering a 20% price decline. That puts the rise at 234%, well above the 22.81% median rise for broadening tops with upward breakouts.

CASE STUDY 2

What happens when the score is below zero? Figure 6.8 illustrates this case study, a situation that results in a negative score and meager gains. As you look at the figure, you can see a well-defined broadening formation in December 1999, a pattern type not included in this study. I used only broadening tops or bottoms, not the right-angled or wedge varieties. Still, the flat base of the right-angled chart pattern has to scream *resistance zone* in your mind. Any investor buying after the April broadening top breakout was probably wondering who took the cork off his lunch.

Since you know how the scoring system works, I quickly run through the tables.

Table 6.1: Trend start. I ignored any overshoot or undershoot leading to the start of the chart pattern when determining where the trend started. In this case, the result is the same as the trend is short term. Score: −1.

Table 6.2: Horizontal consolidation region. Since the region must be in the price path from the trend start to the formation, an HCR does not appear

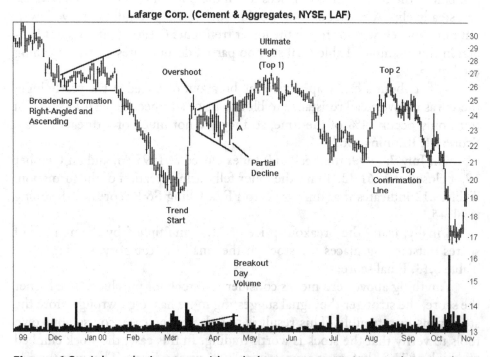

Figure 6.8 A broadening top with a below-zero score. Ignore the overshoot when determining where the trend starts. An ascending, right-angled broadening formation appears in December and the twin peaks of an Eve & Adam double top appear in May and August.

(a downward breakout would put it in the price path). Score: +1. Running total: 0.

In my opinion, a trade is either a win or loss probably due to a support or resistance zone. Those zones are the most critical element when choosing a stock to trade. In this case, the right-angled broadening formation would limit or at least slow any upward move. When buying a stock, be sure to look for any overhead resistance zones and trade accordingly.

Table 6.6: Yearly price range. The yearly high occurred at a price of 37.56 and the yearly low at 18.81, with the breakout at 25.25. Splitting the yearly price range into thirds (that is, (37.56 − 18.81)/3) places the breakout in the middle, 25.06 to 31.31, range. Score: −1. Running total: −1.

Table 6.7: Short or tall. The height represents 13% of the breakout price (that is, (25.25 − 22.06)/25.25) making the pattern a short broadening top. Score: −1. Running total: −2.

Table 6.8: Volume trend. Figure 6.8 shows volume trending upward. Score: −1. Running total: −3.

Table 6.9: Breakout volume. Breakout day volume is below average, scoring −1. Running total: −4.

Table 6.10: Partial decline. Since the breakout is upward, look for a partial decline where prices touch the top trendline, drop, but do not touch or come that close to the lower trendline. I show one example of a partial decline on the chart. If you think the low comes too close to the trendline, then use point A. Prices touch the top trendline and start heading down before curling around and moving up. Either way, score it −1 because of the wasted energy looping down and back up again. Running total: −5.

Table 6.11: Bull trap. Since the breakout is upward, is a bull trap predicted? Yes. For a trap to occur, prices must rise by less than 10% then drop below the formation low. I would argue that the December right-angled broadening formation doomed any rise. Coupled with the sharp, quick climb beginning a week or so before the April broadening top, I would expect prices to tumble and retrace their gains, probably dropping back to the trend start. Thus, I would expect a bull trap. Score: −1. Running total: −6.

Table 6.12: Market trend. From the formation start to the formation end, the S&P declined over those dates. Score: −1. Running total: −7.

Table 6.13: Market capitalization. The stock is a mid cap. Score: −1. Final total: −8.

How did the stock do? From the breakout price of 25.25, the stock climbed to a high of 27, for a gain of just 7%. As you look at the figure, you can see that prices reached their ultimate high, climbed again to the old high during August (top 2), then tumbled. In late September, the Eve & Adam double top confirmed when prices closed below the formation low. If you were still in the stock, that was the sell signal. Prices tumbled to a low of 16.69 before recovering.

CASE STUDY 3

What happens when things go bad? Figure 6.9 shows one result. This is not a paper trade, but an actual one in a copper mining company. To save the person possible embarrassment, I call her Mary. Running through the various tables leaves us with a +2 score. Since scores above zero represent buy candidates, it looked like this was a promising opportunity. How did Mary trade it?

Two days after the stock burst out the formation top on high volume, Mary bought the stock and received a fill at 21.13. Her reasons for purchase were manifold: a broadening top with upside breakout, a short-term rising price of copper (even though it was half what it was 3 years earlier), and success with cost-cutting efforts by the company (which is to say, the fundamentals looked good to her).

Since a throwback is no reason to panic and is often another opportunity to add to a position at a good price, Mary bought more shares at 16.56, right at a minor low. The second purchase marked the touch of a trendline formed by connecting the lows in September and December (not shown). She viewed

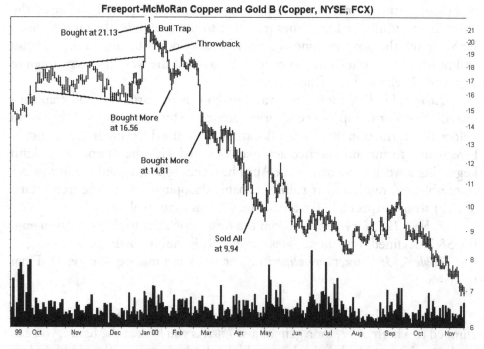

Figure 6.9 Mary bought this stock three times before finally selling her entire position. The tables pointed to a +2 score—a buy candidate. A measured move down formation begins at point 1, through the corrective phase at her second buy point (16.56), suggesting a decline to at least 13.81.

this as a likely support area, as it was in the past. However, copper had reached its high and was now falling while other copper stocks were also heading lower, including the overall market. For this reason, she bought fewer shares than she normally would have, just to be on the safe side.

If things went bad, she expected the stock to find support at 15.50, maybe even down to 15. The upside was more rosy, with the stock predicted to reach the first purchase point of 21.

For a time, it looked as if she was right. After her second purchase, the stock rebounded smartly, even gapping higher on one occasion (an area or common gap in early February). When prices climbed to the broadening top trendline (if you extend it into February), prices stopped climbing there, moved horizontally for a week or two, then tumbled—quickly. The stock punched through support at 15 and continued below 14.

She bought more at 14.81 and, at the time of purchase, the stock was up almost a point in concert with a rising market. Unfortunately, the stock closed lower for the day. About the most recent purchase, she said there was hope in a measured move down (MMD) starting from the high at point 1, through the start of the corrective phase where she bought more at 16.56. The MMD predicted a low price of about 13.81, very close to where the stock was now trading. That gave her confidence to ride the stock a bit lower, anticipating an approaching bottom.

On an almost daily basis, the stock dropped. Eventually, she threw in the towel and sold everything at 9.94, believing that the political turmoil in Indonesia, where the company has mining operations, weighed the stock down. Her last words were something about "limiting losses to just 45%." Ouch!

If there is a silver (or copper, if you prefer) lining to this story, it is that she sold when she did. The stock bottomed at 6.75, or 32% lower than where she sold it.

The big question is, what did Mary do wrong? Averaging down, which is buying more stock as the price declines, is a wonderful strategy providing the stock recovers. Sometimes, as in this case, you sell before that happens and really take a pounding. The proper action was to sell sooner.

Overhead resistance at 21.44 from a peak in April 1998 (not shown in Figure 6.9) spelled possible trouble and that price is exactly where the rise stalled. Mary should not have bought unless prices pierced the resistance zone decisively. Alternatively, she should have expected a throwback and not made the first purchase at 21.13. Clues to the throwback were a high-volume breakout (if everyone buys at once, who remains to support prices?) and overhead resistance from the April 1998 peak (limiting the up move).

When the stock pierced the lower trendline of the broadening top (extended into late February), that was a big hint that prices would continue lower. It was time to sell. Had she sold at that point, around 15, she would have saved a pile of money.

If you ask Mary what she thought her problem was with this trade, she will tell you that she believed the fundamentals—or rather, her interpretation of the fundamentals—was correct. She thought the European, Asian, and South American economies were well into recovery and that recovery would boost copper demand in time. With the company expanding production and mining copper at a cost of just 22 cents per pound (versus a Comex spot price of 88 cents at the mid-January peak), with gold and silver mixed in, it was easy to justify waiting for the market to recognize the improving fundamentals and eventually send the stock higher. After all, that was why she bought in the first place—the stock breaking out to new highs.

Unfortunately, the market was sending her a message that she did not hear until much too late. Her opinion of the facts, no matter how positive, were not enough to sway the market. Hope, alone, would not help this copper balloon fly.

A declining stock price is a message that the company, the industry, and the markets are sending you. Listen to that message. Just because the scoring system says *buy* is no reason to throw caution to the wind.

7

Diamonds

Valentine's day is tomorrow and I think it a strange coincidence that I am writing about diamonds. Both the stone and the chart pattern are rare, but I think the chart pattern leads the gems. Of the two breakout directions, I am only writing about one of them: downward breakouts. Why? Because I was only able to locate 106 patterns with upward breakouts. That is just not enough on which to perform a statistical analysis. Downward breakouts were not much better. I found 184 of them but combined both diamond tops (154) and bottoms (30) to achieve that number.

In case you are unfamiliar with a diamond top or diamond bottom, I define a top as when prices enter the chart pattern from the bottom; diamond bottoms have prices entering from the top. The thinking behind the arbitrary designations is that there are performance differences. For this study, I only worried about the breakout direction, not whether it was a top or a bottom.

THE TYPICAL PATTERN

You can probably guess what a diamond top looks like. It looks like, well, a diamond. Think of a diamond as back-to-back symmetrical triangles, a broadening top followed by a symmetrical triangle, or a complex head-and-shoulders top. Whatever your description, the chart pattern should look something like that shown in Figure 7.1.

As prices climb, they form higher peaks and lower troughs until the process reverses and the range narrows; the peaks are not quite as tall and the minor lows

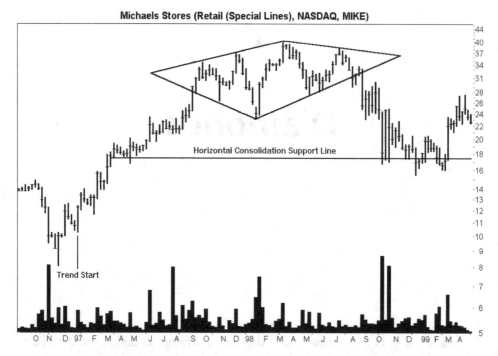

Figure 7.1 A diamond top. Shown on the weekly scale, the large diamond top sees prices break out downward and fall to a support region at 17.63.

are not quite as deep. Eventually, prices drop out of the pattern in a downward breakout, then sometimes pull back to the diamond trendline boundary before slipping away again. If the rise leading to the diamond was unusually quick, the decline after the diamond completes will usually retrace all the gains, leaving investors no better off.

If you are prospecting for diamonds, you might try this trick: Look for the quick rise. Many times that is where you will find a diamond. More about the quick rise later. For now, though, do not expect your diamond to be perfectly symmetrical or diamond shaped. As in Figure 7.1, the trendlines often skew one way or three others, as my dad would say. Watch for a diamond that is really a head-and-shoulders top or a complex head-and-shoulders top. There will be fewer traverses between the trendlines, forming a shoulder, then a higher head, and, finally, a lower right shoulder. Many times, the neckline is the key. If the neckline appears flat, then you have a head-and-shoulders top. Regardless of what you call it, a downward breakout is bad news if you hold the stock. A quick sale is usually best. If you want to short the stock, that is fine, too, just be sure you know what you are doing.

TREND START

Can we make anything of the price trend leading to the diamond top? Yes, and the first set of statistics appears in Table 7.1. Before I discuss the results, let me describe the logic behind the numbers. In my research, I discovered that *when* the trend starts is important to the performance of chart patterns. Most investors define a bull or bear market by a 20% price change, so I decided to apply that rule to the start of a trend.

To find the trend start, move backward in time from the formation start, following prices lower. Make note of each new low and find where prices rise (still moving backward in time!) by 20% or more from the lowest low to the close. When that occurs, the lowest low marks the trend start.

For example, imagine that you have a toboggan about to slide down a large hill. Only a 20% rise will stop the toboggan's downhill run. In Figure 7.1, you climb aboard the toboggan in mid-September 1997 at a price of 31.50 (at the formation start) and begin sliding down, to the left, backward in time. Speed picks up quickly as prices drop away sharply, but soon levels out as prices reach a consolidation zone just below the lowest part of the diamond, at about 21. Prices drop again, plane out, then drop more into late December 1996. You reach bottom at a price of 10.25. Since a minimum 20% rise is the only thing that will stop you (besides a tree—this I know from experience—but I digress), the toboggan starts climbing the next hill, slows, and 3 weeks earlier, at a daily closing price of 12.63, the toboggan stops. Prices continue rising then drop to the November lows, but we have already reached a 20% price change. Thus, the late December low marks the trend start.

Most times, you do not need a calculator to find the trend start, your eyes will usually do. In rare situations like Figure 7.1, the trend appears to start in late November, not December. Whether you use your eyes or a computer to find the trend start in this example, the problem is irrelevant because the trend is long term no matter how you determine its start.

Table 7.1
Average Performance of Diamonds Sorted
by Price Trend Leading to the Pattern

Trend Start to Formation Start	Downward Breakouts	Score
Short term (0 to 3 months)	−25% (97)	+1
Intermediate term (3 to 6 months)	−20% (43)	−1
Long term (over 6 months)	−18% (35)	−1

Note: The number of samples appears in parentheses.

The trend start is a key determination as Table 7.1 shows. Diamonds with long-term rises leading to the pattern result in declines averaging 18% after the formation ends. A short-term rise, by comparison, results in a 25% average decline.

I discuss scoring later in this chapter, so just ignore the scores for now.

HORIZONTAL CONSOLIDATION REGIONS

Table 7.2 shows diamond performance when a horizontal consolidation region (HCR) interferes with the price decline. Before I discuss the table, what does an HCR look like?

Figure 7.2 shows what an HCR looks like. An HCR typically has a flat top, flat bottom, or both. Do not worry if prices spike outside the horizontal line. What you are looking for is a flat region with prices stopping near the same level. The region should be large enough to be easily noticeable as a support zone (at least a week and usually much longer). In the figure, the region I used is 3 weeks long, counting from August 5 to 26. For statistical purposes, I did not count the region before August 5 (where the flat bottom becomes a flat top going back to late June). However, the flat top is important because it shows additional support points.

Returning to Table 7.2, we see that diamonds in which an HCR appears show average declines of 21%. This compares to a 24% decline when the consolidation region is missing. In other words, an HCR tends to support prices and block a price decline.

The average length of an HCR is 37 days, long enough for easy identification. I include this statistic to show you that the region should be relatively long, not just a few day's pause.

Table 7.2
Average Performance of Diamonds with
and Without a Consolidation Region

Description	Downward Breakouts	Score
Consolidation region	−21% (110)	−1
No consolidation region	−24% (71)	+1
Average length (days)	37	
Prices stop within region ±5%	55% (61)	
Prices push through region	36% (40)	
Prices do not reach region	9% (9)	

Note: The number of samples appears in parentheses.

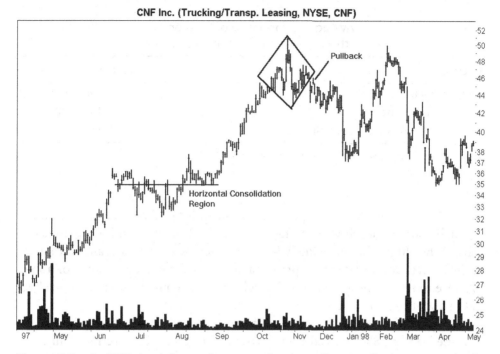

Figure 7.2 An HCR. Look for a price range that has a flat top, flat bottom, or both, between the trend start and the formation low. The area could act as a support zone and stop the decline.

Do prices really stop declining when meeting an HCR? Yes. I added a 5% buffer surrounding the consolidation region to account for those instances when prices fall a bit short or overshoot a smidgen. Fifty-five percent of the time, prices stopped within the consolidation region. In another 36% of the time, prices eventually pushed on through, and the remaining 9% reached their ultimate lows before encountering a consolidation region.

PREFORMATION RISE

Table 7.3 shows statistics for a preformation rise. A more descriptive phrase is *quick rise* because that is what the rise looks like. In a moment, I discuss Figure 7.3 that shows one, but you can see from Table 7.3 that those diamonds with a quick rise leading to the formation decline farther than those without a quick rise, with declines averaging 22.4% and 21.6%, respectively. In an earlier study I conducted, I found that 82% of the time in which a quick rise appears, prices retrace all their gains, sometimes more. Since the numbers are close, the results are not statistically significant, meaning that they could be due to chance.

Table 7.3
Average Performance of Diamonds
with and Without a Preformation Rise

Description	Downward Breakouts
Preformation rise	−22.4% (91)
No preformation rise	−21.6% (90)
Number of times prices retrace all gains	70/85 or 82%

Note: The number of samples appears in parentheses.

Figure 7.3 shows what a preformation rise looks like. The price climb is unusually sharp and short leading to the formation. I would guess that the sharper the climb, the more likely it is that prices will give back all their gains. In the figure, you can see that prices take off from the launch point of about 104, rise to the diamond in about 3 weeks, reverse course, and plunge back to 104 in about the same time.

A quick rise is typical behavior for a diamond. In the 147 diamonds I examined, 85 or 58% showed a quick rise, and of those, 82% retraced all their

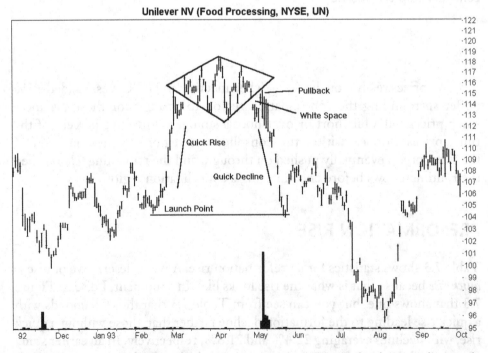

Figure 7.3 A preformation rise. When a quick price rise leads to a diamond, chances are that the decline after the diamond will meet or exceed the preformation rise.

gains. A quick rise can be an identification clue to a diamond formation. If there is a diamond, wait for the downward breakout before selling, or selling short, because the breakout might be upward instead.

INSIDE THE PATTERN

Table 7.4 shows important statistical findings for diamonds. As a rare formation, I only uncovered 184 diamonds in the 700+ stocks I looked at. Still, the number provides enough samples in which to make a valid statistical analysis.

After a downward breakout, prices decline 22%, on average. When you look at all bearish formation types, they sport an average decline of 21%, so diamonds do comparatively well.

I consider the average decline to be a best-case number. Why? Because I measure the rise from the breakout price to the ultimate low, a low that occurs before a 20% rise in prices (signaling a trend change). I have yet to complete a trade that captures both the breakout price and the lowest low at the ultimate low.

Measured from the breakout date to the date of the ultimate low, I found that the S&P 500 Index climbed 3% even as stocks showing diamonds declined 22%. I discuss the influence of the general market later, but the result is interesting. On the surface, the result suggests that the decline from a diamond is powerful enough to swim against the market current.

The median decline is the midrange value such that half the samples are above the median and half are below. To find the median, sort the returns in order and pick the middle one. For diamonds, the median is 21%, very close to the 22% average, suggesting that I found few outliers to distort the average decline.

I am not sure that declines more than 50% are a meaningful measure for bearish formations because it is exceedingly rare for a stock to decline more than 50%. Still, 3% of the diamonds I looked at declined by at least that much.

Table 7.4
Important Statistical Findings

Description	Downward Breakouts
Number of formations	184
Average decline	22%
Standard & Poor's 500 change	+3%
Median decline	21%
Declines more than 50%	6/181 or 3%

FAILURE RATES

Table 7.5 shows the various failure rates for a maximum price decline. For example, 8 or 4% of the diamonds I looked at failed to decline more than 5%. Another 21, for a total of 29 or 16%, declined less than 10%. You can see how the 5% failure rate is deceptively small. The failure rate quadruples to 16% for a price decline of 10%, nearly doubles again to 28%, and again to 47% for price declines of 15% and 20%, respectively. I would like to say that the large percentage increase in failure rates is uncommon, but it appears to be the norm for most chart pattern varieties.

Table 7.6 shows the horizon failure rate. The horizon failure rate is a new concept that compares the breakout price with the price in the future. For example, after 1 week, 8% of the stocks with diamonds had closing prices that climbed above the breakout price, that is, they failed to descend. At the end of the first week, the decline for all diamonds averaged 7%.

You can see in the table that the failure rate stays steady for the first 2 weeks, then begins climbing as more formations have prices rising above the breakout price. At the end of 6 months, over a third are higher than the breakout. Alternatively—and optimistically—64% still show declines.

The average decline marches upward from 7% to 9%, then plateaus at 10%. This trend, how the decline comes quickly, reminds me of the preformation rise. Prices zip up, execute a diamond reversal, then zip back down. It may be that many of the diamonds return to base camp after a month and stay there.

Table 7.5
Maximum Price Decline Versus Failure Rate

Maximum Price Decline (%)	Downward Breakout Failure Rate
5	8 or 4%
10	29 or 16%
15	51 or 28%
20	85 or 47%
25	118 or 65%
30	136 or 75%
35	150 or 83%
50	174 or 96%
75	181 or 100%
100	181 or 100%

Note: The sample count is 181 for each row.

Table 7.6
Horizon Failure Rates and Average Decline

Time Since Breakout	Downward Breakout Failure Rate (%)	Downward Breakout Average Decline (%)
1 week	8	7
2 weeks	8	9
3 weeks	12	9
1 month	15	10
2 months	24	10
3 months	30	10
6 months	36	10

YEARLY PRICE RANGE

Table 7.7 shows the performance after a downward breakout sorted by the breakout price in the yearly price range. Since that may sound confusing, let me explain how I found the results. For each chart pattern, I looked from the breakout date backward 1 year and found the highest high and lowest low over that period. Then I split the high–low price range into thirds and placed the breakout price into one of the three ranges. For each period, I averaged the performance after the breakout and the table shows the results. The best performance comes from those diamonds with breakouts near the yearly low. They declined 29%, but beware of the small sample size (the result may not be accurate). Those diamonds with breakouts in the middle of the yearly price range performed worst, with declines averaging 19%.

The trend, where bearish chart patterns show the best performance near the yearly low, is in agreement with other bearish chart patterns. It suggests you do best when shorting a stock making a new yearly low than when trying to short one making new yearly highs.

Table 7.7
Average Performance Sorted by Breakout Price
According to Prior 12-Month Range

Yearly Price Range	Downward Breakouts	Score
Highest third	–20% (87)	–1
Middle third	–19% (45)	–1
Lowest third	–29% (23)	+1

Note: The number of samples appears in parentheses.

Table 7.8
Performance of Short and Tall Diamonds

Description	Result	Score
Tall (above the median)	–27% (91)	+1
Short (below the median)	–18% (90)	–1
Median percentage of breakout price	12.95%	

Note: The number of samples appears in parentheses.

TALL AND SHORT PATTERNS

Table 7.8 never ceases to amaze me because of the wide performance differ-ence for most of the popular chart patterns. Usually, tall patterns handily out-perform short ones. To find the result, I measured the height of each diamond as a percentage of the breakout price, sorted the results, and chose the median value as the cutoff between short and tall.

Let me give you an example of how I did this. Look back at Figure 7.3. The highest high in the formation is at 118.50, and the lowest low is 112.63, with a breakout price of 114. The height 5.87 (that is, 118.50 – 112.63) as a percentage of the breakout price is 5%, or 5.87/114. Thus, the diamond is a short one. Prices declined 16% on their way to the ultimate low.

VOLUME TREND

Table 7.9 shows the results of a volume trend study. I used linear regression (the trend function in many spreadsheets) to determine the slope of the line from the formation start to its end on the volume data. When volume was trending upward, diamonds declined by an average 23% after the breakout. This result compares to a 22% decline when the volume was trending down-ward. Since the numbers are so close, the differences are not statistically significant.

Table 7.9
Linear Regression Volume Trend and Performance

Description	Result
Rising volume trend	–23% (55)
Falling volume trend	–22% (126)

Note: The number of samples appears in parentheses.

Table 7.10
Breakout Volume and Performance

Description	Result
Average decline on above-average breakout volume	21% (29)
Average decline on average or below-average breakout volume	22% (152)

Note: The number of samples appears in parentheses.

BREAKOUT VOLUME

Table 7.10 shows the results for those chart patterns having a heavy volume breakout compared to an average or below-average volume breakout. Diamonds with heavy breakout volume declined an average of 21%. This result compares to a 22% decline when the breakout volume was average or below average. I would expect a high volume breakout to propel prices down further, but this does not occur, leading me to wonder about the statistics. Since the numbers are so close and with the low sample counts, the differences are not statistically significant.

PULLBACKS

Are there peculiarities to diamonds that occur after the breakout? Yes, and Table 7.11 shows the effects of a pullback.

A pullback is just like a throwback only it occurs after a downward breakout instead of an upward one. By my definition, after a downward breakout, prices return to the breakout price within 30 days, completing the pullback. The 30-day limit is an arbitrary one but one that is commonly recognized. Any return to the breakout price after that is simply normal price action and not the result of a pullback.

To consider a pullback valid, prices must decline low enough to show white space between the breakout price and the daily price range. Take a look at Figure 7.3, and you will see what I mean. The price gaps downward out of the formation on the breakout day, curls around, and closes the gap. Prices return to the breakout price (and continue somewhat higher in the example) with white space between the breakout price and the curling price action. Figure 7.2 shows another example of a pullback, but it is less clear.

Pullbacks are comparatively frequent, occurring 54% of the time in the diamonds I looked at.

I base the score on pullback performance, discussed in a moment.

Table 7.11
Pullback Statistics

Description	Result
Pullbacks	100/184 or 54%
Score if pullback predicted	−1
Score if pullback not predicted	+1
Ultimate low before pullback	25 or 17%
Average decline on above-average breakout volume with pullbacks	20%
Average decline on above-average breakout volume and no pullbacks	22%
Average decline on average or below-average breakout volume and pullbacks	19%
Average decline on average or below-average breakout volume and no pullbacks	26%
Number of pullbacks after a high or very high volume breakout	12/29 or 41%
Number of pullbacks after an average, low, or very low volume breakout	88/155 or 57%
Number of pullbacks that stopped less than 5% from the breakout price	81 or 81%
Number of pullbacks that stopped between the breakout price and diamond top	5 or 5%
Number of pullbacks that stopped above the diamond top	12 or 12%

How often does the ultimate low occur before a pullback completes? In 25 cases, or 17% of the time, prices reach the ultimate low then pull back and continue up. This statistic suggests that it might be wise to cover your short if you detect prices rising on their way to pulling back. After the pullback completes and prices start back down, you can always short the stock again.

Does a pullback influence how far prices will decline? Yes. As you can see from Table 7.11 in the average decline section, when a pullback occurs after a high volume breakout, the average decline from a diamond top is 20%. After a high volume breakout but no pullback, the average decline measures 22%.

The trend is also the same after an average or below-average volume breakout. The average decline from a diamond top showing a pullback with an average or below-average volume breakout is 19%; without a pullback, the loss measures 26%. In other words, a pullback is detrimental to performance, regardless of the breakout volume.

To avoid a pullback, look for a high volume downward breakout, one that has no support zones near the breakout price. The support zones may appear as a consolidation region or prior minor lows or highs.

Are pullbacks more likely to occur after a high or low volume breakout? For diamonds, prices seem to pull back more often after an average or below average volume breakout (41% pull back after a high-volume breakout and 57% after an average or below-average volume breakout). This follows a trend I have seen with other chart patterns. Prices are more likely to *throw back* after an *upward*, high volume, breakout, but pullbacks occur more often after a low volume breakout. I think the reason for this concerns momentum. Technical analysts say that rising prices need comparatively high, sustained volume to push higher, but downward breakouts can fall because of their own weight. A downward breakout on high volume may push prices down too far to recover with a pullback.

The behavior is a lot like spitting. If you spit *with* the wind, your spit travels farther than if you spit against the wind, in which case, you get a face full (I persuaded a friend to test this hypothesis and told him I needed 30 samples!).

After a pullback, where do prices stop? Almost all the time (81%), prices return to within 5% of the breakout price. Another 5% of the time, prices rise to between the breakout price and the diamond top. The remainder of the time, 12%, prices soared above the diamond top. Note that there was no overlap between the three regions.

What these results suggest is that you should place a stop-loss order more than 5% above the breakout price, preferably above a nearby minor low or other resistance area. On average, the stop will be hit once every five trades.

BEAR TRAPS

Table 7.12 shows bear trap frequency. A bear trap occurs when prices drop less than 10%, then climb above the formation top. If investors were to short the stock after the breakout, there is a chance they would be *trapped* in a losing position as prices climbed. The table shows that a bear trap occurs 16% of the time. That result is quite small but not zero, so a bear trap is something you need to be aware of and avoid, if possible.

What does a bear trap look like? Figure 7.4 shows a good example. Prices broke out downward at a price of 15.13, dropped to a low of 13.88—for a decline of 8%—then found support and recovered their losses. Prices pulled back to the breakout price and kept moving upward, finally reaching a high of 16.63, comfortably above the diamond top.

Table 7.12
Bear Traps

Description	Downward Breakouts
Bear trap frequency	29/184 or 16%
Score if trap predicted	−1
Score if trap not predicted	+1

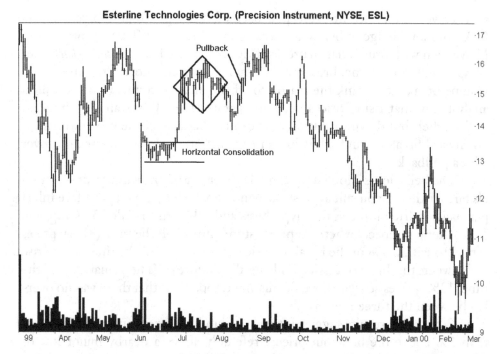

Figure 7.4   A bear trap. Avoid a bear trap by looking for a support region below the breakout price. In this case, an HCR acted as a support zone and prevented prices from descending far, causing a bear trap.

To avoid a bear trap, look for nearby support zones. Sometimes the zone will be an HCR as mentioned in the Table 7.2 discussion, and sometimes prices will hang up on a minor high or low. If you do not see any support zones, and with a trap frequency of just 16%, you should be fine.

GAPS

The results of gap analysis surprise me. Before I explain, look back at the breakout in Figure 7.3. Prices gapped lower, meaning that the daily high price on the breakout day was below the prior day's low, leaving a visible price gap. Four days later, the gap closed when prices climbed and completely covered the gap.

In Table 7.13, we find that only 33 diamonds showed a price gap on the breakout day. When a gap occurred, prices declined an average 18% before reaching the ultimate low and rebounding. This statistic compares to a 23% decline for all diamonds without gaps. Usually, a gap signals enthusiasm and prices decline further, but not in this case. My guess is that the comparatively low sample count is the reason for the unusual results, but it may be that diamonds and gaps just do not get along. In this case, gaps impede performance.

Table 7.13
Gaps and Performance

Description	Result	Score
Average decline after price gap on breakout	18% (33)	−1
Average decline with no price gap on breakout	23% (148)	+1

Note: The number of samples appears in parentheses.

MARKET TREND

Table 7.14 shows the influence of a rising or falling market on diamond performance. During creation of the diamond top (FS to FE), if the market was rising, then prices tended to fall further after the breakout, by 24%, than if the market was falling over the same period (showing a 19% average decline after the breakout). This result is almost opposite the performance from the formation end to the ultimate low. There, a rising tide that usually lifts all boats seems to lift the falling stocks also: They declined by only 20%. When the general market was falling during the breakout to the ultimate low, then those stocks showing diamonds also scored better by declining an average of 23%.

Incidentally, I base the scores on the formation start to end period (FS to FE) because you cannot tell ahead of time how the general market will behave after the breakout.

MARKET CAPITALIZATION

Table 7.15 shows how much better small caps perform than do large caps. I computed the market capitalization of a stock by multiplying the number of shares outstanding times the breakout price. Then, I grouped the associated diamonds into their appropriate capitalization category. Small caps declined farthest, 27%, while mid and large caps declined less—23% and 19%, respectively. If you intend to short a stock, pick a small cap. If you own a stock and it

Table 7.14
Average Price Performance of Diamonds
During a Rising and Falling Market

Market Trend	FS to FE	Score	FE to UL
Rising S&P 500, down breakout	−24% (125)	+1	−20% (64)
Falling S&P 500, down breakout	−19% (56)	−1	−23% (117)

Note: FS = formation start, FE = formation end, UL = ultimate low. The number of samples appears in parentheses.

Table 7.15
Average Price Performance of
Diamonds by Market Capitalization

Capitalization	Down Breakouts	Score
Small cap (up to $1 billion)	–27% (55)	+1
Mid cap ($1 to $5 billion)	–23% (76)	+1
Large cap (over $5 billion)	–19% (48)	–1

Note: The number of samples appears in parentheses.

shows a diamond top, either sell it outright or pray that the stock is a large cap. They hold up best.

SCORES

How do you use the scoring system to improve your trading performance? The case studies that follow give examples of how to score your chart pattern. Generally, you evaluate your diamond according to each table showing a score. Add the scores together. Scores above zero tend to beat the median decline, whereas those below zero usually perform worse than the median.

Table 7.16 shows the statistics for the scoring system. When the scores total above zero, the diamonds with downward breakouts showed losses averaging 28%. This result compares with a 13% loss when the scores were below zero. That is not to say that the system is perfect. The system correctly signaled a sell short candidate 68% of the time. That statistic means the score was above zero and the resulting performance beat the median decline. The system correctly said avoid shorting a stock 83% of the time. That statistic means the score was below zero and the resulting decline was less than the median.

Table 7.16
Formation Performance by Score

Score	Down Breakouts
Average decline of chart patterns with scores above zero	28%
Average decline of chart patterns with scores below zero	13%
Median decline used	20.04%
Percentage with scores above zero beating median decline	68/100 or 68%
Percentage with scores below zero doing worse than median decline	45/54 or 83%

CASE STUDY 1

Throughout this chapter, various tables show scores to assist in the ranking of chart patterns. This case study and Case Study 2 show you how to use those scores.

Consider the diamond top shown in Figure 7.5. At first glance, the diamond may appear oddly placed as it occurs during an upward retrace in a downtrend. Another view shows that the diamond forms at the top of a corrective phase of a measured move down. The first leg is from point A to the trend start; the corrective phase runs from the trend start to the diamond top, and the second leg down starts at the diamond top and finishes at the ultimate low. The theory behind measured moves (either up or down), is that the second leg will approximate the size of the first leg. In this case, the first leg decline measures 11.07 while the second leg measures 7.38. On a percentage basis, the declines are closer: 41% for the first leg and 37% for the second. The corrective phase of the measured move down also looks proportional to the size of the first leg. It reminds me of the three bears story: not too large, not too small.

Finally, look at the short, quick price rise leading to the diamond. In just over 2 weeks the stock climbed 25% from about 16 to 20. It is reasonable to

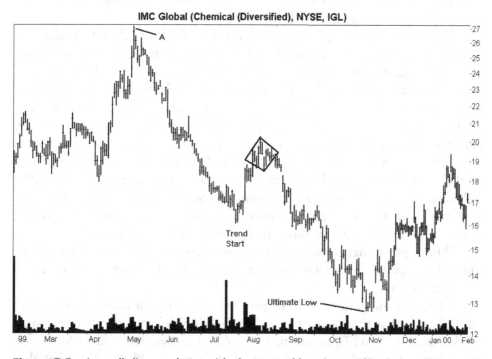

Figure 7.5 A small diamond top with downward breakout. This diamond appears at the top of the corrective phase of a measured move down formation that runs from point A to the ultimate low.

expect that those quick gains would be lost after a downward breakout, and, indeed, they were.

Now, to the scores. Table 7.1 showed the resulting performance of diamonds sorted by the price trend leading to the formation. In Figure 7.5, clearly the trend starts in mid-July, as marked on the figure. Before that low, prices climbed more than 20% (as measured from the lowest low to the close), signaling a trend change. The time from the trend start to the formation start is less than 3 months, placing it in the short-term category, for a +1 score.

Table 7.2 discusses an HCR. From the trend start to the lowest low in the diamond, there is no consolidation region where prices would likely pause. No support beneath the diamond suggests good performance, for a +1 score. Running total: +2.

Skipping to the next table with a score, Table 7.7, we see the diamond performance sorted by the yearly price range. The yearly high, looking backward from the breakout date, is at 27.31, shown as point A. The yearly low, 16.06, occurs at the trend start. The breakout, at 18.81, is within a third of the yearly low. That scores +1 according to Table 7.7. Running total: +3

Is the diamond a tall one? You can probably guess that it is a shorty, but check to be sure. The highest high in the diamond is at 20.13 and the low is at 18.50 with an 18.81 breakout price. The height, 1.63 (or 20.13 − 18.50), expressed as a percentage of the breakout, measures 9% (that is, 1.63/18.81). This result is shorter than the median 12.95% cutoff from Table 7.8. The diamond is short, scoring −1. Running total: +2.

Table 7.11 lists the performance of diamonds and pullbacks. Without a support zone beneath the diamond, and coupled with the quick rise, I consider a pullback unlikely. Since prices stopped declining at 16.06 on the way to the trend start, that price would be the first area in which the stock may find support. A climb back to the breakout point would mean a rise of 21% in less than 30 days. That is not unheard of, but it certainly is unlikely, especially when a pullback only occurs about half the time (54%). Score: +1. Running total: +3.

For the very same reasons that a pullback would not occur, a bear trap is unlikely (see Table 7.12). Recall that a bear trap is a decline of less than 10% followed by a rise above the formation top. Since a sharp decline after the breakout often follows a preformation rise and since a support zone is not nearby, a bear trap would be unlikely. Score: +1. Running total: +4.

The breakout day is the day prices closed outside the diamond trendline. On that day, prices did not gap downward, so Table 7.11 scores that a +1. Running total of +5.

How did the general market perform from the formation start to the end? During that time, the Standard & Poor's 500 Index climbed. A rising market during FS to FE, according to Table 7.14, suggests good performance for a score of +1 and a running total of +6. Let me add that the S&P also declined from the formation end to the ultimate low, but there was no way of predicting that.

The last table, Table 7.15, shows performance sorted by market capitalization. With a breakout price of 18.81, the stock falls into the mid cap category for a score of +1. The final total is +7.

How did the stock perform? From the breakout price of 18.81, you can see that prices quickly dropped to the price of the trend start, then moved sideways for 3 weeks. The decline resumed, reaching a new multiyear low of 12.75 in late October. The decline measured 32%, well beyond the 20.04% median, as predicted.

Let me caution you that sometimes the results of the scoring system are not this clean. On rare occasions, I have seen a perfect score result in below-average performance. Just because the scoring system says the stock is a buy candidate is no reason to throw caution to the wind and mortgage the farm (or to invest some of those millions from your dot.com winnings, to bring the analogy up to date).

CASE STUDY 2

Take a look at Figure 7.6, a diamond hidden in the rough. I did not mention it in this chapter so far, but when a flat base appears, a stock is likely to stop

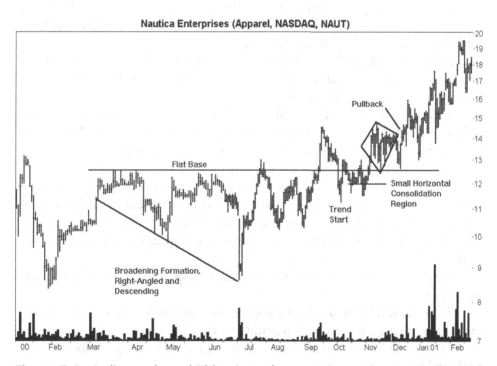

Figure 7.6 A diamond top hidden in a choppy price environment. A partial decline from a broadening formation, right-angled and descending, predicted higher prices. A flat base lent support to prices after the breakout.

declining at that point. Those diamonds springing from a flat base showed declines averaging 19% compared to a 23% average decline without a flat base.

To me, a flat base is a lot like an HCR, where prices either have flat tops, flat bottoms, or both. With a flat base, the consolidation lasts much longer, usually months, with prices touching the same level multiple times. Such is the case in the figure. Prices climbed repeatedly to 12.50 then stalled. The March to mid-June price pattern is a right-angled, descending, broadening formation, one with lower lows, forming the flat base as its top. The twin minor lows in August did not approach the depth of the June low or the down-sloping broadening formation trendline—signaling a partial decline—and suggesting an upward breakout.

What about scoring the diamond top? Running quickly through the tables we find the following.

Table 7.1: Trend start. The trend started in early October, placing the rise in the short-term category for a +1 score.

Table 7.2: Horizontal consolidation region. From the trend start, there are several touches at a price of 12 that are obscured by a few downward spikes. On my charts, I called it an HCR. Certainly the flat base at 12.50 sets up a support zone, one that would make a sustained downward price move less likely. Score: –1. Running total: 0.

Table 7.7: Yearly price range. The yearly high is at 14.75, the yearly low is at 8.38, and the breakout is priced at 14.19. Thus, the breakout is near the yearly high for a –1 score. Running total: –1.

Table 7.8: Tall or short. The formation high is at 14.75, the bottom at 12.50, for a height as a percentage of the breakout of 15.86%. That rates it a tall diamond. Score: +1. Running total: 0.

Table 7.11: Pullback. Is a pullback predicted? Yes. With prices trending higher from the June low, coupled with the small HCR and the longer flat base, there was ample reason to expect a pullback to the breakout price. Score: –1. Running total: –1.

Table 7.12: Bear traps. Knowing that a flat base—a support zone—was at 12.50, I would consider it likely that prices would stop near that level. Factoring in the upward price trend since June, that might be enough to take prices above the diamond top, completing a bear trap. Score: –1 for a running total of –2.

Table 7.13: Gaps. There was no breakout gap. Score: +1 for a running total of –1.

Table 7.14: Market trend. During creation of the formation, the market was falling, giving a score of –1. Running total: –2.

Table 7.15: Market capitalization. The stock is a small cap. Score: +1 for a final total of –1.

Scores above zero mean good performance; below zero mean poor performance. When the score totals zero exactly, the system sounds a note of caution. The closer to zero the score is, the weaker the signal.

How did the stock do? After the breakout at 14.19, prices dropped to a low of 12.63, pulled back and continued higher. On a percentage basis, the decline measured 11%, well below the median 20.04% decline.

8

Double Bottoms

Pretend that it is nearing Christmas and your mom wants you to come visit over the holidays. You call up PU Air and the phone representative (be nice to her; I used to date one) says they have an incredible special. For just $25, they will fly you coast to coast, first class. How can that be, you ask? "We have been having some technical difficulties," she replies candidly. "Of the last three flights, two of them crashed."

If you do not know what you are doing, investing in double bottoms is a lot like flying PU Air. Sixty-four percent of the twin bottom formations will fall below the lowest bottom low without first rising above the confirmation point (the highest high between the two bottoms). In simpler words, you will lose money 64% of the time. Fortunately, there is a simple technique to improve the odds. Call it *waiting for confirmation*. That tip is just one of a number of tips that will improve your chances of success.

THE TYPICAL PATTERN

While doing research for this chapter, I came across two variations of double bottoms—Adam & Eve and Eve & Adam—on the hardrightedge.com Web site. Adam refers to a bottom with a price pattern that appears V-shaped, sharp and deep, perhaps with a long 1-day downward spike. Eve has a more gentle rounded appearance as if someone came along with a file and smoothed the rough edges. I also looked at the two other combinations: Adam & Adam and Eve & Eve.

Figure 8.1 shows an Adam & Adam double bottom. While volume on the right bottom is extremely heavy, most Adam & Adam double bottoms show

142

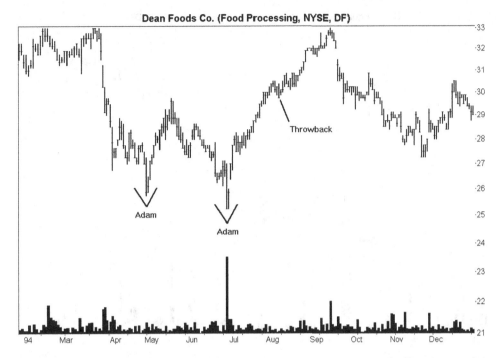

Figure 8.1 An Adam & Adam double bottom. Volume is usually heavier on the left bottom, unlike that shown here. Due to generally poor performance, avoid the Adam & Adam double bottom. Notice that prices climb to the old high, then stall.

volume heavier on the left bottom. The Adam & Adam variety is rare, appearing in just 17% of the 803 double bottoms I reviewed. When compared to the performance of the other double bottom types, this one performs worst.

Figure 8.2 shows an Adam & Eve double bottom. The Adam bottom is sharp, narrow, and deep, whereas Eve appears rounded, wider, and flatter. The left bottom usually shows the heaviest volume. The formation works well when prices rebounded off the same, or nearly the same, low price several times (a flat base region) leading to the double bottom.

Figure 8.3 is an example of an Eve & Adam double bottom. Volume is heaviest on the right bottom, contrasting with the other three varieties of double bottoms. This is the rarest of the four varieties, occurring just 15% of the time. It performs best after a short-term downtrend leading to the pattern.

The Eve & Eve variety represents what most would call a classic double bottom, and Figure 8.4 shows an example. The pattern performs best after a short-term downtrend. Volume is usually heaviest on the left bottom. You could also call the two bottoms in April (the right bottom of the Eve & Eve) a small Adam & Eve double bottom, as it also qualifies.

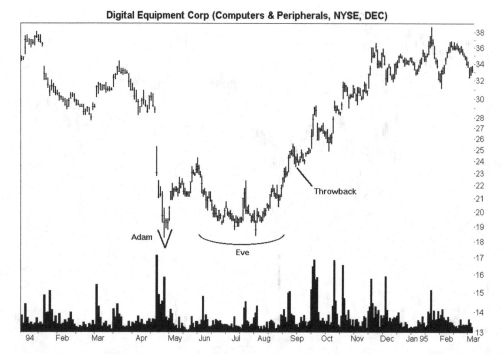

Figure 8.2   The Adam & Eve double bottom. The Adam bottom appears pointed, in a V-shaped depression, whereas the Eve bottom is more rounded. Volume is typically highest on the left bottom.

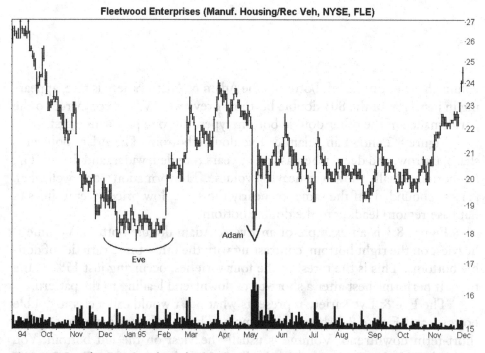

Figure 8.3   The Eve & Adam double bottom. Volume is usually highest on formation of the right bottom.

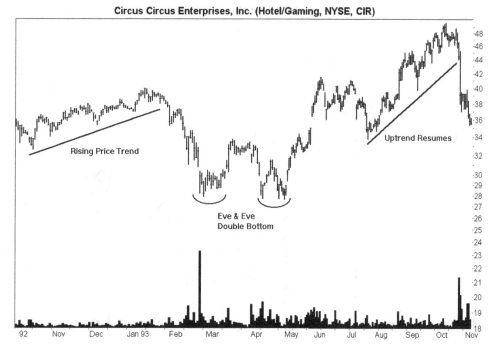

Figure 8.4 A double bottom of the Eve & Eve variety. The bottoms appear rounded with volume highest during creation of the left bottom. This double bottom retraces a portion of the rising price trend before prices resume moving up.

TREND START AND FLAT BASE

The price trend leading to a double bottom comes in three varieties: short-term downtrend, intermediate-term downtrend, and long-term downtrend, with a flat base distinction. I define short-, intermediate-, and long-term downtrends as those having price trends leading downward to the formation for up to 3 months, between 3 and 6 months, and over 6 months, respectively. I define a flat base as when prices rebound off the same low price—or nearly the same—multiple times over several weeks or months. The three downtrends all begin after a 20% change in the price trend.

Figure 8.5 shows two of the three varieties of downtrends. The Eve & Eve double bottom has a price trend that starts just short of the 6-month cut-off. Before January 10, 1992, the price trend was up; after the peak, prices declined to the double bottom. Going backward in time, the change in trend was more than 20%, marking the January 10 high as the start of a new trend.

A short-term downtrend precedes the Eve & Adam double bottom in the center of the figure. I categorize the term as short because prices fall away from the September 17 peak by more than 20% before rising to the highest high on the chart (going backward in time).

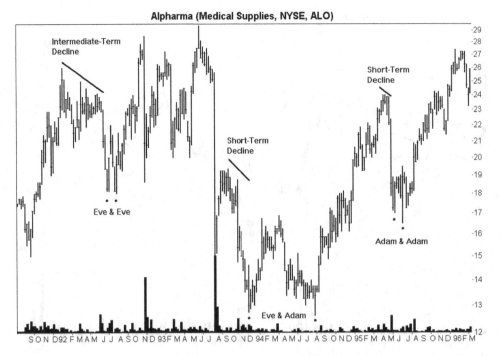

Figure 8.5   These double bottoms appear after short- or intermediate-term downtrends. Two pipe bottom chart patterns make up the Eve & Eve bottom, and they suggest a bullish reversal. Prices appear on the weekly scale. Use the daily scale for identification.

The intent of the figure is to show the price trend, not as good examples of double bottoms, because the Adam and the Eve combinations look different on a weekly scale than they do on the daily charts. Use daily charts for identification.

Figure 8.6 shows a flat base consolidation region followed by a double bottom. Prices rebound off the same low price three times and come close two other times. The flat base should appear near the lows of the double bottom and are easiest to locate on the weekly scale.

An interesting finding for double bottoms appearing in or after a flat price trend is that the double bottom usually forms near the end of a larger formation (on the weekly scale), such as that shown in the figure. The most common patterns for the flat base structure are descending triangles, right-angled ascending broadening tops, symmetrical triangles (where the bottom trendline slopes up, but not too steeply), rectangles, and unconfirmed head-and-shoulders tops.

Why is this important? If you see a flat base—one showing support near the same price over the long term—watch for a double bottom to form. The double bottom may signal an impending upside breakout.

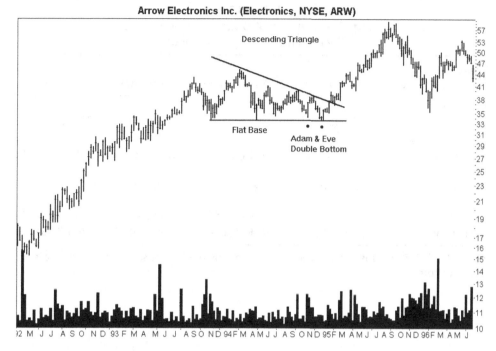

Figure 8.6   A double bottom follows a flat base price trend. The flat base appears within a descending triangle and prices appear on the weekly scale.

Table 8.1 lists the price trend leading to the various types of double bottoms and their corresponding performance. I measured performance from the breakout price to the highest high before a 20% price decline. A 20% decline typically marks a bearish turn for the stock and is usually large enough to say that the up trend is over. In the computation, I used the highest high (called the ultimate high) and close after the ultimate high to flag a 20% price change.

In a similar manner, the trend starts when prices decline by 20%. From the formation start, I followed the price trend backward in time comparing the current closing price to the highest high found so far. Eventually, prices will close 20% below the highest high, marking the highest high as the trend start. Please note that the comparison uses the closing price and not the daily low because, in a few rare circumstances, the daily low price prematurely—and incorrectly—signals the end of the price trend.

Considering the price trend leading to a double bottom, both the Eve & Adam and Eve & Eve patterns perform well. From a flat base, the Adam & Eve double bottom works particularly well, with average price rises of 59%, but the result uses only 19 chart patterns. I would expect the performance to decline after examining more formations.

Look for Eve & Adam double bottoms after a price downtrend of 3 months or less; they will usually give you the best performance. For longer-term downtrends or those springing from flat bases, look for the Adam & Eve

Table 8.1
Average Performance of Double Bottoms Sorted
by Price Trend Leading to the Pattern

Trend Start to Formation Start	Adam & Adam	Adam & Eve	Eve & Adam	Eve & Eve
Short term (0 to 3 months)	27% (55) +1	30% (96) –1	39% (48) +1	38% (128) +1
Intermediate term (3 to 6 months)	27% (37) +1	34% (63) +1	22% (28) –1	33% (73) –1
Long term (over 6 months)	18% (10) –1	41% (23) +1	25% (17) –1	37% (40) +1
Flat base	29% (18) +1	59% (19) +1	44% (15) +1	43% (28) +1
No flat base	27% (98) –1	28% (178) –1	28% (86) –1	36% (233) –1

Note: The first number is the average, followed by the number of samples in parentheses and the score.

variety for best performance. Avoid the Adam & Adam pattern unless you like poor performance.

I discuss scoring later in this chapter, so just ignore the scores for now.

HORIZONTAL CONSOLIDATION REGIONS

Table 8.2 shows the average performance of the various double bottom types when associated with a horizontal consolidation region (HCR). I define an HCR as one that appears between the price at the trend start and confirmation (the highest high between the two bottoms). The region should appear flat (or nearly so) on the bottom or top and horizontal. Individual price spikes pushing through the region are normal—just ignore them. An HCR is a place of resistance in which prices must push through on their way to setting new highs.

I like to think of the resistance area as a pane of glass. If the neighborhood vandal has a tennis ball and he throws it repeatedly against your window, it will eventually break if he throws it hard enough. That analogy is similar to prices burning through resistance. If prices fail to pierce the resistance area, they will tumble, regroup, and gather strength for a future try.

With the exception of Adam & Eve, performance improves if there is no consolidation area posing a challenge to the price rise. In the case of Adam & Adam, the difference is startling: 24% compared to 37%.

You can see the average length of the consolidation regions in Table 8.2. They range from 48 days for Adam & Eve to 55 days for Eve & Adam. When

Table 8.2
Average Performance of Double Bottoms with
and Without a Consolidation Region

Description	Adam & Adam	Adam & Eve	Eve & Adam	Eve & Eve
Consolidation region	24% (85) –1	32% (144) +1	30% (67) –1	35% (184) –1
No consolidation region	37% (31) +1	31% (53) –1	31% (34) +1	41% (77) +1
Average length (days)	52	48	55	49
Prices stop within region ±5%	51%	42%	45%	39%
Prices push through region	39%	47%	48%	52%
Prices do not reach region	10%	11%	7%	9%

Note: The first number is the average, followed by the number of samples in parentheses and the score.

you are looking for an HCR, it should be at least a week long, but the longer the better.

An HCR differs from the flat base pattern mentioned in the Table 8.1 discussion. A flat base appears near the price level of the double bottom lows whereas an HCR appears between the trend start and the confirmation price (by my definition, anyway).

As I was reviewing the charts searching for the HCRs, I noticed that many of the double bottom chart patterns had ultimate highs that stopped within the consolidation region. So, I decided to do an analysis, and the last three rows of Table 8.2 show the results.

I measured where the ultimate high stopped compared to the consolidation region. Since prices often overshoot or undershoot the region a bit, I added a 5% buffer surrounding the consolidation zone to capture those cases. Most of the time, prices move into the consolidation zone without trouble. The consolidation area is where things go bad. About half (51%) of the Adam & Adam patterns show prices stopping within the consolidation area. This result probably explains why the performance is so poor (with gains of just 24% when a consolidation area appears). For the other patterns, most are able to push through the resistance zone nearly half the time.

Figure 8.7 shows what an HCR looks like and how it acts as a resistance zone. The region appears as an ill-formed (it would look better if the minor lows in July and August touched the lower trendline) descending triangle. The resistance area halted the advance after the breakout. Prices formed a head-and-shoulders top, then tumbled to 5.25 before finding traction.

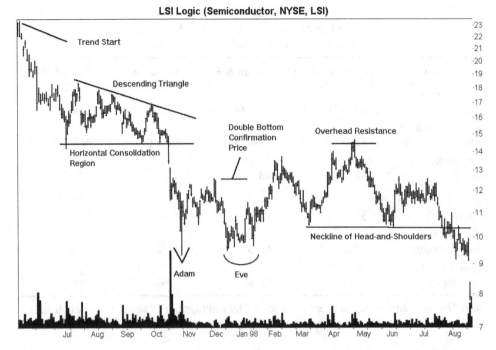

Figure 8.7   An HCR masked as a descending triangle. The region, with lows that near or touch the same price, poses a resistance zone that this stock cannot pierce. Prices eventually drop to a low of 5.25 after the head-and-shoulders formation.

Be sure to look for HCRs or other resistance areas before buying a stock. Often, as in Figure 8.7, resistance zones pose a threat to a continued price advance. Prices reach the resistance zone, then have to burn through it before moving higher.

INSIDE THE PATTERN

Table 8.3 shows important statistical findings for double bottoms. *Only double bottoms with prices climbing above the confirmation point, which is the highest high between the two bottoms, appear in the statistics.* The reason for this requirement is simple: almost two out of three twin bottom patterns never rise to the confirmation point. Instead, prices continue falling. By definition, *if prices do not close above the confirmation point, then the twin bottom is not a double bottom.*

The Adam & Adam and Eve & Adam variety of double bottoms are the rare ones. I included the double bottoms I found while writing *Encyclopedia of Chart Patterns* (Wiley, 2000), and added as many as I could find from the database I use on a daily basis. Together, the statistics cover over 800 patterns in

Table 8.3
Important Statistical Findings

Description	Adam & Adam	Adam & Eve	Eve & Adam	Eve & Eve
Number of formations	134	232	122	315
Average rise	27%	31%	30%	37%
Standard & Poor's 500 change	4%	5%	4%	5%
Median rise	23%	24%	25%	28%
Rises more than 50%	19/116 or 16%	47/197 or 24%	21/101 or 21%	71/261 or 27%
Bottom with highest volume	Left 57%	Left 71%	Right 52%	Left 61%

almost 10 years of data. Since double bottoms are so plentiful, you can afford to be choosy.

I computed the average rise from the breakout price to the ultimate high for all formations for which data was available. The Eve & Eve variety performs best with rises averaging 37%. Your average results will probably be less than this because the statistic assumes that you bought the stock right at the breakout price and sold at the highest high with no commissions, slippage, or other trading costs.

How did the S&P 500 Index perform over the period from the breakout to the ultimate high? I measured the S&P from its close to daily high on the dates the double bottom broke out and reached the ultimate high. You can see in Table 8.3 that the rise was a meager 4% or 5% compared to a minimum 27% rise for double bottoms.

For each double bottom type, I sorted the gains and selected the midrange value, the median, so that half the values were above the median and half below. The median values are important since very large gains may skew the average rise upward. From Table 8.3, you can see that the Eve & Eve formation still performs best (sporting a median rise of 28%), whereas the Adam & Adam pattern performs below the others (with a 23% rise).

I counted the number of patterns with rises more than 50%, just to see how well double bottoms performed. As the table illustrates, the Adam & Eve and Eve & Eve patterns perform best with about a quarter of the patterns rising more than 50%.

Most of the time, the left bottom shows the highest volume except for the Eve & Adam formation, which shows higher volume 52% of the time on the right bottom. To arrive at the result, I added the volume from 2 days before to 2 days after each bottom (5 day's total) then compared the volume totals with the other bottom.

FAILURE RATES

Table 8.4 shows the failure rates for a maximum price rise as measured from the breakout price to the ultimate high. For example, if you consider all Adam & Adam double bottoms that rise less than 5% as failures, then 7 or 6% fall into that category.

Let me give you another example that shows the importance of this table. As an end-of-day trader, I typically buy the day after a breakout, once the price has closed above the confirmation point. This gives me confidence that the formation has indeed made an upside breakout, but it increases my risk of failure and lowers my profit potential. I also know that I never sell at the highest high. In essence, I am getting in a bit late and leaving a bit early—before price's peak—or late, after prices start declining. Adding in commissions and slippage, I decide the stock must rise at least 15% for me to show a profit. Which of the four varieties of double bottoms have the fewest failures for a 15% rise? On a percentage basis, the Adam & Eve pattern has the lowest failure rate with 29% of the patterns failing to rise at least 15%. If I trade often enough, slightly over one in four trades will fail to reach my break-even point.

Another example: If my break-even point is 15%, and I want to make at least a 10% profit (thereby requiring a 25% price rise), then the Eve & Eve pattern is my best bet, but almost half the trades (46%) will fail to reach my profit objective.

Using Table 8.4 only, for a long-term trade, I would concentrate my efforts in locating Eve & Eve formations, because they have the lowest failure rates with the highest price rise. However, 72% of the Eve & Eve double bottoms have rises less than 50%. The larger the rise you hope for, the smaller your

Table 8.4
Maximum Price Rise Versus Failure Rate

Maximum Price Rise (%)	Adam & Adam Failure Rate	Adam & Eve Failure Rate	Eve & Adam Failure Rate	Eve & Eve Failure Rate
5	7 or 6%	11 or 6%	4 or 4%	11 or 4%
10	21 or 18%	29 or 15%	17 or 17%	47 or 18%
15	39 or 34%	57 or 29%	30 or 30%	78 or 30%
20	54 or 47%	76 or 39%	37 or 37%	92 or 35%
25	62 or 53%	101 or 51%	50 or 50%	119 or 46%
30	68 or 59%	115 or 58%	60 or 59%	145 or 56%
35	77 or 66%	126 or 64%	65 or 64%	157 or 60%
50	97 or 84%	150 or 76%	80 or 79%	189 or 72%
75	106 or 91%	179 or 91%	89 or 88%	217 or 83%
100	110 or 95%	186 or 94%	96 or 95%	230 or 88%

chances of attaining it. If you want to double your money (a 100% rise), only 12% (about one in eight) of the Eve & Eve formations will make the cut. Adam & Eve patterns seem to perform well for small rises.

One other observation: look how the failure rates jump for the 5% to 10% maximum price rise. For the Eve & Eve pattern, the failure rate more than quadruples! In all cases, the failure rate at least doubles. The failure rates climb quickly so that if you expect to make a killing in a stock, it is you who might be killed.

Table 8.5 shows the horizon failure rates for the four types of double bottoms. I computed each failure rate entry by looking at the return for the associated double bottom after 1 week, 2 weeks, and so forth, then classified those stocks that closed below the breakout price after each period as failures.

You can see that the Adam & Adam pattern runs into trouble. After 3 months, almost half (45%) of the patterns are below the breakout price, the highest in the group. The Adam & Adam pattern also has only one entry, at 1 month, in which the failure rate is the lowest for its row.

The right half of Table 8.5 shows the results of an analysis of average rise over time. For each double bottom, I looked at the breakout price and compared it with the daily closing price weekly for the first month, monthly for the first quarter and, finally, 6 months after the breakout.

None shows continued price rises over the entire 6 months. The Eve & Eve pattern shows the best performance over many individual time periods when compared with the other double bottom types. It ties or outperforms the others in each period.

If I had to boil down the right half of Table 8.5 into one suggestion, it is this: Place a stop order to buy the stock at the breakout price. You get in at a good price and capture the gains when they are comparatively large (during the first week), but watch for throwbacks. If you are a short-term trader, you might want to sell in a week or two (at the high before the throwback).

YEARLY PRICE RANGE

Does performance vary depending on where the breakout is according to the prior 12-month price range? Yes, and Table 8.6 shows the results. To create the table, I measured from the breakout date backward 1 year and looked at the highest high and lowest low over that span. Then, I split the range into thirds (high, middle, and low) and assigned the breakout price into one of the three ranges.

Most of the time, the breakout occurs in the center third of the yearly price range, but the best performance usually occurs when the breakout price is near the yearly low. Only in the Eve & Adam case does the middle third outperform. Of the group, Eve & Eve shows the best performance, rising 41% when the breakout occurs near the yearly low.

Table 8.5
Horizon Failure Rates and Average Rise

Time Since Breakout	Adam & Adam Failure Rate (%)	Adam & Eve Failure Rate (%)	Eve & Adam Failure Rate (%)	Eve & Eve Failure Rate (%)	Adam & Adam Average Rise (%)	Adam & Eve Average Rise (%)	Eve & Adam Average Rise (%)	Eve & Eve Average Rise (%)
1 week	34	37	27	30	3	2	3	4
2 weeks	28	32	25	26	4	3	4	4
3 weeks	29	27	35	28	4	4	5	5
1 month	30	31	34	31	3	5	5	5
2 months	33	32	34	30	5	4	6	7
3 months	45	33	38	31	4	6	7	8
6 months	38	36	41	39	7	7	4	7

Table 8.6
Average Performance Sorted by Breakout Price
According to Prior 12-Month Range

Yearly Price Range	Adam & Adam	Adam & Eve	Eve & Adam	Eve & Eve
Highest third	20% (18) −1	36% (33) +1	29% (24) −1	37% (59) +1
Middle third	25% (47) −1	30% (77) −1	35% (37) +1	33% (92) −1
Lowest third	32% (32) +1	38% (62) +1	26% (28) −1	41% (83) +1

Note: The first number is the average rise, followed by the number of samples in parentheses and the score.

TALL AND SHORT PATTERNS

Table 8.7 shows the performance sorted by formation height. For many chart patterns, tall formations perform better than short formations and double bottoms follow that trend. That is, except for the Eve & Eve pattern. Before I discuss the results, let me explain how I came up with the numbers.

I measured the formation height from the highest high to the lower of the two bottoms and divided the result by the confirmation price (the highest high). Then, I sorted each chart pattern type and selected the median value as the separation between short and tall. Half the chart patterns were taller than the median value and half were shorter.

Having sorted the results by their short and tall categories, I looked at the resulting performance and found that tall patterns usually creamed the short ones. For example, when the height as a percentage of the breakout price was more than 18.32%, the Adam & Adam double bottoms gained 33%, on average. This compares to a gain of just 24% for the short ones. In the case of Eve & Eve, short ones marginally outperform the tall ones, by 38% to 36%. The differences between the Eve & Eve results are not statistically significant, suggesting they are due to chance. Since most chart patterns show a definite

Table 8.7
Performance of Short and Tall Double Bottoms

Description	Adam & Adam	Adam & Eve	Eve & Adam	Eve & Eve
Tall (above the median)	33% (58) +1	36% (98) +1	33% (51) +1	36% (132) −1
Short (below the median)	24% (58) −1	28% (99) −1	28% (50) −1	38% (129) +1
Median percentage of breakout price	18.32%	17.09%	18.38%	16.39%

Note: The first number is the average, followed by the number of samples in parentheses and the score.

Table 8.8
Linear Regression Volume Trend and Performance

Description	Adam & Adam	Adam & Eve	Eve & Adam	Eve & Eve
Rising volume trend	26% (40)	24% (53)	29% (37)	39% (94)
Falling volume trend	29% (76)	35% (144)	31% (64)	36% (167)
Score: rising trend	–1	–1	–1	+1
Score: falling trend	+1	+1	+1	–1

Note: The number of samples appears in parentheses.

performance improvement for tall patterns, I think the Eve & Eve result is incorrect but have scored it as if the numbers are correct.

VOLUME TREND

Table 8.8 shows the performance results after sorting double bottoms by their volume trend. I used linear regression from the formation start to end to gauge whether volume was trending upward or downward. Linear regression is a fancy way of saying I plotted a *best-fit* line between the points. The slope of the line told me whether volume was trending upward or downward.

With the exception of the Eve & Eve pattern, the double bottom varieties performed best after the breakout if the volume was trending downward from the formation start to end. It is as if investors are saving their bullets for the breakout. After the breakout, they rush back in and push prices higher.

BREAKOUT VOLUME

Speaking of breakout volume, Table 8.9 shows the performance of double bottoms sorted by their breakout volume level compared with the prior 3 months.

Table 8.9
Breakout Volume and Performance

Description	Adam & Adam	Adam & Eve	Eve & Adam	Eve & Eve
Average rise on above-average breakout volume	36% (40)	34% (67)	26% (40)	44% (119)
Average rise on average or below-average breakout volume	24% (76)	30% (130)	33% (61)	32% (142)
Score: high volume	+1	+1	–1	+1
Score: low volume	–1	–1	+1	–1

Note: The number of samples appears in parentheses.

For example, those Eve & Eve double bottoms showing high or very high breakout volume posted gains averaging 44%. This compares to a 32% average rise for patterns with average, low, or very low volume breakouts.

The table suggests that high breakout volume is beneficial in all cases with the exception of Eve & Adam.

THROWBACKS

What happens to prices after the pattern completes? Do prices throw back to the confirmation point then rebound or continue down? Do prices find support near the confirmation point or near the double bottom low? Table 8.10 provides the answers.

A throwback occurs when prices return to the breakout price within 30 days. The 30-day cutoff is an arbitrary limit; it assumes that any price movement beyond that time is due to normal price action and not a throwback. To qualify as a throwback, prices must move above the breakout price (with clear white space), then loop back; prices sliding along or near the breakout price do not qualify as throwbacks. Several of the figures that accompany this chapter highlight throwbacks.

A throwback gives an investor another opportunity to buy the stock at a good price or add to a holding. Most of the double bottom varieties have throwbacks that occur around 60% of the time.

Between 10% and 13% of the double bottoms reach their ultimate high before throwing back to the breakout price and continuing lower. This result is not a huge number, but you might want to sell as prices peak before throwing back. You can always buy again at a lower price if the situation warrants.

In researching the performance of double bottoms with and without throwbacks and associated breakout volume levels, I came across interesting results. The best performance from the various double bottom types usually comes if prices do not throw back after a high or very high volume breakout. Compare the results of the Eve & Adam pattern, for example. Without a throwback the formation scores an average rise of 34%; with a throwback, the rise is almost half, 19%. Both breakouts are on above-average volume. Since the values in the table are averages, your results may vary.

Regardless of the volume level, double bottoms usually perform better without a throwback. The only exceptions are the Adam & Eve and Eve & Adam patterns that perform differently depending on the volume level. The worst performance varies somewhat but relates to average or below-average breakout volume and a throwback.

Removing from consideration whether or not a throwback occurred, compare the performance of double bottoms with above- and below-average volume. Those double bottoms with high or very high volume breakouts outperformed those showing average or below-average breakout volume in nearly

Table 8.10
Throwback Statistics

Description	Adam & Adam	Adam & Eve	Eve & Adam	Eve & Eve
Throwbacks	87 or 65%	138 or 59%	72 or 59%	173 or 55%
Score if throwback predicted	–1	–1	–1	–1
Score if throwback not predicted	+1	+1	+1	+1
Ultimate high before throwback	15 or 11%	26 or 11%	12 or 10%	41 or 13%
Average rise on above-average breakout volume with throwbacks	36%	36%	19%	38%
Average rise on above-average breakout volume with no throwbacks	36%	32%	34%	53%
Average rise on average or below-average breakout volume with throwbacks	22%	29%	33%	28%
Average rise on average or below-average breakout volume with no throwbacks	28%	32%	32%	35%
Number of throwbacks after a high or very high volume breakout	30/44 or 68%	48/79 or 61%	27/43 or 63%	80/135 or 59%
Number of throwbacks after an average, low, or very low volume breakout	57/90 or 63%	89/153 or 58%	45/79 or 57%	93/180 or 52%
Number of throwbacks that stopped ±5% from the breakout price	54 or 62%	74 or 54%	36 or 50%	100 or 58%
Number of throwbacks that stopped between breakout price and double bottom low	25 or 29%	55 or 39%	32 or 44%	55 or 32%
Number of throwbacks that fell below double bottom low	8 or 9%	9 or 7%	4 or 6%	18 or 10%

every column. The widest performance difference comes from the Eve & Eve pattern, with an average rise of 53% for high volume breakouts versus 35% for those showing a weak volume breakout.

I discovered during writing *Encyclopedia of Chart Patterns* (Wiley, 2000) that a stock was more likely to throw back after a high volume breakout. The results in Table 8.10 strengthen that belief (see the third set of statistics). For those breakouts that occurred on above-average volume, the throwback rate ranged from 59% to 68%; when the volume level was average or below, the results ranged from 52% to 63%. In all four double bottom types, throwbacks occur more often after a high or very high volume breakout.

The last rows of Table 8.10 show the percentage of time that a throwback stops descending near the breakout price, between the breakout price and the low of the double bottom, and below the double bottom low (with no overlap among the three regions). You can see that better than half the time, the stock will stop within 5% of the breakout price before rebounding. Another 29% to 44% of the time, the stock will tumble to as low as the lowest low of the double bottom, then rebound. In 10% or fewer cases, prices continue moving below the formation low after a throwback.

The numbers suggest that a stop-loss order placed below the lower of the two bottoms will give the stock every opportunity to turn bullish. A narrower stop placed below the breakout price may work about half the time. As prices climb, raise your stop so you can lock in more profit (or narrow your loss), but do so only after the throwback (so you will not be stopped out prematurely).

Figure 8.8 shows an example of what sometimes happens when a double bottom fails. In this case, prices climbed less than 5% above the confirmation point before heading lower. The resulting plunge saw prices drop from just over 100 in July to 45.88 in January 1993 and down to 40.63 later that August.

BULL TRAPS

I define a bull trap as when prices rise by less than 10%, then move below the lowest low in the double bottom. On the chart, a bull trap appears like the one shown in Figure 8.8, but prices usually climb higher before tumbling.

A bull trap is perhaps an investor's worst nightmare. At first, prices rise to the breakout point and you buy the stock. As you check the quotations each day, the stock continues rising and you feel great; you may even brag about your stock-picking prowess. Then the stock stops rising. You think that it is just retracing a portion of its gains, and after a few days of declining, it closes higher. The decline is at an end, you hope, but 2 days later it gaps down and the decline gathers speed.

Soon, your purchase price is left in the dust, and still the stock tumbles. Should you buy more and average down? If the stock was a buy at 50, you

IBM (Computers & Peripherals, NYSE, IBM)

Confirmation Level

Ultimate High Less Than
5% Above The Confirmation
Level

Eve

Eve

Figure 8.8   Prices moved up less than 5% before tumbling. Not selling when prices drop below the twin lows of a double bottom can be a costly mistake, as in this case. The weekly scale is used.

reason, it must be a good deal at 45 and an absolute steal at 40! You quit looking at the daily quotations and realize that your short-term trade has turned into a long-term holding.

Finally, with much disgust, you sell at 35. A week later, rumors of a takeover make the news, followed by jockeying among several suitors that want to buy the company. The stock closes at 63. You feel like jumping out the window but realize you live on the first floor. You cannot win.

Table 8.11 shows how often bull traps occur in the various types of double bottoms. Adam & Adam has the highest rate of bull traps: 15%, or about one in six. Since the Adam & Adam pattern is such a poor performer, a comparatively high bull trap frequency is another reason to avoid it.

With care and experience, you should be able to reduce the number of bull traps you meet, and by using stop-loss orders, you should limit your losses, too. Many bull traps are the result of prices bumping up against a resistance zone set up by prior price action. Fortunately, a resistance zone is something you can predict ahead of time. Review Chapter 3 on Support and Resistance for tips on how to spot those zones and how to avoid a bull trap.

Table 8.11
Bull Traps

Description	Adam & Adam	Adam & Eve	Eve & Adam	Eve & Eve
Bull trap frequency	20/134 or 15%	26/232 or 11%	16/122 or 13%	43/315 or 14%
Score if trap predicted	–1	–1	–1	–1
Score if trap not predicted	+1	+1	+1	+1

GAPS

One of the benefits of being an author is that people send you investment ideas. I am not talking about investing in the latest fly-by-night enterprise (although they try that, too). One idea came in the form of a question: Had I looked at combinations of patterns, such as a gap after an upside breakout from a double bottom? My answer was yes, but I looked at things such as symmetrical triangles and scallops appearing before a double bottom. The results added value to the investment decision-making process, but analysis resulted in too many tables to include in this book with, perhaps, limited use by the average investor. I did not look at gaps. Since I could easily program my computer to find gaps during a breakout, I decided to test the idea. The results appear in Table 8.12.

Gaps are rare, occurring just 134 times in 803 stocks (17%). The value includes gaps probably too small to see easily, say 6 cents per share. Gaps of 25 cents in size are visible on most charts.

Should you invest only after a gap appears during the breakout (which is to say, a price gap appears the day prices close above the confirmation level)? Table 8.12 suggests that the results are hardly compelling. The best perform-

Table 8.12
Gaps and Performance

Description	Adam & Adam	Adam & Eve	Eve & Adam	Eve & Eve
Average rise after price gap on breakout	29% (20)	26% (35)	30.3% (24)	41% (55)
Average rise with no price gap on breakout	27% (96)	33% (162)	29.9% (77)	35% (206)
Score if gap present	+1	–1	+1	+1
Score if gap absent	–1	+1	–1	–1

Note: The number of samples appears in parentheses.

ing is the Eve & Eve formation with a breakout gap posting a 41% average rise. The Adam & Eve pattern performs better without a gap (33% versus 26%).

MARKET TREND

When I was a young boy, my parents bought a little cottage beside a river. We would visit during the summer and I would sit and watch the boats go by. A real treat was when a barge and tug pushed passed. I would run to the river's edge and watch the water recede as the flat barge sucked the living daylights from everything near shore. When the barge passed, the water would come rushing back in; a miniature tide following the barge upriver.

The general market is a lot like that barge, whereas a company's stock is like you standing waist deep in water. As the barge goes buy, you can feel the rush of water—the undertow—tug at your feet. Most stocks go with the flow and follow the market; a few withstand the forces.

The point I am making is a simple one: Trade with the trend. If the market is rising, then a purchase is more likely to succeed. If the market is declining, check other stocks in the industry. If they are declining, too, then avoid buying.

Table 8.13 shows the effect of the overall market on the performance of individual stocks. The figures measure the average price performance of the associated double bottom during the periods from formation start to end and formation end to ultimate high. The results separate further into two groups: those in which the Standard & Poor's 500 Index was rising and falling.

What does the table suggest? First, a rising market helps stocks perform better. A rising tide does appear to lift all boats except those with holes in them. Furthermore, that so few double bottoms appear when the S&P 500 was falling (denoted by the low sample count) means that you should not buy before prices

Table 8.13
Average Price Performance of Double Bottoms
During a Rising and Falling Market

Market Trend	Adam & Adam	Adam & Eve	Eve & Adam	Eve & Eve
Rising S&P 500, FS to FE	29% (83)	31% (139)	30% (63)	38% (190)
Falling S&P 500, FS to FE	25% (33)	32% (58)	31% (38)	33% (71)
Score: rising S&P	+1	−1	−1	+1
Score: falling S&P	−1	+1	+1	−1
Rising S&P 500, FE to UH	28% (107)	32% (187)	30% (95)	37% (230)
Falling S&P 500, FE to UH	24% (9)	29% (10)	32% (6)	33% (31)

Notes: FS = formation start, FE = formation end, UH = ultimate high. The number of samples appears in parentheses.

rise to the confirmation point. The low sample count suggests that prices of individual stocks during falling markets decline; they do not reach the confirmation point. Why buy a stock if it is going to tumble?

When selecting your stocks for purchase, be aware of the general market trend. If the trend begins rising after the first bottom, that is a good sign. If the general market continues rising after the second bottom appears and as prices rise to the confirmation point, then the trade is more likely to be a success.

Since the market performance after you buy a stock cannot be known ahead of time, I base the scores on the FS to FE period, that is, when the double bottom is under construction.

MARKET CAPITALIZATION

Table 8.14 shows the average performance of the double bottom varieties sorted by market capitalization, which is the breakout price times the number of shares outstanding. Since Eve & Eve is the only pattern that has a decent sample count, the average rise shows the trend quite well. Small caps outperform large caps, with rises averaging 39% versus 33%, respectively. The other double bottom types show a performance mixture with mid caps performing well in the Adam & Adam and Adam & Eve patterns, but the small caps do well in the other two types. Large caps basically stink all around.

SCORES

To use the scoring system to help select stocks to trade, evaluate your chart pattern following the guidelines in each table with a score, then add the results together. Scores above zero suggest performance that beats the median rise;

Table 8.14
Average Price Performance of Double
Bottoms by Market Capitalization

Capitalization	Adam & Adam	Adam & Eve	Eve & Adam	Eve & Eve
Small cap (up to $1 billion)	29% (55)	33% (103)	32% (49)	39% (130)
Mid cap ($1 to $5 billion)	31% (39)	34% (69)	29% (32)	38% (87)
Large cap (over $5 billion)	22% (21)	23% (21)	30% (19)	33% (41)
Score: small cap	+1	+1	+1	+1
Score: mid cap	+1	+1	−1	+1
Score: large cap	−1	−1	0	−1

Note: The number of samples appears in parentheses.

Table 8.15
Formation Performance by Score

Score	Adam & Adam	Adam & Eve	Adam & Adam	Eve & Eve
Average rise of chart patterns with scores above zero	45%	44%	45%	47%
Average rise of chart patterns with scores below zero	18%	19%	24%	25%
Median rise used	18.40%	26.21%	26.50%	27.79%
Number with scores above zero beating median rise	22/31 or 71%	55/99 or 56%	22/31 or 71%	59/90 or 66%
Number with scores below zero doing worse than median rise	25/37 or 68%	44/67 or 66%	28/43 or 65%	57/86 or 66%

scores below zero suggest underperformance—chart patterns you should avoid. The case studies that follow show you how to use the scoring system in more detail, but how well does the system work? Table 8.15 provides the answer.

I compared each chart pattern with a score above zero with those below zero and evaluated their resulting percentage rise. In two cases, chart patterns with scores above zero doubled the average rise of those with scores below zero. For example, Adam & Adam patterns with scores above zero show gains averaging 45% compared to an 18% rise for scores below zero.

Although the differences are quite impressive, do not assume that the system works all the time. I compared the percentage rise for each chart pattern with the median rise of all double bottoms, then assessed whether the scoring system added value. In other words, if the system showed a score above zero (a buy signal) and the resulting rise beat the median rise, then it was a correct buy signal. Similarly, if the score was below zero (an avoid signal) and the resulting rise was at or below the median, then that was a correct avoid signal.

Since the median value is the midrange value, or 50% of the samples, any signal that works more than half the time adds value. You can see in Table 8.15 that all buy and avoid signals add value, but they are far from 100% correct.

CASE STUDY 1

Figure 8.9 illustrates this case study about an actual trade I made. Before I discuss the trade, let us work through the scoring system to see how it predicted the outcome.

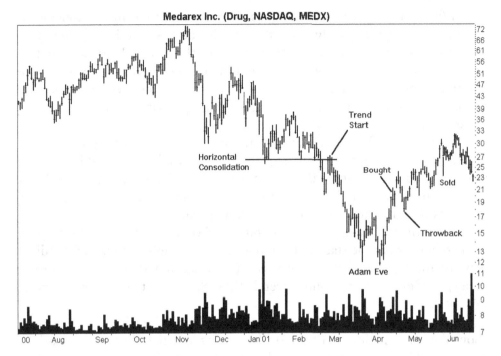

Figure 8.9 An Adam & Eve double bottom. A positive score suggested good performance.

Where does the trend start? From the start of the chart pattern, working backward in time, look for a minor high before which prices decline by 20%. I measure this from the highest high at the minor high to the closing price on each day as we move backward in time. As Figure 8.9 shows, the trend started from a high of 27.38. A 20% decline from this price would be 21.90, and the stock closed below that level 3 days earlier. Thus, the February 27 peak at 27.38 represents the trend start.

Measuring from the trend start to the formation start gives a duration of 23 days, well within the short-term category according to Table 8.1. For the Adam & Eve double bottom, that scores –1.

Also in that table is the flat base pattern. Do prices hover near the double bottom lows for weeks or months? No, so Table 8.1 rates that a –1. Running total: –2.

Is there an HCR between the trend start and the formation top? Yes. As the figure shows, I allow the HCR to span the trend start. The region has several days in which prices near or touch the same level, setting up a resistance zone. Table 8.2 scores a consolidation region as +1. I think the score is strange since a consolidation region may stop a price rise, but that is what the statistics say, so who am I to argue? Running total: –1.

Where in the yearly price range is the breakout price? Just by looking at Figure 8.9 you can probably guess that it is in the lowest third of the yearly price range, and that turns out to be correct. For the record, I looked from the breakout date backward 1 year and found the highest high and lowest low in that time. Then, I split the range into thirds and placed the breakout price (the highest high between the two bottoms) into the appropriate range. Table 8.6 scores the lowest third with a +1 score. Running total: 0.

Is the double bottom short or tall? Computing the formation height is easy. Subtract the lowest low (11.75) from the highest high (17.63) in the pattern and divide the result by the breakout price (17.63). That gives a height to breakout price of 33%. Table 8.7 says the median value is 17.09%, so this double bottom is quite tall. Score: +1. Running total: +1.

From the formation start to its end, is the volume rising or falling? I use the two bottoms as the start and end points, so the volume is clearly receding between those points. Linear regression (the trend function in some spreadsheets) verifies the falling volume trend. Table 8.8 scores that +1 for a running total of +2.

Is the breakout volume anything to write home about? No. Prices close above the confirmation point on April 12, a day in which the volume was just average. Table 8.9 says average or below-average volume rates a –1 score. Running total: +1.

Is a throwback predicted? This can be a tricky question to answer but not in this case. With an HCR hanging over the chart pattern like a dark cloud, a throwback is likely. This couples with a 59% throwback rate from Table 8.10 suggesting one is slightly more likely to occur. Score: –1. Running total: 0.

Is a bull trap going to occur? Since a throwback is likely due to overhead resistance, there is a larger tendency for a bull trap. Table 8.11 shows a trap rate of just 11%. For a trap to occur, prices must climb less than 10% above the breakout price then tumble below the lowest low in the double bottom. I see nothing on the chart that would indicate a bull trap is likely, so I would score that +1. Running total: +1. If you disagree with this assessment and rate a bull trap likely, the score difference will not affect the outcome.

Does a gap, where prices jump above the prior day, occur on the breakout? No. Table 8.12 rates a missing gap as +1. Running total: +2.

Is the market trending upward or downward over the course of the formation? The S&P, on the date the chart pattern made its first bottom, closed at 1117.58. When the pattern made its second bottom, the S&P 500 Index closed at 1103.25. Thus, the general market declined as the pattern was under construction. Table 8.13 scores a falling market trend as +1. Running total: +3.

Finally, the stock is a mid cap, as found by multiplying the breakout price of 17.63 by the number of shares outstanding (you can find this on many Web sites or call your broker). Table 8.14 rates a mid cap as +1. Final score: +4.

Even if you include a bull trap, the score would be +2. Any score above zero suggests performance that beats the median rise of 26.21%. In this case, my computer tells me the stock climbed to 24.20 on April 19 before prices dropped by more than 20% (measured from the high to close). From the breakout price of 17.63, that means a gain of 37%, well above the median.

How did I do? Chapter 3 on Support and Resistance discusses this trade in detail, so I will only say that I made 45%.

CASE STUDY 2

Before I trade a stock, I make notes in my computer about the likelihood of success and the reasons for purchase or sale. (Refer to Figure 8.10.) Here is what I wrote.

"7/19/00. I bought today at 18.38. The stock has confirmed an Eve & Adam double bottom from a small horizontal [flat] base from mid-February to May. Notice a large up move on 6/30 followed by week-long shelf, then upside continuation. I have seen this on other stocks with good earnings' surprises. The stock will continue higher. However, there is resistance at 19, so expect a stall there. The industry is poor. Most apparel stocks are near their lows but some are recovering, like this one. Earnings were good, moving up nicely on higher revenues. Volume yesterday was also high. Downside is a return to the 15 area for a 18.3% loss. I could put a stop at 15.88, dropping the loss to 13.6%. It is just below the horizontal [flat] base support. Upside, resistance at 19, 20, 21, 22. If it pushes through these, it could rise to 28–29. That is what I am shooting for."

Should I have bought the stock? Running briefly through the tables with scores gives some suggestions.

Table 8.1: Trend start and flat base. The trend started back in June 1999 (not shown) after prices climbed from a low of 21.56 and peaked at 29.75. From that point on, prices dropped steadily to the double bottom. The stock, having declined nearly a year before the double bottom formed, falls into the long-term category, scoring –1.

If you consider the congestion from February through May, with an Eve & Adam poking out the bottom, as a flat base (like that shown in Figure 8.6), that is a plus. As the Figure 8.6 discussion describes, a double bottom can form after such a consolidation area and it implies an upside breakout. A few words of caution: This flat base is not long term in nature, although there is additional support at that price level going back to 1995–1996. Table 8.1 shows a +1 score for the Eve & Adam with a flat base. Running total: 0.

Table 8.2: Horizontal consolidation region. There is a flat top in late December 1999 and I label it on the chart as an HCR. Volume is low during this congestion, suggesting there is not much of a threat from other investors wanting to sell their shares when the stock recovers to 20. But 20 is a round number and often a sell point. Table 8.2 says that the Eve & Adam formation with a consolidation region may underperform, scoring a –1. Running total: –1.

Table 8.6: Yearly price range. The breakout occurs near the yearly low. Score: –1. Running total: –2.

Table 8.7: Short or tall. The double bottom is a short one, measuring 11.76%, below the median 18.38%. Score: –1. Running total: –3.

Table 8.8: Volume trend. From the Eve bottom to the Adam bottom, volume receded. Score: +1. Running total: –2.

Table 8.9: Breakout volume. Breakout volume is very high. Score: –1. Running total: –3.

Table 8.10: Throwbacks. I knowingly avoided buying on the high volume breakout, expecting a throwback. What I should have done is place a stop order to buy at the breakout price. That would have lowered my purchase price from 18.38 to 17, an 8% improvement. I also know that trying to chase a stock as it zooms upward is a loser's game. The large daily range on June 30 (15.88 to 18) also reinforced the likelihood of a throwback, which is what happened. I waited for prices to climb and top the June 30 high before buying, just to be safe. Since I waited for prices to surpass the old minor high of June 30, it was reassuring that Table 8.10 indicates that only 10% of the Eve & Adam patterns reach their ultimate high before throwing back. A throwback is a negative, since buying enthusiasm and momentum is wasted as prices return to the breakout price. Running total: –4.

Table 8.11: Bull traps. On the weekly scale, back in late 1995 through the fall of 1996, prices peaked at 19.25 three times but eventually pushed through resistance in December 1996. These three peaks suggested a possible bull trap at that level. However, the release of earnings 2 days before I bought and favorable market reaction to those earnings suggested prices would continue moving higher. I felt confident that I could avoid the trap. Avoiding a bull trap rates a +1, giving a running total of –3.

Table 8.12: Breakout gaps. There are no gaps on the breakout date. However, notice the breakaway gap the day before I bought as a reaction to the earnings news. That breakaway gap is a good sign especially since it was not closed (when prices returned to fill the gap) immediately. A continuation gap appears between 1 and 2 days after I bought, another good sign. Score: –1. Running total: –4.

Table 8.13: Market trend. The S&P 500 climbed between the dates of the formation start (the first bottom) and end (the second bottom). I base the scores in Table 8.13 on the FS to FE dates, that is, while the formation is under construction. Score: –1. Running total: –5.

Table 8.14: Market cap. Oxford is a small cap, scoring +1. That gives a final score of –4, an avoid score.

How did the trade turn out? After the double bottom, prices climbed rapidly on high volume and pierced the confirmation point at 17. Seeing the

1-day rise of almost 1.50 on high volume, I expected a throwback and held off buying.

An earnings announcement occurred 2 days before I bought, and the stock gapped (breakaway gap) upward on the news, suggesting the results were better than expected. This sent the price above the prior minor high of 18 (see June 30). This was the buy signal. I bought the next day and received a fill at 18.38.

Another gap appeared, this time a continuation gap. Prices moved steadily higher traveling along a steep (too steep, really) uptrend line. I know from experience that a quick decline often follows a quick rise, so as prices climbed, I became more worried (I have a receding hairline, so pulling out more hair is not an option).

A review of the other stocks in the apparel group suggested that the industry fundamentals were deteriorating. I made a note in my log about the weakness and the day I penned the note appears in Figure 8.10—just 5 days from the high.

A week later, prices reached their peak, then move horizontally for about 3 weeks before gapping downward. The up move was over. Here is where it gets interesting and nasty. This is what I wrote in my trade log. "9/25/00. Sold my holdings this morning. Just after the open, the stock was off only 0.13 at 20.69

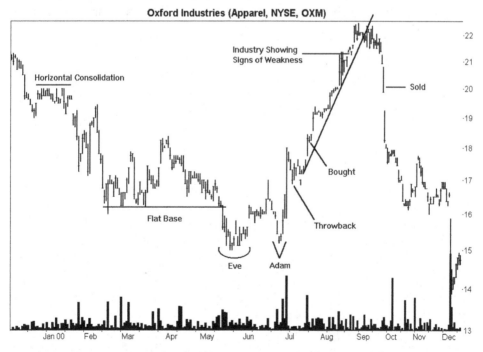

Figure 8.10 An Eve & Adam double bottom. The shelf area at point 1 and good earnings suggested this stock would do well. The breakaway gap on high volume the day before I bought followed by a continuation gap gave added confidence to a successful trade.

on 500 shares volume. Twenty-five minutes later, it had fallen to 20.38 on 2,700 shares. With a gap downward on Friday (the last trading day), I should have known that it was going lower. I did not expect such a large decline so quickly. Since the stock was trending lower, and since it opened lower, I should have sold everything after the first quote, not wait for the usual check in."

I have found that if you wait for the dust to settle, say one-half to an hour into the trading session, it often gives you a clue to how the stock will close. If it is down in the morning, then it is likely to get worse and tumble further. If a stock is rising, it should hold onto its gains and close up. Of course, this varies from stock to stock and industry to industry, so do not bet the farm that it will hold true.

As you can see in Figure 8.10, the stock moved rapidly lower before I chose to dump it. Fortunately, I sold the day before an earnings announcement. This time, the earnings were not up to expectations, and the news sent the stock tumbling—quickly. Another continuation gap, this time much larger, signaled that the downtrend would continue. The stock found support around 16 to 18, then tumbled again on a new earnings warning.

For scoring, Table 8.15 uses a 26.50% median rise. If you traded this one perfectly, you would have made 32%. I made just 10%. Things could have been much worse if I held onto the stock. Recently, it was trading in the low 14s, 23% below the purchase price. Even though the scoring system incorrectly predicted a poorly performing trade, you could also say that it warned of a bumpy ride.

9

Double Tops

Double tops: perhaps one of the best known chart patterns that even novice investors can correctly identify. However, like many topping patterns, double tops do not work very well. But, there are techniques that you can apply to make them pay, sometimes handsomely. First, some identification tips.

THE TYPICAL PATTERN

Like double bottoms, tops appear in one of four varieties: Adam & Adam, Adam & Eve, Eve & Adam, and Eve & Eve. These are not names I made up, but ones I found at the hardrightedge.com Web site, where I first learned of the types.

Figure 9.1 shows the first type of double top: the Adam & Adam formation. The twin peaks are at approximately the same price with a trough between them that represents a 10% to 20% decline, sometimes more. In this case, prices recede 31% between peaks.

Figure 9.2 shows an Adam & Eve double top. If you were a mountaineer climbing the Adam peak, you might fear toppling off the summit or perhaps hurting yourself if you sat down. On the Eve peak, there would be plenty of room to walk around, maybe even catch a helicopter ride back down to the base.

Figure 9.3 shows an Eve & Adam double top with a wide first peak and a slender second one. This double top forms after a short but steep price run starting in late July. Prices top out, then almost as quickly decline back to the level where the straight-line run began. For many chart patterns, a straight-line run is dangerous because quick gains are just as quickly lost when prices retrace the entire rise.

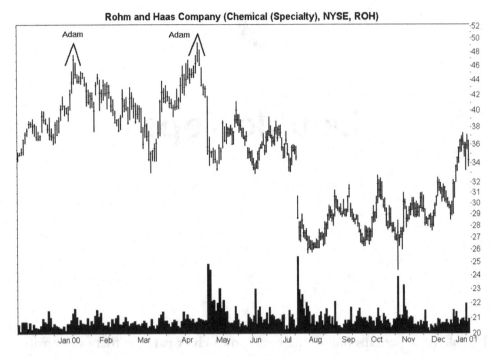

Figure 9.1   Adam & Adam double top. Twin sharp, pointed, narrow peaks mark this double top.

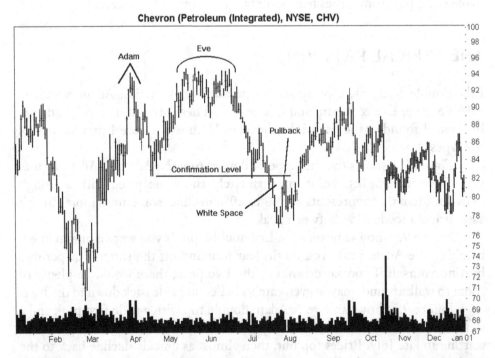

Figure 9.2   Adam & Eve double top. The Adam peak is narrow, pointed and sharp, but Eve appears more rounded.

Figure 9.3 Eve & Adam double top. The Eve peak is much wider than Adam, a clue to make identification easier.

Figure 9.4 shows the last of the four varieties: an Eve & Eve double top. The peaks look alike, both rounded and wide. The left peak on this one is more pointed than I like to see, but the entire width suggests it is an Eve, not an Adam, peak.

By now, you may think that differentiating between Adam and Eve peaks is easy. It is not. If all the charts you examined looked like these four, then selection would be simple. Unfortunately, there is wide variation in the appearance of double tops, but here are some rules to make identification easier.

First, compare the two peaks. Do they look alike or different? If they appear the same, or nearly the same, then the formation is either Adam & Adam or Eve & Eve. Adam peaks appear pointed, sometimes with a tall 1-day price spike. Eve may also have spikes but there are more of them and they are closer together, like the Eve peak in Figure 9.2. The spikes are not tall, but they are plentiful.

Perhaps the easiest way to make a correct identification is to look at the width of each peak. Adam is narrow and pointed—like an upside-down V— whereas Eve is fatter, wider, and more rounded. If you are still unsure, look at other peaks on the same chart and compare those peaks with your double top.

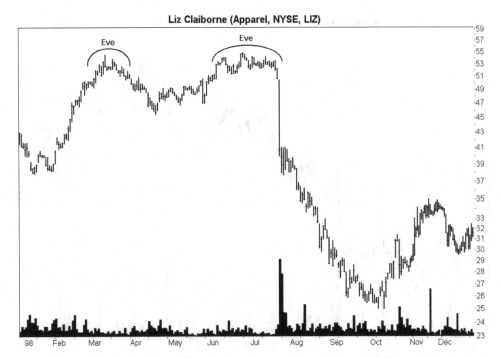

Figure 9.4 A traditional double top. The Eve & Eve formation has both peaks appearing rounded and wide. The stock dropped precipitously in mid-July on a revenue warning.

TREND START

If a 20% trend change in an index signals a bull or bear market, why not apply that benchmark to individual stocks? That is what I did to determine the trend start. From the start of the double top, follow prices backward in time as they descend away from the top. Eventually, the low will be found when prices begin climbing. If they climb by more than 20%—still moving backward in time—then we have found the low point before the double top. I call the low point the *trend start*.

For reference, I use the lowest low and compare the price with the daily close as I progress backward in time, searching for a 20% price rise.

Once we have found where the price trend starts, we can sort the double tops according to the elapsed time from the trend start to the formation (the top of the first peak). Do double tops with a short-term price trend leading to the pattern perform better than those with a longer-term trend? Yes, and Table 9.1 shows the results.

Scan across each row. Which formation type performs best? In two out of three price trends leading to the formation, the Eve & Eve double top shows the largest decline. Look next at the columns. Short-term price rises leading to

Table 9.1
Average Performance of Double Tops Sorted
by Price Trend Leading to the Pattern

Trend Start to Formation Start	Adam & Adam	Adam & Eve	Eve & Adam	Eve & Eve
Short term (0 to 3 months)	–17% (57) –1	–17% (86) +1	–16% (98) +1	–22% (102) +1
Intermediate term (3 to 6 months)	–20% (36) +1	–16% (53) +1	–18% (50) +1	–14.7% (54) –1
Long term (over 6 months)	–15% (26) –1	–13% (42) –1	–13% (43) –1	–15.3% (51) –1

Note: The first number is the average, followed by the number of samples in parentheses and the score.

a double top imply a larger loss when compared with the long-term category. To be fair, the intermediate term wins twice if it is included in the comparison.

HORIZONTAL CONSOLIDATION REGIONS

Table 9.2 shows the effects of price support during the downtrend after the breakout. To generate the figures, I first made a definition of what a consolidation region (support region, in this case) was. By my definition, a consolidation

Table 9.2
Average Performance of Double Tops with
and Without a Consolidation Region

Description	Adam & Adam	Adam & Eve	Eve & Adam	Eve & Eve
Consolidation region	–17% (99) –1	–15% (152) –1	–15% (150) –1	–18% (166) –1
No consolidation region	–22% (32) +1	–17% (42) +1	–19% (47) +1	–20% (49) +1
Average length (days)	38	40	39	37
Prices stop within region ±5%	59%	65%	64%	57%
Prices push through region	34%	29%	28%	34%
Prices do not reach region	7%	6%	8%	10%

Note: The first number is the average, followed by the number of samples in parentheses and the score.

region is one that forms between the trend start and confirmation level (the lowest low between the two tops). Prices should have either tops or bottoms that are near the same price for at least a week (but strict time guidelines are unimportant). In fact, the average length of a consolidation region is over a month, as shown in Table 9.2. The consolidation area lends prices a base in which to rest. Sometimes prices will fall through the support and, at other times, prices recover.

Figure 9.5 shows what a horizontal consolidation area looks like. The Adam & Eve double top has uneven peaks and some would recognize the April–May flat top as the start of a large broadening top (which includes the double top peaks as well). When prices dropped below the confirmation level, that drop confirmed the validity of the double-top formation. Days later, prices pulled back to the middle of the formation before resuming their downward plunge. In December, prices retreated to the price level of the large consolidation area formed in late December 1998 to April. This support area was strong enough to stop the decline and send prices climbing 26% just after Christmas, but prices collapsed and reached a low of 4.69 in May 2000.

Let me highlight a few things about Figure 9.5. When I wrote that I look for a consolidation area between the trend start and confirmation level, I also

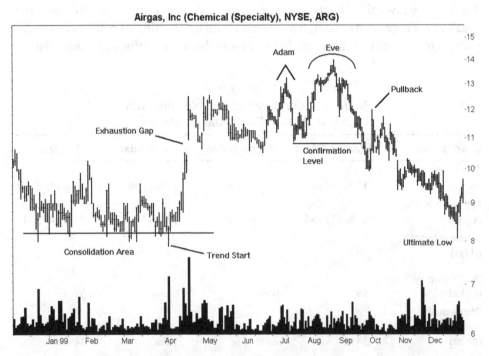

Figure 9.5 A horizontal consolidation area stops prices from declining further. Look for a horizontal consolidation area between the trend start and the confirmation level. The flat top in mid-April starts a large broadening top that includes the double top.

include areas that span the trend start, as shown. The uptrend began on April Fool's Day, near the end of the consolidation area, climbed rapidly on high volume—signaling an end to the horizontal price movement—and included an exhaustion gap in mid-April.

Returning to Table 9.2, we see that in all cases, the declines are larger when no consolidation area exists to support prices as they tumble. Consolidation areas average between 37 and 40 days long, so they are easy to spot.

The remaining three lines in the table show where prices stop around the consolidation region. For example, Adam & Adam double tops had prices that stopped within a consolidation region (including a 5% buffer to catch the ones that stopped nearby) 59% of the time. Another 34% of the time, prices may stop at the consolidation region but eventually push through and tumble further. Finally, just 7% never make it down to the region.

When trying to gauge whether prices will likely pierce the consolidation area, look for a wide area of consolidation, like that shown in Figure 9.5. A wimpy, 1-week horizontal price movement will likely not stop or even slow a determined decline. Apply heavier weight to closer consolidation zones than ones farther away (by price, not time). Remember, two out of three stocks will not drop substantially below the consolidation area, so you can predict how far your stock will decline and determine whether the double top is worth investing in before making a trade.

INSIDE THE PATTERN

Table 9.3 shows important statistical findings for double tops. The only twin-peak formations counted in the statistics are those with prices closing below the confirmation point. If unconfirmed before prices rise above the highest

Table 9.3
Important Statistical Findings

Description	Adam & Adam	Adam & Eve	Eve & Adam	Eve & Eve
Number of formations	134	196	200	216
Average decline	18%	15%	16%	18%
Standard & Poor's 500 change	+1%	+1%	+1%	+2%
Median decline	14%	13%	14%	15%
Declines more than 50%	2/131 or 2%	2/194 or 1%	4/197 or 2%	5/215 or 2%
Top with highest volume	Left 60%	Left 72%	Right 56%	Left 53%

peak high, then the twin-peak pattern is not a double top. You must wait for confirmation before investing. If you decide to jump the gun and sell short early—or sell your long holdings early—the chances are two out of three (65%) that prices will resume rising before reaching the confirmation point.

Judging by the number of formations, double tops are plentiful with the exception of Adam & Adam, which has significantly fewer formations than the others. Combined, I looked at 746 double tops.

I measure average decline from the breakout price to the lowest low. For all four double-top types, the average decline is quite stable, from 15% to 18%, which compares to a 21% average decline for all bearish chart patterns (not just double tops). Simply put, double tops are light on performance.

The S&P 500 changed little over the course of each formation. I measured performance from the close of the S&P, when the formation broke out downward to the day the formation reached its ultimate low (using the daily low of the S&P). Even though the average decline for each formation type was in the range of 15% to 18%, the S&P 500 Index rose over the same period by 1% to 2%. It appears that double tops are able to swim against the rising tide.

The median decline is the midrange value such that half the samples fall below the median and half above. This is the return I expect experienced investors to achieve when trading double tops. The values range from 13% to 15%, in line with the 14% median decline for all bearish chart patterns.

A small number of formations declining more than 50% is not unusual for topping patterns, and double tops are no exception. Clearly, it is easier to climb more than 50% than to decline by that amount, especially during a bull market from which the statistics were gathered. Eve & Eve has the largest number that declined more than 50%, but it happened just 5 times out of 215.

Both double tops and double bottoms show the heaviest volume on the left side with one exception: Eve & Adam. Why Eve & Adam shows higher volume on the right is a mystery to me, but that is the way it behaves. Incidentally, I used the 5-day volume total, from 2 days before to 2 days after the peak, in the comparison.

FAILURE RATES

Table 9.4 shows the maximum price decline versus failure rate for the various double-top types. What do the numbers mean? Look at the Adam & Adam column, 20% maximum price decline row. The total number of Adam & Adam double tops in which prices declined less than 20%, were 81 or 62%. Look how the Adam & Adam pattern, with 11% of them declining less than 5%, suddenly triples to 33%, declining less than 10%. Well over half decline less than 15%. Wow! Or, more accurately, yuck!

Table 9.4
Maximum Price Decline Versus Failure Rate

Maximum Price Decline (%)	Adam & Adam Failure Rate	Adam & Eve Failure Rate	Eve & Adam Failure Rate	Eve & Eve Failure Rate
5	14 or 11%	29 or 15%	23 or 12%	27 or 13%
10	43 or 33%	68 or 35%	71 or 36%	68 or 32%
15	73 or 56%	108 or 56%	111 or 56%	106 or 49%
20	81 or 62%	132 or 68%	136 or 69%	144 or 67%
25	93 or 71%	154 or 79%	158 or 80%	165 or 77%
30	106 or 81%	168 or 87%	175 or 89%	177 or 82%
35	118 or 90%	181 or 93%	181 or 92%	189 or 88%
50	129 or 98%	191 or 98%	193 or 98%	210 or 98%
75	131 or 100%	194 or 100%	197 or 100%	215 or 100%
100	131 or 100%	194 or 100%	197 or 100%	215 or 100%

As you scan down the entries, you see that the Adam & Adam and Eve & Eve patterns usually have the lowest failure rates for a given maximum price decline. If you want few failures, these are the two to concentrate on, and both have higher average declines (see Table 9.3) than the other two types.

Table 9.5 shows the horizon failure rates for double tops. To compute the rates, I compared the daily closing price at the end of each period with the breakout price. If the price was above the breakout price, then I marked it a failure. For example, 1 week after the breakout, almost half (40%) of the Adam & Adam double tops had prices above the breakout price. By definition, at the close of the first day, the horizon failure rate is 0%, so a 40% failure rate after the first week is huge.

As you scan down the columns, you see that the Eve & Adam and Eve & Eve patterns usually have the lowest horizon failure rates. With failure rates starting over 30% after a week, clearly double tops are strongest early, then fade. Another way of saying it is the failure rate increases over time. The longer you hold a stock, the more likely it is to rise instead of continuing its decline.

The right half of the table shows the average price decline over time. You can see that the Adam & Eve double top holds its ground for the first month then jumps to the worst performer with gains averaging 1% to 3% during months two through six. All hold their ground during the first month then weaken. It appears that downward momentum is strongest soon after the breakout, then weakens as prices recover. A negative average decline means a price rise.

Table 9.5
Horizon Failure Rates and Average Decline

Time Since Breakout	Adam & Adam Failure Rate (%)	Adam & Eve Failure Rate (%)	Eve & Adam Failure Rate (%)	Eve & Eve Failure Rate (%)	Adam & Adam Average Decline (%)	Adam & Eve Average Decline (%)	Eve & Adam Average Decline (%)	Eve & Eve Average Decline (%)
1 week	40	41	35	32	2	2	2	3
2 weeks	44	41	35	38	2	2	2	2
3 weeks	40	46	34	40	2	2	3	3
1 month	47	44	40	45	2	2	3	3
2 months	53	52	44	44	1	-1	1	4
3 months	56	54	51	49	1	-2	0	3
6 months	50	61	51	57	1	-3	0	-2

Table 9.6
Average Performance Sorted by Breakout Price
According to Prior 12-Month Range

Yearly Price Range	Adam & Adam	Adam & Eve	Eve & Adam	Eve & Eve
Highest third	–18% (35) +1	–15.8% (35) +1	–18% (43) +1	–20% (58) +1
Middle third	–16% (45) –1	–16% (99) +1	–15% (90) –1	–18% (89) –1
Lowest third	–17% (19) –1	–12% (32) –1	–14% (42) –1	–18% (52) –1

Note: The first number is the average, followed by the number of samples in parentheses and the score.

YEARLY PRICE RANGE

Where in the yearly price range does the breakout reside and is it an indicator of future performance? Table 9.6 provides one answer, and the results are statistically significant.

From the breakout date backward for 1 year, I found the highest high and lowest low over that time, then split the yearly price range into thirds. For each chart pattern, I placed the breakout price into one of the three ranges, then looked at the resulting performance after the breakout.

I find the results surprising because the best-performing bearish patterns usually show a breakout near the yearly low. However, since we are talking about double tops, clearly the majority of the patterns appear in the middle or highest third of the yearly range. The few that do appear in the lowest third seem to underperform.

The results agree with what I found when I researched double tops while writing *Encyclopedia of Chart Patterns* (Wiley, 2000). That is, the best performers usually reside in the middle or upper third of the yearly price range.

TALL AND SHORT PATTERNS

Do tall patterns outperform short ones? Yes, and Table 9.7 shows the statistical results. To compare formation height, I used the median height as a percentage of the breakout price as the separator between short and tall. The median height is the midrange value, chosen from a sorted list, such that half the values are above the median and half below.

Look at the Adam & Eve double top in Figure 9.5 as an example. Take the difference between the higher of the two peaks and the confirmation level—the lowest price between the two peaks. In this example, the high, 14, is at the Eve peak and the low is at 10.88, giving a formation height of 3.13.

Table 9.7
Performance of Short and Tall Double Tops

Description	Adam & Adam	Adam & Eve	Eve & Adam	Eve & Eve
Tall (above the median)	–19% (66) +1	–16% (97) +1	–19% (99) +1	–20% (107) +1
Short (below the median)	–17% (65) –1	–15% (97) –1	–13% (98) –1	–17% (108) –1
Median percentage of breakout price	17.07%	16.85%	16.51%	17.86%

Note: The first number is the average, followed by the number of samples in parentheses and the score.

Divide the height by the breakout price (10.88) to get a percentage (28.77%). Clearly this is a tall double top since it is above the 16.85% benchmark from Table 9.7. The table shows that tall patterns outperform short ones in every double–top category.

VOLUME TREND

I used linear regression to determine the slope of the volume line. Linear regression is a fancy way of saying I plotted a *best fit* line with the slope of the line determining the trend. Some spreadsheets call it the trend function, so it is easy to use.

Table 9.8 shows the performance results after the breakout when volume was trending upward or downward, between the tops. The results pair off, meaning that double tops with a rising volume trend as they were being created resulted in slightly better performance when the double top was an Adam & Adam or Adam & Eve. For the two Eve varieties, a falling volume trend worked better. The differences are statistically significant.

Table 9.8
Linear Regression Volume Trend and Performance

Description	Adam & Adam	Adam & Eve	Eve & Adam	Eve & Eve
Rising volume trend	–18.0% (55)	–16% (59)	–15% (109)	–17% (116)
Falling volume trend	–17.6% (76)	–15% (135)	–17% (88)	–20% (99)
Score: rising trend	+1	+1	–1	–1
Score: falling trend	–1	–1	+1	+1

Note: The number of samples appears in parentheses.

Table 9.9
Breakout Volume and Performance

Description	Adam & Adam	Adam & Eve	Eve & Adam	Eve & Eve
Average decline on above-average breakout volume	19% (46)	18% (48)	17% (53)	20% (64)
Average decline on average or below-average breakout volume	17% (85)	14% (146)	15% (144)	18% (151)
Score: high volume	+1	+1	+1	+1
Score: low volume	−1	−1	−1	−1

Note: The number of samples appears in parentheses.

BREAKOUT VOLUME

Table 9.9 shows the performance of double tops after high and low volume breakouts. The way I determined the volume level is somewhat complicated, so refer to Glossary and Methodology for more information. In short, I compared a 3-month volume average with the breakout volume to determine the volume level. When the breakout volume was high or very high, the double top outperformed by 17% to 20%. When the breakout volume was average or below average, the results were smaller, 14% to 18%.

PULLBACKS

Table 9.10 shows the influence of pullbacks on price behavior, but before I discuss the table, let us look at some illustrations. Figures 9.2 and 9.5 show what pullbacks look like. A pullback occurs after prices break out (a close below the confirmation price), then return to the confirmation price. The initial decline should be large enough so that there is white space between the confirmation price and the low as prices curl around. Contrast Figure 9.2 with Figure 9.3. In Figure 9.2, the white space is clear and obvious, emphasizing the pullback when it occurs. Prices in Figure 9.3 do not fall far enough after the breakout (they return to the breakout price the next day) to show white space.

One more rule: Prices must return to the confirmation price within 30 days. Thirty days is a commonly recognized but arbitrary limit. It assumes that prices after 30 days resort to their normal behavior.

Table 9.10 shows the pullback frequency for the various double-top types. They occur between 57% and 61% of the time, not frequent enough to build a reliable trading strategy around (such as waiting for the pullback before selling

Table 9.10
Pullback Statistics

Description	Adam & Adam	Adam & Eve	Eve & Adam	Eve & Eve
Pullbacks	77 or 57%	114 or 58%	118 or 59%	132 or 61%
Score if pullback predicted	−1	−1	−1	−1
Score if pullback not predicted	+1	+1	+1	+1
Ultimate low before pullback	27 or 20%	50 or 26%	51 or 26%	61 or 28%
Average decline on above-average breakout volume with pullbacks	16%	13%	15%	15%
Average decline on above-average breakout volume and no pullbacks	23%	22%	21%	29%
Average decline on average or below-average breakout volume and pullbacks	16%	14%	13%	17%
Average decline on average or below-average breakout volume and no pullbacks	18%	15%	18%	20%
Number of pullbacks after a high or very high volume breakout	24/46 or 52%	25/49 or 51%	32/54 or 59%	40/64 or 63%
Number of pullbacks after an average, low, or very low volume breakout	53/88 or 60%	89/147 or 61%	86/146 or 59%	92/152 or 61%
Number of pullbacks that stopped less than 5% from the breakout price	42 or 55%	57 or 50%	78 or 66%	68 or 52%
Number of pullbacks that stopped between the breakout price and double top high	30 or 39%	49 or 43%	34 or 29%	51 or 39%
Number of pullbacks that climbed above the double top high	5 or 6%	8 or 7%	6 or 5%	13 or 10%

short). If you happen to short a stock, be aware that prices may pull back to the confirmation price before continuing down; you do not want to be stopped out early in such a situation. A pullback does give you another opportunity to increase your short position or sell a holding before the decline resumes.

I talk about the score in the case study at the end of this chapter, but I consider pullbacks to be a negative. Why? Read on.

Having looked at hundreds of double tops and the resulting price decline, it still surprises me how poorly they work. Between 20% and 28% of the time prices reach the ultimate low (the lowest low before a 20% price rise) before pulling back and continuing up. I base the percentages in the table on all double tops, not just those experiencing a pullback.

The lesson is that should your stock pull back to the confirmation price, wait for prices to resume declining, before adding to (or initially placing) your short position. If you do not wait, prices will continue rising between 35% and 46% of the time. Those numbers are the portion of pullbacks that reach their ultimate low before pulling back. For example, 27/77 or 35% of the Adam & Adam double tops with pullbacks reached their ultimate low before pulling back.

The next four table rows show the influence of volume and pullbacks. For each chart pattern, I sorted the breakout volume level into one of five categories: very high, high, average, low, and very low. When the volume was high or very high, the performance differed significantly, depending on whether a pullback occurred or not. *If a pullback occurs, performance decreases.* In the case of Eve & Eve, the difference is huge, 15% versus 29%.

What happens after an average, low, or very low volume breakout? The trend does not change, but the percentages narrow. Formations with average or below-average breakout volume perform best when no pullback occurs.

Other observations concern the volume level itself. A breakout on above-average volume *without* a pullback shows the best performance; it beats all other combinations. An above-average volume breakout *with* a pullback underperforms almost all other combinations.

Do more pullbacks occur after a high volume breakout? No. All, except the Eve & Eve pattern, either tie or show that more pullbacks occur after an average or below-average volume breakout. This result is common sense, really. If a trend begins with high volume pushing prices downward, it is that much harder for them to recover and climb back to the breakout price.

After a pullback, where do prices stop rising? The last three rows in Table 9.10 provide the answer. From 50% to 66% of the time, prices stop rising within 5% of the confirmation or breakout price. Another 29% to 43% of the time, prices continue rising but stop at or below the double-top high. The remainder of the time (from 5% to 10%), prices climb above the highest double-top high.

The results are important when choosing where to place a stop-loss order. If you short a stock and place your stop near but above the confirmation price (say 6% away), the order will be tripped between half and two-thirds of the time. A worst-case stop placed 0.15 above the highest double-top high would be executed only when things get really bad, or about 5% to 10% of the time. Unfortunately, since the price difference between the double-top high and confirmation point can be quite large (usually between 10% and 20%), you will be giving up a lot of profit by holding on so long. A better choice would be to place a stop above a nearby minor high (between the confirmation price and double-top high), then move the stop lower as prices drop.

BEAR TRAPS

When I think of a bear trap, I envision a cruel mechanical device used to trap bears and, in some cases, people. As the term applies to the financial markets, the picture is worse because it is *my* money that is being trapped.

Consider the bear trap shown in Figure 9.6. When prices drop below the lowest low between the peaks, the breakout price, that confirms the validity of

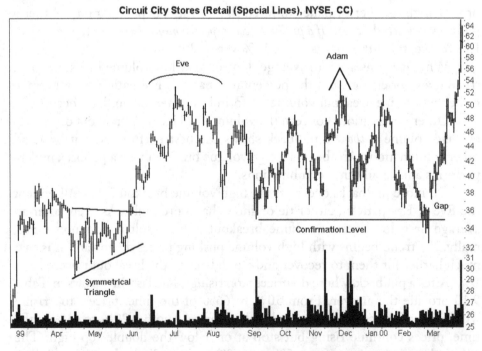

Figure 9.6 A bear trap in an Eve & Adam double top. Prices drop 7% below the confirmation level before recovering and zooming above the double-top peaks. A breakaway gap hints of a rising price trend.

Table 9.11
Bear Traps

Description	Adam & Adam	Adam & Eve	Eve & Adam	Eve & Eve
Bear trap frequency	37/134 or 28%	66/196 or 34%	64/200 or 32%	65/216 or 30%
Score if trap predicted	–1	–1	–1	–1
Score if trap not predicted	+1	+1	+1	+1

the double top. However, prices meet support set up by a consolidation region masquerading as a symmetrical triangle (April to June) and stop declining. A breakaway gap then signals the start of a rising trend. From that point on, prices zoom up and shoot above the formation top.

I define a bear trap as when prices break out downward and reach the ultimate low less than 10% below the confirmation price, then climb above the double-top high. When the breakout occurs, traders short the stock hoping for an extended decline. Instead, they are trapped into a losing position as prices recover. If they are not careful, the losses can grow huge since there is no limit on how far prices can climb.

Table 9.11 shows the frequency of bear traps. The Adam & Eve pattern has the most bear traps, 34%, or one in three, but the others are close behind.

Since a bear trap is always negative for shares sold short, I score it –1. Through an analysis of support zones and horizontal consolidation areas, you should be able to minimize the chances of a bear trap. If your prediction is that you can avoid a trap, then score it +1.

GAPS

Figure 9.7 shows what a price gap looks like. On the breakout day, prices gapped down $1.88, then pulled back to the confirmation point in about 2 weeks. Prices held steady for a little over a week before resuming their decline. In 8 months' time, prices dropped by half.

When you compare the first two lines of Table 9.12, you can see the performance difference between having a gap and not having a gap on the breakout day. Only the Eve & Adam pattern shows a gap underperforming the no-gap statistic, but the differences in that case are not statistically significant (meaning they may be due to chance). Generally speaking, *a gap improves performance.*

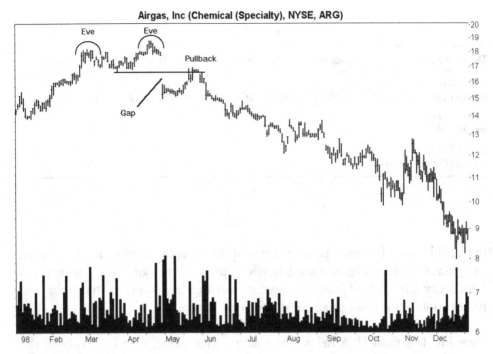

Figure 9.7 A gap after an Eve & Eve double top. This breakaway gap is unusually large and prices pull back to the confirmation level before tumbling.

Table 9.12
Gaps and Performance

Description	Adam & Adam	Adam & Eve	Eve & Adam	Eve & Eve
Average decline after price gap on breakout	21% (31)	18% (36)	15% (33)	19% (43)
Average decline with no price gap on breakout	17% (100)	15% (158)	16% (164)	18% (172)
Score if gap present	+1	+1	−1	+1
Score if gap absent	−1	−1	+1	−1

Note: The number of samples appears in parentheses.

MARKET TREND

Table 9.13 shows the effect of the general market on the performance of prices after a double top. Does a receding tide lower all boats? Yes. As you compare the first two rows, the general trend is for larger declines associated with a falling market, as represented by the S&P 500 Index.

Table 9.13
Average Price Performance of Double
Tops During a Rising and Falling Market

Market Trend	Adam & Adam	Adam & Eve	Eve & Adam	Eve & Eve
Rising S&P 500, FS to FE	−17.5% (80)	−15% (134)	−15% (127)	−18% (153)
Falling S&P 500, FS to FE	−18.1% (51)	−17% (60)	−17% (70)	−20% (62)
Score: rising S&P	−1	−1	−1	−1
Score: falling S&P	+1	+1	+1	+1
Rising S&P 500, FE to UL	−16% (62)	−16% (95)	−16% (84)	−17% (69)
Falling S&P 500, FE to UL	−19% (69)	−15% (99)	−15% (113)	−19% (146)

Notes: FS = formation start, FE = formation end, UL = ultimate low. The number of samples appears in parentheses.

After the breakout, from the formation end to the ultimate low, the message appears mixed. Sometimes a rising market makes a sinking boat fill faster (Adam & Eve and Eve & Adam) and sometimes a falling market has greater pull (Adam & Adam and Eve & Eve).

Since you cannot know ahead of time how the general market will behave after the breakout, I base the score values on the FS to FE period, that is, when the double top is under construction.

MARKET CAPITALIZATION

Does market capitalization affect the behavior of stocks? Table 9.14 gives us clues to the answer. I sorted the chart formations, based on the number of shares outstanding multiplied by the breakout price, to compute market capitalization.

For the most part, the performance results are in line with other chart patterns. The most straightforward trend comes from the Adam & Eve formation. As you look down the column, you find that small caps perform best, declining 18%, and large caps do worst by declining only 13%.

There are two ways to play this. If you own a stock and a double top confirms, then compute the market capitalization. If the stock is a large cap, then the resulting decline should be less severe than a small cap. There are no guarantees here, but that is the way to play the percentages.

If you are considering shorting a stock, look for small caps to give you the best overall performance, with the exception of Eve & Eve, which shows the best performance from mid caps.

Table 9.14
Average Price Performance of Double
Tops by Market Capitalization

Capitalization	Adam & Adam	Adam & Eve	Eve & Adam	Eve & Eve
Small cap (up to $1 billion)	–21% (64)	–18% (83)	–18% (82)	–17% (89)
Mid cap ($1 to $5 billion)	–16.3% (45)	–16% (71)	–14% (68)	–19% (89)
Large cap (over $5 billion)	–15.9% (21)	–13% (40)	–16% (47)	–18% (37)
Score: small cap	+1	+1	+1	–1
Score: mid cap	–1	+1	–1	+1
Score: large cap	–1	–1	–1	–1

Note: The number of samples appears in parentheses.

SCORES

To use the scoring system, first evaluate your chart pattern by each table showing a score. Add the scores together. Scores above zero suggest performance that will beat the median decline; scores below zero suggest underperformance. In the case studies, I show you how to score a chart pattern in more detail, but first, how well does the system work?

Table 9.15 shows the results for scores above or below zero and when compared to the median decline. For example, those Eve & Adam double tops having scores above zero showed losses averaging 21%. This compares with a loss of just 11% for those with scores below zero. That is a substantial difference. However, it does not mean that the system is infallible. The scoring system only adds value if it removes the poor performers and keeps the winners. Thus, the median decline—where half the values are above the median and half below—would seem to be the obvious benchmark. If the system worked, the median decline would rise after removing the losers and keeping the winners, which is what happens.

For example, the table shows that 76% of the Adam & Eve double tops with buy signals (scores above zero) posted declines that were above the median decline. In other words, they were correct sell short signals. Avoid signals, those with scores below zero, performed worse than the median 71% of the time. That means they were correct avoid signals. In all cases, for both sell short and avoid signals, the scoring system improved results.

Table 9.15
Formation Performance by Score

Score	Adam & Adam	Adam & Eve	Eve & Adam	Eve & Eve
Average decline of chart patterns with scores above zero	24%	22%	21%	24%
Average decline of chart patterns with scores below zero	15%	12%	11%	17%
Median decline used	12.40%	13.26%	12.44%	14.81%
Percentage with scores above zero beating median decline	19/26 or 73%	55/72 or 76%	58/74 or 78%	33/48 or 69%
Percentage with scores below zero doing worse than median decline	42/73 or 58%	65/92 or 71%	67/100 or 67%	85/151 or 56%

CASE STUDY 1

I confess that I am not keen on shorting a stock. If you are wrong, you can not only lose your money, but the house, car, wife, and kids (or in my case, a dog and a small concrete cow in the backyard). So, let us approach the case study in two ways, first from the long side.

Pretend that you own stock in the utility pictured in Figure 9.8. From April through December 1999 (not shown) the price moved horizontally in a trading range from 16 to 20. During February 2000, prices gapped up and you hoped that it was the beginning of a strong up move, as many breakaway gaps portend. Unfortunately, the up move was short-lived as it formed a twin-peak top. When prices closed below point 1, the confirmation price, an Adam & Adam double top confirmed. With confirmation, the question to be answered is, do you sell the stock?

Let us run through the tables with scores to help gauge the severity of the coming decline. Where does the trend start? Prices reach a low of 15.52 in early January 2000 before climbing to a closing price of 19.01 in November

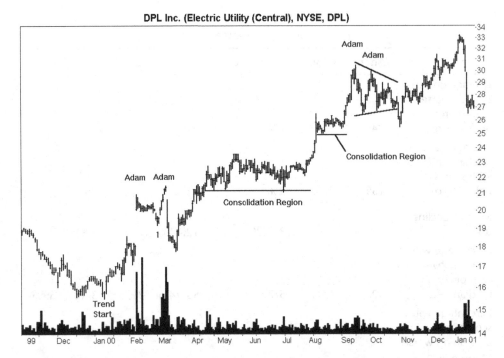

Figure 9.8 Two Adam & Adam double tops. If you own this stock, do you sell or hang on and hope the declines are not too severe? The September–October Adam & Adam double top appears as a symmetrical triangle.

1999 (going backward in time). The climb represents a rise over the 20% needed to mark a trend change. Therefore, the January low represents the start of a new trend (as marked on Figure 9.8). The trend start to the formation start is about a month long, so that falls into the short-term category. Table 9.1 says that a short-term uptrend leading to the formation scores a −1 for an Adam & Adam double top.

Table 9.2 lists performance for consolidation regions located between the price at the trend start and the confirmation point (point 1 on the figure). From the January low of 15.52 in Figure 9.8, to the confirmation price of 19.17, is there a horizontal consolidation region? Yes, but it appears quite small: The days before the February gap show a flat-top formation about a week long. If you could look backward in time, you would see many tops stopping at or near that price. So even though the consolidation appears only a week long, it has additional support going back many months. Table 9.2 says that a consolidation region scores −1. Running total: −2.

Where in the yearly price range does the breakout occur? The yearly high, as measured from the breakout, is at 21.50, the right top high. The yearly low occurs in early April at a price of 14.88. The breakout, at 19.17, is in the middle of the yearly price range. Table 9.6 says the middle third scores –1. Running total: –3.

Is the double top short or tall? With the right top being the higher of the two and the confirmation point being the lowest low in the pattern (point 1), that gives the double top a height of 21.50 – 19.17, or 2.33. The height, as a percentage of the breakout price is 2.33/19.17 (12%). This is below the 17.07% median, so the double top is a short fella. Table 9.7 says size matters and it scores –1. Running total: –4.

Does volume trend upward or downward? Looking at Figure 9.8, you can probably guess that volume, although U-shaped, is heavier surrounding the right top than the left. Thus, the trend appears to slope upward. Linear regression from the left top to right top on the volume numbers confirms a rising volume trend. Table 9.8, for the Adam & Adam pattern with a rising volume trend, scores +1. Running total: –3.

Staying with volume for the moment, the breakout volume is high, as denoted by the volume spike the day prices closed below the confirmation price. Table 9.9 says a high volume breakout rates a +1 score. Running total: –2.

Can we expect a pullback? According to Table 9.10, a pullback occurs 57% of the time in an Adam & Adam formation. Since prices are likely to drop to the horizontal consolidation region mentioned earlier, a zone of significant support going back months, a pullback is likely for a score of –1. Running total: –3.

Table 9.11 lists bear trap frequency. Although you cannot see the support region just mentioned, it poses a significant threat to any downward thrust. Going back to early 1999, there are other minor highs that peak at 19, suggesting additional support. A bear trap, where prices decline less than 10% then zoom upward, is thus more likely. Also, the Dow Jones utility average was approaching the December lows, suggesting a support region with a recovery nearby. Score: –1. Running total: –4.

A breakaway gap appears when prices take their 1-day plunge and close below the confirmation point. The gap size is nearly half a point. Table 9.12 shows that a gap on the breakout day scores +1. Running total: –3.

When the formation was forming in February, the S&P 500 Index rose, as measured on the dates of the two peaks. According to Table 9.13, a rising S&P scores a –1, for a running total of –4.

The final table concerns market capitalization. Using the breakout price of 19.17 multiplied by the number of shares outstanding places the stock in the mid cap category. Table 9.14 says that an Adam & Adam double top in a mid cap scores –1, for a final total score of –5.

Scores above zero mean good performance (that is, a large decline). A negative score implies a wimpy decline—one that should fall short of the median. Should you sell the stock? Probably not.

As you can see in Figure 9.8, prices declined to 17.79 then rebounded, for a 7% decline below the breakout price. The stock pulled back and when prices climbed above the double-top high, we could say that it was also a bear trap. Anyone that shorted the stock expecting a large decline probably lost money.

Fast forward to the second Adam & Adam double top, the one in September. Do you sell now (assume that you cannot see what happened after prices dropped below the confirmation level of 26.48)? You have been collecting dividends from the utility and have held it quite a long time with prices climbing from the January low of 15.52 to a double-top high of 30.51. When you include dividends, you have probably doubled your money. Is the stock ripe to fall?

Running through the tables gives a total score of –7. What changed? The trend start is at the March low, qualifying the double top as having a long-term uptrend. The yearly price range has widened and the breakout is now in the highest third of the yearly range (score: +1). The volume trend is downward (–1), and the breakout volume is just average (–1). There is no breakout gap (–1) and the general market is falling (+1).

What else can we say about the stock? A pullback is likely because of the closeness of the August consolidation region and average breakout volume. Table 9.10 says that 60% of the time, an Adam & Adam formation will pull back after an average or below-average volume breakout. The August consolidation region also suggests a heightened probability of a bear trap. In short, with a –7 score, it is not time to sell.

As you look at Figure 9.8, the two peaks in the September–October double top appear uneven. They only differ by 49 cents, or 2%, still qualifying the formation as a double top. However, I have drawn in the outlines of a symmetrical triangle. Lower tops and higher bottoms outline the triangle. With a rising price trend, you would expect prices to break out of the triangle upward, but they do not. Instead, they drop just 4%, well short of the median decline and just as the scoring system predicted.

The downward performance of this double top is just like the prior one. In both cases the horizontal consolidation region stops the downward plunge. If prices did pierce the region, we could expect prices to stop at the lower consolidation area, about 22 to 24. Before selling your holdings, you should compute the percentage decline if prices dropped to those two areas. For the first area, the price drop represents a decline of 4%, as I have already mentioned. A decline to 22, from the breakout price of 26.48, represents a 17% decline (9% if the drop stops at 24, the top of the support area).

The way I would play it would be to put a stop-loss order below the August consolidation region, say 24.88. That stop-loss order would limit my loss to 6% below the breakout.

CASE STUDY 2

Now for the short side. As a seasoned investor who is comfortable taking risk, you watch the semiconductor industry with delight. Of the nine stocks you follow in the industry, all were showing signs of topping during 2000. Some peaked in March, and were headed down, whereas others held out to the fall before turning color and dropping their leaves. Figure 9.9 shows one of the holdouts.

Year 2000 was a time when the high technology industry, after soaring the prior year, declined dramatically. If you were going to short a high-tech stock, this was the time to do it. Let us quickly run through the tables to see how Micron Technology stacked up.

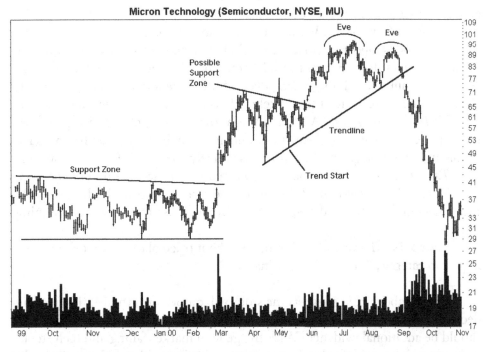

Figure 9.9   An Eve & Eve double top. The semiconductor industry started having trouble in March and by October, even the strongest were tumbling.

Table 9.1: Trend start. By definition, the trend started on May 10, 2000, when prices dipped to a low of 51.06. A 20% rise means a close above 61.27, and that occurred just 4 days earlier. From trend start to the Eve & Eve double top places the trend in the short-term category, for a +1 score.

Table 9.2: Horizontal consolidation. From the trend start to the confirmation point, prices pass through congestion starting in March and ending in May (spanning the trend start), with flat tops at 67 and 71. Score: –1. Running total: 0.

Table 9.6: Yearly price range. The yearly high was at 97.50, the low at 29.13, and the breakout at 73. Thus, the breakout occurs in the middle third of the yearly price range, just squeaking under the 74.71 high third limit. Score: –1. Running total: –1.

Table 9.7: Tall or short. The highest top is at 97.19, the lowest low is at 73, placing the pattern in the tall category. Score: +1. Running total: 0.

Table 9.8: Volume trend. The volume trend, suggested by the slope of the line, found using linear regression between the two tops, is downward. Score: +1. Running total: +1.

Table 9.9: Breakout volume. The day prices closed below the confirmation price, a gap occurred and volume spiked to a very high level. Score: +1. Running total: +2.

Table 9.10: Pullbacks. The breakout occurred on very high volume and an above-average breakout volume increases the chance of a pullback, but not by much (from 61% to 63%). With a consolidation region in the way of a declining price trend (supporting prices), I would bet that a pullback is likely. After the breakout, prices do move up in mid-September, but not to the confirmation point, so a pullback did not, in fact, occur. Still, we would not have known this ahead of time, so score it –1 for a likely pullback occurrence. Running total: +1.

Table 9.11: Bear trap. Although the horizontal consolidation region may block prices for a while, since the semiconductor industry was having such problems, I would suggest a bear trap was unlikely. Score: +1. Running total: +2.

Table 9.12: Gaps. A breakout gap occurred for a +1 score. Running total: +3.

Table 9.13: Market trend. From double top peak to peak, the S&P 500 Index declined on those dates, giving another boost to the score. Running total: +4.

Table 9.14: Market cap. Using the breakout price places the stock into the large cap category for a –1 score. Final total: +3.

A score above zero suggests the stock will outperform the 14.81% median decline, but does not guarantee it. When you are considering shorting, there should be additional evidence. With the general market falling and tech stocks taking hits right and left, that is certainly supporting evidence. Industry weakness also adds to the likelihood of success. Prices topping out near September, the worst performing month of the year, is also a good sign. Looking at Figure 9.9, a piercing of the up-sloping trendline is a good indicator of weakness. This line had three prior touches before being pierced. Applying the 1–2–3 method to identify a trend change (see Chapter 2) also suggests the uptrend was over.

You can see how the trade turned out. The score predictions were correct as the stock tumbled in a near straight-line run to 28, a decline of 62% from the breakout price, and well beyond the median decline. Notice that the stock stopped at the bottom of the large support zone (shown in Figure 9.9 as two roughly parallel lines through February 2000). After bottoming out in October, the stock has stayed within or near the trading range of 28 to 43 for several months.

10

Head-and-Shoulders Bottoms

As with most chart patterns, the head-and-shoulders name accurately describes the way the formation looks: There are shoulders on opposite sides of the head. In the bottom variety, the head is below the shoulders, and a rise above the neckline usually signals a breakout. What does the typical pattern look like?

THE TYPICAL PATTERN

Figure 10.1 shows a good example of a head-and-shoulders bottom. Prices tumbled from the Eve & Eve double top in a measured move down (MMD) pattern (that is, a stair-step pattern: decline, retrace, and second decline nearly matching the first). The end of the MMD marked the left shoulder low on very high volume. Prices recovered and peaked at the left minor high, dropped to the head and recovered to form a lower minor high. A line drawn across the two minor highs between the shoulder lows is called a neckline. When prices close above a down-sloping neckline, the formation confirms as a true head-and-shoulders bottom and stages an upward breakout. In Figure 10.1, after the breakout, prices soon rounded over and retraced to the neckline in a classic throwback before continuing their journey upward.

Volume is usually highest during formation of the left shoulder or head and diminished on creation of the right shoulder, like that shown in Figure 10.1. The neckline can slant in any direction, including horizontally, but there is a slight tendency (55% of the time) for it to slope downward.

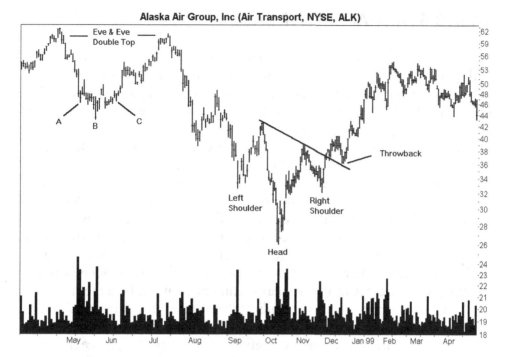

Figure 10.1   A head-and-shoulders bottom. An Eve & Eve double top precedes the decline to the head-and-shoulders bottom. Volume is typically highest on the left shoulder or head, but diminished on the right shoulder. The A–B–C pattern is not a head-and-shoulders bottom because the two shoulders are not distinct minor lows.

Symmetry is important when identifying a head-and-shoulders bottom. The right half of the formation should mimic the left half, the shoulder bottoms should be near the same price, and the distance from the shoulders to the head should be approximately the same. There is wide variation in their appearance, so if yours does not fit the classic pattern, do not be too concerned.

Let me warn you of an identification problem. Look at the A–B–C pattern marked in Figure 10.1. Never try to create a chart pattern where one does not exist. In this case, the low marked by point A is a feeble left shoulder whereas C shows no significant decline at all. The two presumed shoulders, A and C, are not shoulders because the minor lows are not distinct and separate from the prevailing price trend. If you remove the A–B–C labels, you will find just a gradual turn in prices, not a shoulder-head-shoulder pattern.

When trying to identify any chart pattern, ask yourself this question: Will others see the same pattern? If the answer is no, then look for a pattern that everyone can agree on. If you are having trouble identifying a pattern, then others are too.

TREND START AND FLAT BASE

I determine a trend change by a 20% rise or decline in prices. From the start of the formation (the left shoulder low), moving backward in time, prices rise. When they stop rising and decline by 20% or more—still moving backward—then I have found the trend start. In Figure 10.1, for example, the downward trend started in July, at the second Eve top. Working backward, the decline before the second Eve top represents a 29% price decline (from a high of 61.19 to a close of 43.50), far exceeding the 20% trend change minimum.

I used the same technique to determine the trend start for all formations in which data was available. Then, I sorted the time prices took to decline to the start of the chart pattern and computed the resulting average gain. Table 10.1 shows the results. You can see that head-and-shoulders bottoms with a short-term downtrend result in the best performance, with gains averaging 38%. This is above the average 34% gain for all head-and-shoulders bottoms and it handily beats the other two periods (intermediate and long term).

I discuss scoring in the case studies at the end of this chapter, so do not concern yourself with the scores now.

Table 10.1 also lists flat bases. I define a flat base as a long price structure leading to a head-and-shoulders bottom with either flat bottoms, flat tops, or both, on or below the confirmation price. The confirmation or breakout price is the price at which the stock closes above a down-sloping neckline, or closes above the highest minor high between the head and right shoulder when the neckline slopes upward.

In essence, I want to see prices move horizontally for weeks or months before the head-and-shoulders bottom. After the head-and-shoulders pattern confirms, I do not want to see the flat base become an impediment to a price rise; it should act as a support zone, not a resistance area. Think of the flat base as an area where strength is gathering, waiting, for an upside breakout.

Figure 10.2 shows an example of a flat base. During late April and May, prices topped out at 30, then pushed higher in June when 30 became a support

Table 10.1
Average Performance of Head-and-Shoulders Bottoms
Sorted by Price Trend Leading to the Pattern

Trend Start to Formation Start	Result	Score
Short term (0 to 3 months)	38% (215)	+1
Intermediate term (3 to 6 months)	34% (76)	0
Long term (over 6 months)	20% (42)	−1
Flat base	41% (52)	+1
No flat base	33% (314)	−1

Note: The first number is the average, followed by the number of samples in parentheses.

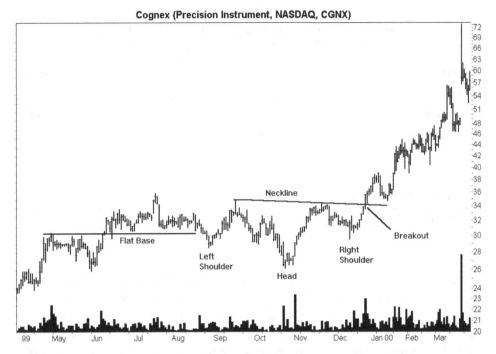

Figure 10.2   A flat base. Head-and-shoulders bottoms perform better after a flat base. In this case, prices soared 118% above the breakout price.

area. A head-and-shoulders bottom appeared with a breakout price above the flat base.

Do not expect to see flat bases often; they occurred only 79 times in the 456 bottoms I looked at (17% of the time). For the 52 formations with flat bases and usable data (those old enough to have reached the ultimate high via a 20% trend change), the formations posted an average gain of 41%, compared to a 33% rise for those patterns without a flat base.

Before you select a pattern, look at the prior few months. If a long, flat base appears *below* the confirmation price, then consider an investment. If the flat base is *above* the confirmation price, then the base could act as a resistance zone to further price advances, and the resulting gain may be disappointing.

HORIZONTAL CONSOLIDATION REGIONS

When a flat base appears between the trend start and the confirmation price, I call that a horizontal consolidation region (HCR). It is an area that could pose a threat to any upward advance. As you can see in Table 10.2, those head-and-shoulders bottoms with an HCR showed gains of just 30%, but gained 46% when consolidation was absent.

Table 10.2
Average Performance of Head-and-Shoulders Bottoms
with and Without a Consolidation Region

Description	Result	Score
Consolidation region	30% (262)	–1
No consolidation region	46% (104)	+1
Average length (days)	50	
Prices stop within region ±5%	42%	
Prices push through region	50%	
Prices do not reach region	8%	

Note: The number of samples appears in parentheses.

Figure 10.3 shows what an HCR looks like. The consolidation region appears mostly flat, between the trend start (I allow it to span the trend start when necessary, as in this case) and the formation top. The location of the region is important because it can act as a resistance zone to an upward price move. For example, the figure shows prices climbing to the base of the consolidation region before tumbling on their way to 20.

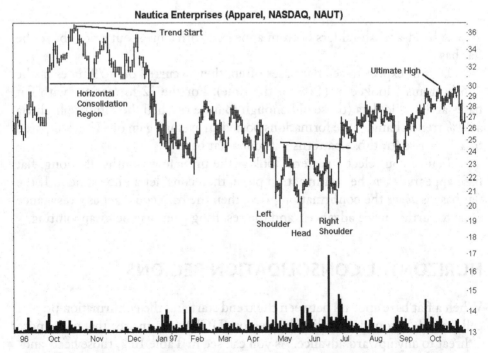

Figure 10.3   An HCR. Half the time, prices push through the consolidation region, but not in this case.

I measured the average length of the consolidation region and found it to be 50 days, or almost 2 months long. The reason I mention this is that the support zone should stick out by being comparatively large, not just a few days worth of congestion. It should be large enough to resist rising prices, preferably with flat tops, flat bottoms, or both. Sometimes the consolidation region takes the shape of another chart pattern, such as a broadening top or symmetrical triangle.

Table 10.2 shows how often prices run into trouble when they meet an HCR. A little less than half the time (42%), prices stop somewhere between the consolidation region high and low, with a 5% buffer surrounding the region. I added 5% to include those prices that stop just above or below the region.

Half the time (50%), prices eventually push through the region on their way to the ultimate high. The remainder of the time, 8%, prices never make it up to the region before tumbling. In short, if you see an HCR above the breakout price, expect prices to stop somewhere in the consolidation region. Prices may continue higher, but to be safe, do not bet the farm on it.

INSIDE THE PATTERN

Table 10.3 shows important statistical findings for head-and-shoulders bottoms. Only those formations with upside breakouts appear in the table. I do not consider price patterns that are unconfirmed (prices do not close above the confirmation point) to be valid head-and-shoulders bottoms, by definition.

The head-and-shoulders bottom is a plentiful formation, appearing 456 times in the stocks I reviewed. However, a substantial number were either too recent to have prices reach the ultimate high, or the data did not go back far enough. I base the table statistics (in this book) only on those formations for which complete data were available and appropriate to use.

I measured the average rise from the breakout price to the ultimate high, but sometimes locating the breakout can be a challenge. The traditional method says that a breakout occurs when prices pierce the neckline. That is

Table 10.3
Important Statistical Findings

Description	Result
Number of formations	456
Average rise	34%
Standard & Poor's 500 change	6%
Median rise	31%
Rises more than 50%	96/366 or 26%
Shoulder with highest volume	Left 68%

fine for down-sloping necklines, but consider Figure 10.4, a head-and-shoulders bottom with an up-sloping neckline. Prices never pierce the neckline, hence, no breakout.

I determine the breakout in two ways. If neck point A is above point B, meaning the neckline slopes downward, then I use a close above the neckline to signal a breakout. Figures 10.1, 10.2, and 10.3 all show downward-sloping necklines in which a close above the neckline marks the breakout. When the neckline slopes upward, as in Figure 10.4 with point B above point A, I use the highest high (point B) to mark the breakout price. In Figure 10.4, the breakout occurs at a price of 29.50 on October 16; that is the day prices close above point B.

Using the 366 chart patterns for which the ultimate high exists, the average rise measures 34%.

The Standard & Poor's 500 change is the change in value of the index from the date the formation staged a breakout to the ultimate high. I compared the closing value of the S&P on the breakout day with the S&P high price on the day when the stock reached its ultimate high. Over the period, the S&P climbed 6% while head-and-shoulders bottoms rose 34%.

Since large values can skew an average, I calculated the median rise. The median is the midrange value in a sorted list; half the values will be below the

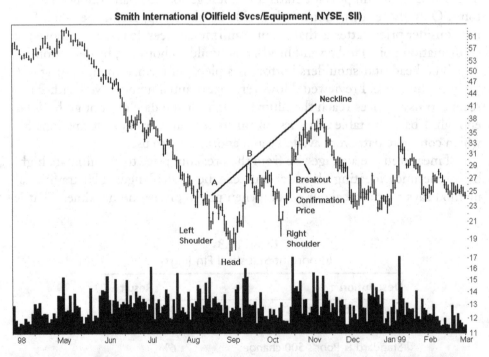

Figure 10.4 A steep neckline means another method must be used to determine the breakout. For all up-sloping necklines, I used the highest high in the formation as the breakout price. For down-sloping necklines, a close above the neckline signals an upward breakout.

median and half above. I view the median as a more realistic return than the average. For head-and-shoulders bottoms, the median rise is 31%.

As a gauge of how successful a chart pattern can be, I counted the number of patterns in which prices climbed at least 50%. Just over a quarter of the patterns (26%), had rises of more than 50%—a strong showing!

As an identification tip, many cite high volume on creation of the left shoulder as a key ingredient to a head-and-shoulders bottom. Indeed, that situation occurs 68% of the time. However, just because the right shoulder has higher volume is no reason to discard the chart pattern. If the pattern shows symmetry, three minor lows—with the center below the other two—and a close above either a down-sloping neckline or the highest high in the formation, then you have a good head-and-shoulders candidate.

NECKLINES AND SHOULDERS

Table 10.4 shows interesting statistics I uncovered when doing research for my previous book, *Encyclopedia of Chart Patterns* (Wiley, 2000). The statistics include more formations, so the results are more meaningful.

The first three rows in Table 10.4 show the results of those formations with up, horizontal, and down-sloping necklines. Recall that the neckline is a trendline drawn across the minor highs on each side of the head. The best performance, with rises averaging 40%, comes when necklines slope downward; the worst performance is when they slope upward (28%).

Even though the results of left and right shoulders are close together, I include them in the table because the *Encyclopedia of Chart Patterns* showed a wider, but consistent result. When the left shoulder is higher than the right

Table 10.4
Neckline Slope, Shoulders, and Volume

Description	Result	Score
Average rise of formations with up-sloping necklines	28% (152)	−1
Average rise of formations with horizontal necklines	32% (18)	−1
Average rise of formations with down-sloping necklines	40% (196)	+1
Average rise of formations with higher left shoulder lows	35% (168)	+1
Average rise of formations with higher right shoulder lows	33% (174)	−1
Average rise of formations with even shoulder lows	40% (24)	+1
Average rise of formations with left shoulder volume above right shoulder	32% (254)	−1
Average rise of formations with left shoulder volume below right shoulder	40% (112)	+1

Note: The average rise is the first number and the number of samples is in parentheses.

one, the formations meeting that criteria had rises averaging 35%. The average rise of formations with a higher right shoulder is 33%. To clarify, Figure 10.2 shows a formation with a higher right shoulder low. The right shoulder low is at 21.19 but the left shoulder low is lower, at 20.31. Before you get too excited at the 40% rise when the shoulders are even, the result uses just 24 samples, so be skeptical.

To me, the results do not make intuitive sense. I would expect that a higher right shoulder would lead to better performance simply because it is more bullish; if prices stop declining sooner because of buying enthusiasm, then that is positive. However, a lower right shoulder could imply an oversold condition—where prices have tumbled unjustifiably low during panic selling—inviting investors to buy the stock.

The last two lines of Table 10.4 list the performance of formations with volume higher on the left shoulder or right shoulder. The best performance occurs with left shoulder volume below the right shoulder (with an average rise of 40%), but that occurrence is also the more rare of the two.

FAILURE RATES

Table 10.5 shows the number of head-and-shoulders bottoms that do not climb more than the associated maximum price rise. For example, the failure rate quadruples, to 12%, when counting those formations that do not rise more than 10%. Although the 5% failure rate, at 3%, is small, it rapidly climbs as the maximum price rises. The results are not unique as other chart patterns

Table 10.5
Maximum Price Rise Versus Failure Rate

Maximum Price Rise (%)	Failure Rate
5	11 or 3%
10	45 or 12%
15	91 or 25%
20	119 or 33%
25	149 or 41%
30	182 or 50%
35	213 or 58%
50	269 or 73%
75	314 or 86%
100	337 or 92%

Note: The sample count is 366 for each row.

show a deceptively small 5% failure rate that doubles, triples, or more, for maximum price rises of 10% or 15%.

How is this useful? Suppose your trading cost is 10% after including commissions, SEC fees, slippage and any other costs. Further, suppose that you want to make a 10% profit margin on your trades. Total cost: 20%. What is the failure rate for a 20% price rise? Answer: 33%, or one in three trades will fail to meet your profit objectives.

Table 10.6 shows another way of looking at failure rates, this one called the horizon failure rate. To create the table, I counted the number of stocks in which prices were above the breakout price weekly for the first month, monthly for the first quarter, and 6 months after the breakout. For example, 21% of the head-and-shoulders bottoms had closing prices below the breakout price at the end of 3 weeks.

Although the failure rates appear large, they are smaller than many other classic chart patterns. By definition, the horizon failure rate after the first day is 0%, because all formations must close above the breakout price. From there, the failure rate climbs to 23% after 2 weeks, and stabilizes in the low 20s until sometime between the first and second month. At the end of 3 months, the horizon failure rate is still in the 20s. A more optimistic way of looking at the numbers is to realize that after 3 months, 75% of the stocks had prices above the breakout.

I computed the average rise by taking snapshots of the closing price at each time interval and comparing it to the breakout price. You can see that the average rise climbs from 5% after the first week to 10% after 6 months. Clearly, the best performance comes in the first week because prices rise an average of 5%. After that, the rise is more sedate. This suggests a buy order placed slightly above the breakout price will capture most of the early-stage gains.

Table 10.6
Horizon Failure Rates and Average Rise

Time Since Breakout	Failure Rate (%)	Average Rise (%)
1 week	17	5
2 weeks	23	5
3 weeks	21	6
1 month	22	7
2 months	28	8
3 months	25	9
6 months	33	10

Table 10.7
Average Performance Sorted by Breakout Price
According to Prior 12-Month Range

Yearly Price Range	Result	Score
Highest third	36% (74)	+1
Middle third	32% (139)	−1
Lowest third	34% (107)	0

Note: The number of samples appears in parentheses.

YEARLY PRICE RANGE

Table 10.7 shows the performance of head-and-shoulders bottoms after sorting by the breakout price in the yearly price range. By that I mean I found the yearly high and low starting from the breakout day, looking backward in time, then I split the price range into thirds: highest third, middle third, and lowest third. Finally, I placed the breakout price into one of the three price ranges and looked at the associated performance.

Head-and-shoulders bottoms with a breakout price near the yearly high performed best, showing gains averaging 36%. Those in the middle of the pack performed worst, with rises of 32%.

TALL AND SHORT PATTERNS

Table 10.8 lists the performance of short and tall head-and-shoulders bottoms. What makes a chart pattern a tall one? That was the question I answered by computing the formation height, from the higher of the minor highs on each side of the head, to the low price at the head. Then I divided by the breakout price and sorted the results. For tall patterns, I chose anything larger than the median or midrange percentage; short patterns had heights as a percentage of the breakout price less than the median.

Table 10.8
Performance of Short and Tall Head-and-Shoulders Bottoms

Description	Result	Score
Tall (above the median)	39% (182)	+1
Short (below the median)	31% (184)	−1
Median percentage of breakout price	19.89%	

Note: The number of samples appears in parentheses.

Table 10.9
Linear Regression Volume Trend and Performance

Description	Result	Score
Rising volume trend	32% (115)	–1
Falling volume trend	35% (251)	+1

Note: The number of samples appears in parentheses.

After sorting the results into short and tall patterns, I found that tall head-and-shoulders bottoms had rises averaging 39%. This result compares to a 31% rise for short patterns. If you are confused, the case studies at the end of this chapter make the calculation clearer.

VOLUME TREND

Table 10.9 shows the performance of head-and-shoulders bottoms after sorting by the volume trend during the chart pattern. To find the trend, I used linear regression, (called the trend function in some spreadsheets) which is a fancy way of saying I mathematically plotted a line using the volume data (from the date of the left shoulder low to the right shoulder low) then looked at the slope of the line.

Those chart patterns with a falling volume trend showed gains averaging 35% compared to a 32% rise when the volume trend was climbing.

BREAKOUT VOLUME

Table 10.10 shows the results of a study of breakout volume. Before I discuss the results, let me say that a table of volume trends does not appear in this chapter because the results were statistically insignificant, meaning that they could be due to chance. However, Table 10.10 shows statistically significant differences between the results.

Table 10.10
Breakout Volume and Performance

Description	Result	Score
Average rise on above-average breakout volume	39% (108)	+1
Average rise on average or below-average breakout volume	33% (258)	–1

Note: The number of samples appears in parentheses.

I computed the average volume and created five volume categories: very high, high, average, low, and very low. Then, I sorted the breakout volume into the appropriate category. See Glossary and Methodology for more details on how I accomplished this. Grouping the categories together shows that those chart patterns with above-average volume, that is, high or very high, had rises averaging 39%. Those with average or below-average breakout volume showed gains of just 33%. In short, high breakout volume is like chocolate: It is wonderful!

THROWBACKS

Table 10.11 gives some clues as to the behavior of prices after a head-and-shoulders bottom.

A throwback occurs when prices return to, or come very close to, the breakout price within 30 days. Figure 10.1 shows a good example of a throwback. Prices staged a breakout when they closed above the neckline on November 25,

Table 10.11
Throwback Statistics

Description	Result
Throwbacks	183 or 40%
Score if throwback predicted	–1
Score if throwback not predicted	+1
Ultimate high before throwback	28/456 or 6%
Average rise on above-average breakout volume with throwbacks	31%
Average rise on above-average breakout volume with no throwbacks	44%
Average rise on average or below-average breakout volume with throwbacks	29%
Average rise on average or below-average breakout volume with no throwbacks	36%
Number of throwbacks after a high or very high volume breakout	50/127 or 39%
Number of throwbacks after an average, low, or very low volume breakout	133/329 or 40%
Number of throwbacks that stopped ±5% from the breakout price	132 or 72%
Number of throwbacks that stopped between breakout and right shoulder low	29 or 16%
Number of throwbacks that stopped between right shoulder low and head	14 or 8%
Number of throwbacks that stopped below the head low	8 or 4%

1998. Prices climbed to a high of 40.44 before rounding over and approaching the down-sloping neckline. Notice that there is white space between the neckline and prices as they round over. If prices slide along the neckline, with no white space, then I do not count it as a throwback. If prices return to the breakout price beyond 30 days, they also are not counted as throwbacks. The 30-day limit is an arbitrary one, but one that is commonly recognized.

Only 40% of the chart patterns had throwbacks. This result is too low to formulate a trading plan, meaning that you should not depend on prices returning to the breakout price.

In my paper trading, what occurs most often is being stopped out during a throwback. I buy the day after prices close above the breakout price and set a stop point. As prices climb, I raise my stop until I get taken out during a throwback (when it occurs, that is).

In my other trading, when I spend real money, I can usually predict when a throwback will occur and wait for it to complete before buying. In that way, I am not trying to make a few bucks as prices climb; I trade for the longer term.

A danger for most chart patterns is a throwback in which prices continue falling. In other words, prices reach the ultimate high before the throwback. For the head-and-shoulders bottom, this occurs just 6% of the time.

The next four lines concerning average rise in Table 10.11 compare the performance of formations sorted by breakout volume and throwbacks. When the breakout volume was above average, those formations throwing back had rises averaging 31%, but they averaged 44% if no throwback occurred, which is a substantial difference, and why the score is –1 when a throwback occurs.

A similar situation occurs when the breakout volume is average or below average. In those formations when a throwback occurs, prices rise an average of 29%, but climb 36% if no throwback occurs.

In this book, it has often been the case that a stock is more likely to throw back after a high volume breakout. The jury is still out on head-and-shoulders bottoms as the numbers are too close to call. When you look at all breakouts on high volume, only 39% of them throw back. When the breakout volume is average or below, the throwback rate is similar, 40%.

After a throwback, do prices recover or continue down? The last four rows in Table 10.11 provide the answer. I counted the number of throwbacks that stopped within 5% of the breakout price, between the breakout and right shoulder low, between the right shoulder low and head, and below the head. All four regions do not overlap.

In almost three out of four cases (72%), prices stopped near the breakout price; 16% of the time they continued down to the shoulder low; another 8% dropped to the head, and the remainder (4%) continued lower. If you place a stop-loss order 0.15 below the right shoulder low, that should protect your position the vast majority of the time. Even a stop just below the breakout price has a good chance of remaining intact. Be sure to raise your stop as prices climb so you can capture additional profits while helping to protect against a catastrophic loss. Besides, placing a stop gives the market makers something to aim for!

BULL TRAPS

Table 10.12 shows how often a bull trap occurs. In case you are not familiar with bull traps, I define them as when prices break out upward and travel less than 10% higher before tumbling and declining below the formation low. A bull trap seduces investors into expecting a gain, but they usually wind up with a loss.

Bull traps are rare for head-and-shoulders bottoms, occurring just 9% of the time. I know that is little comfort when you invest in a stock like the one shown in Figure 10.5. In mid-March, prices closed above the breakout price of 67.50, confirming the head-and-shoulders bottom. If you bought the stock near that price, you probably lost money. Prices threw back and continued down to 63.50, then moved up and posted a new minor high, at 71.75. After rising just 6%, prices completed an island-top reversal, tumbled, and slipped below the formation low on their way to 43.88 in late August.

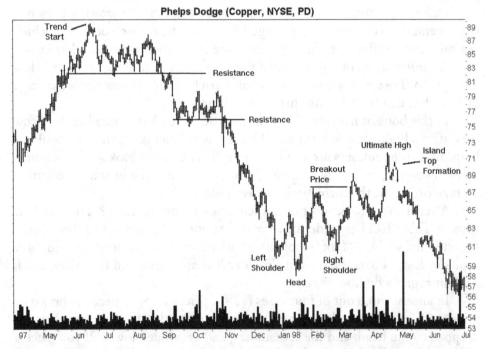

Figure 10.5   A bull trap. Traps occur when prices rise less than 10% then decline below the formation low. Look for significant overhead resistance before investing. If you assume that prices will stop at the resistance area, then you can determine whether the investment is worth risking. An island top marks the ultimate high.

Table 10.12
Bull Traps

Description	Result
Bull trap frequency	40/456 or 9%
Score if trap predicted	–1
Score if trap not predicted	+1

The figure is an example of a bull trap, but could you have avoided the situation? Look at the two formidable resistance levels, one at 75 and another at 83. From the breakout price of 67.50, the two areas represent gains of 11% and 23%, respectively. I usually do not invest in a stock unless the reward is at least 20%. Such a rule would disqualify this formation as an investment. Both of the resistance areas qualify as horizontal consolidation zones that I mentioned in the discussion of Table 10.2. Look for such zones before you invest.

GAPS

Table 10.13 shows an analysis of gaps and performance. The head-and-shoulders bottom is one of the few formations in which a price gap on the breakout day results in no performance difference. Before I explain what a gap looks like, the statistics may be the result of the way I flagged a breakout. The traditional method is when prices rise above the neckline. I only use that method for down-sloping necklines. With up-sloping necklines, the highest minor high in the formation represents the breakout price. As Figure 10.4 shows, trying to trade a stock using an up-sloping neckline sometimes does not work. Additionally, since the breakout can be far removed from the chart pattern, it may be that investors fail to notice the breakout and so gaps are less likely. Whatever the reason, I do not provide a score for gaps.

Figure 10.6 shows what a gap looks like, and it is huge, measuring $3.59. It helped thrust the stock to a 93% gain. The buying enthusiasm was so powerful that prices easily drove through the resistance zone partially shown by the two areas marked A. When prices reached overhead resistance between 50 and

Table 10.13
Gaps and Performance

Description	Result
Average rise after price gap on breakout	34% (81)
Average rise with no price gap on breakout	34% (285)

Note: The number of samples appears in parentheses.

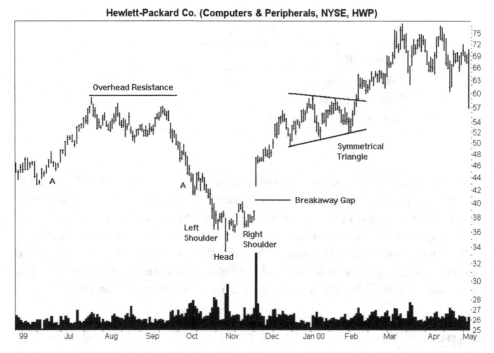

Figure 10.6   A breakaway gap. A huge price gap appears the day prices rise above the confirmation price of 40.22. The two areas labeled A mark portions of a large resistance zone.

60, prices oscillated up and down eventually forming a symmetrical triangle top. An upside breakout suggested the rise would continue.

MARKET TREND

Table 10.14 shows the effect of the general market on the performance of head-and-shoulders bottoms. You would expect bullish chart patterns to perform best when the general market is rising and to underperform when the market is declining. The performance results meet those expectations.

In a rising market, during creation of the head-and-shoulders bottom, the stocks show a 35% average gain after the breakout; in a declining market over the same period, the gain measures 32%.

If you can predict how the general market will perform after you buy a stock, then the FE to UH column is of interest to you. When the general market was rising from the formation end to the ultimate high, the gains were 35%. In a falling market, the gains averaged only 24% (but the result uses only 26 samples). I would expect the 24% number to rise as more samples become available.

Table 10.14
Average Price Performance of Head-and-Shoulders
Bottoms During a Rising and Falling Market

Market Trend	FS to FE	Score	FE to UH
Rising S&P 500	35% (276)	+1	35% (340)
Falling S&P 500	32% (90)	−1	24% (26)

Note: FS = formation start, FE = formation end, UH = ultimate high. The number of samples appears in parentheses.

Since most of us cannot accurately foretell the future, I base the score on the market performance during creation of the chart pattern, from formation start to end (FS to FE).

MARKET CAPITALIZATION

Table 10.15 shows the performance results of head-and-shoulders bottoms sorted by market capitalization. I determined market capitalization by multiplying the breakout price times the number of shares outstanding.

Small caps perform best, with average gains of 42%. Mid and large caps do worse than the benchmark 34%. Mid caps showed gains averaging 33%, whereas large caps climbed only 27%. Many other classic chart patterns show the same performance trend. If you have a choice, and you always do, invest in small caps during a bull market.

SCORES

To use the scoring system, evaluate your chart pattern and compare your results with each table showing a score. Add the scores together. Scores above zero suggest performance that will beat the median price rise; scores below

Table 10.15
Average Price Performance of Head-and-Shoulders
Bottoms by Market Capitalization

Capitalization	Result	Score
Small cap (up to $1 billion)	42% (154)	+1
Mid cap ($1 to $5 billion)	33% (147)	−1
Large cap (over $5 billion)	27% (64)	−1

Note: The number of samples appears in parentheses.

zero suggest underperformance. The case studies that follow give examples of how to score a chart pattern.

Since we are dealing with probabilities, there is no guarantee that a good score will result in good performance or a bad score in poor performance, but that is the way to trade.

To show how the system performs, I computed the performance for those head-and-shoulders bottoms having scores above and below zero (Table 10.16). For positive scores, the stocks climbed 48%; negative scores showed gains averaging half that (24%).

Since I use the median rise (29.03%) as the benchmark because it is the midrange value, a buy (scores over zero) or avoid signal (scores below zero) that works more than half the time adds value. As Table 10.16 shows, buy signals correctly exceed the median rise 72% of the time and avoid signals correctly predict underperformance 70% of the time.

CASE STUDY 1

Figure 10.7 illustrates this first case study. A head-and-shoulders bottom appeared at the end of a flat base, rounding top. This particular bottom was probably more difficult to identify because of the many large downward spikes in the preceding months.

Take a close look at the three minor lows marked by the letters A, B, and C (pretty inventive labeling, huh?). Is this a head-and-shoulders bottom? The pattern has all the makings of a head-and-shoulders bottom except for one thing: Prices are rising leading to the pattern.

How would you score the August to September head-and-shoulders bottom? Running through the tables with scores, let us review the scoring mechanism.

Where does the price trend start in Figure 10.7? Moving backward in time from the start of the formation, we find that prices reach a minor high on June 7, 1999, at 13.41. Is this the trend start? If it is, then prices must decline

Table 10.16
Formation Performance by Score

Score	Result
Average rise of chart patterns with scores above zero	48%
Average rise of chart patterns with scores below zero	24%
Median rise used	29.03%
Percentage with scores above zero beating median rise	95/132 or 72%
Percentage with scores below zero doing worse than median rise	101/145 or 70%

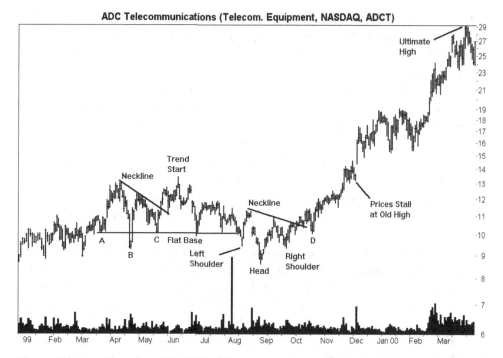

Figure 10.7 A head-and-shoulders bottom with a score of +4. The stock posted a rise of 181%.

by at least 20% from this point, going backward in time. A 20% decline from 13.41 means a *closing* price of 10.72, which occurred in mid-May, when prices declined to 10.08, forming a minor low (shown as point C in Figure 10.7). The time between the trend start and the formation start (left shoulder low) was 64 days, placing it in the short-term category. Table 10.1 rates a short-term decline as +1.

Table 10.1 also mentions a flat base. I have drawn a horizontal line across what I call a flat base. Many of the minor lows declined to about 10, and the base is below the confirmation price. If prices were to decline to this point, you could expect support. Indeed, this happened at point D when prices slipped, found support at 10.06, then recovered. A flat base scores +1 for a running total of +2.

Is there an HCR between the trend start and the formation top? If you slide a ruler horizontally from the formation top upward, there is a small region in July that shows a flat top, but I consider it too close to the formation top to be a valid HCR. A region more likely to pose a threat is the three peaks marking the trend start. They are at about the same price level and the April peak also is near the same price. I consider this a valid resistance zone, so Table 10.2 scores a consolidation region with a –1 score. Running total: +1.

Inside the formation, we find that the neckline slopes downward. A downsloping neckline, according to Table 10.4 scores +1. The price at the left shoulder low is 9.44 and the right shoulder low is 9.33. A higher left shoulder scores +1. If you look carefully at Figure 10.7, you can see that the volume on the left shoulder is lower and more sparse than that on the right shoulder. Score: +1. Running total: +4.

Where does the breakout reside in the yearly price range? The yearly high is at 13.41 and the low, 3.94, with a 10.47 breakout. Splitting the yearly price range into thirds shows that the breakout just makes it into the highest third. Table 10.7 scores that +1. Running total: +5.

Is the chart pattern short or tall? A high price of 11.28 and a head low of 8.59 gives a height of 2.69. Dividing this by the 10.47 breakout price gives a height-to-breakout price of 25.69%, which is well above the median 19.89%, so according to Table 10.8 the formation is tall and scores +1. Running total: +6.

Is volume trending up or down? Looking at Figure 10.7, you can probably guess that volume is sloping downward. It appears heaviest to the left of the head and diminished on the right side. Verifying the result from the date of the left shoulder low to the right shoulder low using linear regression confirms a falling volume trend. Table 10.9 scores that +1 for a running total of +7.

For down-sloping necklines, the breakout price is a close above the neckline. Volume on the day that occurred was just average. It is even difficult to pick out on the chart, so Table 10.10 scores that –1. Running total: +6.

Is a throwback predicted? Yes. How can you tell that a throwback will occur? The throwback rate is just 40%, a little more frequent than one in three, suggesting a throwback is unlikely. Most of the time, though, overhead resistance is what causes a throwback. I mentioned the HCR set up by the three trend start peaks. That is a likely resistance zone and one that might repel prices. Also, the July flat top may pose a nearer resistance point. I would guess that one of these zones would throw prices back. Table 10.11 scores this scenario a –1. Running total: +5.

What about a bull trap? Bull traps only occur 9% of the time, making them highly unlikely. If I were considering buying this chart pattern, I would look at the two peaks in early April and early June—at a price of about 13—as warning areas. I would expect prices to reach this point and stall, just as they did on those two occasions, and possibly form a triple top. If you look to the right in Figure 10.7, you can see that prices did stall—briefly—near 13 during late November. From a breakout price of 10.47, a climb to 13 would represent a rise of 24%, well above the maximum climb of 10% for a bull trap.

If prices climbed to the flat top in July, that still represents a climb of 15%. Again, the rise is outside the bull trap arena. Table 10.12 scores no bull trap as +1. Running total: +6.

Table 10.14 discusses the effects of a rising market on the performance of head-and-shoulders bottoms. The S&P 500 Index, on the date of the left shoulder bottom, was 1281.43. On the right shoulder bottom, when I consider the formation ended, the S&P was 1280.41. Thus, the general market declined, albeit marginally, from the formation start to end. That scores -1 for a running total of +5.

At a breakout price of 10.47, the stock is a large cap due to the preponderance of shares outstanding. According to Table 10.15, a large cap scores –1 for a final total of +4.

A score above zero means the stock is likely to do well. The higher the score, the better the performance but a high score is no guarantee of success. Your trading skills, analysis of the situation, and perhaps a dose of luck are all key ingredients for investment success. If you timed the trade perfectly, placed a stop order to buy at the breakout price, and sold exactly at the ultimate high, you would have made 181%.

If you were tardy in selling, the shares would have backtracked to 21.50, then continued rising to 49. Selling at 49 would have given you a gain of 368%. About a year later, the stock bottomed at 5.50!

CASE STUDY 2

What happens when the score is negative? Figure 10.8 shows the stock I use in this case study. The first thing you may notice is how small the formation is. It is a commonly held belief that the smaller the chart pattern, the less powerful it will be. I do know that the 1 or 2 day chart patterns I tested (inside days, outside days, weekly reversals, and so forth) had some of the most alarming failure rates (for example, 56%). With failure rates like that, you would improve your performance by ignoring the pattern and just throwing darts at the newspaper for stock selection.

It always pays to look for prior chart patterns because they can sometimes give you a clue to future performance. In the case of Figure 10.8, a measured move down—marked A and Head—warned of a retrace to the corrective phase, B to C. The retrace also coincided with a resistance area at 29, precisely where the stock stopped climbing. Prices formed a triple top then tumbled to a recent low of 13.15.

How do you evaluate the chart pattern using the scoring system? Let us run through the tables.

Table 10.1: Trend start. Marked on the figure is the trend start, a location from which prices declined by more than 20% (moving backward in time to gauge this, by the way). The trend start to the left shoulder low is 134 days (go ahead, count them!), placing it in the intermediate-term category. Table 10.1 says that those formations with an intermediate term downtrend showed gains averaging 34%, for a zero score.

There is no flat base below the confirmation price. Score: –1.

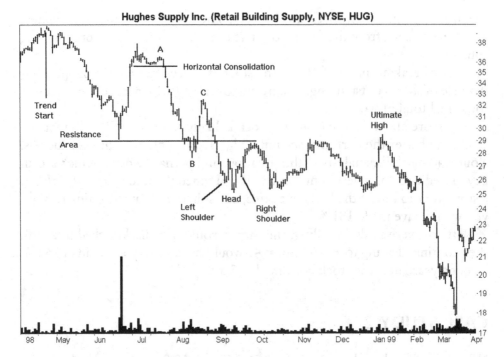

Figure 10.8 A small head-and-shoulders bottom. The scoring system predicted this chart pattern would be a stinker and it was right, with a below average gain of 8%. The head-and-shoulders bottom formed at the end of a measured move down (marked A, B, C, and Head).

Table 10.2: Horizontal consolidation. Is there an HCR? Yes, and it is marked on the chart. This region falls between the trend start and the formation top, where you would expect prices to find resistance and run into trouble. However, in this case, with the region at 36, a climb from the breakout price of 27.31 would represent a climb of 32%. That is a nice return if you can get it. Still, Table 10.2 scores an HCR as a –1, for a running total of –2.

Table 10.4: Neckline shapes. The neckline slopes downward (score: +1), the right shoulder low is higher than the left (score: –1), and the left shoulder volume is higher than on the right (score: –1). Running total: –3.

Table 10.7: Yearly price range. The yearly high is at 39.21, the low at 24.74, and the breakout is at 26.90. Thus the breakout is closest to the yearly low. Score: 0.

Table 10.8: Tall or short. Is the pattern tall or short? Just by looking at it, you can probably guess it is pint sized. A formation high of 27.15 and the head low at 24.74 gives a height-to-breakout price ratio of 8.93%. The chart pattern is, indeed, short. Score: –1. Running total: –4.

Table 10.9: Volume trend. Even as small as the pattern in Figure 10.8 appears, you can see that volume is trending downward. Score: +1. Running total: –3.

Table 10.10: Breakout volume. If you take out a magnifying glass, you can probably spot the breakout volume. It is average, scoring –1. Running total: –4.

Table 10.11: Throwbacks. The formation has a throwback that almost takes prices below the head. If that occurred, then the ultimate high would have been on the throwback hump, instead of in early January 1999. As mentioned previously, the corrective phase of a measured move down is a common resistance area, so a throwback was more likely. With further resistance at 29 from the downward spike in mid-June and another consolidation area not shown, we could expect a throwback. Score: –1. Running total: –5.

Table 10.12: Bull trap. Can you predict the bull trap that occurred? If so, then score that a –1. To be fair, I think a bull trap in this instance is difficult to predict. Remember, they only occur 9% of the time. Certainly there is resistance at 29, but is it strong enough to keep the stock down and send prices below the head low? I will score this one a +1 (trap not predicted), for a running total of –4.

Table 10.14: Market trend. Take my word for it, the S&P 500 Index was rising at the date of the left shoulder low compared to the right shoulder low. Score: +1 for a running total of –3.

Table 10.15: Market capitalization. Hughes Supply, using a breakout price of 26.90, fits into the small cap category, for a score of +1. Final total: –2.

With a negative score, the system predicted underperformance and the stock only climbed 8%. Investors in this building supply stock got, well, hosed. Had you correctly predicted a bull trap then the score would have dropped to –4, a stronger avoid signal.

11

Head-and-Shoulders Tops

If you ask any investor to name a chart pattern, he or she will probably say either double tops or head-and-shoulders. Investors may not know anything more than that about chart patterns, but those two patterns are the most well known. When I think of a head-and-shoulders top, my mind wanders to a wall outside my old office. There, I hung a picture of a head-and-shoulders top in the company's stock. I remember the stock suddenly rising above the surroundings, forming a head-and-shoulders top, then dropping just as swiftly back to the base from which it came. There is a lesson in that memory: a quick decline often follows a quick rise.

THE TYPICAL PATTERN

Figure 11.1 shows an example of a head-and-shoulders top. Prices begin their climb from 52.63 and rise to 80.13 before retracing a portion of the climb, leaving the left shoulder visible. The head forms at 84.44, a new high that towers above the left shoulder. The right shoulder appears at 79.50, quite close in price to the left shoulder high but below the head.

On the time line, the two shoulders are nearly symmetrical about the head. Usually the left shoulder shows the highest volume, followed by the head, and much diminished volume on the right shoulder.

Once prices *close* below the neckline, which is a line drawn connecting the two minor lows on either side of the head, the pattern confirms as a valid head-and-shoulders top. Only then should an investor get nervous because he holds

Figure 11.1   A head-and-shoulders top. Two shoulders flank the head in this chart pattern. Volume is usually higher on the left shoulder than the right.

stock in the company, or only then place a short sale to take advantage of the predicted decline.

Are there ways to choose head-and-shoulders tops that improve performance? Yes. Read on.

TREND START

One selection method that improves performance is to measure the price trend leading to the pattern. First, work backward from the left shoulder, moving downward in price, comparing the lowest found price with the current closing price. When prices rise by 20%, the lowest low marks the start of the trend. It may sound complicated but it is not: work backward and find the lowest low before a 20% trend change. Many times, you can find the trend start just by looking at the chart.

Once you have found where the trend begins, look at the distance from the trend start to the left shoulder high and compare it to Table 11.1. Head-and-shoulders tops with the best performance are those with a short-term price rise from the trend start to the left shoulder. The worst performance comes with long-term rises. Apparently, a long-term rise implies inherent upward strength, strength that a head-and-shoulders top cannot overcome for long.

Table 11.1
Average Performance of Head-and-Shoulders Tops
Sorted by Price Trend Leading to the Pattern

Trend Start to Formation Start	Result	Score
Short term (0 to 3 months)	–24% (225)	+1
Intermediate term (3 to 6 months)	–19% (130)	–1
Long term (over 6 months)	–18% (126)	–1

Note: The number of samples appears in parentheses.

The chart pattern shown in Figure 11.1, for example, has a trend that begins in mid-January. Prices drop to a low of 52.63 then rise to a close of 64.69 in early December 1997 (working backward). That represents a rise of 23% from the low to the close, signaling a trend change. The elapsed time from the trend start to the formation's left shoulder high is over 3 months, placing the up trend in the intermediate-term category.

I discuss the scores in the Scores section of this chapter, so ignore them for now.

HORIZONTAL CONSOLIDATION REGIONS

Table 11.2 shows the performance of head-and-shoulders tops when a support zone, which I call a horizontal consolidation region (HCR), intersects a declining price trend. In a moment, I show you what an HCR looks like, but, for now, the table shows that prices decline further when a support region is missing.

Figure 11.2 shows what an HCR looks like. Look for prices to form flat tops, flat bottoms, or both. These areas are the most likely support zones, regions where prices decline to but have trouble penetrating. The figure highlights two of them. In the first case during January 2000, a small symmetrical triangle with

Table 11.2
Average Performance of Head-and-Shoulders Tops
with and Without a Consolidation Region

Description	Result	Score
Consolidation region	–20% (406)	–1
No consolidation region	–25% (108)	+1
Average length (days)	40	
Prices stop within region ±5%	56%	
Prices push through region	35%	
Prices do not reach region	9%	

Note: The number of samples appears in parentheses.

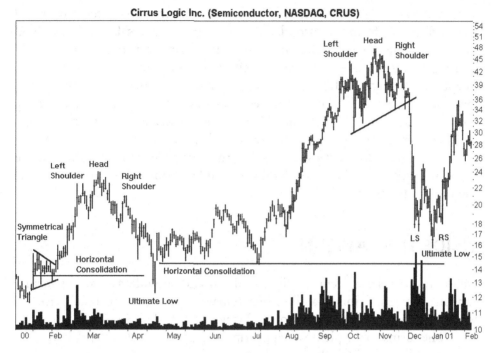

Cirrus Logic Inc. (Semiconductor, NASDAQ, CRUS)

Figure 11.2   An HCR. When a consolidation region appears between the neckline low and trend start, it can act as a support zone and stop any further decline. A symmetrical triangle (January 2000) and head-and-shoulders bottom (December) also appear on the chart.

a horizontal center (ignore the 3 downward spikes) acts as the bottom of a weak support zone.

In the second case, the HCR appears more pronounced, lasting from April through July. In December, prices approach the support region and recover by forming a small head-and-shoulders bottom.

The consolidation regions I examined averaged 40 days long. There is a wide variety, but look for a zone between the trend start and the formation low, one that is at least a week long with prices that touch or near a common price. If you spot a consolidation region before the trend start and want to consider using that, then do so. For simplicity, I allowed the consolidation area to span across the trend start, but that was as far back as I went.

How often do these areas support prices? Table 11.2 has the answer. In 9% of the cases, prices do not decline to the consolidation region at all; they reach the ultimate low somewhere above the region. In 56% of the cases, prices stop declining within 5% of the consolidation region. I include the 5% buffer because a number of patterns overshoot or undershoot the HCR a little before recovering. The mid-April decline in Figure 11.2 shows an example of over-shoot. The remainder of the time (35%) prices eventually push through the consolidation region and continue lower.

In researching chart patterns, I often see one trait that occurs over and over: Prices rise from a consolidation area, form a reversal, then retrace all their gains. This situation often happens in the diamond pattern, but it occurs with regularity in other patterns as well. The head-and-shoulders top is no exception, and Figure 11.2 shows what I am talking about. Look at the July to September quick rise leading to the head-and-shoulders top. Prices start rising from a base at about 14.50 and quickly climb to the head-and-shoulders reversal. Then, prices even more quickly drop back almost to where they started.

If you intend to short a stock, look for a chart pattern to form after a quick rise from a horizontal base. After a downward breakout, prices may fall all the way back to the base.

INSIDE THE PATTERN

Table 11.3 shows important findings for head-and-shoulders tops. Any formation that is unconfirmed—a close that remains above the breakout price—is not a valid head-and-shoulders top and is not included in this study.

The formation is plentiful, appearing 531 times in the stocks I looked at. If you question your identification of a head-and-shoulders top, then you might want to skip it and move on to the next one. After all, if you are having problems identifying it, others are too, and the formation may not perform as expected.

The average decline measured 21%, exactly matching the average decline for all bearish chart pattern types. I measured this from the breakout price to the ultimate low, without taking slippage, commissions, or other factors into consideration. As such, you should view the average decline as a best-case scenario, one you are unlikely to achieve.

From the breakout date to the ultimate low date for each formation, I measured the percentage change in the S&P 500 Index. Over that time, the index rose an average of 1%.

An unduly large value can skew the average, so I provide the median decline as well. I find the median value by sorting the declines and selecting the

Table 11.3
Important Statistical Findings

Description	Result
Number of formations	531
Average decline	21%
Standard & Poor's 500 change	+1%
Median decline	18%
Declines more than 50%	11/514 or 2%
Shoulder with highest volume	Left 69%

middle one so that half the values are below the median and half are above it. I consider it a value that many investors can approach if they trade often enough. In this case, I think the 18% median decline is probably unrealistic because it is too close to the *best-case* average decline of 21%.

Even though stocks rarely drop more than 50%, I use the value to judge how successful a bearish pattern can be. Only 11 or 2% of the formations I looked at declined by more than 50%. By comparison, head-and-shoulders *bottoms* have over a quarter of the patterns rising more than 50%.

Some people place an unduly heavy emphasis on volume. I do not. However, at times it can help with pattern identification. For head-and-shoulders tops, 69% of the time the left shoulder will show a higher volume pattern than the right shoulder. Since high volume can appear over a range of days and not at the exact top, I used the 5-day total of each shoulder, that is, 2 days before the shoulder top to 2 days after, to find the statistic.

NECKLINES AND SHOULDERS

The statistics in Table 11.4 are disappointing. Although the differences are statistically significant (except for the last two rows), the statistics are probably close enough not to worry about. However, they may give you a better guide to investment performance.

Is the neckline slope significant? Yes. Those formations having a horizontal or up-sloping neckline perform better than those with a down-sloping neckline. In case you are wondering what sloping necklines look like, Figure 11.3 shows a head-and-shoulders top with an up-sloping neckline, whereas Figure 11.4 shows a down-sloping neckline.

Table 11.4
Neckline Slope, Shoulders, and Volume

Description	Result	Score
Average decline of formations with up-sloping necklines	22% (261)	+1
Average decline of formations with horizontal necklines	22% (24)	+1
Average decline of formations with down-sloping necklines	20% (229)	−1
Average decline of formations with higher left shoulder highs	22% (214)	+1
Average decline of formations with even shoulder highs	20% (43)	0
Average decline of formations with higher right shoulder highs	19% (257)	−1
Average decline of formations with left shoulder volume above right shoulder	21% (356)	
Average decline of formations with left shoulder volume *below* right shoulder	20% (158)	

Note: The number of samples appears in parentheses.

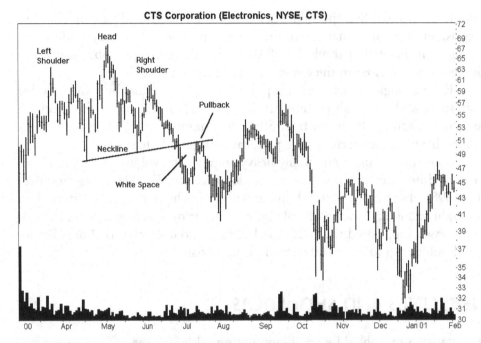

Figure 11.3 A pullback. A pullback occurs when prices return to the breakout price within 30 days, providing there is white space between the breakout point and the pullback low.

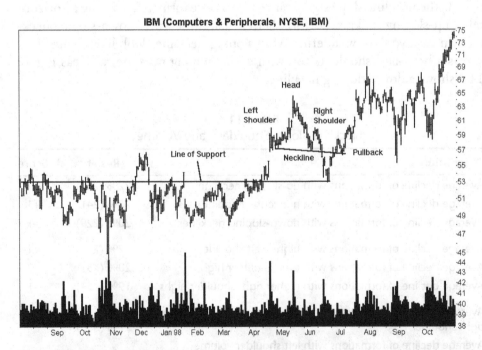

Figure 11.4 A bear trap. When prices drop less than 10%, then climb above the head, a bear trap occurs, snaring those investors that expected a sustained decline. Look for a flat base or other consolidation region below the chart pattern to act as an impenetrable support layer.

Comparing the high price of each shoulder, we find that those head-and-shoulders tops with a higher left shoulder peak show declines of 22%, but those with a higher right shoulder decline 19%, on average.

Regardless of which shoulder has higher volume, performance does not vary much. That is to say I found no statistical difference between shoulder volume (measured over 5 days: 2 days before to 2 days after the shoulder high) and performance.

FAILURE RATES

Table 11.5 shows the failure rate for a given price decline. I used a frequency distribution to count the number of formations according to how far prices declined. Thirty-two chart patterns (6%) showed declines of less than 5%, for example. Well over half the formations declined less than 20%.

Look how the failure rate increases as the maximum price decline rises. For those stocks declining less than 10%, the 5% failure rate triples to 18%; at a 15% price decline, the failure rate more than doubles to 39%. The numbers suggest that it is unlikely you will see a large decline, but be sure to protect yourself with stops just in case you own the stock.

Table 11.6 shows another type of failure rate: the horizon failure rate. I counted the number of chart patterns that were below the breakout price weekly for the first month, monthly for the first quarter, and at the end of 6 months. After 1 week, for example, 18% of the patterns were above the breakout price so they were failures. Over the same period, the average decline measured 5%.

Table 11.5
Maximum Price Decline Versus Failure Rate

Maximum Price Decline (%)	Failure Rate
5	32 or 6%
10	95 or 18%
15	198 or 39%
20	294 or 57%
25	354 or 69%
30	399 or 78%
35	444 or 86%
50	503 or 98%
75	514 or 100%
100	514 or 100%

Note: The sample count is 514 for each row.

Table 11.6
Horizon Failure Rates and Average Decline

Time Since Breakout	Failure Rate (%)	Average Decline (%)
1 week	18	5
2 weeks	21	5
3 weeks	20	6
1 month	23	7
2 months	34	7
3 months	38	7
6 months	43	5

As you scan the table, you can see that the failure rate remained in the low 20s during the first month, then shot up to 34% during month 2, and climbed to 43% at the end of 6 months. During this time, the average head-and-shoulders top continued to decline until sometime after month 3, when the average decline changed from 7% to 5%. The table suggests the need for patience because, after the first week, declines come gradually. Between months 3 and 6, the strength of the decline weakens and prices begin rebounding. Be prepared to close out your short position.

YEARLY PRICE RANGE

Table 11.7 shows the performance of head-and-shoulders tops after sorting by the breakout price in the yearly price range. I looked from the breakout date backward 1 year and found the highest high and lowest low over that span and split the range into thirds. Then, I placed the breakout price within one of the three ranges. The unremarkable performance is not statistically significant, meaning it could be due to chance, so it is not scored.

Table 11.7
Average Performance Sorted by Breakout Price
According to Prior 12-Month Range

Yearly Price Range	Result
Highest third	−20% (197)
Middle third	−21% (178)
Lowest third	−20% (49)

Note: The number of samples appears in parentheses.

Table 11.8
Performance of Short and Tall Head-and-Shoulders Tops

Description	Result	Score
Tall (above the median)	–24% (278)	+1
Short (below the median)	–18% (256)	–1
Median percentage of breakout price	17.65%	

Note: The number of samples appears in parentheses.

TALL AND SHORT PATTERNS

Table 11.8 shows the performance of head-and-shoulders tops after sorting by their height as a percentage of the breakout price. I measured from the high price at the head to the lowest low between the shoulders, then divided by the breakout price to find the formation height. Sorting the results and choosing the median value marked the difference between short and tall. I know this sounds complicated, but it really is not, and the results are worth the effort.

The table shows that tall patterns, those with heights above the median, have losses averaging 24%. This compares to an 18% decline for short patterns.

VOLUME TREND

Table 11.9 shows how the chart patterns performed if the volume trend was rising or falling from the left shoulder to the right shoulder. I measured the volume trend by performing linear regression on the data and looking at the slope of the resulting line. Linear regression is somewhat complicated, but many spreadsheets call it the trend function, so it is easy to use.

Those head-and-shoulders tops with a rising volume trend showed declines averaging 22% after the breakout. Those with a falling volume trend showed a statistically significant difference by declining just 20%.

Table 11.9
Linear Regression Volume Trend and Performance

Description	Result	Score
Rising volume trend	22% (201)	+1
Falling volume trend	20% (313)	–1

Note: The number of samples appears in parentheses.

Table 11.10
Breakout Volume and Performance

Description	Result
Average decline on above-average breakout volume	21.4% (127)
Average decline on average or below-average breakout volume	20.5% (387)

Note: The number of samples appears in parentheses.

BREAKOUT VOLUME

Table 11.10 shows how little breakout volume influences the depth of the decline. I computed an average volume and compared the breakout volume with the average (see Glossary and Methodology for more details). Those formations with high or very high breakout volume showed declines averaging 21.4%. When the volume was average, or below average, the declines measured 20.5%, a statistically insignificant difference.

PULLBACKS

What is the behavior of prices after the breakout? Table 11.11 provides some of the answers.

A pullback occurs within 30 days after a breakout, by conventional definition, and is when prices come very close to or return to the breakout price. A pullback is the same as a throwback but occurs after a downward breakout.

Figure 11.3 (page 228) shows a good example of a pullback. I have changed the definition of what I consider a valid pullback to include white space between the breakout price and prices as they curl around. Sometimes, prices will slide along the neckline for days or weeks before tumbling. I do not classify those as pullbacks. As in the figure, the white space should be obvious and the pullback should return to the breakout price within 30 days to qualify.

Why so much focus on pullbacks? For novice investors holding a stock, a pullback seems as if the downward breakout was false. Prices recover and there is little need to worry. Then, prices peak and begin heading down again. The novice investor—instead of selling near the top of the pullback—hangs on for the ride back down.

For seasoned investors, a pullback is another opportunity to make a short sale or add to a short position. If you own the stock, it gives you one last chance to sell it before the decline really begins.

Predicting whether a pullback will occur usually rests on how close a consolidation area is to the predicted price path. In other words, if prices are headed down and there is a significant consolidation region a few points below

Table 11.11
Pullback Statistics

Description	Result
Pullbacks	248 or 47%
Score if pullback predicted	−1
Score if pullback not predicted	+1
Ultimate low before pullback	85 or 16%
Average decline on above-average breakout volume with pullbacks	17%
Average decline on above-average breakout volume and no pullbacks	25%
Average decline on average or below-average breakout volume and pullbacks	20%
Average decline on average or below-average breakout volume and no pullbacks	21%
Number of pullbacks after a high or very high volume breakout	66/135 or 49%
Number of pullbacks after an average or below-average volume breakout	182/396 or 46%
Number of pullbacks that stopped less than 5% from the breakout price	176 or 71%
Number of pullbacks that stopped between the breakout and right shoulder high	48 or 19%
Number of pullbacks that stopped between right shoulder high and head	14 or 6%
Number of pullbacks that stopped above the head	10 or 4%

the bottom of the formation, then expect prices to bounce off the region and pull back to the breakout price. For head-and-shoulders tops, a pullback occurred 47% of the time.

In the chart patterns I looked at that had pullbacks, 16% of them reached the ultimate low before the pullback. That means prices completed a pullback and kept on rising. Of course, that is bad news if you shorted the stock. On the plus side, that situation does not happen very often.

The next several lines in the table (average declines) compare the breakout volume with the occurrence of pullbacks. For those stocks in which the breakout volume was above average and there was a pullback, the average stock declined 17%. Without a pullback, under the same conditions, the decline measured 25%. In short, *prices decline further without a pullback.*

Does the trend continue when the breakout volume is average or below average? Yes, with declines averaging 20% with a pullback and 21% when no pullback occurs.

Is a stock more likely to pull back after a high volume breakout? Yes, but the difference is narrow, at 49% versus 46%.

When a pullback occurs, where do prices stop climbing? Most, 71%, stop within 5% of the breakout price. Another 19% continue higher, stopping below the right shoulder high. An additional 6% move to the head and the remainder, 4%, rise above the highest high in the formation (the head).

These statistics suggest where to place a stop-loss order. A stop placed above the breakout price will work better than two out of three times, on average. A safer place is above the right shoulder high; that will only trigger 10% of the time but may be too far away from the breakout price. If you do get stopped out, your losses may be significant.

BEAR TRAPS

Table 11.12 shows how often bear traps occur. What is a bear trap? A bear trap is when prices break out downward, decline less than 10%, then climb above the highest high in the formation. That is my definition, at any rate, and it emphasizes the risk careless investors sometimes endure. After a downward breakout, investors short the stock and prices head down—for a time—until reaching a support level. Prices recover, pull back to the breakout price, and continue moving up. Those with short positions are caught in a death grip as prices spiral higher and their losses mount.

Figure 11.4 (page 228) shows what a bear trap looks like. The head-and-shoulders top has high volume on the left shoulder, diminished volume on the head, and even lower volume on the right shoulder—just the sort of pattern you would expect to see from well-behaved patterns. Prices break out on high volume but soon encounter a line of support. This support line stretched back to mid-July 1997—almost a year long. Prices touched the line briefly, as if the line were a bed of hot coals, then gapped higher and continued rising in a near straight-line advance, cresting at 64.66. Prices bobbed up and down with indecision and almost retreated back to the support line at 53 before restarting their stair-step climb to higher territory.

Returning to Table 11.12, you can see that bear traps are scarce, occurring just 17% of the time. Look for a support zone below the breakout point,

Table 11.12
Bear Traps

Description	Result
Bear trap frequency	89/531 or 17%
Score if trap predicted	–1
Score if trap not predicted	+1

Table 11.13
Gaps and Performance

Description	Result
Average decline after price gap on breakout	22% (114)
Average decline with no price gap on breakout	20% (400)

Note: The number of samples appears in parentheses.

like that shown in Figure 11.4. The support area need not be very long to cause trouble, sometimes just a week or two of flat prices (flat tops, flat bottoms, or both) will set up an impenetrable wall. Sometimes the zone is just a prior minor high but one with high volume; at other times, resistance created by a previous chart pattern will indicate a problem area.

GAPS

Table 11.13 shows the performance statistics related to gaps. First, what is a gap? Look back at Figure 11.1, which shows a good example of a breakaway gap the day prices closed below the breakout price. The gap measured 3.13— huge for a gap. Table 11.13 only concerns gaps that occurred on the day prices closed below the breakout price.

You can see that a gap sends prices lower by 22% versus 20% for those chart patterns not having a breakout day gap. Unfortunately, the differences are not statistically significant, meaning that they may be due to chance, so I do not provide a score.

MARKET TREND

For many chart patterns, we have seen that a rising market helps to lift bullish stocks; a falling market tends to send stock prices lower. For head-and-shoulders tops, the influence is limited. When the chart pattern is under construction and the general market is rising, the average decline after the breakout is 20.86%. This compares with a decline averaging 20.51% for those patterns in which the market was falling while the pattern was under construction. The same trend applies from the formation end to the ultimate low.

Why a rising general market would send a stock's price lower is a mystery to me, but since the differences are not statistically significant, they are probably due to chance.

Table 11.14
Average Price Performance of Head-and-Shoulders
Tops During a Rising and Falling Market

Market Trend	FS to FE	FE to UL
Rising S&P 500	−20.86% (342)	−21.81% (200)
Falling S&P 500	−20.51% (172)	−20.05% (314)

Note: FS = formation start, FE = formation end, UL = ultimate low. The number of samples appears in parentheses.

MARKET CAPITALIZATION

Table 11.15 shows the performance of stocks after a head-and-shoulders top, sorted by market capitalization. I base market capitalization on the breakout price multiplied by the number of shares outstanding. The trend is clear: Small caps perform best while large caps perform worst. Putting it optimistically, large caps hold up best in a falling market. Keep that in mind during the next bear market.

SCORES

How do you use the scoring system? The case studies that follow give examples that make the process clear. Essentially, you score your chart pattern according to the information provided in each table, then add the scores together. Scores above zero suggest performance that will beat the median decline; scores below zero suggest underperformance. There are no guarantees, but Table 11.16 shows a study of the system's performance.

Those chart patterns with scores above zero, representing the sell-short signals, showed declines averaging 25%. This statistic compares to a 16% average decline for those head-and-shoulders tops with scores below zero—the "avoid selling short" signals. As an additional measure of how well the system

Table 11.15
Average Price Performance of Head-and-Shoulders
Tops by Market Capitalization

Capitalization	Result	Score
Small cap (up to $1 billion)	−22% (213)	+1
Mid cap ($1 to $5 billion)	−21% (192)	0
Large cap (over $5 billion)	−19% (106)	−1

Note: The number of samples appears in parentheses.

Table 11.16
Formation Performance by Score

Score	Result (%)
Average decline of chart patterns with scores above zero	25
Average decline of chart patterns with scores below zero	16
Median decline used	17.37
Percentage with scores above zero beating median decline	65
Percentage with scores below zero doing worse than median decline	65

works, I compared the sell-short and avoid-selling-short signal results with the median decline. Those chart patterns with scores above zero had declines beating the median 17.37% decline 65% of the time. With scores below zero, meaning to avoid shorting, the system correctly anticipated poor performance 65% of the time (the decline was smaller than the median decline). In short, the system adds value in about two out of three trades.

CASE STUDY 1

Look at the head-and-shoulders top pictured in Figure 11.5. That is the stock I discuss in this case study. First, the fundamentals. In June 1996, the semi-conductor industry's book-to-bill ratio rose in May after falling since January, a sign that chip pricing and demand in the United States were beginning to rebound. After June, the ratio climbed steadily until hitting 1.15 in November. A book-to-bill ratio greater than 1.00 suggests chip orders were growing, a bad indicator if you intend to short a semiconductor stock such as Cirrus.

In July, the company reported a loss on slowing sales. In August, you read of a money manager that shorted the stock. Also in August, an alliance of 36 chip makers announced plans to develop 'systems on a chip' technology. Cirrus is one of them.

In September, shares of memory chip manufacturers rose after analysts forecasted that prices of semiconductors used in personal computers had stabilized. Chips used in PCs are a key market for the company.

In October, a brokerage firm raised its rating of the stock to buy from neutral. The quarterly report said the company earned money on shrinking sales, but the profit was a surprise as the consensus estimate was for a loss. The Semiconductor Industry Association forecast that fourth quarter semiconductor sales would grow 3.5%.

These few fundamental factors sound bullish to me, on balance, but you need to do more in-depth research before considering shorting a company. Although the fundamental news is positive, the technical situation sometimes

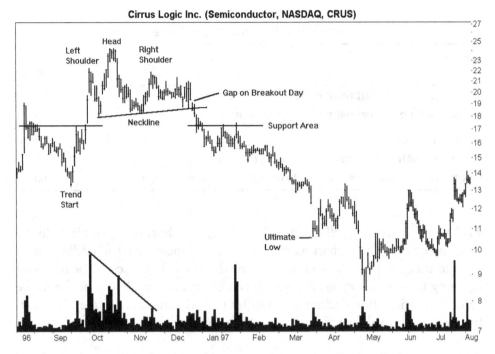

Figure 11.5 A head-and-shoulders top in a semiconductor stock. Do you risk shorting the stock?

tells a different story, a story suggesting the bullish outlook is not what it seems. What about the technical side?

You know from experience that shorting a stock making new highs is a recipe for disaster, but a stock making new lows is the way to profitability. You look back a year ago and see that Cirrus was trading at 42 in November 1995 after having peaked at 61.13 in September, along with most other semiconductor stocks. Cirrus is not at its yearly low, 12.63, that much is clear from Figure 11.5 (assume everything to the right of the breakout date is blank). The breakout price is 19.13.

To evaluate the head-and-shoulders top, let us run through those tables with scores.

Table 11.1 lists performance measured from the trend start to the formation. You look at the chart and guess that the trend starts in September at a *low* of 13.25. A 20% rise from this price is almost 16, a *closing* price reached about 2 weeks before (I use the lowest low to the daily close as the measure for a trend change). The rise means a trend change and that you have found the correct trend start. The climb from the trend start to the formation start (the left shoulder high) is less than a month, falling into the short-term category according to the table. Score: +1.

Table 11.2 suggests checking for a consolidation region between the trend start and the formation low. In our case, there is no HCR to slow the descent, so the score increases by 1 to +2.

Buried in the discussion of Table 11.2 is a mention of quick rises. The quick rise from the trend start to the formation is steep, but it does not spring from a flat base. Still, expect that prices will retrace all their gains, which means a decline to 13 is a real possibility. That represents a 32% drop from the breakout price.

Table 11.4 lists performance for neckline slope and shoulder price levels. Recall that the neckline is a trendline connecting the minor lows that form between the shoulders. In Figure 11.5, the neckline slopes upward, scoring +1. That gives a running total of +3.

When the left shoulder high is higher than the right shoulder high, as in this case, that merits a +1 score, too. The thinking behind this is that a lower right shoulder denotes an especially weak technical situation. If prices cannot climb as far as they did in the recent past, then there is a better chance that they will fall further when the decline comes. Running total: +4.

Is the chart pattern short or tall? First, compute the formation height from the head to the lowest low in the pattern. The head is at 24.25 and the lowest low (the minor low on the left) is at 18, for a height of 6.25. Expressing the height as a percentage of the breakout price (19.13) is 33%, well above the 17.65% median height from Table 11.8. Score +1 as this pattern is tall. Running total: +5.

Is volume trending upward or downward? I make this easy by showing the down-sloping volume trend in Figure 11.5. Table 11.9 scores this trend as −1. Running total: +4.

Will a pullback occur? According to Table 11.11, a pullback occurs almost half the time, usually after touching a support zone. If I were the one selling this stock short, I would guess that a pullback would occur after declining to 17. Why? You cannot see it in Figure 11.5, but in February 1996 there was a nearly horizontal consolidation region with a bottom at 17, which lasted over 2 months. In late June, early August, and again in September, prices hesitated briefly at 17, as illustrated in Figure 11.5 by the horizontal line in August through September.

One factor against a pullback occurring is the quick rise mentioned in the Table 11.2 discussion. A quick decline often follows a quick rise, implying no pullback. Even though no pullback actually occurred, let us assume a −1 score because one seems to be predicted. That would leave a running total of +3.

Table 11.12 shows the bear trap frequency. Since a trap only happens 17% of the time, and since the factors predicting a pullback were mixed at best, my guess would be that a bear trap would not occur. For a trap to happen, prices must decline less than 10%, then soar above the chart pattern high (the head, in this case). With the quick rise implying a quick decline, I suggest a bull run pushing prices vastly higher would be quite unlikely. No bear trap rates a score of +1 for a running total of +4.

Cirrus Logic is a mid cap stock at the breakout price of 19.13, which rates a score of zero in Table 11.5, for a final total of +4. A score above zero means that you should consider trading the stock. In this case, a short sale could prove profitable, but I must warn you that a positive score is no guarantee of profit. Even if the stock does decline, you could flub your entry, botch your exit, and pay big bucks to your full-service broker, leaving you with a loss for your trouble.

How did the trade go? Figure 11.5 shows the result. Prices declined from the 19.13 breakout price through the 17 support area, then attempted to pull back, but the same area that showed support at 17 now acted as resistance. Prices touched 17 twice but failed to penetrate very far. Soon, the stock was heading down again.

On the fundamental side, there were factors helping the stock down. In mid-January the book-to-bill ratio for December was 1.10, down from a revised 1.16. Five days later, the company reported earnings that fell well short of the consensus estimate. Analysts started revising their earnings estimates downward. Year-over-year worldwide chip sales fell. In early February, reports surfaced of insider selling.

The stock reached its ultimate low on March 17, at a low of 10.63, or 44% below the breakout price. From the low, the stock recovered to close at 13, more than a 20% rise, signaling the end of the down trend (at least for statistical purposes). But the decline was not really over. Prices tumbled again and reached a new yearly low of 8 before a sustained rally ensued. Had you traded this stock perfectly, and weathered the rise in April from the March low, you would have made 58%.

CASE STUDY 2

Figure 11.6 illustrates this case study. Let us run through the tables to check the likelihood of superior performance.

Table 11.1: Trend start. The trend start occurred at the lower of the two downward spikes in October, placing the trend rise into the intermediate-term category. Score: –1.

Table 11.2: Horizontal consolidation region. An HCR appears as the base of a right-angled, ascending, broadening formation. The base of this formation touches or nearly touches 10, a whole number at which investors commonly place stops. Score: –1 for a running total of –2.

Table 11.4: Necklace shape. The neckline is very steep, sloping downward and scoring –1. The left shoulder high is higher than the right one, scoring +1 and leaving the running total unchanged at –2.

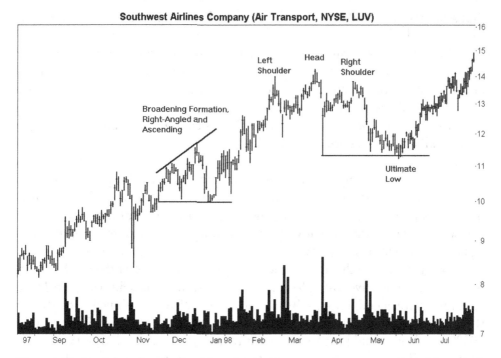

Figure 11.6 A head-and-shoulders top with a negative score. A right-angled, ascending, broadening formation forms a horizontal consolidation area, potentially supporting prices.

Table 11.8: Short or tall. The head is at 14.25, the lowest low is at 11.33, and the breakout price is 11.33, for a height to breakout ratio of 26%, which is well above the median for a +1 score. Running total: –1.

Table 11.9: Volume trend. From Figure 11.6 it seems clear that volume is heavier on the left side of the formation than on the right, and linear regression from the dates of the left shoulder high to the right shoulder high confirms this. Score: –1. Running total: –2.

Table 11.11: Pullback. Is a pullback predicted? We have a support zone at 10 to 11 with a flat base and irregular tops. Betting that a pullback will occur because of this zone is a smart move. Score: –1. Running total: –3.

Table 11.12: Bear trap. What about a bear trap? Again, if prices decline to 10, that places the decline at nearly 12%, beyond the 10% maximum. The 10% maximum decline for a bear trap is an arbitrary limit, but one that suggests anything larger and you should be able to close out your short with a profit. Also, should prices drop to 10, they would need to climb above the formation high to qualify as a bear trap. Such a rise would mean a massive climb of 43%. The likelihood of a bear trap occurring is just 17%, so I would argue that a bear trap is unlikely. The absence of a bear trap means a +1 score for a running total of –2.

As you look at Figure 11.6, you can see that just the reverse occurred. A throwback did not occur because of the lack of white space between the break-out price and ultimate low, but a bear trap occurred when prices rebounded and climbed above the formation top.

Table 11.15: Market capitalization. The stock is a small cap, and the table gives small caps a +1 score. Final total: –1.

A negative total suggests underperformance. The stock dipped to a low of just 11.22, or 1% below the breakout price, well short of the 17.37% median decline, as predicted. Although it is not clear from the figure, prices did *close* below the lowest formation low (represented by the horizontal line), thereby signaling a downward breakout.

Had you shorted the stock at the closing price the day after the breakout and held it, you would have lost 29%. In other words, the stock climbed from 11.61 to 14.92 before encountering a 20% trend change. If you continued to hold your short position, your losses would grow as the stock climbed to 23.58, for a tidy 103% loss. You would have lost your entire investment and still owed your broker money. Think about that the next time you consider shorting a stock.

CASE STUDY 3

When I wrote *Encyclopedia of Chart Patterns* (Wiley, 2000), I said that you need not wait for confirmation if you *knew* the formation was a head-and-shoulders top and you owned shares in the company. You could sell anytime after the right shoulder peak. That statement is true providing you are confident of your assessment. If prices do not fall to the breakout price, then you will be throwing away profits when prices rise above your sell point.

For most people and for most chart patterns, waiting for confirmation is the right thing to do. If you want to sell your shares before confirmation, run an analysis of the pattern and compute its score. If the score is above zero, then sell immediately. If the score is below zero, meaning that the formation is likely to underperform (but no guarantee), then consider holding on with the expectation that prices will decline; just hope that they do not go down too far.

If you want to short a stock, wait for confirmation unless the fundamentals look exceedingly bad and there is reason to expect a decline. Just because the fundamentals suggest the company is heading toward bankruptcy, in your opinion, is not an impediment to a buyout specialist offering to grab the company on the cheap.

Figure 11.7 shows the same stock as the prior case study, but a different situation. Here are my notes from the trade.

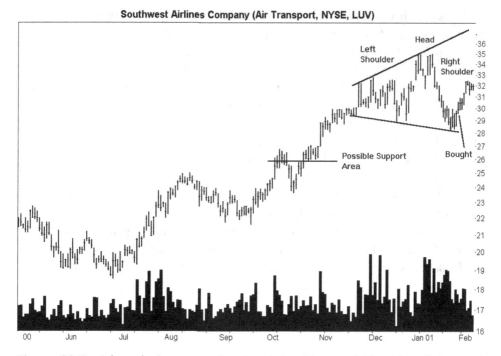

Figure 11.7 A broadening top or head-and-shoulders top? Should I sell the stock immediately or hope that prices resume their climb to the broadening-top boundary?

"1/28/01. I bought at the market on a broadening-top formation with prices at the lower trendline, but moving up. The company is successfully hedging fuel costs. I expect oil prices to decline, the Federal Reserve to ease interest rates next week [which they did], and the economy to slowly rebound. The broadening top scores −1, assuming an upward breakout, 0 for a downward breakout. Not a compelling situation, but I am buying early, before the breakout, playing an intraformation trade. I expect a partial rise with downside breakout. Upside is formation top at 35, downside is stop loss at 27.30, call it 27.25, for a 10% decline. If it closes below 28, that is a sell signal. Dump immediately. Filled at 30.39."

The intent of the trade was to buy near the bottom of the broadening top—once prices started climbing—and sell near the top, pocketing the difference between the two trades. If prices pierced the top of the broadening top, then that would be a plus and reason to hold the stock longer, hoping the −1 score was inaccurate.

A week or two into the trade, prices stalled at about 32, as shown in the figure, looking suspiciously like the right shoulder of a head-and-shoulders top. Alternatively, prices could eventually continue up in a measured move stair-step pattern and touch 35. The general market was weak, with the technology sector being battered. A slowing economy means fewer business travelers will take to the skies. However, as a low-fare operation, the company may end up acquiring market share from other, higher priced, competitors.

If prices do round over and head down, then a partial rise from the broadening top would be a negative. The stock would be a sell candidate, with a downside breakout predicted. It could also mean that the stock is a head-and-shoulders top, with a complex left shoulder.

If the stock moves lower, what type of performance can we expect from the head-and-shoulders top? Running through the tables gives a +1 score, suggesting it is wise to sell a holding. That is what I did. Here is my notebook entry. "2/12/01. I sold at 31.18 because of partial rise on a broadening top. Since I believe this is going down, there is no sense to wait for it to close below 28 before dumping. I made a small profit, about 2.5%."

The stock continued lower from a split-adjusted sell price of 20.79 to a low of 16, a drop of 23%, above the 17.37% median decline correctly predicted by the scoring system for a head-and-shoulders top.

12

Rectangles

When a chart pattern fails to perform up to expectations, what do novice investors blame? Identification. Perhaps they are right. You would think that rectangles, with their flat tops and bottoms, would be easy to pick out of a historical price trend. That would be true if all rectangles were perfect, with no solitary peaks poking through the trendlines, with straight, horizontal price boundaries. Examples purporting to be rectangles are commonly far from perfect, though, making good examples rare.

There are four varieties of rectangles: Tops with up and down breakouts and bottoms with up and down breakouts. Tops have prices entering the pattern from the bottom, whereas bottoms have prices entering from the top. Since this book deals with *classic* chart patterns, I collapsed my arbitrary tops and bottoms definition back into the generic *rectangles*. I make no distinction between tops and bottoms. However, there were not enough samples to catalog anything but rectangles with upward breakouts, and even then I had trouble finding the pesky critters.

THE TYPICAL PATTERN

Figure 12.1 shows what a rectangle looks like. Prices started the upward trend with a large, one-day reversal bottom in early April, climbed to an old resistance level at 28.38, and moved sideways—forming the rectangle—bounded on the top and bottom by invisible resistance and support zones.

When prices pierced the top trendline, a breakout occurred. About half the time, prices throw back to the breakout price but not in this case. With the breakaway gap, prices had enough upward momentum to gap again, this time

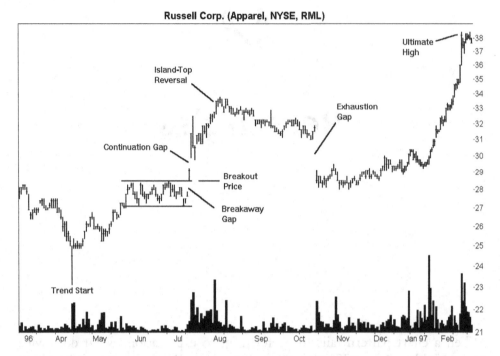

Figure 12.1 A rectangle with upward breakout. A high volume, large downward spike—called a one-day reversal—marks the start of the upward price trend in April. Prices enter the rectangle from the bottom and shoot out the top in a break-away gap on high volume. Continuation and exhaustion gaps set off the island top.

a continuation gap that also showed high volume. Prices backpedaled for a few days before resuming the uptrend at a more leisurely pace.

In mid-October, prices gapped downward, this time an exhaustion gap, leaving behind an island-top reversal. Prices slowly recovered from the brisk tumble and meandered upward, eventually closing the gap and making a new high. Prices reached the ultimate high in mid-February just 2 months before dead-cat bouncing down to 25, a decline of 35%.

TREND START

Table 12.1 shows the average performance from rectangles, sorted by the preceding price trend. To find the trend start, search backward beginning from the rectangle start, and look for a 20% price trend change. If prices decline away from the rectangle start (again, moving backward in time), after the trend change, prices should rise. A 20% rise, measured from the lowest low to the close, signals that you found the trend start. If prices rise leading away from the rectangle, then you will be looking for a peak before prices drop more than 20%, measured from the highest high to the close.

Table 12.1
Average Performance of Rectangles Sorted
by Price Trend Leading to the Pattern

Trend Start to Formation Start	Result	Score
Short term (0 to 3 months)	39% (165)	+1
Intermediate term (3 to 6 months)	42% (54)	+1
Long term (over 6 months)	23% (37)	−1

Note: The number of samples appears in parentheses.

Having found the trend start, compute the time between the trend start and the formation start, then use Table 12.1 to gauge the expected performance.

As you can see in the table, the best performance comes from rectangles with price trends that last between 3 and 6 months, scoring rises averaging 42%. The short term (up to 3 months) follows close behind, with rises after the breakout measuring 39%, and the long term does worst, gaining just 23%. For long-term trends leading to the rectangle, it is as if the stock appears tired, nearing its end. Prices continue rising, sure, but missing the enthusiasm that accompanied the early days, and the trend ends shortly thereafter.

Ignore the scores for now; I discuss them later.

HORIZONTAL CONSOLIDATION REGIONS

At this point in the chapter, I would regale you with tales of horizontal consolidation regions—resistance zones positioned above the chart pattern. Unfortunately, there were too few chart patterns with prices descending into the pattern and exiting upward to make a statistically sound sampling.

INSIDE THE PATTERN

Turn your attention to Table 12.2, which shows important statistical findings. I unearthed 305 rectangles with upward breakouts, substantially more than I found when doing research for *Encyclopedia of Chart Patterns* (Wiley, 2000). The new patterns help place the results on a firmer statistical foundation.

The average rise is 37%, as measured from the breakout price (the top trendline) to the ultimate high. This is a good showing for a classic chart pattern. The result does not include any trading cost, and should be viewed as the best-case basis because it assumes an investor buys at the breakout price and sells at the highest high before a 20% trend change.

Table 12.2
Important Statistical Findings

Description	Result
Number of formations	305
Average rise	37%
Standard & Poor's 500 change	6%
Median rise	29%
Rises more than 50%	78/272 or 29%

From the day the rectangle breakout occurred to the day prices reached the ultimate high, I compared the price change in the S&P 500 Index using those dates. On average, the S&P climbed by 6%, one of the more robust showings for the index. However, the 6% rise pales in comparison with the 37% average rise from rectangles.

The median rise measures 29%. I sorted the rises and chose the median or midrange value. The median is a number in which half the values are above the median and half below. As such, I think it gives an investor a more realistic target, one that a good trader should be able to achieve over time.

To show the opportunity to score outsized gains, listed are the number of rises of more than 50%. For rectangles, this turned out to be 29%, placing rectangles second from the top of the pack, compared to other chart pattern types. Only descending triangles with upward breakouts do better.

FAILURE RATES

Table 12.3 shows the failure rate for rectangles compared with the maximum price rise. It begins with the 5% failure rate. To explain, I grouped rectangles with gains of less than 5% before encountering a 20% trend change. There were 27 of them, representing 10% of the rectangles. Another group, those rising less than 10%, numbered 52 or 19%. You can see in the table why the 29% median rise falls in the middle of the group, and that the average rise, at 37% (from Table 12.2), is harder to reach (about 60% do not make it). If you want to double your money, be aware that only 13% make the cut (87% fail).

Why is Table 12.3 important? Suppose you wanted to make 25% from your trading. What percentage of rectangles fail to rise more than 25%? The answer: 43% or almost half will fall short of your expectations. When you factor in trading costs, such as commissions, slippage, and taxes, you might want to boost the return to 30% or 35%. With a 35% maximum price rise, more than half your trades (58%) will fail to meet your goal.

Table 12.3
Maximum Price Rise Versus Failure Rate

Maximum Price Rise (%)	Failure Rate
5	27 or 10%
10	52 or 19%
15	75 or 28%
20	101 or 37%
25	118 or 43%
30	142 or 52%
35	159 or 58%
50	193 or 71%
75	227 or 83%
100	237 or 87%

Note: The sample count is 272 for each row.

Table 12.4 puts the failure rate into a different perspective. I computed the horizon failure rate by counting the number of chart patterns in which the closing price is below the breakout price a set time in the future. For example, 1 week after the breakout, 19% of the chart patterns had declined below the breakout price, but the average rise was 4%. At the end of 2 weeks, the failure rate had climbed to 21%, but more stocks climbed higher than declined, boosting the average rise to 5%.

You can see in the table that the failure rate is quite stable for the first month then climbs and seems to level off in the low 30% range. During that time, the average rise climbs steadily until reaching 15% after 6 months, one of the best performances I have seen. To put this in perspective, the average rise nearly quadruples for a 63% increase in failures.

Table 12.4
Horizon Failure Rates and Average Rise

Time Since Breakout	Failure Rate (%)	Average Rise (%)
1 week	19	4
2 weeks	21	5
3 weeks	23	6
1 month	22	7
2 months	27	8
3 months	31	10
6 months	31	15

Table 12.5
Performance of Partial Declines

Description	Result	Score
Partial decline correctly predicts upside breakout	80/113 or 71%	
Performance after a partial decline	34%	−1
Performance without a partial decline	37%	+1
Intraformation partial decline frequency	33/113 or 29%	

PARTIAL DECLINES

Table 12.5 shows the results of a study of partial declines. Before I discuss the results, take a look at Figure 12.2, a good example of a partial decline.

Figure 12.2 shows a partial decline in a rectangle. A partial decline occurs when prices retreat from the top trendline and approach, but do not touch, the bottom trendline. A partial decline is a good hint that prices will break out

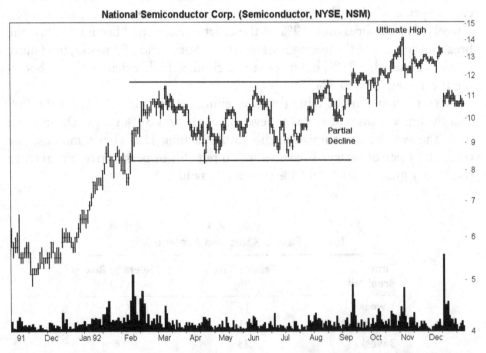

Figure 12.2   A partial decline. Prices tag the top trendline, drop toward the lower rectangle trendline, curl around, and struggle to push through the top trendline, staging an upward breakout. A partial decline correctly predicts an upward break-out 71% of the time.

upward. To correctly identify a partial decline, first look for a rectangle. The rectangle must be established, meaning that there must be at least two touches of each trendline (that is, two distinct minor highs and two distinct minor lows). Only after the second touch of each trendline can you expect a partial decline. Prices must touch the top trendline, then decline, but not come too close to the bottom trendline. Buy the stock once it is clear that prices are rising again.

Returning to Table 12.5, 71% of the rectangles with partial declines correctly predicted an upward breakout. I included the results from rectangles with up and down breakouts to get a correct reading of the failure rate.

Although a partial decline can alert you to the possibility of an upward breakout, the resulting performance of the rectangle after a partial decline is slightly below average, at 34%. This statistic compares to a 37% average rise for those rectangles without partial declines, following the trend I have seen for other chart patterns. It is as if a partial decline takes energy away from the upward momentum; instead of breaking out immediately, prices retrace, curl around, then break out. The human equivalent may be something like taking one step backward for every few forward as you shop the grocery aisle.

Sometimes a partial decline occurs within the rectangle itself and does not result in an immediate breakout. I call these intraformation partial declines. To an investor, they look like a regular partial decline, but when prices reach the top trendline, they head back down and continue bouncing between the trendlines. Intraformation partial declines occur 29% of the time in the rectangles with up and down breakouts that I looked at. Again, before an intraformation partial decline may occur, the rectangle must have two distinct touches of each trendline. In other words, the rectangle must be a valid chart pattern.

YEARLY PRICE RANGE

Table 12.6 shows how placement in the yearly price range affects performance. To find the results, I located the highest high and lowest low looking back 1

Table 12.6
Average Performance Sorted by Breakout Price
According to Prior 12-Month Range

Yearly Price Range	Result	Score
Highest third	35% (165)	−1
Middle third	41% (52)	+1
Lowest third	42% (20)	+1

Note: The number of samples appears in parentheses.

year from the breakout date. Then, I split the yearly price range into thirds and assigned the breakout price to one of the three categories.

When the breakout price was near the yearly low, the rectangles tended to perform the best, showing rises averaging 42%. This compares to a gain of just 35% when the breakout happened near the yearly high.

I consider the results to be unusual because many chart patterns with upward breakouts show the best performance when the breakout occurs near the yearly high, which is what upward momentum is all about. Buy high, sell higher. It may be that there were more rectangle bottoms (they appear after a downward price trend) occurring than tops in the study.

TALL AND SHORT PATTERNS

I uncovered the significance of tall and short patterns after thinking how shy this chapter was with tables of information that you can use to score a chart pattern. I first checked to see if long rectangles performed better than short ones. Some analysts will tell you that a large chart pattern is more powerful than a small one, but when I looked at other chart pattern types, I found no statistical difference. For rectangles, I reasoned that they might act like coiled springs. The longer the rectangle, the tighter wound it would become, and the larger the resulting rise. The performance differences between large and small rectangles turn out to be statistically insignificant.

So, I checked the rectangle height. There was a huge, statistically significant difference in performance between the tall boys and the vertically challenged. Table 12.7 shows the results. I computed the rectangle height as a percentage of the breakout price and sorted the results, then used the median value, 11.24%, as the dividing line between tall and short. The table shows that short rectangles score gains averaging 27%, whereas those over the median height show gains of 50%. Thus, tall rectangles perform better than short ones.

Table 12.7
Performance of Short and Tall Rectangles

Description	Result	Score
Tall (above the median)	50% (136)	+1
Short (below the median)	27% (136)	−1
Median percentage of breakout price	11.24%	

Note: The number of samples appears in parentheses.

Table 12.8
Linear Regression Volume Trend and Performance

Description	Result
Rising volume trend	37% (86)
Falling volume trend	36% (186)

Note: The number of samples appears in parentheses.

VOLUME TREND

Table 12.8 shows the volume trend from the formation start to its end, and the resulting performance of the associated rectangle. Those rectangles with a rising volume trend showed gains of 37% compared to a 36% rise when the volume trend was falling. The results are not statistically significant, meaning they may be due to chance, so are not scored.

BREAKOUT VOLUME

Table 12.9 shows the performance results after the breakout for rectangles sorted by their breakout volume. I used the breakout volume compared to the prior 3-month average to determine one of five volume levels: very high, high, average, low, and very low. Combining the volume levels into two groups, above average and average or below gave enough samples to make the comparison statistically significant.

You can see in the table that those rectangles accompanied by a high volume breakout showed rises averaging 47%. Those with average or below-average breakout volume soared just 32%. For the best average performance, *invest in rectangles showing a high volume breakout.*

Table 12.9
Breakout Volume and Performance

Description	Result	Score
Average rise on above-average breakout volume	47% (100)	+1
Average rise on average or below-average breakout volume	32% (172)	−1

Note: The number of samples appears in parentheses.

THROWBACKS

Table 12.10 shows the results of a study of throwbacks. A throwback occurs when prices break out upward then return to the breakout price within 30 days. The 30-day time limit is an arbitrary one, but one that is commonly recognized. If prices return to the breakout price *after* 30 days, then it is considered normal price action and not a throwback. There should also be white space between prices and the rectangle, assuring that investors can recognize the hooking action of a throwback and discard those breakouts in which prices slide along the top rectangle trendline before climbing.

Figure 12.3 shows an example of a throwback. Within days after the breakout, prices rounded over and returned to the breakout price. Instead of rebounding upward at that point, prices continued down until finding support at the prior minor low. After that, it was off to the races as prices climbed in a stair-step manner on their way to the ultimate high.

Table 12.10
Throwback Statistics

Description	Result
Throwbacks	156 or 51%
Score if throwback predicted	−1
Score if throwback not predicted	+1
Ultimate high before throwback	35 or 11%
Average rise on above-average breakout volume with throwbacks	42%
Average rise on above-average breakout volume with no throwbacks	52%
Average rise on average or below-average breakout volume with throwbacks	26%
Average rise on average or below-average breakout volume with no throwbacks	40%
Number of throwbacks after a high or very high volume breakout	55/110 or 50%
Number of throwbacks after an average, low, or very low volume breakout	101/195 or 52%
Number of throwbacks that stopped ±5% from the breakout price	118 or 76%
Number of throwbacks that stopped between rectangle trendlines	25 or 16%
Number of throwbacks that stopped below the rectangle	13 or 8%

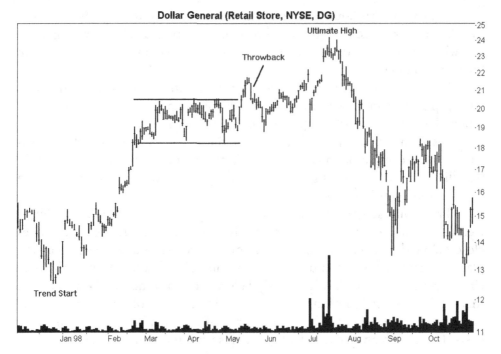

Figure 12.3 A rectangle throwback. Prices return to the breakout price within 30 days, with good white space, qualifying the action as a throwback.

Table 12.10 shows statistics related to throwbacks. A throwback occurs just over half the time, 51%. This result is not high enough on which to base a trading rule, such as wait for the throwback before buying.

To protect yourself against a throwback, look for overhead resistance. Is there a horizontal consolidation region above the rectangle? How about a prior chart pattern hiding on a nearby top? Consult Chapter 3 on Support and Resistance for more ideas on how to tell if prices stand a good chance of throwing back.

How often do prices find the ultimate high before throwing back? That situation occurs just 11% of the time, probably not enough to worry about . . . unless, of course, it happens to you!

How do breakout volume and throwbacks influence performance? I computed the average volume leading to the breakout and compared it to five volume categories: very high, high, average, low, and very low. When breakout volume was above average and a throwback occurred, the average stock climbed 42% compared to a 52% rise without a throwback.

Making the same comparison after an average or below-average volume breakout, with and without throwbacks, gives consistent results. When a throwback occurred after a meager volume breakout, the stocks averaged a 26% rise. Without a throwback, prices climbed 40%. Clearly, *a high volume breakout is preferable to a low volume one, and no throwback is preferable to a throwback.*

Does a low breakout volume mean a throwback is more likely to occur? Yes, but not by much. When the breakout volume was above average, the throwback rate was 50%, compared to 52% for average or below-average breakout volume.

After a throwback occurs, where do prices stop falling? Most of the time (76%), prices drop to within 5% of the breakout price, then rebound. The rebound may not take prices up much, but it is enough to signal that the throwback has completed. In another 16% of the cases, the throwback stopped within the rectangle boundaries, which is to say, between the two rectangle trendlines. In the remaining 8%, prices dropped below the lower rectangle trendline and continued down.

The results suggest that a stop-loss order placed slightly below the lower trendline will protect you from a massive loss 92% of the time. If prices close below the lower trendline, then you should sell immediately. If a stop placed below the lower trendline would mean a significant loss from the purchase price, then place a stop slightly below the top trendline. Not only will this cut the potential loss but it should work in three out of four trades. Sometimes placing the stop just below the price of a nearby minor low will work best—far enough away not to be hit but close enough to minimize losses.

BULL TRAPS

Table 12.11 shows how often bull traps occur. I define a bull trap as when prices break out upward but climb less than 10% before tumbling and falling below the lower rectangle boundary. This scenario is called a bull trap because those bullish investors who buy the stock on the breakout are corralled and headed for slaughter as prices drop into loss territory. They are trapped in the chutes with just one way to go: down.

You can defend yourself against a bull trap by searching for overhead resistance. Look for price congestion, where prices seem to congregate at the same level. Flat tops, flat bottoms, or both mark horizontal consolidation regions that could spell trouble to a price advance. Prior chart patterns, minor

Table 12.11
Bull Traps

Description	Result
Bull trap frequency	49/305 or 20%
Score if trap predicted	−1
Score if trap not predicted	+1

Table 12.12
Gaps and Performance

Description	Result	Score
Average rise after price gap on breakout	42% (58)	+1
Average rise with no price gap on breakout	35% (214)	−1

Note: The number of samples appears in parentheses.

highs, and minor lows also indicate resistance areas. Review Chapter 3 on Support and Resistance for more information.

A bull trap occurred just 20% of the time in the rectangles I looked at.

GAPS

Table 12.12 lists the performance of stocks after a price gap on the breakout day, and Figure 12.1 shows a good example of what a gap looks like. For upward breakouts, a price gap occurs when the daily low is above the prior day's high. My tests show that if a breakout gap occurs, the average stock climbs 42%. This result compares to a 35% rise for those stocks not having breakout gaps.

MARKET TREND

Table 12.13 lists the performance after a rectangle upward breakout when the general market was rising and falling. As measured by the Standard & Poor's 500 Index, stocks showing rectangles under construction (that is, from formation start to formation end) performed better when the general market declined, with gains of 48% versus 33%. The table also shows the performance from the formation end to the ultimate high when the general market is rising and falling. The common belief is that a rising tide lifts all boats. That situation appears to be the case with rectangles, as a rising market helps push prices higher than a falling market, by 38% to 27%, respectively. However, be aware that the sample size on the falling market is comparatively small (33 samples).

I base the scores on how the general market affects the rectangle during the construction phase, from formation start to end (FS to FE), because you cannot tell with certainty, at the time of purchase, how the market will behave as prices rise to the ultimate high.

Look at Table 12.13 again. Notice how the best performance comes during a falling market when the formation is under construction, then a rising market after the formation ends. This V-shaped market trend is the same that

Table 12.13
Average Price Performance of Rectangles
During a Rising and Falling Market

Market Trend	FS to FE	Score	FE to UH
Rising S&P 500	33% (196)	−1	38% (239)
Falling S&P 500	48% (76)	+1	27% (33)

Note: FS = formation start, FE = formation end, UH = ultimate high. The number of samples appears in parentheses.

other formations have shown in which they also perform well. After you buy a stock when prices close above the top trendline in a falling market, pray that the general market quickly rebounds, helping to lift your stock also. Before you buy, you might also guess the general market direction in the weeks ahead. Yes, it is only a guess, but sometimes an educated guess is better than nothing, and practice should improve your results.

MARKET CAPITALIZATION

Table 12.14 shows the performance of rectangles sorted by market capitalization. I define market capitalization as the number of shares outstanding multiplied by the breakout price. The results shown in the table conform to what we have seen with other chart pattern types. Small caps perform best, with gains averaging 45%, followed by mid caps with a 36% rise, and large caps scoring a 31% gain.

SCORES

The scoring system for chart patterns is easy to use. Evaluate your rectangle by each table showing a score, then total the scores. Scores above zero suggest performance that may beat the median rise; scores below zero suggest under-

Table 12.14
Average Price Performance of
Rectangles by Market Capitalization

Capitalization	Result	Score
Small cap (up to $1 billion)	45% (108)	+1
Mid cap ($1 to $5 billion)	36% (99)	0
Large cap (over $5 billion)	31% (64)	−1

Note: The number of samples appears in parentheses.

Table 12.15
Formation Performance by Score

Score	Result
Average rise of chart patterns with scores above zero	55%
Average rise of chart patterns with scores below zero	22%
Median rise used	28.98%
Percentage with scores above zero beating median rise	62%
Percentage with scores below zero doing worse than median rise	65%

performance. The case studies that follow provide examples of how to score your chart pattern.

Table 12.15 shows how the scoring system performs. Rectangles with scores above zero showed gains averaging 55%. This result compares to a 22% rise for those scoring below zero. Zero scores were not evaluated.

I use the median rise of 28.98% as the mark between a winner and a loser. Those chart patterns with scores above zero and rises above the median, I consider successful buy signals. Sixty-two percent placed in that category, that is, the rectangles with positive scores beat the median rise. When the score was below zero meaning to avoid buying the rectangle, the signal was correct 65% of the time, or nearly two out of three, which means that the negative score correctly predicted that the resulting rise would be less than the median.

Let me warn you that a 62% or 65% recording of beating the median is no guarantee of success. The system is not perfect. I prefer to think of the scoring system not as a system, but as a checklist of trading tactics. Just because you find a rectangle with a perfect score is no reason to assume it will do well. After all, your trading skill comes into play, and even a skilled trader makes mistakes.

Since much of this chapter deals with probabilities, it reminds me of the weather service predicting a 100% chance of rain tomorrow. It does not mean that it will rain, it means that on those days with similar conditions, it rained every day. Tomorrow may be the first exception. Consider chart patterns to be like the weather.

Having put the excuses behind us, let us score a rectangle.

CASE STUDY 1

Figure 12.4 shows the rectangle we study first. This rectangle is probably one of those chart patterns that you are likely to miss. It is not very long or very tall. In fact, it is really not exceptional at all. Prices touch the top and bottom horizontal trendlines numerous times, setting up a valid rectangle.

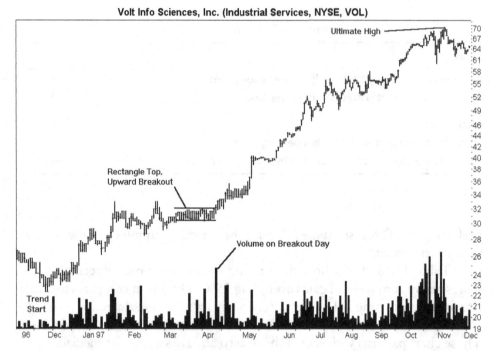

Figure 12.4 A flat rectangle with upward breakout. The scoring system predicted superior performance, and this stock did not disappoint with a rise of 120%.

Evaluating the tables with scores we find the following.

Where does the trend start? I programmed my computer to automatically locate the trend start by finding the lowest low before a 20% trend change, moving backward in time. In late November, prices reached a low of 22.33. A 20% rise from this low would be a *close* above 26.80. This occurred on October 25, about a month before the trend start, and it does not appear in Figure 12.4.

Measuring from the trend start to the rectangle start gives a time of 104 days, placing the rise in the intermediate-term category. Table 12.1 lists the best performance coming from rectangles with intermediate- or short-term rises leading to the rectangle, for a +1 score.

Does the rectangle have a partial decline? No. Prices touch the bottom trendline, then push out the top in one easy motion. Table 12.5 says that a rectangle missing a partial decline is likely to outperform for a +1 score. Running total: +2.

Where is the breakout in the yearly price range? Although you cannot see the yearly range in Figure 12.4, the yearly high is at 33 and the low at 15.50. That places the breakout price of 32 near the yearly high. Table 12.6 scores that a –1. Running total: +1.

Table 12.6 lists rectangle heights. Although this little stinker looks short, the price scale may make it appear smaller than it really is. It is best to check. The top trendline is at 32 and the bottom one is at 30.33. The difference is 1.67, and, as a ratio of the breakout price, it measures 5.21%, well short of the 11.24% cutoff. Our little stinker is indeed short for a −1 score. Running total: 0.

Is the breakout volume high? Yes! Figure 12.4 shows the volume spike, the highest up to that date. Table 12.9 scores a high volume breakout as +1 for a running total of +1.

A throwback does not occur and, according to Table 12.10, that rates a +1 score. How could you have guessed that a throwback would not happen? First, the table says that a throwback occurs 51% of the time, almost the rate that heads will turn up on a fair coin toss. Looking further down the table, we find that a high volume breakout has a throwback rate of 50%. This result is not much help, although a low volume breakout has a higher throwback percentage (52%).

If we look backward in time to the fall of 1996 (not shown), we find a large support zone at 30 set up by many peaks touching that price. The base of the rectangle is at 30.33, so there appears to be no overhead resistance to prevent an upward climb, thus, no throwback is predicted. Running total: +2.

Again, for the same reasons that a throwback is not likely, a bull trap is also not predicted. Coupled with a bull trap frequency of 20%, that supports the no-bull trap scenario. Table 12.11 scores a missing trap as +1. Running total: +3.

Does a gap occur on the day prices stage a breakout? No. That scores −1, so the running total is +2.

Is the general market rising or falling? Taking two snapshots, one on the day the formation starts and another when it ends, indicates that the S&P 500 Index is falling. A falling market rates a +1 score. Running total: +3. Incidentally, the S&P turned around and ended higher the day prices climbed to the ultimate high, exactly the V-shaped performance we hope for.

Finally, the stock is a small cap using the breakout price of 32 in the calculation. Small cap stocks do unusually well, for a score of +1 and a total score of +4.

Scores above zero tend to outperform scores below zero. How did the stock do? You can see in Figure 12.4 that the breakout price was at 32, and prices climbed nicely until reaching the ultimate high of 70.25, for a gain of 120%, well above the median rectangle performance of 28.98%.

CASE STUDY 2

When a negative score appears, will the rectangle underperform? Take a look at Figure 12.5. This rectangle is one that you would probably miss. The numbers one through five show the pattern having two touches on the bottom, three on the top—if you are charitable and include the one where prices close above the top trendline (number five).

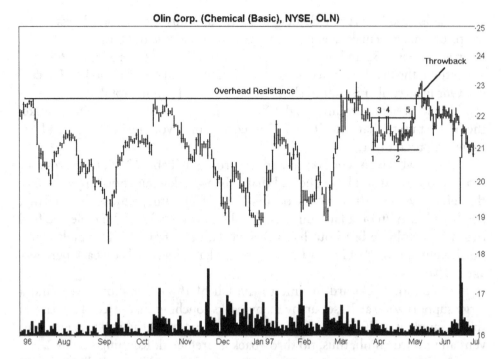

Figure 12.5 A rectangle with a rise of just 4%. A negative score correctly predicted performance falling short of the median rise.

Now, let us see how this rectangle scores.

Table 12.1: Trend start. I measure from the highest high to the closing price moving backward in time. Since prices enter the formation from the top, I am looking for the highest high before prices drop by 20%. That places the trend start off the figure on May 20, 1996. Between that point and the formation start, prices do not close 20% below the highest high. The duration measures 311 days, well into long-term territory. Score: –1.

Table 12.5: Partial declines. Since prices touch the bottom trendline at point two then exit at point five, there is no partial decline. Score: +1. Running total: 0.

Table 12.6: Yearly price range. The breakout is at 22.18, the yearly high at 23.89, and the yearly low at 18.29. Thus, the breakout is near the yearly high for a –1 score. Running total: –1.

Table 12.7: Tall or short. The top rectangle line is at a price of 22.18 and the bottom trendline is at 20.91 for a difference of 1.27. Expressed as a percentage of the breakout price (22.18), gives 5.7% (that is, 1.27/22.18). The rectangle is short. Score –1 for a running total of –2.

Table 12.9: Breakout volume. A quick look at Figure 12.5 shows low break-out volume. Score: –1. Running total: –3.

Table 12.10: Throwbacks. Is a throwback predicted? Yes. I marked the overhead resistance line on the figure, but it really continues further back in time, to the trend start. If you were a helium balloon, you would be bobbing against the ceiling for a long time before punching through. Although not shown, it took the stock almost 2 months of determined pressure to finally pierce the resistance zone and post a new high. With resistance so close by, it would pay to wait for prices to push through before buying. Score: –1. Running total: –4.

Table 12.11: Bull traps. With overhead resistance, I would be scared to death that this was going to bull trap. Checking other stocks in the industry shows dismal results. Most were trending downward and the few that were still working their way higher had a resistance zone approaching, suggesting an impending downturn. Thus, I would assume a bull trap is likely. Score: –1. Running total: –5.

Table 12.12: Gaps. There is no gap the day prices close above the top trendline. Score: –1 for a running total of –6.

Table 12.13: Market trend. The general market is rising as the formation is being created for a score of –1. Running total: –7.

Table 12.14: Market capitalization. The stock is a small cap, scoring +1 for a final total of –6.

A negative score means the stock is likely to underperform (but there is no guarantee). How did the stock do? From the breakout price of 22.18, prices climbed to a high of 23.14, reaching the ultimate high just before throwing back and eventually declining below the formation low. The rise measured just 4%, well short of the 28.98% median.

13

Scallops, Ascending

I received the phone call from someone I had never met, never heard of, and cannot remember his name anyway; a person who seemed intent on determining whether I was going to market my formation-finder program. You see, having sold his software company, he was looking to start another and had promising results from his pattern-recognition algorithms. Somehow, the conversation turned to scallops and the caller admitted that he had never heard of them until reading *Encyclopedia of Chart Patterns* (Wiley, 2000). That begs the question, are scallops classic chart patterns?

I would argue that since they have been around for decades, even though not well known, they still qualify. However, even I was tempted to remove this chapter from the book, mostly because of the work involved in analyzing 760 patterns.

THE TYPICAL PATTERN

Figure 13.1 shows two examples of ascending scallops. Prices reach a minor high (points A in the figure) then round downward into a saucer-shaped bowl. Usually the daily low prices form a smooth, rounding curve but sometimes the daily high prices (the inside of the bowl) appear more smooth. Either way, the bowl should be easy to recognize. After completing the bowl, prices rise forming the handle, usually in a straight-line, nearly vertical advance, as in the July scallop, but prices can ease over, as in the October pattern. Prices reach another minor high at points B, then retrace to points C (the hook). Incidentally, the amount of hook retrace does not indicate future performance.

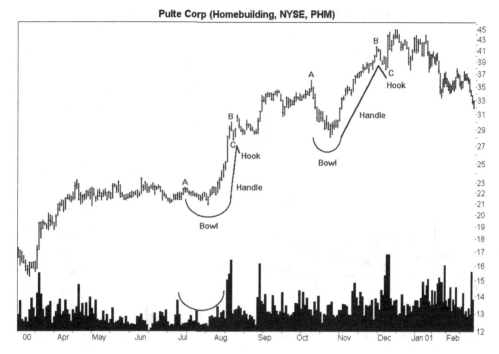

Figure 13.1   Ascending scallops with upward breakouts. Two ascending scallops begin at points A, form the bowl, rise to the handle top at points B, then hook downward to finish at points C.

Sometimes, the volume pattern also appears bowl shaped, as in the July scallop. The volume pattern during the October scallop also appears rounded, but you may need to be really drunk to see it.

There are two types of ascending scallops: those with upward breakouts and those with downward ones. Figure 13.1 shows what upward breakouts look like, and Figure 13.2 shows the downward variety. I label an upward breakout as when prices close above the highest high in the formation; a downward breakout is when prices close below the lowest low in the formation.

TREND START

As with other chart pattern types, the trend leading to the formation can help predict the performance of the stock. Ascending scallops are no different as Table 13.1 shows.

To use the table, first find where the trend starts. From the formation start, look backward and follow prices lower. Eventually, prices will rise by at least 20% from a minor low. When that happens, the minor low represents the trend start (Case Study 1 at the end of this chapter gives an example). Having

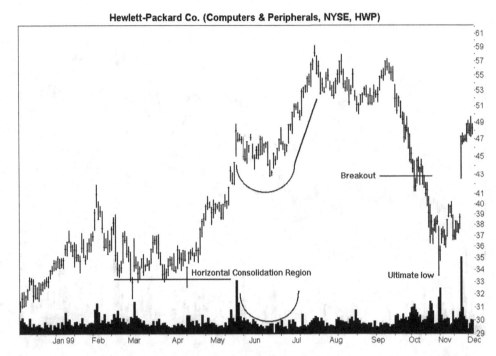

Hewlett-Packard Co. (Computers & Peripherals, NYSE, HWP)

Figure 13.2 Ascending scallop with downward breakout. When prices drop below the formation low, I call it a downward breakout. In this case, the horizontal consolidation region supports prices. The February to May period is another ascending scallop.

found the trend start, compute the time between that point and the formation start, then look up the term category in the table.

You can see in the table that the best performance comes after a short-term rise leading to the scallop, regardless of the breakout direction. For upward breakouts, the short-term uptrend is also the most frequent; for downward breakouts, the samples split about equally.

I discuss scoring in the Scores section of this chapter, so do not concern yourself with them now.

Table 13.1
Average Performance of Ascending Scallops
Sorted by Price Trend Leading to the Pattern

Trend Start to Formation Start	Upward Breakout	Score	Downward Breakout	Score
Short term (0 to 3 months)	31% (266)	+1	−16% (28)	+1
Intermediate term (3 to 6 months)	24% (85)	−1	−13% (30)	+1
Long term (more than 6 months)	19% (117)	−1	−10% (42)	−1

Note: The number of samples appears in parentheses.

HORIZONTAL CONSOLIDATION REGIONS

Table 13.2 shows the effect of a horizontal consolidation region (HCR) when it gets in the way of falling prices. Before I discuss the table further, what does an HCR look like? Consider Figure 13.2. A consolidation region has flat tops, flat bottoms, or both. It acts as a support zone for falling prices and tends to prop them up, sometimes permanently and sometimes not. Support regions are bad news if you want to see lower prices, as in the case of a short sale: You sell the stock at a high price and hope to buy back at a lower one.

To locate an HCR, look between the trend start and the formation bottom. When prices break out downward (and only downward as the consolidation region does not apply to upward breakouts), that is the area of recent price activity and one that is in the path of falling prices. Look for at least a week of horizontal price movement, but the region usually lasts much longer, averaging nearly a month. Prices should touch or approach the same price on several days, but if downward or upward price spikes appear—as in Figure 13.2—do not be concerned. What is important is the flat region and its length. It should look as if it will support prices.

If you find an HCR, then there is a chance that should prices decline to that level, they will decline no further. For performance statistics, return to Table 13.2. For those scallops with downward breakouts that stumbled across an HCR, the declines averaged 12%. When they did not hit a support zone, the decline was larger—19% (but based on only 14 samples).

The average length of an HCR was comparatively long, 27 days or almost a month. The region should be large enough and flat enough to alert investors that prices might find support there.

How often did an HCR show support? Just over half the time, 53%, prices stopped within the consolidation region with a 5% buffer surrounding it. I added the buffer because prices sometimes fall just short of, or overshoot,

Table 13.2
Average Performance of Ascending Scallops
with and Without a Consolidation Region

Description	Downward Breakout	Score
Consolidation region	−12% (93)	−1
No consolidation region	−19% (14)	+1
Average length (days)	27	
Prices stop within region ±5%	53%	
Prices push through region	32%	
Prices do not reach region	14%	

Note: The number of samples appears in parentheses.

the region. Another 32% of the time, prices push through the region and the remainder of the time, 14%, prices never decline to the consolidation zone before rebounding.

INSIDE THE PATTERN

Table 13.3 shows important findings for ascending scallops. The first thing you may notice is that ascending scallops are plentiful. I uncovered 760 of them in the 700+ stocks I looked at. Most break out upward but do not move too much higher before heading down. Certainly, the performance is below average when compared to other bullish and bearish chart patterns.

For upward breakouts, the formation high to the ultimate high before a 20% trend change measures the average rise. For the stocks I looked at, the rise averaged 26%, well short of the 38% average rise for all bullish chart patterns.

For downward breakouts, I changed the way I measured the average decline from *Encyclopedia of Chart Patterns* (Wiley, 2000). In this book, I use the lowest low in the formation as the breakout point because that is the price at which one can be sure that prices are heading down. Therefore, ascending scallops with downward breakouts showed declines averaging 12%, well short of the 21% average for all bearish chart patterns.

As measured from the day prices closed above the breakout price to the date of the ultimate high, the S&P climbed 4% for upward breakouts. The S&P for downward breakouts, measured from the breakout date to the day prices reached the ultimate low, was flat.

In a sorted list, the median value is the midrange value such that half the samples are above the median and half below. For upward breakouts, the median rise registers 21%; for downward breakouts, it is 11%. The median value is sometimes a better gauge of performance because it removes the effect of large rises or declines on the average.

Rises or declines more than 50% are the benchmark that separates the strong performers from the also-rans. In ascending scallops with upward break-

Table 13.3
Important Statistical Findings

Description	Upward Breakouts	Downward Breakouts
Number of formations	645	115
Average rise or decline	26%	12%
Standard & Poor's 500 change	+4%	0%
Median rise or decline	21%	11%
Rises or declines over 50%	86/508 or 17%	1/107 or 1%

outs that I looked at, 86 climbed more than 50%. Only one scallop with a downward breakout suffered a loss of more than 50%. Compared to other chart pattern types, the results are poor.

FAILURE RATES

The next two tables take an in-depth look at failure rates because they seem to be of importance to investors. The 5% line of Table 13.4 reads: 11% of the ascending scallops with upward breakouts failed to rise more than 5%. For downward breakouts, 27% failed to decline more than 5%. Here is another example. Almost half (44%) of the ascending scallops with upward breakouts did not rise more than 20%, and 76% of those scallops with downward breakouts failed to decline more than 20%.

As you scan down the columns in the table, you should marvel at how fast the failure rates climb. Although the 11% failure rate for a 5% rise seems comparatively small, it doubles to 22% for a 10% rise, then doubles again to 44% for rises of 20%. Downward breakouts start out poorly, with a 27% failure rate, and get worse, shooting to 45% for a 10% decline. These statistics suggest that you should avoid shorting an ascending scallop with a downward breakout unless you like losing money.

For upward breakouts, do not invest in an ascending scallop with the hope of doubling your money. Only 4% do, that is, 96% fail to rise 100%.

Table 13.5 shows the horizon failure rates for ascending scallops. The horizon failure rate is a new idea but one that is easy to understand. Take a look

Table 13.4
Maximum Price Rise or Decline Versus Failure Rate

Maximum Price Rise or Decline (%)	Upward Breakout Failure Rate	Downward Breakout Failure Rate
5	58 or 11%	29 or 27%
10	113 or 22%	48 or 45%
15	163 or 32%	67 or 63%
20	223 or 44%	81 or 76%
25	279 or 55%	90 or 84%
30	326 or 64%	97 or 91%
35	357 or 70%	103 or 96%
50	422 or 83%	106 or 99%
75	469 or 92%	107 or 100%
100	489 or 96%	107 or 100%

Note: For upward breakouts, the sample count is 508 and for downward breakouts, 107.

Table 13.5
Horizon Failure Rates and Average Rise or Decline

Time Since Breakout	Upward Breakout Failure Rate (%)	Average Rise (%)	Downward Breakout Failure Rate (%)	Average Decline (%)
1 week	30	3	49	1
2 weeks	34	3	48	1
3 weeks	32	3	49	1
1 month	33	4	51	0
2 months	35	5	61	−3
3 months	37	5	62	−4
6 months	41	4	59	−9

at the failure rates at the end of the first week. I counted the number of scallops having closing prices below (for upward breakouts) or above (for downward breakouts) the breakout price. For upward breakouts, this number amounted to 30%; for downward breakouts, 49% were above the breakout price. The numbers represent the failure rate for their respective breakout direction.

As time goes by, you can see that upward breakout failures hold quite steady, only climbing to 41% after 6 months. Downward breakout failures start high and drop marginally to 48% the following week, climb to 62% after 3 months, then back off to 59%. Since the horizon failure rate at the end of the first day is zero, by definition, both breakout direction failure rates are horrible.

For the intervals shown in the table, you can see that ascending scallops with upward breakouts had gains averaging 3% after the first week. Performance improved until sometime between months 3 and 6 when the average rise moved from 5% to 4%. For downward breakouts, the "signal" is strongest for the first 3 weeks, with an average decline of 1%. After that, prices climb. The results suggest that if you are daft enough to short an ascending scallop with a downward breakout, watch it carefully because it might not stay down for long. After 3 weeks, your scallop might become fish food. Negative declines mean a price rise.

YEARLY PRICE RANGE

Table 13.6 shows the performance after sorting scallops by the breakout price in the yearly price range. To find the values, I looked 1 year before the breakout date and found the highest high and lowest low over that time. Then, I split the yearly price range into thirds and assigned the breakout price to one of the three categories. For upward breakouts, when prices closed above the formation high, those having a breakout near the yearly low, performed best, with rises averaging 52%. Do not get too excited as the results use only nine samples, so the statistic is probably unrealistic.

Table 13.6
Average Performance Sorted by Breakout Price
According to Prior 12-Month Range

Yearly Price Range	Upward Breakouts	Score	Downward Breakouts	Score
Highest third	25% (370)	−1	−14% (31)	+1
Middle third	29% (61)	+1	−10% (48)	−1
Lowest third	52% (9)	+1	−14% (16)	+1

Note: The number of samples appears in parentheses.

Downward breakouts tie, with the extremes doing best and the middle third doing worst, with declines averaging 14% and 10%. For downward breakouts, the breakout price is the lowest low in the formation.

Usually, bullish chart patterns do best when the breakout is near the yearly high; bearish patterns do best near the yearly low. The results for upward breakouts do not support that thesis, and my guess is that the small sample counts for the middle and lowest thirds are the reason. With larger sample counts, the results for downward breakouts might change also.

TALL AND SHORT PATTERNS

Table 13.7 shows the performance of ascending scallops when the formation is either tall or short. Let me discuss the results and then I will explain the method. You can see that tall ascending scallops with upward breakouts resulted in performance that was above average (31%). Short formations, by comparison, climbed an average of 22%.

Downward breakouts from ascending scallops showed a similar trend but one less pronounced. The best performance came from those formations that were tall, with declines measuring 16%. Short scallops showed declines averaging 10%.

What is short or tall? I calculated the formation height, from the highest high to the lowest low, then divided the result by the breakout price. After sort-

Table 13.7
Performance of Short and Tall Ascending Scallops

Description	Upward Breakout	Score	Downward Breakout	Score
Tall (above the median)	31% (253)	+1	−16% (53)	+1
Short (below the median)	22% (255)	−1	−10% (54)	−1
Median percentage of breakout price	20.00%		18.27%	

Note: The number of samples appears in parentheses.

ing the results, I chose the median height as the separator between short and tall. Short formations were those less than or equal to the median height; tall ones were those above the median.

When you calculate the height, be sure to use the correct breakout price. An upward breakout uses the highest formation high as the breakout price; for downward breakouts, the lowest low marks the breakout price.

Let me give you an example using the scallop pictured in Figure 13.2. The formation height is the difference between the highest high, at 59.22, and the lowest low, at 42.81, or 16.41. The height expressed as a percentage of the breakout price is 38% (that is, 16.41/42.81). Since 38% is above the 18.27% median listed in Table 13.7, the scallop is considered tall. The results predict an above-average decline from the tall scallop, and the actual decline measured 22%, about double the 11.01% benchmark (from Table 13.14).

Be forewarned that this calculation does not always work. Consider Figure 13.1. If you do the math, both scallops are tall, with heights in the 30% range but both underperform the median 22.75% rise (with rises of 20% and 8%), contrary to what Table 13.7 predicts. Hence, the need for a scoring system to balance the outliers.

VOLUME TREND

Table 13.8 shows the scallop performance after sorting by the volume trend from formation start to its end. I used linear regression (some spreadsheets call it the trend function) to determine a *best-fit* line; the slope of the line indicates the volume trend. For more details, refer to Glossary and Methodology.

Those scallops with a rising volume trend showed better results (27% and 13%) than those with a falling volume trend (23% and 11%). Although the differences are statistically significant, recall that scallops sometimes show a curving volume trend (for example, see Figure 13.1). I would probably have to use curvilinear regression to accurately map the volume shape. Curvilinear regression is beyond the scope of this book and, also, my desire to perform such a feat.

Table 13.8
Linear Regression Volume Trend and Performance

Description	Upward Breakouts	Score	Downward Breakouts	Score
Rising volume trend	27% (380)	+1	−13% (73)	+1
Falling volume trend	23% (128)	−1	−11% (34)	−1

Note: The number of samples appears in parentheses.

Table 13.9
Breakout Volume and Performance

Description	Upward Breakouts	Score	Downward Breakouts	Score
Average rise or decline on above-average breakout volume	31% (186)	+1	14% (30)	+1
Average rise or decline on average or below-average breakout volume	24% (322)	−1	12% (77)	−1

Note: The number of samples appears in parentheses.

BREAKOUT VOLUME

What can we learn about breakout volume and how it affects performance? Table 13.9 provides some answers. I programmed my computer to assign rankings to the breakout volume compared to the prior 90-day average. The rankings were very high, high, average, low, and very low.

When the breakout volume ranked high or very high, ascending scallops with upward breakouts showed rises averaging 31%. This compares to average or below-average breakout volume and rises of just 24%, a statistically significant difference.

Downward breakouts show the same trend, but the numbers are much closer and the sample size is much smaller. For above-average breakout volume, the declines were 14% compared to 12% for those scallops with average or below-average breakout volume.

For improved performance, select scallops that show above-average breakout volume.

BULL AND BEAR TRAPS

Table 13.10 shows how often a bull or bear trap occurs. A bull trap happens after an upward breakout when prices rise by less than 10%, then tumble below the formation low. A bear trap is similar; prices break out downward but soon rise much higher—above the formation top after declining less than 10%.

In a moment, we look at a bear trap, but first, review the table statistics. You can see that bull traps, those associated with upward breakouts, occur 19% of the time in the ascending scallops I looked at. Bear traps, on the other hand, happen almost half the time (43%). If your ascending scallop has a downward breakout and you intend to short the stock (which is probably a mistake due to the scallop's poor performance), then you should begin to worry about a bear trap.

Table 13.10
Bull and Bear Traps

Description	Upward Breakouts (Bull Traps)	Downward Breakouts (Bear Traps)
Trap frequency	97/508 or 19%	46/107 or 43%
Score if trap predicted	−1	−1
Score if trap not predicted	+1	+1

Look for support areas below the purchase price. HCRs (see Table 13.2), a series of prior minor highs or lows, other chart patterns, trendlines connecting the peaks or valleys—all are indications of support. Search for them, then consider if the trade is worth making should prices decline to the support zone and stop.

Figure 13.3 shows a bear trap where prices close below the formation bowl—staging a downward breakout—drop another 8%, then climb above the formation top. Can we predict this trap? Sometimes. In this case, if you were to look at the price history, you would find a minor low near 34 in early 1998, setting up what looked like a large head-and-shoulders bottom on the weekly scale. Additional support at the 34 level extended into earlier years. One could

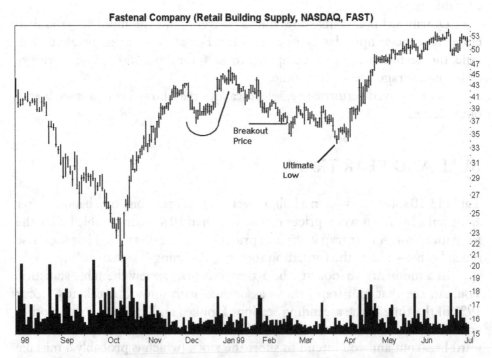

Figure 13.3 A meager decline from an ascending scallop. Prices decline less than 10%, then rise above the formation top in a bear trap.

Table 13.11
Gaps and Performance

Description	Upward Breakouts	Downward Breakouts
Average rise or decline after price gap on breakout	25% (92)	12% (22)
Average rise or decline with no price gap on breakout	26% (416)	13% (85)

Note: The number of samples appears in parentheses.

make the assumption that prices would stop near the price level of the left shoulder, setting up the symmetry necessary for a head-and-shoulders bottom. In other words, prices may drop to 34, then rebound, springing a bear trap on unwary investors.

GAPS

Table 13.11 shows the results of a study of price gaps in ascending scallops. Gaps are comparatively rare, with 92 and 22 samples for up and down breakouts, respectively, so I would view the statistics with a large dose of skepticism. Couple that finding with the results, where the performance after a gap is worse than without a gap, and you see what I mean. The differences are not statistically significant, therefore, I attach no score.

For upward breakouts, a price gap occurs when the daily low is above the prior day's high; for downward breakouts, the daily high is below the prior day's low. I only examined gaps occurring on the breakout day and the resulting performance from the scallops.

The average gain for stocks with gaps and upward breakouts was 25%, marginally below the 26% rise without a breakout gap. For downward breakouts, the average decline was 12% with gaps and 13% without gaps. I believe the results are due to chance and likely to change.

MARKET TREND

Table 13.12 lists the average performance resulting from ascending scallops during rising and falling markets as measured by the Standard & Poor's 500 Index. I measured the performance of the scallops during two periods: when the scallops were under construction (from formation start to end) and from the formation end to the ultimate high (upward breakouts only) or low (downward breakouts only).

Those stocks in a rising general market, when the scallops were under construction, outperformed those in a declining market by 26% to 25%. For

Table 13.12
Average Price Performance of Ascending Scallops
During a Rising and Falling Market

Market Trend	FS to FE	Score	FE to UH	FE to UL
Rising S&P 500, up breakout	26% (390)	0	27% (410)	
Falling S&P 500, up breakout	25% (118)	0	22% (98)	
Rising S&P 500, down breakout	–12% (84)	–1		–14% (51)
Falling S&P 500, down breakout	–15% (23)	+1		–11% (56)

Note: FS = formation start, FE = formation end, UH = ultimate high, UL = ultimate low.
The number of samples appears in parentheses.

downward breakouts, the results were opposite those of upward breakouts: A falling market improved performance by 15% versus 12% for a rising market.

If you could foretell the market direction after you purchased the stock, then the period from formation end to ultimate high or low would be of interest. A rising market after an upward breakout shot prices upward, with gains averaging 27%. During a falling market over the same period, stocks only climbed 22%.

For downward breakouts, the results are opposite of what you would expect. A rising market tended to push prices down further (by 14%) than a falling market (by 11%). It may be that a rising tide lifts all boats, but if your dinghy has a leak and you are taking on water faster than you can bail, you had better climb back into your yacht. In many cases, a rising market will not save a sinking stock.

I only show one meaningful set of scores because the results for downward breakouts were the only statistically significant differences, and the results to the ultimate high or low—although interesting—have no real value unless you can accurately predict the future.

MARKET CAPITALIZATION

Table 13.13 shows the scallop performance after sorting by market capitalization. To find a stock's market capitalization, I multiplied the number of shares outstanding by the breakout price. Then, I sorted the results into three groupings: small, mid, and large.

You can see that small caps perform best after an upward breakout with rises averaging 31%. For downward breakouts, mid caps do best by declining 15%, on average. In both breakout directions, large caps do worst: a 21% average rise for up breakouts and an 8% loss for down breakouts. Optimistically, you should own large caps in a falling market (or when the industry is suffer-

Table 13.13
Average Price Performance of Ascending
Scallops by Market Capitalization

Capitalization	Up Breakouts	Score	Down Breakouts	Score
Small cap (up to $1 billion)	31% (238)	+1	−14% (47)	+1
Mid cap (1 billion to $5 billion)	24% (197)	−1	−15% (40)	+1
Large cap (over $5 billion)	21% (72)	−1	−8% (20)	−1

Note: The number of samples appears in parentheses.

ing) because they decline least. In a rising market, stick with the small caps for best performance.

SCORES

In many tables in this chapter, scores appeared along with performance numbers. Those scores are part of a ranking system to determine the likely performance of ascending scallops. To use the system, find the scores in each table according to your chart pattern's behavior. Add the scores together. Totals above zero mean the chart pattern is likely to outperform the median; those below zero mean an investment in the stock may be unwise. There are no guarantees, but the system helps to guide you toward more profitable situations and to avoid the takedowns.

As is shown in Case Study 3, the scoring system is not perfect. However, comparing the scoring results from ascending scallops is telling, and Table 13.14 shows the findings. For scores above zero with upward breakouts, the gains averaged 35%; scores below zero showed gains of only 18%. For downward breakouts, the losses averaged 18% for scores above zero and 9% for scores below zero.

How often does the system work? To determine success or failure, I used the median rise (22.75%) or decline (11.01%) as the benchmark. The median cited in Table 13.14 is different from that shown in Table 13.3. Table 13.14 includes those chart patterns that have valid information for *all* tables showing scores. For example, if the ultimate high could not be determined because the breakout occurred yesterday, I would remove the chart pattern from consideration.

Those ascending scallops with upward breakouts and scores above zero beat the median rise 62% of the time. When the system said avoid an investment because the score was below zero, the signal correctly predicted a rise worse than the median 65% of the time.

Table 13.14
Formation Performance by Score

Score Value	Up Breakouts	Down Breakouts
Average rise or decline of chart patterns with scores over zero	35%	18%
Average rise or decline of chart patterns with scores below zero	18%	9%
Median rise or decline used	22.75%	11.01%
Percentage with scores over zero beating median rise or decline	147/237 or 62%	29/43 or 67%
Percentage with scores below zero doing worse than median rise or decline	128/198 or 65%	33/52 or 63%

In a similar manner, down breakouts showed correct sell-short signals 67% of the time, and correct avoid signals 63% of the time.

CASE STUDY 1

Look at Figure 13.4. The ascending scallop started life at point A, curled down and around, then soared to the minor high at point B, marking its end. Prices staged a breakout 4 days later when they closed above point B. Prices continued moving up until a one-day reversal at the ultimate high signaled the start of a new trend. After that point, it was all downhill.

Could the performance of this ascending scallop be predicted? Let us put the tables and the scoring system to work.

Table 13.1 lists the performance sorted by the trend leading to the formation. First, where does the trend start? From point A in Figure 13.4, work backward and compare the *lowest low* with the highest daily *close*. We find that the trend starts on January 21, at a low of 18. A 20% trend change from this point would mean a rise to 21.60, which occurred about a week earlier when prices closed at 21.81. Therefore, the January 21 low marks the trend start.

From the trend start, how much time elapses until the formation begins? The formation starts on February 4, placing the rise in the short-term category. For upward breakouts, Table 13.1 says a short-term trend leading to the scallop scores +1.

Since the breakout is upward, Table 13.2 does not apply. Skipping to the next table with a score, we come to Table 13.6, which lists the performance according to the yearly price range. Looking back over the year before the breakout gives a yearly high of 26.69 (point B) and a low of 14.75 (not shown

Figure 13.4   An ascending scallop with a 38% gain. The scoring system predicted good performance. A one-day reversal formation marks the ultimate high.

in Figure 13.4). With a breakout price of 26.69, clearly the breakout is in the highest third of the yearly high. Table 13.6 scores that –1. Running total: 0.

Table 13.7 shows short and tall scallop performance. Taking the difference from the formation high at point B, 26.69, from the low at point C, 18.94, gives a height of 7.75. Dividing this by the breakout price at point B gives 29%, the formation height expressed as a percentage of the breakout price. Scallops over 20% are tall and receive a score of +1. Running total: +1.

Is volume trending upward or downward? Despite the curved volume pattern shown in Figure 13.4, volume under point A is less than that leading to point B. Therefore, the volume trend is rising and Table 13.8 scores that +1. Running total: +2. Performing linear regression on the volume data from point A to point B also verifies a rising volume trend.

Table 13.9 compares breakout volume and performance. Figure 13.4 shows breakout volume that is above most of the prior 90 days. My computer informs me that it considers the volume rank to be high, scoring +1. Running total: +3

Table 13.10 lists bull traps. They only occur 19% of the time, so we can assume that they will not occur unless we can determine otherwise. Looking on the weekly chart for the stock, there were several peaks at the 24 level and one week that reached a high of 26.63, back in late 1996. Since the breakout occurred above those prices, there is no reason to suspect a bull trap. You can see in the figure that prices paused at these two support zones on the way down. Score +1 for a running total of +4.

Table 13.13 lists market capitalization. Using the breakout price of 26.69 multiplied by the number of shares outstanding places the stock in the mid cap category. This scores –1 for a final total of +3. Scores above zero suggest that the stock will do well and it does, posting a 38% rise, well above the 22.75% median.

CASE STUDY 2

Figure 13.5 illustrates this case study. Investing is sometimes difficult because of contradictions. Several times in this book, I have remarked that the best bullish chart patterns have their breakout near the yearly high. This theory is what the momentum players hang their hat on: buy high and sell higher. Sometimes, as in Figure 13.5, the uptrend is long in the tooth, looking tired and ready to collapse. If you know the signs, you can get out in time with the majority of your profits intact.

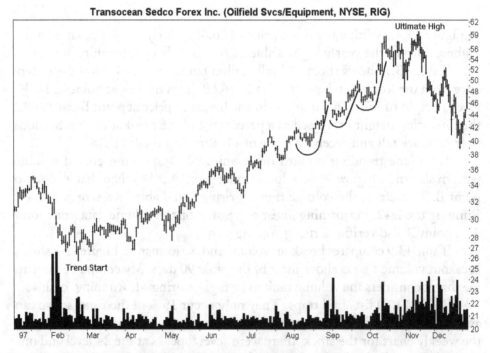

Figure 13.5 Three ascending scallops near the trend end. All have scores below zero, suggesting underperformance. The best gains 23%, the worst, just 2%.

Let us quickly run through the tables for the August scallop.

Table 13.1: Trend start. The uptrend begins in mid-February for all three scallops, placing the rise into the intermediate-term category for the August scallop, but the long term for the others. Score: –1.

Table 13.6: Yearly price range. The yearly high is at 48.47, the low at 25.73, placing the 48.47 breakout price at the yearly high. Score: –1. Running total: –2

Table 13.7: Tall or short. The scallop low is at 39.22 and tops out at 48.47, for a height-to-breakout-price ratio of 19%. For upward breakouts, that result is considered a short scallop. Score –1 for a running total of –3.

Table 13.8: Volume trend. Linear regression shows a rising volume trend and this trend is clear from Figure 13.5 too. Score: +1. Running total: –2.

Table 13.9: Breakout volume. The breakout volume is average according to my computer (the breakout occurs when prices *close* above the highest formation high, September 19, the day before the middle scallop high). Average breakout volume scores –1 for a running total of –3.

Table 13.10: Traps. Is a bull trap predicted? With no overhead resistance to impede upward price movement and a trap rate of just 19%, a bull trap is unlikely. Score: +1. Running total: –2.

Table 13.13: Market capitalization. The stock is a large cap for a –1 score. Final total: –3, suggesting underperformance.

How did the stock do? From the 48.47 breakout price, the stock scalloped its way upward to a high of 59.73, a climb of 23%, essentially tying the median rise. The middle scallop has a final score of –5 and a rise of 20%. The last scallop has a total score of –1 and rises just 2%. On the last scallop, the drop to almost the scallop lows should have been a warning of weakness. Although prices closed above the formation high, the trend lasted one additional day before prices tumbled.

CASE STUDY 3

Figure 13.6 illustrates this case study. The utility stock is one that I considered buying but did not. During the volatile markets in 2000, I moved mostly out of stocks and into cash (a money market fund yielding between 5% and 6% at the time), sidestepping a disastrous year for most investors. Since I am a stock market player, I like to keep my feet wet and buy when interesting situations appear. Since the technology stocks were getting slaughtered, I thought of moving into utility stocks, slow growers with good yields and a defensive holding in a turbulent market.

In my computer program, there is a note remarking about the quick, massive February decline. It says, "Down on prospect of higher interest rates, slower economy." You can see what the gloomy outlook did to the stock.

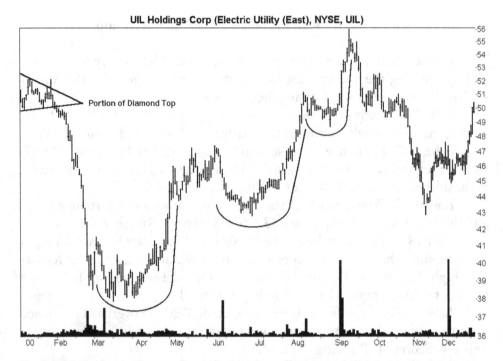

Figure 13.6 Ascending scallops that grow narrower and shorter as they rise, suggesting the uptrend will end. A diamond top reversal signals a downward price trend.

Prices tumbled from a diamond top at 53.63 (a portion of which appears in the figure), to a low of 37.88, a decline of 29% in about 3 months—massive for a stodgy utility.

I took notice of this stock well into the uptrend and thought of buying it. The scoring system shows a total score of +1 for the March scallop and prices climbed 25%, just above the 22.75% benchmark. The middle scallop has a –1 score and rises only 11%, while the highest scallop, the one with a downward breakout, scores –2 and declines 10.68%, shy of the median decline, as predicted (for all scallops).

The reason I show this figure is not for the scoring system, but to have you take note of something I found when doing research for *Encyclopedia of Chart Patterns* (Wiley, 2000). Notice how the scallops get shorter and narrower as they climb. In many consecutive series of ascending scallops, I have noticed this behavior, which suggests the uptrend is ending. In this case, the narrowness of the August scallop was enough to warn me off. I made the right decision to avoid the stock.

14

Scallops, Descending

On my property, I have two bird feeders at one end and a gazebo at the other. A cardinal family comes to visit, along with blue jays, sparrows, house wrens, and, of course, pigeons. What I call pigeons are really flying cows in disguise. They feast at the bird feeder, have their favorite beverage and catch some sun at the bird bath, then use the gazebo as target practice. Clearly, there are some birds you invite into your sanctuary and some you would rather not. Just as with chart patterns. Some chart patterns work better than others, some you actively seek, some you avoid. Descending scallops, with performance that is undistinguished even on a charitable day, are unusual at best, perhaps even contradictory. Do they possess no redeeming qualities? You decide.

THE TYPICAL PATTERN

Figure 14.1 shows the first type of descending scallop, one with downward breakouts. Of the two breakout directions, the downward breakout is the most prevalent, being almost twice as numerous as upward breakouts. Prices form the scallop handle at point A, a minor high at the top of the pattern. From there, prices usually take a near vertical plunge, then round upward forming the bowl. Prices climb to another minor high, represented in the figure as point B—the right bowl lip. Finally, prices close below the bowl low, staging a downward breakout. The complete chart pattern looks like a backward J or ladle, with a long handle and bowl as the main features.

Figure 14.2 shows the second variety of descending scallop. This one looks like the prior one, but the breakout is upward. For an upward breakout to occur, prices must *close* above point B, the right bowl lip. Another scallop appears in the

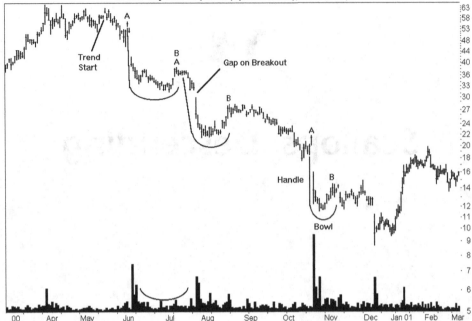

Figure 14.1 Three descending scallops with downward breakouts. Each scallop starts at point A and ends at the following point B. A breakout occurs when prices close below the lowest price in the bowl. Sometimes the volume trend appears bowl shaped, too, as in the June scallop.

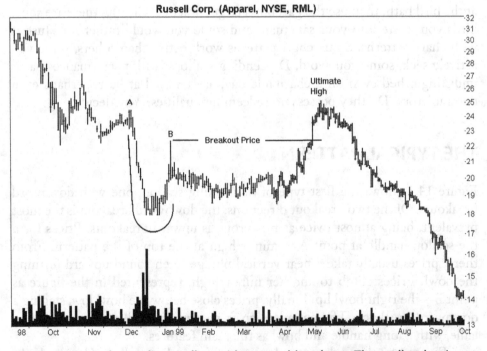

Figure 14.2 A descending scallop with upward breakout. The scallop begins at point A and ends at B. When prices close above point B, a breakout occurs. A wide, ascending scallop begins at point B and ends at the ultimate high.

Table 14.1
Average Performance of Descending Scallops
Sorted by Price Trend Leading to the Pattern

Trend Start to Formation Start	Upward Breakout	Score	Downward Breakout	Score
Short term (0 to 3 months)	15% (86)	−1	−18% (209)	+1
Intermediate term (3 to 6 months)	19% (35)	+1	−12% (66)	−1
Long term (over 6 months)	20% (32)	+1	−15% (53)	−1

Note: The number of samples appears in parentheses.

figure, this time a wide *ascending* scallop (starting at point B and rounding up to the ultimate high). The ascending scallop has a downward breakout.

TREND START

We can use the trend leading to the pattern to help predict performance after the scallop ends. To find the trend start, pretend you are a time machine and search backward in time from the formation start, higher, looking for the highest high before prices drop by 20%. For the June scallop shown in Figure 14.1, the trend started in mid-May, at a high price of 63.44. From that point, still moving backward, prices must *close* below 50.75 for a 20% trend change. That occurs about a month earlier, on April 14, when prices closed at 50.44.

Having found the trend start, find the time between the trend start and the formation start (point A). Usually, it will be a short-term duration, such as the 17 days for the June scallop. Once you know the duration, use Table 14.1 to look up the likely performance and determine a score. For the June scallop, which has a downward breakout, the table indicates losses averaging 18%. I discuss scoring in the Scores section near the end of this chapter, so do not concern yourself with scores now.

HORIZONTAL CONSOLIDATION REGIONS

Table 14.2 shows the performance of descending scallops when they encounter overhead resistance. Since the price trend leading to a descending scallop is downward, overhead resistance only applies to upward breakouts.

Before I discuss the results in Table 14.2, look at Figure 14.3. It shows a descending scallop with an upward breakout and prices that meet resistance at a horizontal price line. The horizontal consolidation region poses a threat to the upward price movement.

Believe it or not, this is the best recent example I could find. You might quibble with the breakout direction, but I require a *close* below the bowl to

Table 14.2
Average Performance of Descending Scallops
with and Without a Consolidation Region

Description	Upward Breakout
Consolidation region	18% (124)
No consolidation region	13% (35)
Average length (days)	44
Prices stop within region ±5%	52%
Prices push through region	38%
Prices do not reach region	10%

Note: The number of samples appears in parentheses.

signal a downward breakout, and prices close at 25.31 on October 1, just above the bowl low of 25.25. You also might say that the ultimate high seems to end prematurely. However, the ultimate high occurs at 29.91 and prices decline to a close of 22.94, a tumble of 23%, signaling a trend change and a valid ultimate high.

I examined only those descending scallops with upward breakouts and a line of consolidation between the trend start and the high price at the forma-

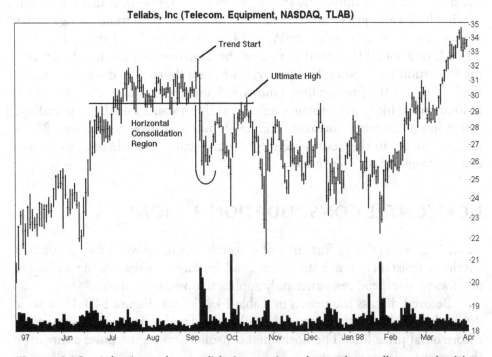

Figure 14.3 A horizontal consolidation region above the scallop repels rising prices. Before trading a stock, look for overhead resistance between the trend start and the formation top. A horizontal price line may mean overhead resistance to the upward price trend.

tion end (the upper right bowl lip). The consolidation line should have flat tops, flat bottoms, or both, and ignore occasional spikes that pierce the resistance line.

In Figure 14.3, after the upward breakout, prices quickly ran into overhead resistance and stalled in early October before giving way to selling pressure. Prices moved essentially sideways for months before trying determinedly in late February to push through to a new high. In March, prices succeeded and reached a high of 46.56 in July 1998 before a significant decline ensued.

Table 14.2 shows the performance results. You can see that when a consolidation region exists above the breakout point, prices climb by 18%, but move higher by just 13% when there is *no* overhead resistance. To my way of thinking, this is clearly wrong. It could be that the low sample count is responsible—all 35 samples might have meager gains. It could be that the consolidation regions are well above the scallop and if prices climb to the region then stop, they have made quite a rise. Whatever the reason, the differences are not statistically significant, so no score is attached.

As a gauge to show how long the consolidation area was, I took the average of all descending scallops (with upward breakouts) showing horizontal consolidation and found the average region to be 44 days long. In other words, the area should be comparatively long, perhaps with several minor highs or lows, touching or nearing a common price level.

How often does overhead resistance stop the upward price momentum? I compared the ultimate high with the consolidation region and found that 10% of the time, prices did not climb to the bottom of the consolidation region. Another 52% of the time, prices climbed into the consolidation region (give or take 5%) and stopped there. I added the 5% buffer to include those prices that peaked slightly above or below the region. The remainder of the time, 38%, prices eventually pushed through the region and continued higher. The results are similar to other chart pattern types.

INSIDE THE PATTERN

Table 14.3 shows important statistical findings for descending scallops. As far as frequency goes, descending scallops are plentiful, with the downward breakout variety almost twice as common as the upward ones. Together, my fishing expedition caught 531 scallops.

How far do prices travel in the breakout direction? For upward breakouts, the average rise is 17%. Upward breakouts use the highest high in the upper right bowl lip as the breakout point (see Figure 14.2). Usually, bullish chart patterns score rises of 38%, so descending scallops with upward breakouts underperform severely. The reason for this underperformance may be downward price momentum. Recall that descending scallops appear in a declining price trend. An upward breakout would run against the receding tide and tend to be short-lived.

Table 14.3
Important Statistical Findings

Description	Upward Breakouts	Downward Breakouts
Number of formations	186	345
Average rise or decline	17%	16%
Standard & Poor's 500 change	+4%	–1%
Median rise or decline	13%	15%
Rises or declines more than 50%	20/159 or 13%	3/345 or 1%

Downward breakouts, which use the lowest low in the bowl as the breakout price, perform almost as well with losses averaging 16%—but not that close to the 21% average decline for all bearish chart pattern types. I would expect a declining price trend to carry prices much lower, but that does not appear to be the case. The underperformance may be due to where the breakout occurs. *If we use the right bowl lip high, the same as that shown in Figure 14.2, as the downward breakout price, then the average decline increases to 26%.*

Knowing that scallops scored gains or losses of about 16%, what happened to the S&P over the same period? Comparing the S&P on the breakout date with the date of the ultimate high or low, the index showed gains of 4% and losses of 1% for upward and downward breakouts, respectively. You might want to consider these as the returns a buy-and-hold investor would receive as compared to a chart pattern player. The numbers do not include dividends or trading costs.

I sorted the rises or declines according to the breakout direction and chose the median value. The median is a midrange value such that half the values are above it and half below. I consider the median a number that experienced investors can achieve if they trade the chart pattern often enough and carefully enough. For upward breakouts, the median is 13%; downward breakouts show a slightly larger decline, at 15%.

As a gauge to assess how successful a chart pattern is, I include the number of rises or declines of more than 50%. For upward breakouts, I found only 20 that soared more than 50%; downward breakouts had 3. This result is a paltry showing for upward breakouts and about right for downward ones (it is unusual for a stock to drop by half, but gains can be unlimited).

FAILURE RATES

Table 14.4 shows the first of two tables listing failure rates. Understanding the table is easiest by example. Just over half, 88 or 55%, of descending scallops with upward breakouts climbed less than 15%, while half with downward breakouts declined less than 15%. In essence, the table shows how many scallops fail to rise or decline a set amount.

Table 14.4
Maximum Price Rise or Decline Versus Failure Rate

Maximum Price Rise or Decline (%)	Upward Breakout Failure Rate	Downward Breakout Failure Rate
5	49 or 31%	45 or 13%
10	69 or 43%	108 or 31%
15	88 or 55%	174 or 50%
20	98 or 62%	232 or 67%
25	109 or 69%	276 or 80%
30	115 or 72%	299 or 87%
35	125 or 79%	318 or 92%
50	139 or 87%	342 or 99%
75	149 or 94%	345 or 100%
100	153 or 96%	345 or 100%

Note: For upward breakouts, the sample count is 159 and for downward breakouts 345.

When I wrote my previous book, *Encyclopedia of Chart Patterns* (Wiley, 2000), some people squealed like stuck pigs that the failure rates seemed too low. In that book, I considered as failures prices that moved in an adverse breakout direction or that moved in the intended breakout direction but by less than 5%. As you look at Table 14.4, you can see why they complained. Look how the failure rate climbs. For downward breakouts, the 13% failure rate more than doubles to 31% for just a 10% decline. For a 15% decline, the failure rate nearly quadruples the rate at 5%. Huge.

Table 14.5 shows another way to calculate failure rates—the horizon failure rate. To determine the horizon failure rate, count the number of stocks

Table 14.5
Horizon Failure Rates and Average Rise or Decline

Time Since Breakout	Upward Breakout Failure Rate (%)	Average Rise (%)	Downward Breakout Failure Rate (%)	Average Decline (%)
1 week	42	0	25	4
2 weeks	48	1	29	4
3 weeks	49	−1	32	4
1 month	54	−2	36	3
2 months	55	−3	38	3
3 months	59	−5	41	3
6 months	57	−3	46	2

with prices below (upward breakouts) or above (downward breakouts) the breakout price at the end of a period. By definition, at the end of the first day, all chart patterns have a horizon failure rate of 0%, but you can see what happens after the first week. Forty-two percent of the descending scallops with upward breakouts were below their breakout prices, and 25% with downward breakouts failed.

The table also shows the average rise and it is just as it sounds: the average difference between the breakout price and the current price at the end of each period. For example, at the end of week 1, scallops with upward breakouts did not budge (a 0% rise), whereas those with downward breakouts showed losses averaging 4%.

What this table tells me is that scallops with upward breakouts occur in downtrends, and the downward momentum quickly overwhelms any rise (notice how the average rise starts off slow, peaks at 2 weeks, then declines). Do not buy a stock showing a descending scallop with an upward breakout. Chances are, the upward rise will be meager. Downward breakouts do fine for the first 3 weeks, then weaken.

YEARLY PRICE RANGE

Where in the yearly price range do the best performing scallops reside? Table 14.6 provides the answer. For the year before the breakout date, I found the highest high and lowest low, then divided the high–low range into thirds and compared the breakout price with each third. Excluded were those scallops that did not have a full year of prior data.

Descending scallops with upward breakouts seated in the lowest third of the yearly price range performed best, showing gains averaging 23%. Presumably, these were the ones that marked the end of the downtrend. For downward breakouts, the best performers were scallops with breakouts in the highest third of the yearly price range, but just six scallops qualified. They showed declines averaging 23%.

Table 14.6
Average Performance Sorted by Breakout Price
According to Prior 12-Month Range

Yearly Price Range	Upward Breakouts	Score	Downward Breakouts	Score
Highest third	8% (16)	−1	−23% (6)	+1
Middle third	14% (52)	−1	−17% (78)	+1
Lowest third	23% (75)	+1	−16% (223)	0

Note: The number of samples appears in parentheses.

Table 14.7
Performance of Short and Tall Descending Scallops

Description	Upward Breakout	Score	Downward Breakout	Score
Tall (above the median)	23% (81)	+1	–17% (173)	+1
Short (below the median)	12% (78)	–1	–15% (172)	–1
Median percentage of breakout price	24.44%		22.62%	

Note: The number of samples appears in parentheses.

TALL AND SHORT PATTERNS

Table 14.7 shows the performance of tall and short scallops. I computed the height from the highest formation high to the lowest low and expressed it as a percentage of the breakout price. Then, I sorted the results according to the breakout direction and chose the median, or midrange, value as the dividing line between short and tall.

The performance of upward breakouts is the most startling. Those descending scallops that fell into the tall category climbed an average 23%; short scallops showed gains of just 12%. Downward breakouts showed a similar trend with tall scallops outperforming the short ones by 17% to 15%.

VOLUME TREND

Table 14.8 shows the performance of descending scallops after sorting by the volume trend from formation start to end (handle high to right bowl lip). To determine the volume trend, I found the slope of the line using linear regression on the volume data. Some spreadsheets call linear regression the trend function, but you need not worry about that. Why? Because the differences are statistically insignificant.

For rising volume trends, scallops showed gains after an upward breakout of 16%, compared to a 17% rise when volume was trending downward.

Table 14.8
Linear Regression Volume Trend and Performance

Description	Upward Breakouts	Downward Breakouts
Rising volume trend	16% (77)	–16% (160)
Falling volume trend	17% (82)	–16% (185)

Note: The number of samples appears in parentheses.

Table 14.9
Breakout Volume and Performance

Description	Upward Breakouts	Downward Breakouts
Average rise or decline on above-average breakout volume	23% (42)	19% (92)
Average rise or decline on average or below-average breakout volume	15% (117)	15% (253)
Score: High volume	+1	+1
Score: Low volume	−1	−1

Note: The number of samples appears in parentheses.

Downward breakouts tied at 16% declines regardless of the volume trend. I can sum the results of Table 14.8 in two words: never mind!

BREAKOUT VOLUME

Although the volume trend during construction of the scallop did not tell us anything about the resulting performance, breakout volume says, well, volumes (see Table 14.9).

I programmed my computer to sort the breakout volume into one of five categories: very high, high, average, low, and very low compared with the average volume. For upward breakouts, when the volume was above average (that is, high or very high), descending scallops soared 23% on average. When the breakout volume was average or below average, the rise was only 15%, a sizable difference.

For downward breakouts, the trend remained the same with high volume breakouts (losses averaging 19%) outperforming those with average or below-average volume (a 15% average loss).

In the case of descending scallops, the Wall Street folklore that high breakout volume suggests superior performance is true, at least for this chart pattern.

BULL AND BEAR TRAPS

Table 14.10 shows how frequently bull and bear traps occur. A bull trap (upward breakouts) occurs twice as often as a bear trap (downward breakouts), but both occur less than 50% of the time.

What is a trap, anyway? Figure 14.4 shows an example of a bear trap. I define a bear trap as when prices break out downward and reach the ultimate low less than 10% below the breakout. Prices must then rise above the forma-

Table 14.10
Bull and Bear Traps

Description	Upward Breakouts (Bull Traps)	Downward Breakouts (Bear Traps)
Trap frequency	68/159 or 43%	74/345 or 21%
Score if trap predicted	−1	−1
Score if trap not predicted	+1	+1

tion top to qualify as a bear trap. In Figure 14.4, prices drop to a low of 41, then climb to 51, a rise of 24%, signaling that the ultimate low has been found (just 63 cents below the breakout price). Then, but not shown in the figure, prices rose above the formation top of 51.94 in early October and continued climbing.

Those investors selling the stock short, with the expectation of buying it back later at a lower price, became trapped in a losing position as prices rose. If they did not cover their short, they would have lost a bundle on paper as the stock peaked over 70.

A bull trap is similar. The breakout is upward, seducing investors into buying the stock. Prices move up less than 10% before plummeting and shooting out the formation bottom.

Figure 14.4 A bear trap. Prices break out downward and decline to the support level of the ultimate low then rebound. Prices eventually climbed to just over 70 before falling back into the 40s.

How can you avoid a trap? Look at Figure 14.4 again. See how prices touch a support zone and stop declining at that point? Prices push a little lower in early August but still find support. To predict a trap, look for a horizontal consolidation region in the recent past. This is easier for upward breakouts from descending scallops because the price trend is usually downward leading to the scallop and so covers recent price action. Refer to the Table 14.2 discussion for more information.

Downward breakouts, trendlines, minor highs or lows, horizontal consolidation regions, and sometimes even prices touching the level of a moving average will form support and stop a downward decline. Search for those anomalies before investing to get a better handle on how far prices are likely to move.

GAPS

Table 14.11 shows the performance of scallops when a price gap appears on the breakout day. In Figure 14.1, for example, a gap appears on the day prices closed below the bowl low after the June scallop. Gaps are a sign of trading enthusiasm, and as the table shows, they are beneficial to performance. When a gap appears during an upward breakout, prices rise an average of 19%, compared to a 16% rise when no gap appears. Downward performance is similar, only the differences are wider, at 21% and 15%, respectively.

MARKET TREND

Table 14.12 shows the influence of the general market, as measured by the Standard & Poor's 500 Index, on individual stocks. I looked at the market from the day the scallop started to its end and to the ultimate high or low. For upward breakouts when the formation was under construction (FS to FE), a falling market seemed to make prices perform better after the breakout, an 18% rise versus 16%. Downward breakouts were even.

Table 14.11
Gaps and Performance

Description	Upward Breakouts	Downward Breakouts
Average rise or decline after price gap on breakout	19% (25)	21% (69)
Average rise or decline with no price gap on breakout	16% (134)	15% (276)
Score if gap present	+1	+1
Score if gap absent	−1	−1

Note: The number of samples appears in parentheses.

Table 14.12
Average Price Performance of Descending Scallops
During a Rising and Falling Market

Market Trend	FS to FE	FE to UH	FE to UL
Rising S&P 500, up breakout	16% (83)	18% (137)	
Falling S&P 500, up breakout	18% (76)	9% (22)	
Rising S&P 500, down breakout	−16% (202)		−17% (136)
Falling S&P 500, down breakout	−16% (143)		−16% (209)

Note: FS = formation start, FE = formation end, UH = ultimate high, UL = ultimate low.
The number of samples appears in parentheses.

From the formation end to the ultimate high or ultimate low, a rising market helped both breakout directions, with gains of 18% versus 9% for upward breakouts, and 17% versus 16% for downward breakouts.

No scores appear in the table because the differences for the FS to FE period are not statistically significant. However, if you correctly guess that the general market will rise after an upward breakout, then your chart pattern could do well. Also note the V-shaped market trend: falling from FS to FE, and rising thereafter, gives the best performance. This result is similar to other chart patterns explored in this book.

MARKET CAPITALIZATION

Table 14.13 shows the performance after a breakout from a descending scallop, sorted by market capitalization. Market capitalization is the number of shares outstanding multiplied by the breakout price. You can see in the table the dollar size of each capitalization category. For small cap stocks with descending scallops and upward breakouts, the average rise was 21%, more than double the large cap performance of 9%. Downward breakouts were not

Table 14.13
Average Price Performance of Descending
Scallops by Market Capitalization

Capitalization	Up Breakouts	Score	Down Breakouts	Score
Small cap (up to $1 billion)	21% (73)	+1	−18% (166)	+1
Mid cap (1 billion to $5 billion)	17% (60)	0	−17% (116)	+1
Large cap (over $5 billion)	9% (24)	−1	−13% (61)	−1

Note: The number of samples appears in parentheses.

as startling, but the trend was similar: Small caps outperformed the other two categories.

The results follow trends shown by other chart pattern types, that is, small caps perform best for bullish chart patterns and large caps lose least in bearish markets.

SCORES

Evaluate your chart pattern by the items in each table that have a score. Total the scores. Scores above zero suggest the descending scallop will outperform the median; avoid scallops with scores below zero as they may underperform. The case studies at the end of this chapter make this procedure clear.

There are no guarantees about how the chart pattern you select will do. Your trading skill, the markets, the industry, and the company will all work together to shape a successful investment. If you decide to trade scallops, select your fish food carefully.

The first few lines of Table 14.4 list the average gain or decline for scores above and below zero. For example, the average rise from descending scallops with upward breakouts and scores above zero was 34%. That rise was more than triple the 10% rise for scallops showing a negative score. That statistic is an impressive difference.

How well does the system perform? I used a median rise or decline to serve as a benchmark between good and bad performance. If the system added value, then more scallops with upward breakouts would have scores above zero and rises above the median rise; more scallops would have avoid signals (scores

Table 14.14
Formation Performance by Score

Score	Upward Breakouts	Downward Breakouts
Average rise or decline of chart patterns with scores above zero	34%	21%
Average rise or decline of chart patterns with scores below zero	10%	10%
Median rise or decline used	12.52%	14.86%
Percentage with scores above zero beating median rise or decline	41/52 or 79%	99/149 or 66%
Percentage with scores below zero doing worse than median rise or decline	53/76 or 70%	70/91 or 77%

below zero) with rises below the median. The same logic applies to downward breakouts.

For upward breakouts, I found that 79% of the time, the system correctly said buy and correctly said avoid 70% of the time. For downward breakouts, the correct sell-short signals were 66% and the avoid signals were right 77% of the time. In other words, the system adds value, but it is not perfect.

CASE STUDY 1

The case studies in this chapter concern only downward breakouts as they are the most prevalent. Take a look at the situation shown in Figure 14.5. You can see that the downtrend from the trend start was not very long. At the bottom of the two scallops lay a minefield of support, potentially blocking any downward thrust; that may be why the scallops formed their bowls near that price point.

Let us work our way through the tables for the most recent scallop, the one in February. Beginning with Table 14.1, where does the trend start? From

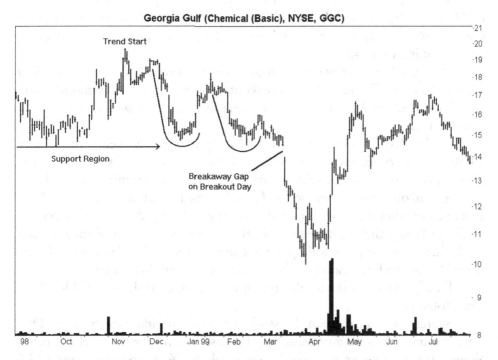

Figure 14.5 Two descending scallops with positive scores. The scores suggested a profitable opportunity to short the stock, and it did not disappoint, with losses over 30%.

the formation start in mid-January, work backward and find the highest high price before prices drop by at least 20%, measured from high to close. At the top of the scallop, prices reached a high of 18.25. A 20% decline from that price would be at close below 14.60. The December scallop has a close of 14.75, just above the 20% mark, so the trend start must be further back in time.

Prices reach a new high in early November, at 19.69, just after a steep rise. Checking this point as the trend start yields success. A 20% decline from the November high would be 15.75, and the stock closed below that price in mid-October.

From the trend start to the formation start, the time difference is 68 days, placing the downtrend in the short-term category. A short-term decline leading to the formation scores +1 from Table 14.1.

Table 14.6 is the next table with a score and it lists the yearly high and low. Prices break out downward when they gap below the formation low, on March 11, 1999. Scanning the price chart over the prior year (not shown in Figure 14.5), finds that prices reached a high of 32.19 and a low of 14.50. Comparing the breakout price (14.56, the lowest low in the scallop) with the yearly high–low range, clearly the breakout price is in the lowest third of the range. That scores 0, for a running total of +1.

Is the scallop tall or short? The scallop has a high price of 18.25 and a low of 14.56, giving it a height of 3.69. As a percentage of the breakout price (3.69/14.56 or 25%) it ranks as a tall scallop for a +1 score, according to Table 14.7. Running total: +2.

Does the breakout occur on above-average volume? Yes. Although it is difficult to see in Figure 14.5, the breakout volume is above the 3-month average. Table 14.9 ranks above-average breakout volume with a +1 score for a running total of +3.

Table 14.10 lists trap frequency. Once prices pushed below the nearby 14.50 support zone, there was nothing to stop prices from tumbling. That means a bear trap is not predicted, rating a score of +1. Running total: +4.

A breakout occurs when prices *close* below the formation low. For the February scallop, they did so with a burst of energy and gapped lower on March 11. Table 14.11 says that a gap helps performance for a score of +1. Running total: +5. Incidentally, the prior scallop did not share the same breakout price. Prices closed below the formation low the day before the gap, March 10.

Finally, the stock is a small cap, for a +1 score according to Table 14.13. Final total: +6.

Scores above zero mean the stock is a good candidate for trading. That does not mean it is an automatic buy because you may want to check other things, such as your sanity. How did the stock do? You can see in Figure 14.5 that the stock dropped in short order to 10, for a 31% decline. As predicted, that is well above the 14.86% median.

Incidentally, the December scallop finished with a score of +2 and it posted a 32% decline. Lower breakout volume and no breakout gap were the only differences.

CASE STUDY 2

Figure 14.6 illustrates this case study, an example of when the score predicts underperformance. I concentrate on the January scallop. The first thing you might notice is that the bottom of the scallop appears ragged, not rounded. The inside, however, shows a smoother surface as if running water over centuries etched the inside of the bowl. Despite its rough exterior, I consider it a valid descending scallop. Quickly running through the tables we find the following.

Table 14.1: Price trend. The downward trend starts in early October, and 92 days later the formation begins. That pushes the duration into the intermediate-term category for a −1 score.

Table 14.6: Yearly price range. The yearly high was 49.25 and the low was 34.44, placing the breakout price of 42.25 in the middle third of the yearly price range. That scores +1, for a running total of 0.

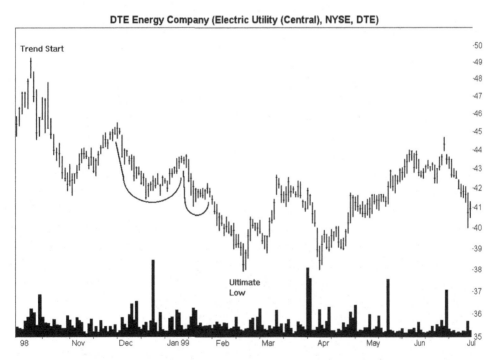

Figure 14.6 Two descending scallops with downward breakouts. Both have scores predicting underperformance and both declines measure about 8%.

Table 14.7: Scallop height. The height represents 7% of the breakout price, placing the scallop in the short category. Score: –1. Running total: –1.

Table 14.9: Breakout volume. The breakout volume was average when compared to the prior 3 months. Score: –1. Running total: –2.

Table 14.10: Bear trap. Not shown in Figure 14.6 is a long, horizontal line of support starting in June and lasting into August, with another patch in September touching the same price of 40. This warned of a support zone beneath the scallop, suggesting a bear trap. Score: –1. Running total: –3. It turns out that prices tumbled through the support zone without pause, but hindsight does not affect the bear trap prediction.

Table 14.11: Gaps. There is no breakout gap. Score: –1. Running total: –4.

Table 14.13: Market capitalization. The utility is a large cap for a –1 score and a final score of –5.

How did the stock do? From the breakout price of 41.06, the stock dropped to 37.94, a decline of just 8%. The December scallop had a total score of –3 and it declined 7%. The only difference between the two was the length of the trend start. The December scallop has a short-term downtrend leading to it for a +1 score.

15

Triangles, Ascending

When I was a hardware design engineer at a major defense contractor, the wife of one of the bosses there had a baby. If the baby was anything like its photo, it was the ugliest baby I have seen! Oddly enough, that reminds me of ascending triangles. The picture of an ascending triangle seems pretty enough, but, in reality, triangles suffer from overshoots or undershoots on the way in and premature breakouts on the way out. That is not to say that you should avoid this chart pattern. Like many chart patterns, ascending triangles can be profitable if traded correctly.

THE TYPICAL PATTERN

Figure 15.1 shows what an ascending triangle looks like, at its best. You can draw a horizontal trendline along the peaks. Connecting the minor lows along the bottom forms an ascending trendline, giving the formation its name.

Prices cross the chart pattern plenty of times and the minor highs and lows touch the two trendlines at least twice each. The volume trend shows a receding volume pattern that is typical for triangles. A breakout occurs when prices close above the horizontal trendline, as in this case, or close below the up-sloping trendline along the bottom.

Figure 15.2 shows a variation of an ascending triangle that you may come across. Prices descend into the formation but overshoot, meaning that prices travel slightly above the formation trendline on entry. On exit, prices poke their head through the formation top for 1 day, but close lower, then prematurely break out downward, curl around, and move much higher. I consider the true breakout direction to be upward, but that is little consolation if you

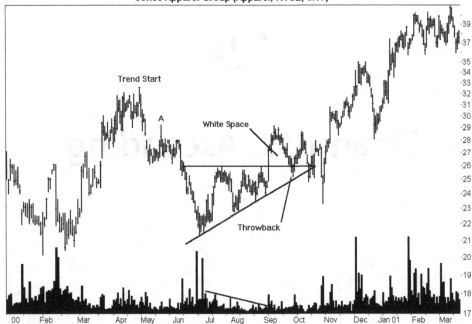

Figure 15.1 An excellent ascending triangle. Plenty of price crossings within the formation and a receding volume trend sets up a perfect triangle.

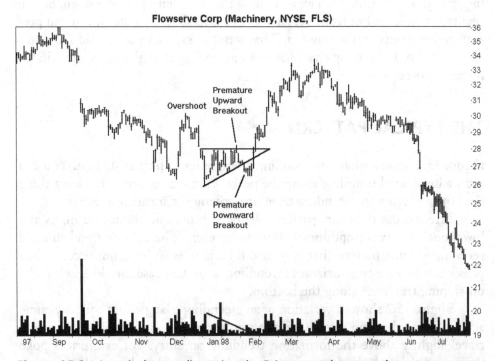

Figure 15.2 A typical ascending triangle. Prices overshoot on the entry, prematurely break out upward and downward before moving significantly higher in the true breakout direction.

bought on the premature upside breakout, then cut your losses when prices dropped out the bottom only to see prices move higher.

On entry, prices can overshoot (moving above the top trendline) or undershoot (moving below the formation bottom) and break out prematurely in either direction. When drawing trendlines, ignore these anomalies; when trading, pray you never come across them.

TREND START

The price trend leading to a chart pattern is one key to predicting how prices will perform after the formation ends. On rare occasions, the chart pattern will be nearly equidistant between the trend start and the ultimate high (upward breakouts) or ultimate low (downward breakouts). Keep that in mind when guessing where the ultimate high or low will be.

Where does the trend start? To answer this question, begin with the formation start and work backward in time. For those price trends moving downward, away from the formation, find the lowest low before prices climb more than 20%. For upward price trends leading away from the triangle, look for the highest high before a 20% trend change.

Incidentally, the 20% value is one that I use to find both the trend start and the ultimate high or low. For the general market, a 20% decline in a bull market means prices have entered bear territory; a rise of 20% in a bear market means a bull market has begun. I used the conventional gauges and applied them to individual stocks.

Figure 15.1 provides an example that we can use to illustrate how to find the trend start. Since prices enter the formation from the top, we will look for a high price before a 20% trend change. Work backward and find the highest high before prices drop off. One point, shown as point A, is a minor high in mid-May with a daily high price of 29.25. To signal a trend change, prices must decline by 20% and *close* below 23.40. However, prices only decline to 26.25 before posting a new high. We keep searching, moving backward in time, and see the late April peak at a high price of 32.56. A 20% decline from this price would be a close below 26.05, a level reached in mid-March. Thus, the April peak represents the trend start for this chart pattern.

When searching for the trend start, ignore any overshoot or undershoot just before the formation starts. Sometimes, using the high or low price in these periods will incorrectly signal a trend start. As an example, look at Figure 15.3. From the formation start working backward in time, point A is above the formation. You might conclude that point A represents the trend start since prices drop more than 20%. However, I would argue that the price trend is really downward (again, working backward in time) so we need to look for a 20% rise in prices. The trend starts in mid-April at 16.75, the low before prices climb in early March to nearly 21, a rise of 25%.

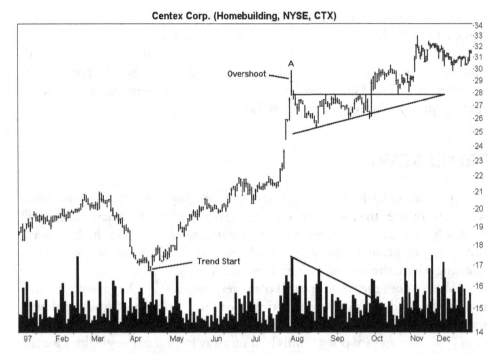

Centex Corp. (Homebuilding, NYSE, CTX)

Figure 15.3   A good example of overshoot. Prices rise rapidly in the days leading to the formation then overshoot before settling down.

With practice, you should be able to accurately guess where the trend starts without need for any calculation.

Table 15.1 shows the performance resulting from ascending triangles when sorted by the price trend leading to the chart pattern. For both upward and downward breakouts, the short-term trend leading to the pattern results in the best performance, and the long-term category shows the worst performance.

I base the score column on the performance relative to the average performance, and discuss scoring in the Scores section of this chapter. Do not concern yourself with the scores now.

Table 15.1
Average Performance of Ascending Triangles
Sorted by Price Trend Leading to the Pattern

Trend Start to Formation Start	Upward Breakout	Score	Downward Breakout	Score
Short term (0 to 3 months)	38% (241)	+1	−21% (152)	+1
Intermediate term (3 to 6 months)	31% (77)	−1	−18% (57)	−1
Long term (over 6 months)	25% (98)	−1	−15% (63)	−1

Note: The number of samples appears in parentheses.

HORIZONTAL CONSOLIDATION REGIONS

Table 15.2 shows the performance of ascending triangles when a horizontal consolidation region (HCR) interferes with prices. Before I explain the results, let me discuss what a consolidation region is.

Take a look at Figure 15.4, which shows an HCR. When an ascending triangle acts as a reversal of the prior price trend, look for a region where prices move horizontally, or nearly so. The region should have flat tops, flat bottoms, or both, and be positioned between the trend start (which the consolidation region can span) and the formation start (for downward price trends leading to the formation, use the highest high in the chart pattern; otherwise, use the formation low as the cutoff price). In essence, you are looking for a support or resistance zone that is both nearby and in the breakout direction.

Figure 15.4 shows a price trend leading down to the formation with an upward breakout—a short-term reversal of the prevailing price trend. After the breakout, prices rise to 11 before meeting resistance set up by the consolidation region from October through November.

A support zone below an ascending triangle comes into play when prices climb into the triangle, then break out downward. Prices tumble to the zone and find support, sometimes rebounding upward and sometimes pushing on through.

Returning to Table 15.2, we see that consolidation regions pose a threat to performance. When a consolidation region is in the price path, prices rise after upward breakouts by 29%, well below the 36% gain when no consolidation region exists. For downward breakouts, the trend is the same only the numbers change: Prices decline by an average 18% when a consolidation region exists and 19% without one. Clearly, it pays to look for a consolidation

Table 15.2
Average Performance of Ascending Triangles
with and Without a Consolidation Region

Description	Upward Breakouts	Score	Downward Breakouts	Score
Consolidation region	29% (149)	–1	–18% (88)	–1
No consolidation region	36% (310)	+1	–19% (206)	+1
Average length (days)	40		36	
Prices stop within region ±5%	35%		24%	
Prices push through region	59%		52%	
Prices do not reach region	6%		24%	

Note: The number of samples appears in parentheses.

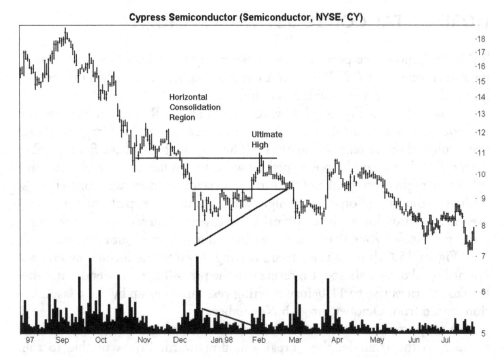

Figure 15.4 An HCR. Prices near or touch 10.69 from October through November, setting up a resistance zone that February prices cannot pierce.

region between the trend start and the formation start before buying or shorting a stock.

As an indication of what to look for, I measured the average length of an HCR. For upward breakouts, the regions averaged 40 days long and 36 days for downward breakouts. In essence, the regions should be easily visible on the daily time scale and appear large enough to pose a threat to continued price movement.

How often does the consolidation region repel prices? I compared the ultimate high to the top and bottom of the consolidation region, and Table 15.2 shows the results. For upward breakouts, 35% of the time prices stop within the region (including a 5% buffer surrounding the region to include those prices that stop near the region). Six percent of the time prices never climb into the zone, and the remaining 59% of the time prices pierce the consolidation region and continue climbing. There is no overlap between the zones.

For downward breakouts, prices stop within 5% of the region 24% of the time, and another 24% of the time, prices do not make it down to the consolidation region. The remainder, 52% of the time, prices push on through and continue lower. Again, there is no overlap between zones.

INSIDE THE PATTERN

Table 15.3 shows important statistical findings for ascending triangles. I found 850 ascending triangles in the 700+ stocks I looked at using up to a 10-year period. Since triangles are so plentiful, you can be selective when choosing one in which to invest.

I measured the average rise from the formation top to the highest high before a 20% trend change; for downward breakouts, the average decline is from the breakout price to the ultimate low—the lowest low before a 20% price rise. I ignored premature breakouts, either up or down, and those breakouts that curl around the end of the formation before moving off in the eventual breakout direction. *Encyclopedia of Chart Patterns* (Wiley, 2000) provides a dozen statistics on premature breakouts if you need more information.

For example, look at Figure 15.2. The first close outside the formation boundaries is downward but it lasts just 6 days. Prices climb back into the formation then shoot out the top and continue moving higher. The sustained rise indicates that the actual breakout direction is upward. Therefore, determining the breakout direction in a historical price series is subjective.

Premature breakouts are a problem with ascending triangles and one you should be aware of. When researching my previous book, I found that premature breakouts occurred 25% of the time or less (for both breakout directions) and when they did occur, they agreed with the actual breakout direction between 40% and 42% of the time. My advice is simple: Trade in the direction of the breakout *when it agrees with the prevailing price trend*, and if prices then go against you, close out your position quickly.

For the ascending triangles I looked at, the gains averaged 34% (upward breakouts) and the losses averaged 19% (downward breakouts).

The 34% rise and 19% loss compares to a gain of 6% and loss of 0%, respectively, for the Standard & Poor's 500 Index, as measured from the breakout date to the date of the ultimate high or low. Consider the S&P change as the rise or decline that an owner of an index mutual fund would have.

Table 15.3
Important Statistical Findings

Description	Upward Breakouts	Downward Breakouts
Number of formations	552	298
Average rise or decline	34%	19%
Standard & Poor's 500 change	6%	0%
Median rise or decline	27%	19%
Rises or declines more than 50%	116/459 or 25%	8/294 or 3%

The median rise or decline is the midrange value after sorting the returns such that half the values are above the median and half fall below it. For upward breakouts, the median is 27%—quite far from the 34% average, whereas the median decline is 19%, tying the average decline.

Since the average rise or decline represents a *best-case* scenario, because it is measured from the breakout price to the ultimate high or ultimate low, your results will probably be lower. When you include your trading skill, commissions, slippage, and other trading costs, your actual return may differ substantially from the average or median.

To gauge the peak performance, I counted the number of ascending triangles that rose or fell more than 50%. For upward breakouts, 25% climbed above the 50% mark, but just 3% of downward breakouts dropped by 50%. These results sound about right for bullish and bearish chart patterns. So, if you expect your short sale to drop by half, you will probably be wrong.

FAILURE RATES

Since investors seem to place an emphasis on failures, I show two types of failures. The first type appears in Table 15.4. I sorted ascending triangles by their breakout direction and used a frequency distribution to further sort the performance into 10 bins. For example, 27 or 6% of the ascending triangles with upward breakouts climbed less than 5%. Six percent, or 17, of the downward breakouts failed to decline by more than 5%.

Table 15.4
Maximum Price Rise or Decline Versus Failure Rate

Maximum Price Rise or Decline (%)	Upward Breakout Failure Rate	Downward Breakout Failure Rate
5	27 or 6%	17 or 6%
10	77 or 17%	72 or 24%
15	117 or 25%	118 or 40%
20	175 or 38%	162 or 55%
25	220 or 48%	207 or 70%
30	248 or 54%	232 or 79%
35	280 or 61%	266 or 90%
50	343 or 75%	286 or 97%
75	391 or 85%	294 or 100%
100	419 or 91%	294 or 100%

Note: The sample count is 459 and 294 for upward and downward breakouts, respectively, for each row.

Table 15.5
Horizon Failure Rates and Average Rise or Decline

Time Since Breakout	Upward Breakout Failure Rate (%)	Average Rise (%)	Downward Breakout Failure Rate (%)	Average Decline (%)
1 week	10	5	6	6
2 weeks	15	6	7	7
3 weeks	20	6	12	7
1 month	22	7	16	8
2 months	27	8	28	7
3 months	30	10	36	5
6 months	30	13	44	2

As you scan down the table, look at how quickly the failure rate rises. Those formations rising or declining less than 10% show triple or quadruple the failure rates of the prior row. For downward breakouts, half the formations will decline less than 20%; for upward breakouts, half will rise less than 27%. Only 9% of the stocks I looked at had prices that doubled after an upward breakout.

Table 15.5 shows a new concept called the horizon failure rate. To find the horizon failure rate, count the number of stocks with upward breakouts in which the closing price is below the breakout price after 1 week, 2 weeks, and so forth. For downward breakouts, count the number above the breakout price. Then divide the results into the total number of formations for their respective breakout directions. The result is the horizon failure rate.

For example, after 1 week, 10% of the ascending triangles with upward breakouts had closing prices below the breakout price; 6% with downward breakouts were in failure territory—above the breakout price. During that time, those with upward breakouts showed rises averaging 5%, and those with downward breakouts declined by an average of 6%.

By definition, after the first day the horizon failure rate is 0%, so you can see how the failure rates climb as time passes. For the most part, ascending triangles do quite well. For upward breakouts, the horizon failure rate triples from 10% to 30% after 6 months. Downward breakouts, however, go from 6% to 44%, a multiple of seven in the failure rate over the same span.

For upward breakouts, the average rise almost triples, too, moving from 5% to 13% with steady increases. For downward breakouts, the best performance comes after 1 month with a decline averaging 8%, then the decline shallows. At the end of 6 months, the average decline is just 2%.

In summary, for upward breakouts it appears worth the added risk to hold onto a stock showing good performance. For downward breakouts, beware that after 1 month you may have seen the maximum depth of the decline.

Table 15.6
Average Performance Sorted by Breakout Price
According to Prior 12-Month Range

Yearly Price Range	Upward Breakouts	Score	Downward Breakouts	Score
Highest third	37% (184)	+1	–18% (89)	–1
Middle third	30% (107)	–1	–18% (84)	–1
Lowest third	31% (74)	–1	–20% (70)	+1

Note: The number of samples appears in parentheses.

YEARLY PRICE RANGE

Table 15.6 shows the performance of ascending triangles sorted by the breakout price over the prior 12-month price range. For those stocks in which data was available for the 12 months leading to the breakout, I found the highest high and lowest low over that period and divided the price range into thirds: highest third, middle third, and lowest third.

For upward breakouts, breakouts in the highest third of the yearly price range posted rises averaging 37%. Downward breakouts showed the best performance in the lowest third of the yearly price range with declines averaging 20%.

If you have a choice, and you always do, select ascending triangles with upward breakouts near the yearly high; find triangles with downward breakouts near the yearly low for best performance. The results are in keeping with the belief that those stocks making new highs continue making new highs, and those making new lows are the ones to short—not the other way around.

TALL AND SHORT PATTERNS

Table 15.7 shows some astounding results. Tall ascending triangles with upward breakouts post gains averaging 51%, more than double the 24% rise for short ones. Downward breakouts show a similar trend but are less spectacular: losses of 22% and 16% for tall and short, respectively.

How did I come up with those results? I computed the formation height from the highest high to the lowest low in the formation, then divided the result by the breakout price. Following that, I sorted the results according to their breakout direction and chose the median value as the cutoff between short and tall. For upward breakouts, the cutoff was 10.80% and downward breakouts had a 11.61% cutoff. The case studies at the end of this chapter give examples of how to make the calculation.

Table 15.7
Performance of Short and Tall Ascending Triangles

Description	Upward Breakout	Score	Downward Breakout	Score
Tall (above the median)	51%, (229)	+1	−22% (147)	+1
Short (below the median)	24%, (230)	−1	−16% (147)	−1
Median percentage of breakout price	10.80%		11.61%	

Note: The number of samples appears in parentheses.

VOLUME TREND

A key identification tip for ascending triangles is a receding volume trend over the length of the formation, from start to breakout. As you can see by the sample sizes in Table 15.8, a receding volume trend occurs most often. For downward breakouts, declining volume is fine because performance improves over a rising volume trend, with losses averaging 20% and 16%, respectively. For upward breakouts, the results are just the reverse. The average gain after ascending triangles showing a rising volume trend is 39%, compared to 32% for those triangles with falling volume trends.

To determine the volume trend, I used linear regression, which is explained in Glossary and Methodology. Many times, you can come to the same conclusion as linear regression just by looking at the volume graph. For example, look at Figure 15.1. Clearly, the volume trend is downward as the line on the chart illustrates. Indeed, many of the figures in this chapter have receding volume trends, according to the slope of the line found using linear regression. If you want to use linear regression, I suggest loading up a spreadsheet with the volume numbers and using the spreadsheet's built-in formula (usually called the trend function) to compute it.

Table 15.8
Linear Regression Volume Trend and Performance

Description	Upward Breakouts	Score	Downward Breakouts	Score
Rising volume trend	39% (106)	+1	−16% (72)	−1
Falling volume trend	32% (353)	−1	−20% (222)	+1

Note: The number of samples appears in parentheses.

BREAKOUT VOLUME

Consider breakout volume and the resulting performance from ascending triangles, as shown in Table 15.9. Those triangles with above-average breakout volume scored gains of 46%, whereas those with average or below-average breakout volume performed less well, with gains averaging 31%. For downward breakouts, the results were essentially flat, at 18% and 19%.

For the longest time, I did not give much credence to volume patterns. Just because you have heavy breakout volume is no reason to assume that your triangle will outperform. Many analysts will tell you that high breakout volume is a good sign and my research into volume trends suggests they are right. Table 15.9 reinforces that opinion, at least for upward breakouts.

What is average breakout volume? I compared the breakout volume with the average from the prior 90 days and assigned the breakout volume reading into one of five categories: very high, high, average, low, and very low. Usually, you can come to the same conclusion just by looking at a chart. Visually compare the breakout volume with the last 3 months. If the breakout volume is higher than most volume peaks, then you are probably dealing with above-average volume.

I do not score downward breakouts because the differences (18.3% versus 18.7%) are not statistically significant.

THROWBACKS AND PULLBACKS

Table 15.10 shows an analysis of throwbacks (upward breakouts) and pullbacks (downward breakouts). A throwback or pullback occurs when prices return to the breakout price within 30 days of the breakout and there is white space between the curl of the throwback or pullback and the breakout price. Figure 15.1 shows an example of a throwback. Figure 15.2 shows an example of a pullback, if you consider the premature downward breakout as the actual breakout. I use the white space requirement to distinguish a throwback or pullback

Table 15.9
Breakout Volume and Performance

Description	Upward Breakouts	Score	Downward Breakouts	Score
Average rise or decline on above-average breakout volume	46% (94)	+1	18% (48)	0
Average rise or decline on average or below-average breakout volume	31% (365)	−1	19% (246)	0

Note: The number of samples appears in parentheses.

Table 15.10
Throwback and Pullback Statistics

Description	Upward Breakouts (Throwbacks)	Downward Breakouts (Pullbacks)
Throwbacks or pullbacks	286/552 or 52%	128/298 or 43%
Score if throwback or pullback predicted	–1	–1
Score if throwback or pullback not predicted	+1	+1
Ultimate high or low before throwback or pullback	84/552 or 15%	41/297 or 14%
Average rise or decline on above-average breakout volume with throwbacks or pullbacks	36%	17%
Average rise or decline on above-average breakout volume with no throwbacks or pullbacks	54%	19%
Average rise or decline on average or below-average breakout volume with throwbacks or pullbacks	26%	14%
Average rise or decline on average or below-average breakout volume with no throwbacks or pullbacks	37%	22%
Number of throwbacks or pullbacks after a high or very high volume breakout	55/159 or 35%	19/159 or 12%
Number of throwbacks or pullbacks after an average, low, or very low volume breakout	231/691 or 33%	109/691 or 16%
Number of throwbacks or pullbacks that stopped ±5% from the breakout price	216 or 76%	115 or 90%
Number of throwbacks or pullbacks that stopped between formation high and low	44 or 15%	3 or 2%
Number of throwbacks or pullbacks that stopped below/above formation low/high	26 or 9%	10 or 8%

from prices sliding along the breakout price. There should be enough space between the throwback or pullback and the breakout price to make the curling pattern obvious.

Throwbacks occur just over half the time (52%), whereas pullbacks are more rare, coming in at 43%.

How often does a throwback or pullback reach its ultimate high or low before curling back to the breakout price? For both up and down breakouts, the rate is nearly the same, 15% and 14% for throwbacks and pullbacks, respectively.

The next several lines of Table 15.10 show the price performance after a throwback or pullback when accompanied by high or low volume. If you compare the results carefully, you can see that a throwback or pullback impedes performance. For example, when a throwback occurs, prices score an average rise of 36%, compared to a rise of 54% when no throwback occurs. In both cases, the breakout volume is above average.

Performance also varies with breakout volume. A high volume breakout pushes prices further than a low volume breakout. For example, a high volume upward breakout with a throwback has an average rise of 36%, but the gain is only 26% when the breakout volume is average or below. The trend is the same regardless of whether a throwback or pullback occurs except for downward breakouts with no pullbacks. They show that a high volume breakout and no pullback has losses averaging 19%, compared to a 22% average loss for low volume breakouts.

In research I have done for other chart patterns, a throwback is more likely to occur after a high volume breakout, a pullback after a low volume breakout. Ascending triangles agree with other patterns. A throwback is more likely to occur after an above-average volume breakout (35% versus 33% of the time) and pullbacks occur more often after a low volume breakout (12% versus 16% for high, low volume, respectively).

When a throwback or pullback occurs, where do prices usually stop? This is important to know so you can place a stop-loss order outside the usual trigger range. For both throwbacks and pullbacks, prices usually stop within 5% of the breakout price. Since the table may be confusing, let me describe the statistics for throwbacks. When a throwback occurred, 76% of the time prices stopped descending within 5% of the breakout price. Another 15% of the time, prices continued down into the formation before recovering. Finally, the remaining 9% of the time, prices not only threw back, but plunged out the bottom of the formation and continued down. A similar scenario exists for pullbacks, only the direction is upward.

In all cases, I measured from the first minor low or high after the throwback or pullback reached the breakout price. If a stair-step decline took place, for example, I only measured the first step, even though prices tumbled lower.

BULL AND BEAR TRAPS

A bull (upward breakout) or bear (downward breakout) trap occurs after a breakout when prices move in the breakout direction less than 10%, then return to the formation and shoot out the other side. The term bull trap or bear trap is descriptive because the price action seduces investors into buying or shorting the stock, then traps them into a losing position as prices move in the adverse direction.

For ascending triangles, bull traps are rare, occurring only 17% of the time (see Table 15.11). Bear traps occur more often, 24% of the time, but I consider that low, too. To determine whether a trap is likely to occur, look for

Table 15.11
Bull and Bear Traps

Description	Upward Breakouts (Bull Traps)	Downward Breakouts (Bear Traps)
Trap frequency	77/459 or 17%	72/294 or 24%
Score if trap predicted	–1	–1
Score if trap not predicted	+1	+1

anything that might interfere with price travel, such as support or resistance zones set up by prior chart patterns, HCRs, trendlines, minor highs or lows; even popular moving averages sometimes influence buying or selling behavior.

MARKET TREND

Table 15.12 shows the performance after ascending triangles break out during rising and falling markets, as measured while the formation is under construction and to the ultimate high or low. I took a snapshot of the Standard & Poor's 500 Index on the day the formation started, ended, and the date the stock reached its ultimate high or low. The differences between those points indicated whether the general market was rising or falling over that span. Then, I compared the performance of prices after an ascending triangle, sorted by the breakout direction and market trend.

For both breakout directions, performance is best when the formation is under construction and the market is falling. After the breakout, you would expect a rising market to lift all boats and prices to rise higher than if the market were falling, which is the case as Table 15.12 shows. However, a falling market should make it easier for prices to decline, but that does not seem to happen with ascending triangles. Prices drop by 21% in a rising market but by only 17% in a falling market.

Table 15.12
Average Price Performance of Ascending Triangles During a Rising and Falling Market

Market Trend	Upward Breakouts FS to FE	FE to UH	Downward Breakouts FS to FE	FE to UL
Rising S&P 500	33% (334)	35% (402)	–18% (230)	–21% (129)
Falling S&P 500	35% (125)	23% (57)	–20% (64)	–17% (165)

Note: FS = formation start, FE = formation end, UH = ultimate high, UL = ultimate low. The number of samples appears in parentheses.

For both breakout directions, the performance differences are not statistically significant, so are not scored.

MARKET CAPITALIZATION

Table 15.13 shows the performance after sorting stocks by market capitalization. To compute the market capitalization, I used the shares outstanding times the breakout price. You can see that small and mid caps performed better than large caps for both market directions.

The table says two things: First, for rising stocks, buy small caps because they perform best; second, large caps decline least in a falling market.

SCORES

Throughout this chapter tables contain score values. Use the scores to rank your chart pattern. I show you how to do that in the case studies, but it amounts to comparing your chart pattern with the table listings, then adding the scores together. Scores above zero mean an investment is worth considering; scores below zero suggest avoiding the stock. These results apply to both upward and downward breakouts.

To assess how effective the scoring system is for ascending triangles, Table 15.14 lists the performance results.

Ascending triangles with scores above zero show gains averaging 50%. When the score is below zero, the rises average just 21%. For downward breakouts, the declines are 23% and 12% for above zero and below zero scores, respectively.

To further evaluate the system's performance, I found the median rise or decline for those ascending triangles in which all the information was available. For example, if the ultimate high was unavailable because the breakout occurred yesterday, then I removed that formation from the tally.

Table 15.13
Average Price Performance of Ascending
Triangles by Market Capitalization

Capitalization	Upward Breakouts	Score	Downward Breakouts	Score
Small cap (up to $1 billion)	41% (263)	+1	–19% (177)	0
Mid cap ($1 to $5 billion)	30% (143)	–1	–20% (75)	+1
Large cap (over $5 billion)	24% (44)	–1	–15% (34)	–1

Note: The number of samples appears in parentheses.

Table 15.14
Formation Performance by Score

Score	Upward Breakouts	Downward Breakouts
Average rise or decline of chart patterns with scores above zero	50%	23%
Average rise or decline of chart patterns with scores below zero	21%	12%
Median rise or decline used	26.82%	17.21%
Percentage with scores above zero beating median rise or decline	130/192 or 68%	93/146 or 64%
Percentage with scores below zero doing worse than median rise or decline	117/165 or 71%	54/68 or 79%

Chart patterns with above zero scores (buy signals) beat the median rise 68% of the time. I consider anything above 50% to add value. Those chart patterns with scores below zero (avoid buying signals) correctly fell short of the median 71% of the time.

Downward breakouts tell a similar tale with correct sell-short signals 64% of the time, and correct avoid shorting 79% of the time.

As always, your trading skill will be the deciding factor in any trade, regardless of whether or not the triangle has a good score. The system is not perfect, as the table shows, so consult other indicators or techniques before making a trading decision.

CASE STUDY 1

Since upward breakouts occur twice as often as downward ones, I concentrate on the upward direction. Consider the triangle shown in Figure 15.5. Where does the trend start? Starting with the beginning of the formation, working backward in time, we see that prices generally trend downward, so we look for prices to rise by 20% after reaching the trend start.

Prices make a minor low in late October at a price of 15.25. A 20% rise from this price would be a *close* above 18.30, and prices cleared that hurdle just 4 days earlier. Therefore, the October low represents the trend start. Using Table 15.1, the time from the trend start to the formation start is less than 3 months, for a +1 score (upward breakout direction).

Is there an HCR between the trend start and the formation? No. That is because prices enter the formation from the bottom and shoot out the top, so there is no resistance zone to hold prices down. Table 15.2 indicates that

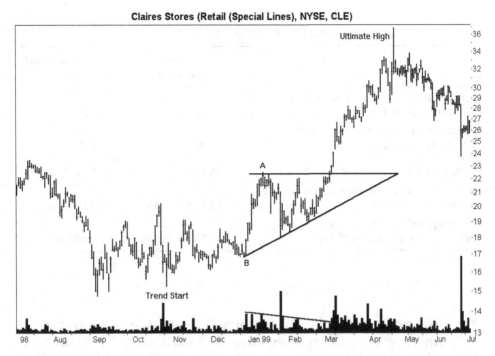

Figure 15.5 An ascending triangle with upward breakout. The scoring system ranked this a +5 and prices climbed 62% after the breakout.

ascending triangles showing no consolidation regions work best, for a +1 score. Running total: +2.

I skip to Table 15.6 because that is the next table with scores. Where in the yearly price range does the breakout occur? You can almost see the yearly price range in Figure 15.5. The yearly high was 24.13, and the low was 14.75, with a breakout price of 22.75—the price of the horizontal trendline. Clearly, the breakout resides near the yearly high for a +1 score. Running total: +3.

How tall is the triangle as a percentage of the breakout price? At the widest part where prices touch the trendlines, the top is at the breakout price of 22.75 (point A), and the low is at 16.94 (point B), for a difference of 5.81. Divide the result by the breakout price, 22.75, for a height of 26% of the breakout price. According to Table 15.7, the triangle is a tall one because its height is above the median 10.80%, for a +1 score. Running total: +4.

What is the volume trend from the formation start to the breakout (or formation end, if you prefer—they are the same point)? You can use linear regression to determine the slope of the volume trendline, but why bother? Clearly, volume is trending downward. Table 15.8 says a falling volume trend rates a –1 score. Running total: +3.

Is the breakout volume above average? My computer rates it high and, if you look at Figure 15.5, I am sure you will agree. Table 15.9 says high breakout volume is bitchin', dude, for a +1 score. Running total: +4.

What is the likelihood of a throwback? With prices so close to the yearly high, the breakout might clear any prior resistance zone. The July 1998 minor high poses no real threat to upward price movement, so I would suggest a throwback is unlikely. Table 15.10 says no throwback rates a +1 score, for a running total of +5. After the breakout, you can see that prices moved higher almost without pausing and without throwing back.

For the same reason—no overhead resistance—a bull trap was also unlikely. Looking at the weekly chart since 1996, prices reached a high of 26.63 briefly in September 1996 and touched 24 three other times along the way. If the 24 level is questionable, either from a bull trap or throwback standpoint, simply wait to be sure prices punch through that level before buying. However, waiting raises your risk of failure and decreases your potential profit. No predicted trap means a score of +1. Running total: +6.

Using the 22.75 breakout price and multiplying it by the number of shares outstanding places the stock in the mid cap category. According to Table 15.13, mid caps score −1, so the final total is at +5.

Any score above zero suggests the stock is worth considering. That does not mean it is an automatic buy, but it improves the chances of the stock performing above the median. In this case, prices reached their ultimate high in mid-April at a price of 36.88, or 62% above the breakout price and well above the 26.82% median rise.

CASE STUDY 2

What happens when the score is negative? Figure 15.6 shows this case study and one that results in a negative score. Running quickly through the tables gives the following analysis.

Table 15.1: Price trend. The trend started in mid-July, placing it in the intermediate term for a −1 score.

Table 15.2: Consolidation region. By definition, there was no HCR between the trend start and the formation. Since the breakout was upward and prices trended into the formation from the bottom, an HCR would only interfere if prices broke out downward. Score: +1. Running total: 0.

Table 15.6: Yearly price range. The breakout price was at 22.38, the yearly high was at 29.25, and the yearly low at 18.38, placing the breakout in the center third of the yearly price range. Score: −1. Running total: −1.

Table 15.7: Triangle height. A breakout price of 22.38 and a formation low of 20.38 gives a height expressed as a percentage of the breakout price of 2/22.38 or 9%. It is a short fella for a −1 score. Running total: −2.

Table 15.8: Volume trend. You can see in Figure 15.6 that the volume trend slopes downward for a −1 score. Running total: −3.

Figure 15.6 An ascending triangle with upward breakout and highly negative score. The stock climbed just 6%.

Table 15.9: Breakout volume. The breakout volume was nothing to write home about as it was lower than many of the days over the last 3 months. My computer calls it average, for a –1 score. Running total: –4.

Tables 15.10 and 15.11: Throwback and bull trap. With a solid resistance zone and a flat top hanging over prices, it is no wonder prices struggled, but failed, to move much higher. A throwback occurred after hitting the resistance zone. When prices dropped below the formation low, a bull trap confirmed. If you owned the stock, it was time to sell when prices closed below the triangle apex (where the two triangle trendlines meet). Actually, with overhead resistance, you would have to be crazy to buy this one. Score –1 for the throwback and –1 for the bull trap. Running total: –6.

Table 15.13: Market capitalization. The stock is a small cap for a +1 score. Final total: –5.

With a score below zero, an investment risks underperforming the median rise. In fact, the stock climbed by just 6%, to 23.63 before tumbling, coming up well short of the 26.82% median rise.

CASE STUDY 3

Consider Figure 15.7. If you run through the tables you come up with a –1 score, suggesting poor results after an upward breakout. Why an upward breakout? On June 9, prices closed at 21.50, a whisker above the formation top of 21.38. I saw the ascending triangle forming and this is my notebook entry for June 9.

"6/9/99. Ascending triangle with upside breakout. I decided to stay away from this because it might do a rounding turn and head down. The other machinery stocks are weak today and with interest rates due to rise at the end of June (Federal Open Market Committee meeting then), this could be a disaster. I'll paper trade it."

Another clue was the quick price rise in the 2 weeks before the formation. Prices zipped from 15.38 to 21.31, a rise of almost 40% in just 14 trading days. Quick declines often follow quick rises. Keep that in mind the next time you see a similar situation.

Fortunately, I made the right decision to stay away from this one. The next day, prices moved back into the formation, dropped out the bottom, then

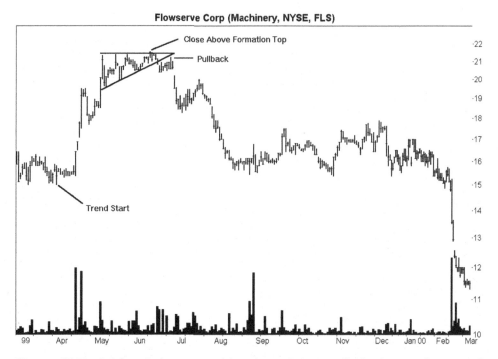

Figure 15.7 A false, 1-day upward breakout. Prices really broke out downward and declined by 50%.

pulled back, struggling to hold on. By mid-August, prices were down to 16 where they traded horizontally for 6 months before completing their tumble. Prices reached bottom at 10.56 in early March 2000, just to the right of Figure 15.7, a decline of 50% from the downward breakout price.

This scenario is an example of when the scoring system accurately predicted a disaster. The good news is that if you bought into the upward breakout, there was plenty of time to exit when prices closed below the bottom trendline boundary. You had nine trading days to get out of the situation with a small loss. If you were a novice investor and decided to hold on for the long term, it would be a long time, indeed. A year and a half later, in mid-December 2000, you would have received an early Christmas present when prices fully recovered to break even.

Study this chart carefully. If you cannot close out a losing position quickly, do not give up your day job. You will need the money to cover your massive losses.

16

Triangles, Descending

Descending triangles seem to be as messy as their ascending cousins. With premature breakouts and real breakouts that quickly curl around the triangle apex, it is a wonder that people even consider these chart patterns for trading. Indeed, the name *descending* is mildly misleading since 45% of the descending triangles I looked at had upward breakouts. However, their performance is quite good, and that makes up for all the messiness. To make money trading descending triangles, trade in the direction of the breakout, then visit your favorite place of worship (pray, in other words). Close out your position quickly if prices go against you.

THE TYPICAL PATTERN

I am not sure there is such a thing as a *typical* pattern for descending triangles. However, Figure 16.1 shows a decent example of one. Prices enter from the bottom and form a new minor high, retrace to the bottom trendline, and continue bouncing between the trendlines until breaking out downward. Prices return to the triangle base before eventually moving lower, reaching a low of 29.56 in early January 2000, for a decline of 29%.

The volume trend in this example is not typical. Usually, the trend is downward (82% of the time), not upward as it appears in Figure 16.1.

Figure 16.2 shows another example of a descending triangle, but this one has a premature breakout upward. Why premature? Because prices briefly close above the top trendline, then throwback and fall substantially lower. Prices rejoin the prevailing downward trend that was in effect from January through April, before the formation began. Clearly, this is a judgment call that

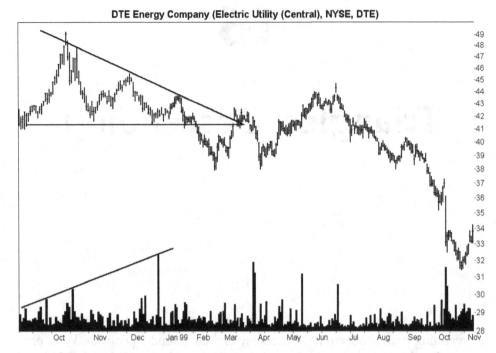

Figure 16.1   A descending triangle. This is a good example of a descending triangle but even it has problems. In a classic descending triangle, the volume trend slopes downward, instead of rising as shown here.

can have an impact on the statistics. Regardless, keep in mind this curling situation, and remember that tight stops would have prevented a major loss.

TREND START

Many times the price trend leading to a chart pattern helps predict the performance after the breakout. To make searching for the trend start consistent, I adopted a set of rules. Begin with the formation start and work backward in time, following the price trend until a 20% trend change occurs. Measure this from the current closing price to the highest high or lowest low price.

For example, consider Figure 16.2. Except for the 2 days before the triangle starts, prices are trending downward toward the triangle. Therefore, working backward in time, we are looking for the highest high before a 20% decline in prices. First, we come across the minor high shown as point B, at 35.19. A 20% decline from that price would be a close below 28.15. Clearly, prices did not decline that far, so we move further backward in time, stopping at point A. A 20% decline from 45.25, would be a close below 36.20. Again, prices did not decline that far. Eventually, we find the trend start at 45.75. A

Figure 16.2 A descending triangle with a premature upward breakout. Prices curl around the triangle apex and head lower . . . much lower.

20% decline from this price would be a close below 36.60, and prices reach this level on December 4. So, the 45.75 price represents the trend start.

Measuring from the trend start to the formation start gives us the length of the trend. For Figure 16.2, it measures 101 days (just over 3 months). Using Table 16.1, we find that descending triangles with downward breakouts and intermediate-term price trends leading to the formation show declines averaging 19%.

Table 16.1
Average Performance of Descending Triangles
Sorted by Price Trend Leading to the Pattern

Trend Start to Formation Start	Upward Breakout	Score	Downward Breakout	Score
Short term (0 to 3 months)	49% (170)	+1	−20% (246)	+1
Intermediate term (3 to 6 months)	43% (65)	+1	−19% (88)	+1
Long term (over 6 months)	30% (60)	−1	−13% (97)	−1

Note: The number of samples appears in parentheses.

You can see that the best performance comes from short-term—under 3 months—price trends. From the results, you can guess that a descending triangle occurring after a long-term price rise or decline is probably forming near, but not quite at, the end of the trend, which is why the average rise or decline is comparatively poor.

Incidentally, I explain scoring in the Scores section of this chapter, so do not be concerned with the values now.

HORIZONTAL CONSOLIDATION REGIONS

Figure 16.3 shows what a horizontal consolidation region (HCR) looks like. Sometimes, a consolidation region can get in the way of further price travel. In this case, prices stop in the 41 area after encountering overhead resistance.

How can you determine if a consolidation region will act as a deterrent to price movement? For upward breakouts, look for consolidation between the trend start and the formation top, if prices entered the formation from the top (the formation acts as a U-shaped reversal). For downward breakouts, look for a support zone between the trend start and the formation bottom, assuming

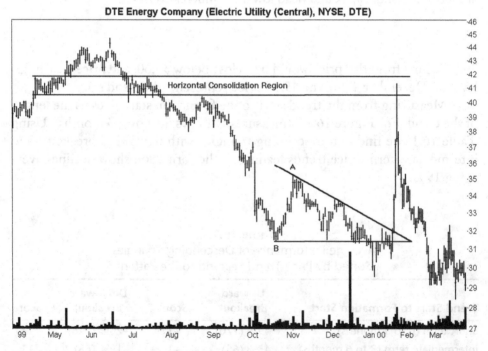

Figure 16.3   An HCR. Sometimes overhead resistance is an impediment to upward price travel, as in this case. The price difference between points A and B mark the formation height.

prices entered the formation from the bottom (an inverted U-shaped reversal). For example, Figure 16.3 shows prices entering from the top and staging an upward breakout. As prices rise, they have to push through prior price action—layers of resistance—to reach new highs.

Once you determine that the price trend looks like a U or inverted U, then look for flat tops, flat bottoms or both. It is not mandatory that prices all stop at the same level, but many prices must reach the same level over several days or weeks. In Figure 16.3, there are two HCRs, one in April and one in July. Together, they act as a formidable barrier to upward price movement.

Table 16.2 shows statistics related to HCRs. For downward breakouts, when an HCR is in the price path, prices decline 16%. When no support region exists, prices tumble an average of 19%.

For upward breakouts, the results are the reverse. A consolidation region apparently acts as a springboard since prices climb 54% but climb just 39% without overhead resistance. The differences are statistically significant, meaning that they are not likely due to chance.

Why this is the case is a mystery to me, but I suspect the comparatively small sample count (62) is the reason. Feel free to pencil in the scores you want to use. For other chart pattern types, a consolidation region usually scores –1 and no consolidation region scores +1.

How long must a consolidation region be to be effective? There is no set limit, but the average length was about 5 weeks for both breakout directions. Of course there is wide variation as you might expect.

Where do prices stop in relation to the consolidation region? Just 16% of those formations with upward breakouts could not quite make it up to the consolidation region. Another 26% stopped within the region (including a 5% buffer so as to include those that stopped a bit short or wide of the mark), and the remainder, 59%, pushed through the resistance zone and continued higher,

Table 16.2
Average Performance of Descending Triangles with and Without a Consolidation Region

Description	Upward Breakouts	Score	Downward Breakouts	Score
Consolidation region	54% (62)	+1	–16% (173)	–1
No consolidation region	39% (259)	–1	–19% (280)	+1
Average length (days)	36		37	
Prices stop within region ±5%	26%		53%	
Prices push through region	59%		40%	
Prices do not reach region	16%		7%	

Note: The number of samples appears in parentheses.

which says a lot about the effectiveness of overhead resistance, or rather, the lack of effectiveness.

Downward breakouts performed better. Seven percent of the time prices did not make it down to the region. Another 53% of the time, prices stopped within 5% of the region, and the remainder of the time, 40%, prices pushed on through. In all cases, the regions did not overlap.

For downward breakouts, there is a decent chance that a consolidation zone below the chart pattern will support prices. For upward breakouts, it seems that price momentum easily overcomes the resistance set up by the consolidation region. That may be one reason (but not a complete explanation) why a consolidation region is not an impediment to upward price movement—for descending triangles at any rate.

INSIDE THE PATTERN

Table 16.3 shows important statistical findings for descending triangles. The first thing you may notice is that descending triangles are plentiful, occurring 824 times in the stocks I looked at. If I told you I had to search a gazillion stocks to find those 824, that might take the wind out of your sails. However, I looked at 500 stocks over 5 years with an additional 230 stocks ranging from 1 to 5 years of nonoverlapping data. Compared with other formation types, descending triangles are quite common.

For upward breakouts, I measured from the breakout price (when prices close outside the trendlines) to the highest high before a 20% trend change; for downward breakouts, I used the lowest low. Upward breakouts score quite well, averaging gains of 42%, whereas downward breakouts show losses of 18%, on average. This compares with a rise of 38% and a decline of 21% for all bullish and bearish chart pattern types, respectively.

As descending triangles were posting 42% gains and 18% losses, the S&P 500 Index was scoring rises of just 5% and losses of 1%, respectively. To get

Table 16.3
Important Statistical Findings

Description	Upward Breakouts	Downward Breakouts
Number of formations	368	456
Average rise or decline	42%	18%
Standard & Poor's 500 change	5%	−1%
Median rise or decline	34%	17%
Rises or declines more than 50%	109/321 or 34%	11/453 or 2%

this result, I measured from the day the descending triangle broke out to the date prices reached the ultimate high or low.

The median rise or decline is the midrange value from a sorted list of values such that half the samples are above the median and half below it. You could consider this to be the rise or decline that an experienced investor can expect to receive if he trades descending triangles often enough.

Many factors influence trading results, such as commissions, slippage, and skill, all of which are not included in the numbers. However, the median value suggests that a few large values pull the average upward. Even with a large sample size of 321, the average is eight points above the median.

As a gauge of how successful a chart pattern can be when it is not misbehaving, I counted the number of rises or declines of more than 50%. For upward breakouts, a third soared more than 50%; downward breakouts only showed 11 or 2% dropping in excess of 50%. Of all the chart patterns reviewed in this book, upward breakouts from descending triangles had the most rises of more than 50%.

FAILURE RATES

Table 16.4 shows one way to calculate the failure rate. I base failures on how far prices rise or decline. For example, 9 or 3% of descending triangles with upward breakouts climbed less than 5%; 7% of downward breakouts failed

Table 16.4
Maximum Price Rise or Decline Versus Failure Rate

Maximum Price Rise or Decline (%)	Upward Breakout Failure Rate	Downward Breakout Failure Rate
5	9 or 3%	33 or 7%
10	30 or 9%	121 or 27%
15	65 or 20%	196 or 43%
20	90 or 28%	281 or 62%
25	126 or 39%	338 or 75%
30	148 or 46%	378 or 84%
35	165 or 51%	407 or 90%
50	212 or 66%	442 or 98%
75	255 or 79%	453 or 100%
100	277 or 86%	453 or 100%

Note: The sample count is 321 and 453 for upward and downward breakouts, respectively, for each row.

to drop more than 5%. Another example: 39% of triangles with upward breakouts climbed less than 25%, whereas 75% with downward breakouts dropped less than 25%.

You can see how the failure rates associated with a 5% price rise or decline are deceptively small. The 10% rise or decline rate shows the number of failures, on a percentage basis, tripling for upward breakouts and almost quadrupling for downward breakouts. The failure rate gets worse as the percentage price rise or decline column increases. If you buy after an upward breakout with the expectation that prices will double (a 100% price rise), your chances of being correct are just 14%—86% will fail to rise that far.

Table 16.5 shows the horizon failure rate. To compute the rate, I counted the number of stocks in which prices moved into failure territory: they dropped below the breakout price for upward breakouts, or climbed above the breakout price for downward breakouts. For example, after the first week, 4% of the descending triangles with upward breakouts were below the breakout price, and after a downward breakout, 14% were above the breakout price. At the end of the first week, triangles with upward breakouts showed rises averaging 7%, whereas those triangles with downward breakouts showed losses of 5%. At the end of 6 months, downward breakouts had *gains* of 2% (hence, the minus sign in the table).

The table shows that over time, the failure rate increases regardless of the breakout direction. For upward breakouts, there appears to be weakness between months 2 and 3, as the average rise drops from 15% to 14% then climbs to 20% at the end of 6 months. For downward breakouts, the largest declines come quickly, in the first 3 weeks, then the "strength of the signal" weakens. Holding longer than 3 weeks suggests a substandard return. Of course, your results may vary.

Table 16.5
Horizon Failure Rates and Average Rise or Decline

Time Since Breakout	Upward Breakout Failure Rate (%)	Average Rise (%)	Downward Breakout Failure Rate (%)	Average Decline (%)
1 week	4	7	14	5
2 weeks	6	9	19	6
3 weeks	6	11	24	6
1 month	11	12	28	5
2 months	13	15	38	4
3 months	17	14	44	2
6 months	20	20	50	-2

Table 16.6
Average Performance Sorted by Breakout Price
According to Prior 12-Month Range

Yearly Price Range	Upward Breakouts	Score	Downward Breakouts	Score
Highest third	43% (90)	0	−16% (122)	−1
Middle third	43% (86)	0	−18% (119)	0
Lowest third	44% (94)	0	−19% (134)	+1

Note: The number of samples appears in parentheses.

YEARLY PRICE RANGE

Table 16.6 shows triangle performance sorted by the position of the breakout price within the yearly trading range. I used only those formations in which the prior 12-month trading range was available, then split the range into thirds—highest third, middle third, and lowest third.

The best performance for both upward and downward breakouts comes when the breakout price is near the yearly low, with rises averaging 44% and declines averaging 19%, respectively. Usually, upward breakouts perform best in the highest third and downward breakouts perform best in the lowest third. At least descending triangles got half of it right. The differences for upward breakouts are not statistically significant, so they have no score.

TALL AND SHORT PATTERNS

Table 16.7 shows the performance of short and tall descending triangles. Perhaps not surprisingly, tall triangles outperformed the small ones. First, some definitions: I calculated the formation height, from the highest high to the

Table 16.7
Performance of Short and Tall Descending Triangles

Description	Upward Breakout	Score	Downward Breakout	Score
Tall (above the median)	53% (161)	+1	−22% (227)	+1
Short (below the median)	34% (160)	−1	−15% (226)	−1
Median percentage of breakout price	12.62%		11.62%	

Note: The number of samples appears in parentheses.

lowest low in the chart pattern, as a percentage of the breakout price. Then I sorted the results according to their breakout direction and selected the median (midrange) value as the separator between short and tall. For upward breakouts, the median was 12.62% and for downward breakouts, the median turned out to be 11.62%.

Using the descending triangle pictured in Figure 16.3 as an example, point A is at 35.25 and the formation low, point B, is at 31.31. The difference between the two points, 3.94, expressed as a percentage of the breakout price, 31.88, is 12.35%. The result places the triangle in the short category because 12.35% is below the median reading of 12.62%.

For upward breakouts, those triangles taller than the median showed gains averaging an astounding 53%, but short triangles had gains of just 34%. The same trend applies to downward breakouts, with declines of 22% compared to 15%, for tall and short triangles, respectively.

VOLUME TREND

Can the volume trend be used to help predict the performance after the breakout? Yes. I used the slope of the line found using linear regression on the volume data to determine whether volume was rising or falling, from the formation start to the breakout. Usually, you can tell just by looking at the volume trend, but most spreadsheets support linear regression (sometimes called the trend function), too, in case you wish to check your results.

For those descending triangles with upward breakouts and a rising volume trend, the performance was superior, with gains of 48% versus a rise of 40% for those triangles with a receding volume trend. Downward breakouts acted in a reverse manner, with a falling volume trend outperforming a rising one by 18% to 16%, respectively. In all cases, the differences are statistically significant, meaning they are not likely due to chance.

Table 16.8
Linear Regression Volume Trend and Performance

Description	Upward Breakouts	Score	Downward Breakouts	Score
Rising volume trend	48% (58)	+1	−16% (77)	−1
Falling volume trend	40% (263)	−1	−18% (376)	+1

Note: The number of samples appears in parentheses.

Table 16.9
Breakout Volume and Performance

Description	Upward Breakouts	Score	Downward Breakouts	Score
Average rise or decline on above-average breakout volume	41% (83)	0	19% (97)	+1
Average rise or decline on average or below-average breakout volume	42% (238)	0	17% (356)	−1

Note: The number of samples appears in parentheses.

BREAKOUT VOLUME

Table 16.9 shows the importance of breakout volume. I computed the 3-month average volume leading to the breakout and compared the result with the volume level on the day prices closed outside the triangle boundaries—the breakout day. I sorted breakout volume into one of five categories: very high, high, average, low, and very low. For those triangles with upward breakouts and above-average breakout volume, prices climbed an average of 41%. This result compares to a rise of 42% for those triangles showing average or below-average breakout volume.

For downward breakouts, the trend flipped—and is what you would expect. Losses averaged 19% on above-average breakout volume and 17% for average or below-average volume. Since the differences for upward breakouts are not statistically different, I show no score.

THROWBACKS AND PULLBACKS

Figure 16.4 shows an example of a pullback. Throwbacks and pullbacks occur after the breakout when prices return to the breakout price within 30 days and there is white space between the curling action of the throwback or pullback and the triangle trendlines. Thirty days is an arbitrary limit but one that is commonly recognized. I added the white space criterion to remove those cases when prices slide along the triangle trendlines.

Table 16.10 shows statistics related to throwbacks (upward breakouts) and pullbacks (downward breakouts). Throwbacks occur 29% of the time, and pullbacks happen 55% of the time.

How often does the ultimate high or low occur before the throwback or pullback? For upward breakouts, the ultimate high or low occurs 10% of the time, but the statistic is more than double that for downward breakouts—24%.

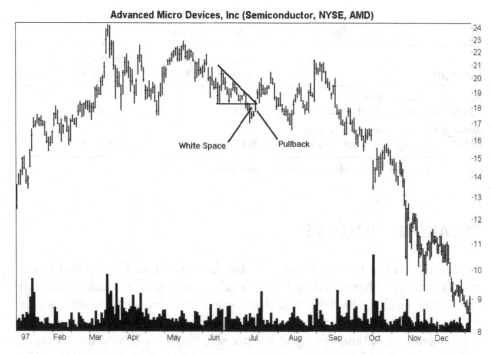

Advanced Micro Devices, Inc (Semiconductor, NYSE, AMD)

Figure 16.4 A pullback from a descending triangle. A pullback occurs when prices return to the breakout price within 30 days and there is white space between the curling price action and the triangle.

The next several lines (average rise and decline) gauge the performance of throwbacks or pullbacks and breakout volume. When breakout volume is above average and no throwback occurs, prices rise an average of 49%, compared to a rise of just 20% after a throwback. That difference is startling. For downward breakouts, a similar trend occurs but the numbers are not as wide, 25% versus 15%.

What happens when the breakout volume is average or below average? Prices climb 48% when no throwback occurs and climb 29% when one does occur. Downward breakouts without pullbacks show losses of 20% compared to losses of 14% for those triangles with pullbacks.

In short, a throwback or pullback hurts performance, regardless of the breakout volume level. The best performance comes after a heavy volume breakout and *no* throwback or pullback.

Is breakout volume an indication that a throwback or pullback will occur? Maybe. For descending triangles, a throwback or pullback occurs more often after an average or below-average volume breakout than a heavy volume breakout. For other chart pattern types, a throwback occurs more often after a high volume breakout, but a pullback happens more often after a low volume breakout.

Table 16.10
Throwback and Pullback Statistics

Description	Upward Breakouts (Throwbacks)	Downward Breakouts (Pullbacks)
Throwbacks or pullbacks	107/368 or 29%	250/456 or 55%
Score if throwback or pullback predicted	–1	–1
Score if throwback or pullback not predicted	+1	+1
Ultimate high or low before throwback or pullback	37/368 or 10%	108/456 or 24%
Average rise or decline on above-average breakout volume with throwbacks or pullbacks	20%	15%
Average rise or decline on above-average breakout volume with no throwbacks or pullbacks	49%	25%
Average rise or decline on average or below-average breakout volume with throwbacks or pullbacks	29%	14%
Average rise or decline on average or below-average breakout volume with no throwbacks or pullbacks	48%	20%
Number of throwbacks or pullbacks after a high or very high volume breakout	22/190 or 12%	55/190 or 29%
Number of throwbacks or pullbacks after an average, low, or very low volume breakout	85/634 or 13%	195/634 or 31%
Number of throwbacks or pullbacks that stopped ±5% from the breakout price	91 or 85%	170 or 68%
Number of throwbacks or pullbacks that stopped between formation high and low	2 or 2%	46 or 18%
Number of throwbacks or pullbacks that stopped below/above formation low/high	14 or 13%	34 or 14%

Where do throwbacks and pullbacks stop? This information is important when trying to decide where to place a stop-loss order. For throwbacks, 85% of the time prices stopped within 5% of the breakout price; 68% of pullbacks stopped near the breakout price. Another 2% and 18%, for throwbacks and pullbacks, respectively, stopped within the price level of the highest high or lowest low of the triangle. The remainder of the time, prices threw back and continued lower or pulled back and continued rising.

For both breakout directions, the horizontal trendline along the bottom of the formation is a good place to put a stop-loss order. Do not place the stop on the price of the trendline, but 0.15 or so below the trendline for upward breakouts, and 0.15 above the trendline for downward breakouts. That way, the line can act as a price support or resistance zone.

BULL AND BEAR TRAPS

Figure 16.5 shows what a bear trap looks like. Bear traps occur when prices break out downward and drop less than 10%, pull back to the formation, and continue rising so that prices climb above the formation top. Bull traps occur

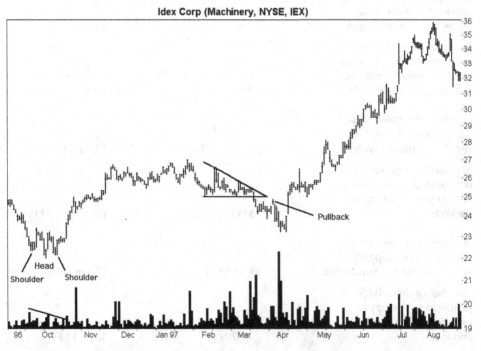

Figure 16.5 A bear trap. Prices break out downward, pull back, and rise above the formation top in a bear trap. A head-and-shoulders bottom forms a consolidation region that supports prices in April.

Table 16.11
Bull and Bear Traps

Description	Upward Breakouts (Bull Traps)	Downward Breakouts (Bear Traps)
Trap frequency	30/321 or 9%	117/453 or 26%
Score if trap predicted	−1	−1
Score if trap not predicted	+1	+1

in a similar manner only if prices throw back after an upward breakout and drop below the lower trendline. In both cases, bear or bull traps, if investors do not sell quickly, they become trapped in a losing position.

Table 16.11 shows how often bear or bull traps occur. For upward breakouts, a bull trap happens only 9% of the time; bear traps occur almost three times as often, or 26%. Both rates are comparatively small.

How can you guard against a trap happening? Look for support or resistance zones in the way of price travel. Figure 16.5, for example, shows a head-and-shoulders bottom that sets up a support zone in which prices cannot penetrate. In April, prices drop to the top price level of the formation, then recover.

GAPS

Table 16.12 shows performance statistics for those descending triangles with and without a price gap on the breakout day. By definition, for upward price gaps, today's low price is above yesterday's high; for downward gaps, today's high price is below yesterday's low.

For upward breakouts, prices climbed an average of 52% after a gap, or fell by 18% for downward breakouts. This compares to an average rise of

Table 16.12
Gaps and Performance

Description	Upward Breakout	Score	Downward Breakouts	Score
Average rise or decline after price gap on breakout	52% (42)	+1	18% (75)	0
Average rise or decline with no price gap on breakout	40% (279)	−1	17% (378)	0

Note: The number of samples appears in parentheses.

40% or a decline of 17% when no gap occurs. In short, *breakout gaps improve performance*.

Unfortunately, I show no meaningful score for downward gaps because the differences are not statistically significant.

MARKET TREND

Table 16.13 shows the average performance after a descending triangle breakout when the general market was trending upward or downward. I measured the overall market performance using the Standard & Poor's 500 Index from the day the formation started, ended, and reached the ultimate high or low.

You can see that the performance difference is quite minor while the formation is under construction, that is, from formation start to end. Measuring from the formation end to the ultimate high or low gives a larger difference. For upward breakouts, a rising market lifts all boats as the performance reaches 43%, whereas prices only rise 31% when the market is trending down (but note the small sample size—46). For some reason, a rising market also helps prices drop lower for downward breakouts. Perhaps the boats have holes in their sides and a rising tide fills them further.

Incidentally, I base the scores on the performance when the formation is under construction (FS to FE), because you cannot know ahead of time if the general market will rise or fall after the breakout. Unfortunately, only the downward breakout direction showed differences that were statistically significant.

MARKET CAPITALIZATION

Table 16.14 shows the performance of descending triangles, sorted by market capitalization. I define market capitalization as the number of shares outstand-

Table 16.13
Average Price Performance of Descending
Triangles During a Rising and Falling Market

Market Trend	Upward Breakouts FS to FE	Score	FE to UH	Downward Breakouts FS to FE	Score	FE to UL
Rising S&P 500	41% (206)	0	43% (275)	–17% (282)	–1	–19% (189)
Falling S&P 500	42% (115)	0	31% (46)	–18% (170)	+1	–16% (264)

Note: FS = formation start, FE = formation end, UH = ultimate high, UL = ultimate low. The number of samples appears in parentheses.

Table 16.14
Average Price Performance of Descending Triangles by Market Capitalization

Capitalization	Upward Breakouts	Score	Downward Breakouts	Score
Small cap (up to $1 billion)	49% (181)	+1	–18% (269)	+1
Mid cap ($1 to $5 billion)	39% (98)	–1	–19% (126)	+1
Large cap (over $5 billion)	31% (40)	–1	–14% (52)	–1

Note: The number of samples appears in parentheses.

ing times the breakout price. Small caps perform best for upward breakouts (49% rise), and large caps do worst (31% rise). For downward breakouts, mid caps squeak ahead of small caps and trounce large caps. However, in a falling market, you want to own large cap stocks as they decline least.

SCORES

In many of this chapter's tables, I listed scores ranked by their performance relative to the average. To use the scoring system, evaluate your chart pattern according to the table suggestions and assign a score. Add the scores together. Total scores above zero means the stock is an investment candidate—either to buy or to sell short. For scores below zero, avoid the stock as it may underperform the median rise or decline. A zero score gives you the option of trading the stock or not.

Even if the chart pattern scores the maximum value, you can botch the trade by shorting the stock when you should go long. Trading skills, general market conditions, the industry, and the company itself all are factors in the success of any trade. Invest carefully.

Table 16.15 shows how the scoring system worked on the database. For those descending triangles with upward breakouts and scores above zero, the triangles showed rises averaging 53%. This result compares to an average rise of just 27% when the score was below zero. For downward breakouts, the pattern was the same only the numbers were smaller. Triangles with scores above zero showed losses of 22%, compared to 12% for those with negative scores.

Since some triangles were excluded from the statistics because all the data were not present, I show the median rise or decline benchmark that I used for comparison. Those triangles with scores above zero beat the median rise 59% of the time. That statistic may not sound like much, but remember that I am comparing it with a 36.55% rise. To beat that rise is a tall order by almost any

Table 16.15
Formation Performance by Score

Score	Upward Breakouts	Downward Breakouts
Average rise or decline of chart patterns with scores above zero	53%	22%
Average rise or decline of chart patterns with scores below zero	27%	12%
Median rise or decline used	36.55%	17.09%
Percentage with scores above zero beating median rise or decline	91/153 or 59%	142/229 or 62%
Percentage with scores below zero doing worse than median rise or decline	40/50 or 80%	76/98 or 78%

measure, so it is no surprise that few make the grade. Any result above 50% means the system adds value.

For the remainder of the table, when the score said avoid a stock, the signal correctly underperformed the median 80% of the time (upward breakouts). Downward breakouts had correct sell-short signals 62% of the time and correct avoid signals 78% of the time.

CASE STUDY 1

In Case Studies 1 and 2, I use downward breakouts from descending triangles because they are the most common. Consider Figure 16.6, a descending triangle that shows prices falling but does not show the complete picture. Measured from the October 1997 peak of 30, the stock tumbled to a low of 4.50 in March 1999. If you shorted this stock at the peak and stuck with it until the low, you would have made a nice chunk of change—85%.

How do you use the scoring system to rate this stock? Let us evaluate the chart pattern using those tables showing scores, beginning with Table 16.1. Where does the trend start? If you were to stand at the base of the triangle and look backward, prices would be climbing away from your position. Therefore, a trend change would mean prices must decline. If you walk backward in time—away from the triangle—you come to a small hilltop at point A. From that high price of 20, a 20% trend change would mean a closing price of 16. That did not occur before prices moved to higher ground. So, continue walking backward in time until you come to the real trend start. That happens at a

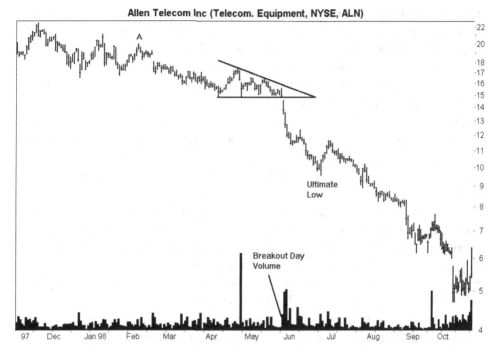

Figure 16.6 A descending triangle with a positive score. Scores above zero suggest good performance and the stock dropped 35% below the breakout price, double the 17% median.

price of 30 on October 1, 1997 (not shown). A 20% drop from the high would mean a close below 24, and that happened in late August 1997. So, the October high marks the trend start.

Measure the time from the trend start to the formation start. I count 188 days, placing the trend in the long-term (over 6 months) category. Table 16.1 says a long-term trend scores –1.

Is there an HCR to interfere with price movement? No. Prices enter the triangle from the top and shoot out the bottom, so the triangle acts as a consolidation of the falling price trend, not a reversal. Consolidation areas only work with reversals. Table 16.2 says no consolidation region scores +1, for a running total of 0.

I skip to Table 16.6 because that is the next table with scores. Where is the breakout positioned in the yearly price range? The yearly high was 30 and the low was 14.81 the day before the breakout. With a breakout price of 14.81, the breakout price is in the lowest third of the yearly price range, scoring +1 for a +1 running total.

Is the triangle tall or short? Looking at Figure 16.6 can be deceptive because of the log scale used, so it is best to check the result mathematically.

The triangle high was at a price of 17.44 with a low of 14.81. The difference, 2.63, expressed as a percentage of the breakout price gives a value of 17.76% (that is, 2.63/14.81). A 17.76% height means the triangle is a tall one for a +1 score according to Table 16.7. Running total: +2.

Does volume recede from the formation start to the breakout point? If you look at Figure 16.6 and exclude the large, 1-day volume spike on April 24, the volume appears to trend upward. However, you cannot just toss out a day's worth of volume, especially one so large. When you include that day and run linear regression (use your spreadsheet's trend function) on the volume data, you find that the volume is trending downward for a +1 score. Running total: +3.

How does volume stack up on the breakout day? The breakout occurs when prices close below the lower trendline boundary. In this case, prices gapped downward but volume did not climb substantially until a day later. If I compare the breakout day volume with the levels over the prior 3 months, my computer tells me the breakout volume is only average. Clearly the following 2 days show high volume and the April peak scores very high volume, too. I think the average reading is appropriate. Table 16.9 says average or below-average breakout volume scores –1 for a running total of +2.

Was a pullback predicted? No. With no support zone in the way of the downward price thrust, the stock making new lows and downward momentum pushing prices lower, a pullback is unlikely. Score: +1. Running total: +3.

Bear traps? No trap is predicted for the same reason that a pullback is unlikely, that is, there is no recent support zone beneath the formation to catch prices. A bear trap would also have to send prices above the formation top, a difficult trick in a falling market (which we get to in a bit). Table 16.11 scores +1 if a trap is not predicted. Running total: +4.

How is the market behaving from the formation start to formation end (in this case, the breakout date)? On the day the formation began, the S&P 500 closed at 1109.55. The day the formation ended, the S&P closed at 1094.02. In short, the market declined. A declining market from FS to FE means a +1 score according to Table 16.13. Running total: +5.

Finally, using the breakout price of 14.81 multiplied by the number of shares outstanding places the stock in the small cap category. A small cap rates a +1 score according to Table 16.14, for a final total score of +6.

Since scores above zero suggest good performance, this stock would be a good short-sale candidate. If you owned the stock on the downward breakout, a +6 score would mean that you should sell immediately, because the price is expected to tumble dramatically.

Using the 20% trend change rule to mark the ultimate low means that the ultimate low as it appears in Figure 16.6 is correct. That price, 9.56, means a decline of 35%, well above the 17.09% median decline for descending triangles. If I used the October low of 4.69 as the ultimate low, that would mean a decline of 68%.

CASE STUDY 2

How does the scoring system work when the final score is below zero? Look at Figure 16.7, a descending triangle that is a lot like me, not handsome, but still in good condition. Prices dangled their feet below the lower trendline boundary at point A, but that did not signal an actual breakout because prices closed within the triangle boundary. The actual breakout came just over a week later in early August. Prices broke out downward, pulled back briefly, then declined to the ultimate low before returning to the triangle base, moved horizontally for several weeks and finally headed higher in a choppy manner.

Let us briefly run through the tables to calculate the score.

Table 16.1: Trend start. Figure 16.7 does not show the trend start, so that is a good indication that it is more than 6 months away from the formation. The trend began on August 12, 1997, at a low price of 17.75. The time from the trend start to the formation start was 321 days—almost a full year. Score: –1.

Table 16.2: Consolidation region. I have shown an HCR that would probably support prices if they dropped that far. From January to March, numerous peaks either touched or came close to the support line setting up a floor to stop any downward decline. Score: –1. Running total: –2.

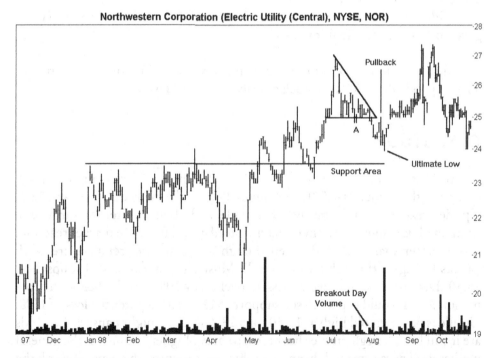

Figure 16.7 A descending triangle with a negative score. The breakout from this triangle is a bear trap with prices declining just 3% before shooting above the formation top.

Table 16.6: Yearly price range. You can guess from Figure 16.7 that the breakout price is near the yearly high and you would be correct. Score –1 for a running total of –3.

Table 16.7: Tall or short. The formation is short, measuring 9% of the breakout price. Score: -1. Running total: -4.

Table 16.8: Volume trend. The volume trend is downward as denoted by the slope of the line found using linear regression even though, to me at least, the trend looks upward in the figure (I might be needing glasses soon). Score: +1. Running total: –3.

Table 16.9: Breakout volume. You can see that breakout volume is nothing special. It rates an average ranking for a –1 score. Running total: –4.

Table 16.10: Pullback. Is a pullback likely? Yes, because of the consolidation region in the path of the downward price trend. Score –1 for a running total of –5.

Table 16.11: Bear trap. Again, the support area would likely repel the downward price trend and may be powerful enough to send prices above the formation top, causing a bear trap. With prices trending upward leading to the pattern, a bear trap is a more plausible scenario. Anytime you are in danger of hitting a trap—either bullish or bearish—avoid the trade. Score: –1. Running total: –6.

Table 16.13: Market trend. The market was trending down from formation start to end (on which I base the score) and as prices reached the ultimate low. Score: +1. Running total: –5.

Table 16.14. Market capitalization. The stock falls into the small cap category, for a +1 score. Final total: –4.

A score below zero, as in this case, means you should avoid an investment. That is good advice for this stock as prices declined just 3%.

CASE STUDY 3

Figure 16.8 shows a descending triangle trade I made. Here is my notebook entry for the trade. "10/5/00. I bought 800 at the market, filled at 12.63. Upside breakout from a descending triangle, and I bought after the throwback completed. Earnings were announced yesterday and from the market reaction, it was better than expected. Even though other apparel retailers are weak (stocks falling), I think this will do well. Must sell point is at 10.13, upside is 15.50. Downside would give a massive decline of 20%, but be below the formation low. I would expect to see support at 11.25, for a potential loss of 11%. Upside is based on old high at 15.50 for a 23% gain. It might pause at 14. Odds are it will be a struggle in the short term to move higher because of the general market weakness expected during October. Going into Christmas, I think the stock could do well. The buy comes after an Eve & Adam double bottom confirmed and throwback completed. This could hit 16.50."

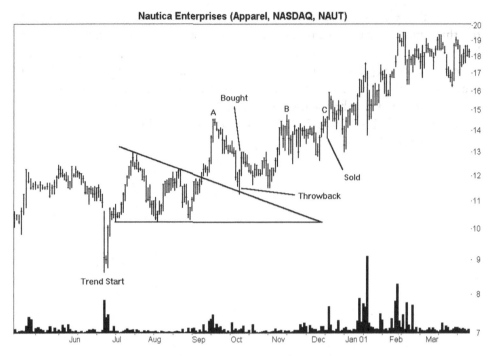

Figure 16.8 A descending triangle that I traded. The positive score suggests good performance but I cashed out too early, for an 11% gain. Points A, B, and C mark a potential triple top that never confirmed. The trend start marks the Adam trough of an Eve & Adam double bottom, part of which appears.

For the sale, here is what I wrote. "12/8/2000. I sold 800 at the market, filled at 14.06. The stock was bid at 14.50. As I was putting in my sell order, it dropped to 14.38 then filled at 14.06. That is a half point change, or $400. Talk about slippage! I sold this one because Russell Corp. took a tumble yesterday for unexplained reasons, Oxford Industries took a tumble because of a profit warning a few days ago. Others in the industry are mixed—about half are rising slowly, half are falling. This stock was one of the better performing, but with slow retail sales this holiday season, I think it spells weakness for the stock. So, I tried to dump it near the third peak of a budding triple top and came close. Made about $1,125 on the trade. Not bad in a falling, tough market!"

I suppose making money in the stock market is a lot like a plane crash: Anytime you can walk away, it is a good landing. There is not much to add except that the scoring system rated the stock +4 and, as I write this, prices topped out at 19.56 in early February 2001, for a gain of 55% above the purchase price of 12.63. I made just 11% because I panicked, with good reason.

I mentioned expecting support at 11.25, and prices dropped to 11.50 on October 26—a good call. In November, prices paused near 14, as I predicted.

On the sell side, I mentioned a triple top, which appears in Figure 16.8 as the three points marked A, B, and C. This scenario is a good example of what happens when selling before confirmation (when prices must drop below the lowest low among the three tops). Triple tops are rare enough that it is good practice to note a potential one, but not to trade on the expectation of confirmation. However, if I had waited and sold if prices dropped below the confirmation price of 11.25, I would have taken a loss instead of booking a profit.

I will take the cash.

17

Triangles, Symmetrical

Symmetrical triangles are the last member of the distinguished triangle family that includes the ascending and descending siblings. When I wrote *Encyclopedia of Chart Patterns* (Wiley, 2000), I split symmetrical triangles into bottoms and tops—the difference being the way prices enter the triangle. With this chapter, I recombine them. Why? Because the performance differences between the two types are minor, and because the classic definition recognizes only one. The real reason is, of course, that I wanted a higher sample count!

THE TYPICAL PATTERN

Figure 17.1 shows a symmetrical triangle with an upward breakout, but prices throw back to the price level of the triangle apex and continue down. When searching for symmetrical triangles, look for a converging price series, one with lower highs and higher lows over time. There should be at least two minor highs and two minor lows with prices crossing from trendline to trendline often enough to remove most white space. Resist the temptation to cut off a rounding turn and call it a symmetrical triangle—a common mistake—for if you do, the interior between the trendlines will be mostly white space.

The volume trend typically slopes downward over time and is usually very low near the breakout. This trend is clear from the figure when the volume drops off, then spikes on the breakout and following days.

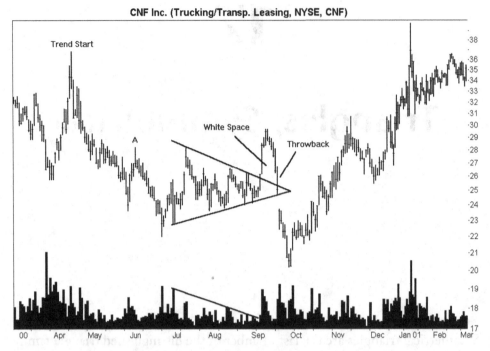

Figure 17.1 A symmetrical triangle. Two trendlines—one sloping upward with the other sloping downward—intersect at the triangle apex. Prices cross from trendline to opposing trendline often enough to fill the space.

TREND START

The trend leading to the chart pattern can give you a hint of future performance. First, we need to find where the trend starts. Consider Figure 17.1. I have shown where the trend starts and it may seem obvious, but sometimes the start may be difficult to find. Here are the rules I follow when searching for the trend start. Begin with the formation start and work backward in time, following the price action. If prices enter the formation from the bottom, you will be looking for a 20% price rise; if entering from the top, look for a 20% price decline. The 20% price change signals a trend reversal.

The figure shows prices entering the formation from the top, so we will be looking for a 20% price decline. Working backward from the formation, we find a minor *high* at 28.25 on June 2, shown as point A. A 20% decline from this value would put the *closing* price at 22.60, but prices only dropped to 24. So, we keep looking, moving backward, up the price trend until we come to the mid-April peak. There, prices reach a high of 36.88. A 20% decline would be a close below 29.50, and prices reached that low just over a week earlier. Therefore, we have found a 20% trend change and the high represents the trend start.

Table 17.1
Average Performance of Symmetrical Triangles
Sorted by Price Trend Leading to the Pattern

Trend Start to Formation Start	Upward Breakout	Score	Downward Breakout	Score
Short term (0 to 3 months)	38% (192)	+1	–23% (181)	+1
Intermediate term (3 to 6 months)	35% (48)	0	–18% (65)	–1
Long term (over 6 months)	28% (44)	–1	–16% (41)	–1

Note: The number of samples appears in parentheses.

Having found the trend start, measure the time from the trend start to the formation start. For Figure 17.1, the duration is 70 days, or just over 2 months. According to Table 17.1, that places the trend in the short-term category. Symmetrical triangles that appear after a short-term trend show price rises averaging 38%. That result is head and antlers above the long-term rate of 28%.

Downward breakouts show the same trend with the short-term trend performing best and the long-term trend performing worst. It is as if a triangle, after a long-term rise or decline, is tired and prices soon reverse.

I discuss the scoring in the Scores section of this chapter, so do not concern yourself with it now.

HORIZONTAL CONSOLIDATION REGIONS

Figure 17.2 shows a horizontal consolidation region (HCR). Look for a region of price congestion with flat tops, flat bottoms, or both, between the trend start and the formation top or bottom, whichever is closer to the consolidation region. You want to find a region that poses a threat to upward or downward price movement, depending on the breakout direction.

The figure shows an upward breakout, so look for resistance above the formation but below—or perhaps spanning (as in this case)—the trend start. A resistance zone in that price range is both nearby and in the expected price flight path. In the figure, you can see a consolidation region where prices move essentially horizontally, with bottoms that touch or near a flat line several times. After trying twice to punch threw the overhead resistance, prices gave up and tumbled, eventually forming another symmetrical triangle in February.

Table 17.2 shows statistics related to HCRs. When a consolidation region gets in the way of upward price travel, prices after a triangle breakout show gains averaging 30%. When no consolidation region exists, the gains are higher, 37%. A similar trend exists for downward breakouts, with losses of 18% and 21%, respectively.

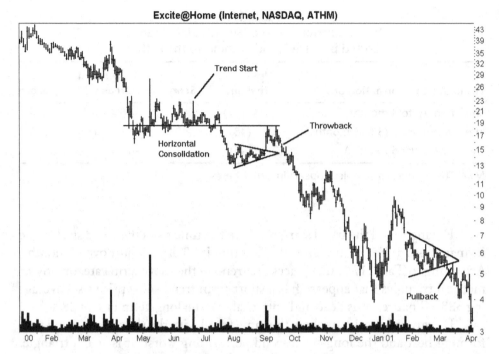

Figure 17.2 Horizontal consolidation. Look for support or resistance zones with flat tops, flat bottoms, or both, between the trend start and the nearest formation trendline boundary. Here, overhead resistance prevented an extended price run.

Table 17.2
Average Performance of Symmetrical Triangles
with and Without a Consolidation Region

Description	Upward Breakouts	Score	Downward Breakouts	Score
Consolidation region	30% (72)	−1	−18% (93)	−1
No consolidation region	37% (238)	+1	−21% (209)	+1
Average length (days)	36		32	
Prices stop within region ±5%	40%		57%	
Prices push through region	53%		28%	
Prices do not reach region	7%		15%	

Note: The number of samples appears in parentheses.

How long is the average consolidation region? About a month long. The length makes looking for consolidation regions a snap as they are clearly visible on the daily price chart and not confined to small squiggles.

When a consolidation region interferes with price travel, how often do prices penetrate the region? For upward breakouts, prices top out within the consolidation region (including a 5% buffer to catch those that fall just short or rise just above the region) 40% of the time. Just 7% of the time prices fail to rise to the bottom of the region and the remainder of the time, 53%, prices push on through.

For downward breakouts, 57% of the time prices stop within the consolidation region (including the 5% buffer). Another 15% do not make it down to the top of the consolidation region. The remaining 28% continue falling, dropping below the consolidation region.

INSIDE THE PATTERN

Table 17.3 shows important statistical findings for symmetrical triangles. For the longest time, I was under the belief that symmetrical triangles were somewhat rare, and yet I saw many of them in the daily charts. It was a contradiction that I could not resolve until I included chart patterns from my more recent database. Symmetrical triangles occur less often than both ascending and descending triangles; those chart patterns had over 800 samples each, whereas symmetricals total only 661.

As you can see in Table 17.3, the number of formations splits almost equally between upward and downward breakouts, with slightly more breaking out upward.

I measured an average rise of 35% and decline of 20%, from the breakout price to the highest high or the lowest low before a 20% trend change. A breakout occurs when prices close outside the formation trendlines and continue in the breakout direction. Sometimes, the breakout direction is difficult

Table 17.3
Important Statistical Findings

Description	Upward Breakouts	Downward Breakouts
Number of formations	356	305
Average rise or decline	35%	20%
Standard & Poor's 500 change	3%	–2%
Median rise or decline	28%	18%
Rises or declines more than 50%	87/310 or 28%	13/302 or 4%

to determine because of premature breakouts or breakouts that curl around the formation apex and zoom off in the opposite direction. I ignored premature breakouts (when prices move outside the triangle boundaries for a few days but quickly return) and usually accepted the first *close* outside the triangle as the breakout day.

Figure 17.1, for example, shows an upward breakout that carries prices high enough to be worth exploiting even though prices quickly rejoin the formation, then shoot out the bottom.

Figure 17.3 shows a good example of what I am talking about. Prices drop below the lower formation trendline and close there, but the next day, prices move back into the formation. The 2-day excursion is a premature breakout that is indistinguishable, as it occurs, from an actual breakout. In this case, the real breakout is upward, as that is the direction prices travel farthest.

I measured the change in the S&P 500 Index from the day prices staged a breakout to the day prices reached the ultimate high or low in the stocks showing symmetrical triangles. For those chart patterns having upward breakouts, the S&P gained 3%; for downward breakouts, the index lost 2% of its value. To put this another way, had you bought every symmetrical triangle showing an upward breakout and sold at the ultimate high, you would have

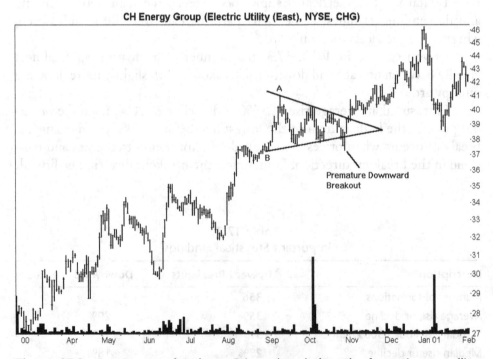

Figure 17.3 A premature breakout. Prices close below the formation trendline but move back inside the formation the next day in a classic premature breakout. The triangle height is the difference between points A and B.

made 35%. If you traded the 500 stocks in the S&P 500 over the same time as your triangles, you would have made just 3%. Clearly, chart patterns add value.

Since the average rise or decline can be misleading because large values can skew the average, I show the median rise or decline. I sorted the performance results according to the breakout direction, then found the midrange, or median value, one that has half the samples above the median and half below. For upward breakouts, the median was 28% and for downward breakouts, it was 18%. I consider these values closer to what an experienced triangle trader could make if he or she traded triangles often enough. The numbers do not account for taxes, commissions, or other trading costs.

I think Mae West said, "Too much of a good thing can be wonderful!" How good can performance get? For upward breakouts, 28% climbed more than 50%; for downward breakouts, just 4% lost over half their value. The results are in the range of what we have seen for other chart patterns.

FAILURE RATES

Table 17.4 shows the failure rate according to the maximum price rise or decline. An example makes this clear. For upward breakouts, 47 or 15% of the triangles I looked at had prices rise less than 10% after the breakout. Downward breakouts had a higher failure rate, with 72 patterns, or 24%, failing to decline more than 10%.

As you scan down the columns in the table, you can see that the failure rate quickly rises. For a 5% maximum price rise, upward breakouts show a 5%

Table 17.4
Maximum Price Rise or Decline Versus Failure Rate

Maximum Price Rise or Decline (%)	Upward Breakout Failure Rate	Downward Breakout Failure Rate
5	15 or 5%	14 or 5%
10	47 or 15%	72 or 24%
15	84 or 27%	127 or 42%
20	120 or 39%	178 or 59%
25	140 or 45%	222 or 74%
30	161 or 52%	251 or 83%
35	175 or 56%	268 or 89%
50	223 or 72%	289 or 96%
75	263 or 85%	301 or 100%
100	286 or 92%	302 or 100%

Note: The sample count is 310 and 302 for upward and downward breakouts, respectively, for each row.

failure rate. For a 10% rise, the failure rate triples to 15% then almost doubles again for a 15% rise. Downward breakouts show a steeper trend with the rate moving from 5% to 24%, almost five times the increase for a doubling in the price decline (from 5% to 10%).

The point of this is that a 5% failure rate, when prices move less than 5%, is deceiving. Imagine that you want to make a 20% return on your investment and experience says that you get in a bit late and exit a bit early. Including commissions, slippage, and other trading costs, you feel that you need a 25% gain to net 20%. How often will symmetrical triangles deliver that kind of performance? According to Table 17.4, 45% of the triangles with upward breakouts will fail to rise more than 25%, which is to say that 55% will bring home the bacon. For downward breakouts, 74% will fail to decline by 25%. The choice is clear: Avoid downward breakouts and either watch your upward breakouts carefully or select another chart pattern type with a lower failure rate.

Table 17.5 shows the horizon failure rate and average rise and decline. The horizon failure rate measures the number of failures over a given time. For example, at the end of the first week, 8% of the chart patterns with an upward breakout had prices below the breakout price. This statistic compares with a 12% failure rate for downward breakouts. In other words, 12% of the stocks failed when prices stayed above the breakout price at the end of the first week. Over that time, prices climbed by an average of 7% (for upward breakouts) or declined by 6% (downward breakouts).

You can see that the failure rate climbs from 8% after week 1 to 33% at the end of 3 months (upward breakouts). The downward breakout failure rate rises steadily from 12% to 44%, a similar rate of increase. Over the 6 months, the average rise climbs quickly in the first week then slows after 1 month. Downward breakouts lose their momentum after the first month too, when the average decline moves from 8% to 7% and eventually to 4%. If you are considering shorting a stock, the downward ride may bottom around week 3 or 4.

Table 17.5
Horizon Failure Rates and Average Rise or Decline

Time Since Breakout	Upward Breakout Failure Rate (%)	Average Rise (%)	Downward Breakout Failure Rate (%)	Average Decline (%)
1 week	8	7	12	6
2 weeks	16	8	15	7
3 weeks	20	9	21	8
1 month	24	10	25	8
2 months	32	10	35	7
3 months	33	11	40	6
6 months	31	12	44	4

Table 17.6
Average Performance Sorted by Breakout Price
According to Prior 12-Month Range

Yearly Price Range	Upward Breakouts	Score	Downward Breakouts	Score
Highest third	36% (128)	+1	−19% (102)	−1
Middle third	34% (75)	−1	−20% (78)	0
Lowest third	40% (57)	+1	−24% (85)	+1

Note: The number of samples appears in parentheses.

YEARLY PRICE RANGE

Table 17.6 shows the performance of symmetrical triangles after sorting by their breakout price over the prior 12-month price range. For example, prices declined 24% when the downward breakout was close to the yearly low. This result compares to a 19% decline when the breakout price was near the yearly high.

With other chart pattern types, we have seen upward breakouts perform best when the breakout occurs near the yearly high, and downward breakouts do best when the breakout is near the yearly low. The table supports that trend for downward breakouts, but not completely for upward breakouts. For downward breakouts at any rate, the results imply the following: If you want to sell short, pick those making new lows.

TALL AND SHORT PATTERNS

Table 17.7 shows amazing performance results for short and tall symmetrical triangles. I sorted the triangles according to their breakout direction, and found the median height expressed as a percentage of the breakout price. For example, the formation height of the triangle shown in Figure 17.3 is point A, at 41, minus point B, at 37.19, or 3.81. Divide the result by the breakout price

Table 17.7
Performance of Short and Tall Symmetrical Triangles

Description	Upward Breakout	Score	Downward Breakout	Score
Tall (above the median)	48% (155)	+1	−24% (151)	+1
Short (below the median)	25% (155)	−1	−17% (151)	−1
Median percentage of breakout price	15.98%		14.66%	

Note: The number of samples appears in parentheses.

of 39.13 to get 9.7%. According to Table 17.7, the triangle is a short one, and prices rise just 18%.

For downward breakouts, the math is the same: the formation height measured from the widest point divided by the breakout price. If the result is less than the median height of 14.66%, then it is a short triangle, otherwise, it is tall. For both breakout directions, tall triangles trounce the vertically challenged.

VOLUME TREND

Table 17.8 shows the performance sorted by the volume trend from the formation start to the breakout. I used the slope of the line, found using linear regression, to determine whether volume was trending upward or downward. Most of the time, as you can see by the sample sizes, volume declined. If you do not know about linear regression, many spreadsheets call it the trend function. Often, you can just look at a chart to determine the volume trend. Figure 17.1, for example, has a downward volume trend.

For both breakout directions, performance seemed to improve if volume climbed over the course of the formation. This result may be due to the small sample size for the rising volume trend. For upward breakouts, the differences were not statistically significant, so no useful scores appear.

BREAKOUT VOLUME

Table 17.9 lists the performance of symmetrical triangles after a high or low volume breakout. The table answers the question, does high breakout volume propel prices farther? Yes. I compared the breakout volume with the average of the prior 90 days, then separated the breakout volume into one of five categories: very high, high, average, low, and very low.

Table 17.8
Linear Regression Volume Trend and Performance

Description	Upward Breakouts	Score	Downward Breakouts	Score
Rising volume trend	37% (45)	0	−22% (42)	+1
Falling volume trend	35% (265)	0	−20% (260)	−1

Note: The number of samples appears in parentheses.

Table 17.9
Breakout Volume and Performance

Description	Upward Breakouts	Score	Downward Breakouts	Score
Average rise or decline on above-average breakout volume	41% (62)	+1	28% (36)	+1
Average rise or decline on average or below-average breakout volume	34% (248)	–1	19% (266)	–1

Note: The number of samples appears in parentheses.

When breakout volume is above average (high or very high), prices after an upward breakout show gains averaging 41%, and downward breakouts show losses averaging 28%. These statistics compare to a rise of 34% and a loss of 19% when the volume is average or below average. In short, *heavy breakout volume is good.*

THROWBACKS OR PULLBACKS

Table 17.10 shows throwback (upward breakouts) and pullback (downward breakouts) related statistics. Figure 17.2 shows an example of a throwback (August formation) and a pullback (February triangle). The difference between the two is that throwbacks curl down from the top, whereas pullbacks curl up from the bottom. By convention, both occur within 30 days after the breakout, and I have added an additional white space requirement. The throwback pictured in Figure 17.1 shows what I am talking about. There is white space between the curling of the throwback and the triangle trendline. White space applies to pullbacks also. I added the requirement to avoid confusion when prices slide along the trendline.

Throwbacks and pullbacks occur often in symmetrical triangles, both just over 50% of the time. This is no big deal except that when one occurs, performance typically suffers as we see in a moment.

Recall that the ultimate high or ultimate low occurs when prices reach a high or low point, then the trend changes and prices move more than 20% in the new direction. How often is the ultimate high or low found during the throwback or pullback? Just 19% to 24% of the time, respectively. This is low enough that it should not be a big worry, but you should still check for resistance or support zones to determine—before you invest—how far prices are likely to move.

Table 17.10
Throwback and Pullback Statistics

Description	Upward Breakouts (Throwbacks)	Downward Breakouts (Pullbacks)
Throwbacks or pullbacks	183/356 or 51%	157/305 or 51%
Score if throwback or pullback predicted	–1	–1
Score if throwback or pullback not predicted	+1	+1
Ultimate high or low before throwback or pullback	67/356 or 19%	73/305 or 24%
Average rise or decline on above-average breakout volume with throwbacks or pullbacks	30%	20%
Average rise or decline on above-average breakout volume with no throwbacks or pullbacks	53%	31%
Average rise or decline on average or below-average breakout volume with throwbacks or pullbacks	25%	16%
Average rise or decline on average or below-average breakout volume with no throwbacks or pullbacks	44%	22%
Number of throwbacks or pullbacks after a high or very high volume breakout	39/106 or 37%	13/106 or 12%
Number of throwbacks or pullbacks after an average, low, or very low volume breakout	144/555 or 26%	144/555 or 26%
Number of throwbacks or pullbacks that stopped ±5% from the breakout price	121 or 66%	25 or 16%
Number of throwbacks or pullbacks that stopped between formation high and low	26 or 14%	101 or 64%
Number of throwbacks/pullbacks that stopped below/above formation low/high	36 or 20%	31 or 20%

The next several lines (average rise or decline) are the interesting ones. They show how performance suffers when a throwback or pullback occurs as well as the influence of breakout volume. After a heavy volume breakout with a throwback, the average rise is 30%, compared to a rise of 53% when no throwback occurs. Similarly, when the breakout volume is average or below, a throwback hurts performance with rises of 25% when a throwback occurs and 44% without a throwback. Downward breakouts for pullbacks show the same trends only the numbers change: *A pullback hurts performance* regardless of the volume trend.

For some chart pattern types, a high volume breakout suggests a throwback is more likely to occur, but a pullback often occurs after a low volume breakout. How about symmetrical triangles? A throwback is more likely to occur after a high volume breakout than a low volume one, by 37% to 26%. Pullbacks show the reverse: A pullback occurs more often after an average or below-average volume breakout.

When a throwback or pullback does occur, where do prices stop? For upward breakouts (throwbacks), prices stop 66% of the time within 5% of the breakout price. Another 14% of the time, prices drop to somewhere between the triangle high and low (in other words, somewhere between the price levels shown by points A and B in Figure 17.3, not including the 5% surrounding the breakout). The remaining 20% of the time, prices drop below the formation low.

For downward breakouts, prices stop near the breakout price only 16% of the time after a pullback. Often, 64%, prices stop somewhere within the triangle high–low price zone. The remaining 20% of the time, prices climb above the triangle high.

Why is this information important? Because it gives you a good clue as to where to place a stop-loss order. Placing a stop below the formation for upward breakouts or above the formation for downward breakouts should protect you about 80% of the time. Of course, this action may entail a large loss, so you may want to tighten your stop by moving it closer to the transaction price.

To predict when a pullback or throwback will occur, review Chapter 3 on Support and Resistance. Look for a support or resistance area near the triangle, one that is in the breakout direction. Minor highs, minor lows, trendlines, prior chart patterns, and even moving averages sometimes stop or slow prices. Look for those also.

BULL AND BEAR TRAPS

Table 17.11 shows how often bull or bear traps occur. First, what is a trap? Look at Figure 17.4, which shows a good example of a bear trap. By my definition, a trap occurs when prices break out and move less than 10% in the breakout direction before retracing and zipping out the other side of the triangle. Price must rise above the top of the triangle, or fall below the bottom of the triangle, to complete the trap.

The figure makes this action clear. Prices stage a downward breakout on May 27, and seem to struggle lower. Then, prices pull back into the triangle and seesaw up and down, eventually climbing above the triangle top and confirming a bear trap. Those investors hoping for a bearish, downhill run were trapped into a losing position as prices climbed above their entry price.

Table 17.11
Bull and Bear Traps

Description	Upward Breakouts (Bull Traps)	Downward Breakouts (Bear Traps)
Trap frequency	47/310 or 15%	71/302 or 24%
Score if trap predicted	−1	−1
Score if trap not predicted	+1	+1

Fortunately, traps do not occur often. For upward breakouts, they happen 15% of the time and for downward breakouts, they occur 24% of the time, on average. Still, I can think of many more things to do with my money than lose it in a silly trap.

How can you guard against a trap? Look again at Figure 17.4. Look for support or resistance zones, prior chart patterns, trendlines, and moving average lines (such as the 200-day moving average) to see where support or resistance may interfere with price travel. If you see something that may block prices, skip the trade and look for a more promising situation.

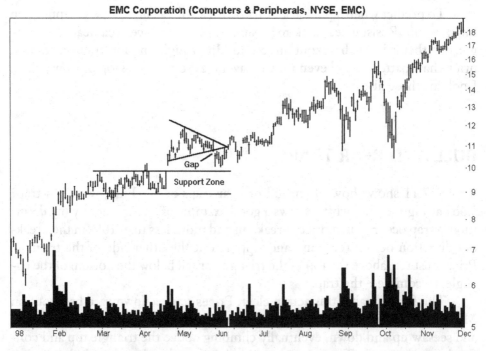

Figure 17.4 A bear trap. Prices break out downward and drop less than 10% before climbing above the triangle top.

Table 17.12
Gaps and Performance

Description	Upward Breakouts	Score	Downward Breakouts	Score
Average rise or decline after price gap on breakout	33% (58)	0	23% (53)	+1
Average rise or decline with no price gap on breakout	36% (252)	0	19% (249)	−1

Note: The number of samples appears in parentheses.

GAPS

Table 17.12 shows gap statistics. Before I discuss the results, look at Figure 17.4 again. It shows a gap the day prices closed below the lower trendline. A price gap occurs when today's low price is above yesterday's high (for upward breakouts), or today's high is below yesterday's low (downward breakouts). Gaps are a sign of exuberance.

Table 17.12 shows the performance of stocks having gaps on the breakout day. When prices gapped upward, prices averaged gains of 33% compared to 36% for symmetrical triangles showing no breakout gaps. Since a gap usually provides an added push, the results are unusual. In fact, the differences are not statistically significant—meaning they could be due to chance—so I show no useful score.

Downward breakouts performed better, with losses of 23% versus 19% for gaps and no gaps, respectively. This result is as it should be, and the differences are statistically significant.

MARKET TREND

How do prices behave in rising or falling markets? Table 17.13 provides some answers. I compared the performance after a symmetrical triangle breakout with the direction of the general market, as measured by the Standard & Poor's 500 Index from the formation start to the formation end, and from the formation end to the ultimate high or low.

If the market is falling when the formation is under construction—from formation start to formation end—that seems to help performance after an upward breakout. As prices are climbing to the ultimate high, a rising market lifts all boats and boosts performance to 37% from 30%. As you would expect, a falling market helps lower all boats with losses averaging 20% versus 19%.

Table 17.13
Average Price Performance of Symmetrical
Triangles During a Rising and Falling Market

Market Trend	Upward Breakouts FS to FE	Score	Upward Breakouts FE to UH	Downward Breakouts FS to FE	Score	Downward Breakouts FE to UL
Rising S&P 500	34% (226)	−1	37% (247)	−20% (203)	0	−19% (99)
Falling S&P 500	39% (84)	+1	30% (63)	−20% (99)	0	−20% (203)

Note: FS = formation start, FE = formation end, UH = ultimate high, UL = ultimate low. The number of samples appears in parentheses.

Since you cannot tell how the market will behave after you buy a stock, I base the scores on the results from FS to FE, that is, while the formation is under construction. To sum the lessons from the table, *look for a falling market while the formation is being built, and hope the market trends in the breakout direction thereafter.*

The differences from the downward breakout direction were not statistically significant, so I show a zero score.

MARKET CAPITALIZATION

Table 17.14 shows the performance results of symmetrical triangles sorted by market capitalization. Market capitalization is the number of shares outstanding multiplied by the breakout price. For upward breakouts, small caps do best followed by mid caps and large caps, in that order, the same as we have seen in other chart pattern types.

For downward breakouts, large caps decline farthest with a 21% loss, but the differences are not statistically significant. Thus, I show a zero score.

SCORES

Many of the tables accompanying this chapter show scores based on the relationship between the results and the average rise or decline. To use the scores, evaluate your chart pattern according to the table and associated discussion, then add the scores together. Totals above zero mean the chart pattern is a good investment candidate. Avoid chart patterns showing scores below zero. A zero score is your call; you can either invest or pass it up.

Table 17.14
Average Price Performance of Symmetrical
Triangles by Market Capitalization

Capitalization	Upward Breakouts	Score	Downward Breakouts	Score
Small cap (up to $1 billion)	38% (123)	+1	−20% (126)	0
Mid cap ($1 to $5 billion)	36% (115)	+1	−20% (111)	0
Large cap (over $5 billion)	32% (67)	−1	−21% (64)	0

Note: The number of samples appears in parentheses.

A chart pattern with a perfect score is no reason to buy, or short, the stock. The score is only the first step in making a trading decision. However, I have found the scoring system performs well in actual trading.

Table 17.15 shows statistics for the scoring system. Symmetrical triangles with scores above zero showed rises averaging 46% for upward breakouts and declines of 29% for downward breakouts. These results compare to scores below zero showing paltry gains of 19% and losses of 16%.

The remainder of the table shows how the system works when compared to the median rise or decline. The median shown in the table is for those chart patterns that had enough information to calculate a score (in other words, the price history was long enough).

For triangles with scores above zero and upward breakouts, 61% beat the median rise of 28.47%. Downward breakouts did even better with 74% beating the median 17.81% decline. When the scores were below zero, suggesting that the chart pattern be avoided, upward breakouts correctly underperformed

Table 17.15
Formation Performance by Score

Score	Upward Breakouts	Downward Breakouts
Average rise or decline of chart patterns with scores above zero	46%	29%
Average rise or decline of chart patterns with scores below zero	19%	16%
Median rise or decline used	28.47%	17.81%
Percentage with scores above zero beating median rise or decline	108/177 or 61%	70/95 or 74%
Percentage with scores below zero doing worse than median rise or decline	55/71 or 77%	100/154 or 65%

the median rise 77% of the time. Downward breakouts showed avoid signals that correctly underperformed the median decline 65% of the time.

To summarize, the system helps differentiate between a good investment candidate and an also-ran, but it is not perfect. Use other indicators or techniques to further refine your trading style.

CASE STUDY 1

How do you use the scoring system? I use tables with scores beginning with Table 17.1 in regard to Figure 17.5. The table shows the performance of symmetrical triangles sorted by the duration from the trend start. First, where does the trend originate?

Beginning at the start of the chart pattern (point B in Figure 17.5), look backward and find that prices rise away from the formation. Therefore, we are looking for a 20% decline in prices from a high point. When that occurs, the high point will mark the trend start. Since the price trend leading down to the formation is essentially a straight line with no appreciable hills or valleys, finding the trend start is easy because it is the first peak we come to. The *high* is at

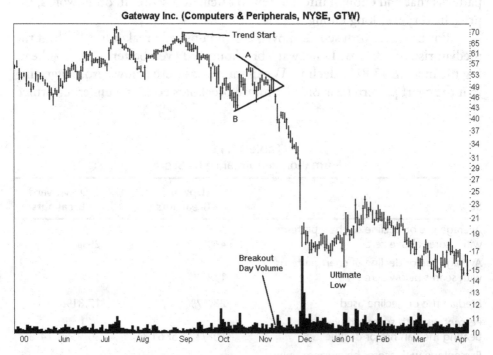

Figure 17.5   A positive score suggests good results. After the breakout, this stock declined 68%.

a price of 69.88. A 20% decline from this point would be a *close* below 55.90. That occurred when prices dropped—looking backward—on August 3, just shy of a month before the peak.

Now that we have found where the trend starts, compute the time from that point to the formation start. Clearly, the trend starts less than 3 months from the triangle (41 days to be precise), placing the duration in the short-term category. Table 17.1 says a short-term trend scores +1 for a downward breakout.

Is there an HCR in the way of falling prices? No. Prices enter the triangle from the top and exit from the bottom, so there is no price overlap that could spell trouble. With a downward breakout, any support zone is probably too far in the past to be of significance. Table 17.2 says no consolidation region scores +1 for a running total of +2.

Where in the yearly price range does the breakout occur? The high occurred at a price of 84 on November 15, 1999, and the low was at 42.15—point B in Figure 17.5. The breakout is just above the yearly low price, placing it in the lowest third of the yearly price range. Table 17.6 rates the lowest third as a +1 score. Running total: +3.

Is the triangle tall or short? Compute the triangle height by subtracting the low (42.15), shown as point B in Figure 17.5, from the high (57.28), point A. The difference, 15.13, expressed as a percentage of the breakout price (48), is 32% or 15.13/48. That result is more than double the median cutoff between short and tall shown in Table 17.7. Thus, the triangle is a tall fella, scoring +1. Running total: +4.

Does volume trend upward or downward? I used linear regression to find the answer: downward. This answer is clear just by looking carefully at Figure 17.5. Score: –1. Running total: +3.

Is the breakout volume above average? Even though prices gapped lower, volume did not rise until a day after the breakout. My computer informs me that the breakout volume is average when compared to the prior 90 days. Average breakout volume scores –1 according to Table 17.9. Running total: +2.

Is a pullback or bear trap predicted? No, for the same reason I mentioned when discussing an HCR. The triangle acts as a consolidation of the price trend. Prices enter the triangle from the top, moving down, and exit from the bottom with no support area to pose a threat to continued lower prices. Score +1 for no pullback (Table 17.10) and score +1 for no trap predicted (Table 17.11). Running total: +4.

A price gap often propels prices lower, at least that is what Table 17.12 says. If the chart is clear enough and you have your contacts in, you can see a price gap on the breakout day. A gap scores +1 for a final total of +5.

Totals above zero suggest performance that will be above the 17.81% median decline for downward breakouts, which is the case here. From the breakout price of 48, prices drop to a low of 15.30 before climbing more than 20% and signaling a trend change. The drop measures 68%.

CASE STUDY 2

What happens when the score is below zero? Consider Figure 17.6, a symmetrical triangle in an electric utility company stock. One of the things you might notice is the volume chart. Every quarter, volume skyrockets. Why? I do not have a clue. This phenomenon has been going on for the 2 years I have been following the stock. In any case, let me quickly run through the tables and add the scores.

   Table 17.1: Trend start. The trend starts from a low of 19.06 in late February (not shown), placing the trend in the long-term category (187 days). Score: –1.
   Table 17.2: Horizontal consolidation region. Is there an HCR in the price path? Yes. Prices enter and exit from the bottom, indicating the triangle acts as a reversal of the price trend. Looking back over the prior price action, we can see several instances where prices near or touch the same price, namely, 22.25. The area around that price is likely to act as a support zone, one that prices will have trouble penetrating. Score: –1. Running total: –2.
   Table 17.6: Yearly price range. The breakout price is 24.13 and the yearly high is at 26.19 (the triangle top) with the yearly low at 18.75, set in mid-

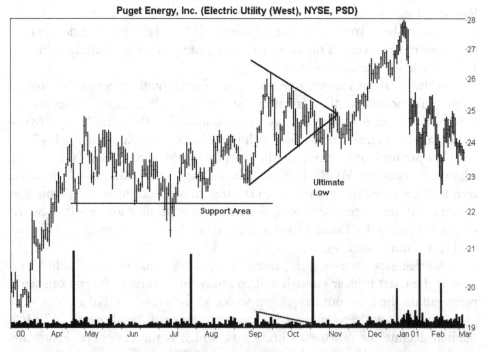

Figure 17.6 A negative score in a symmetrical triangle. A score below zero suggests the stock will underperform, and that was the case here, as prices dropped just 6%.

December 1999. Thus, the breakout is in the highest third of the yearly price range, for a –1 score. Running total: –3.

Table 17.7: Short or tall. The formation high is at 26.19 and the low is at 22.75 with a breakout price of 24.13. That gives a height as a percentage of the breakout price of (26.19 – 22.75)/24.13 or 14.26%. This is a runt, a short triangle, for a –1 score. Running total: –4.

Table 17.8: Volume trend. Volume trends downward, as shown in Figure 17.6. Score: –1. Running total: –5.

Table 17.9: Breakout volume. The breakout day is the day after the tall October volume spike. Compared with the prior 3 months, the breakout volume is low. Score: –1. Running total: –6.

Table 17.10: Pullback and Table 17.11: Bear trap. The support area, discussed in Table 17.2, poses a threat to any downward price movement. A pullback is likely because of the support area. Further, utility stocks during that time were in a wonderful bull market, suggesting that any downturn would be short-lived and likely to carry prices above the triangle top. Score –1 for the pullback prediction and –1 for the bear trap prediction. Running total: –8.

Table 17.12: Gaps. What gap? Score: –1. Final total: –9.

According to the scoring system, avoid stocks with a minus score. That is good advice since the stock only declined 6%. If you shorted this stock expecting a large decline, not only would you be disappointed, there is a chance that you would have lost money *and* had to pay the dividend to whomever you borrowed the stock from.

CASE STUDY 3

Figure 17.7 illustrates an actual trade I made using a symmetrical triangle. Here is my notebook entry for the purchase. "6/15/00. I bought 300 shares at the market as I think this is rising off a triple bottom. Fundamentals, with company predicting it will meet earnings expectations, look good. When I looked at the stock, it was trading at 37.06. When I placed the order, it had risen to 37.25 and I got a fill at 37.56. Ouch! Talk about slippage. Downside is 33, upside is 40."

Figure 17.7 shows the three bottoms of the unconfirmed triple bottom labeled 1, 2, and 3, priced at about the same level. With many chart patterns, it pays to wait for confirmation, that is, wait for prices to rise above the highest high in the formation. I bought in before the expected climb to 50 (the highest high). Big mistake. The formation never confirmed, something I should have expected from a comparatively rare triple bottom. Instead, a fourth bottom appeared and if you draw a line connecting the four bottoms and join it with a down-sloping trendline connecting the tops, you will see a

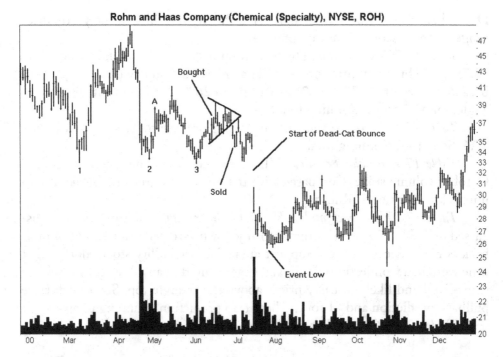

Figure 17.7   An actual trade using a symmetrical triangle. The downward break-out from the triangle indicated it was time to close out the trade. The score (–1) incorrectly predicted a mediocre decline; the stock tumbled 30%. Bottoms 1, 2, and 3 mark the bottoms of an unconfirmed triple bottom that turned into a descending triangle.

descending triangle. A descending triangle predicts a downward breakout with lower prices to follow, but at the time of purchase I did not see it.

When the symmetrical triangle appeared, I took notice. Here is my notebook entry for the sale. "6/30/00. I sold 300 today for a loss of about 6%. Prices broke out of a symmetrical triangle downward and violated a short-term up trendline [connecting point 3 with the triangle apex]. Time to leave as it is headed lower with still-high oil prices [typically used as a feed stock for chemical firms]. Margins will probably remain weak and despite assurances by the company that sales would hold up, I doubt that they will. This could even dead-cat bounce. Earnings are due out July 27. I received a fill at 35.25."

Any time the picture changes from what you thought would happen, especially with chart patterns, take action. When the stock broke out downward from the symmetrical triangle, I sold it. The 2-day delay is because I waited for the breakout and, as an end-of-day trader, I did not find out about it until the following day, when I sold.

On May 2, 2000 (point A in Figure 17.7), news reports indicated the company said it was on track to post a 6% to 8% earnings gain. The stock moved up

3.25 that day. Oil and natural gas prices have an influence on a chemical company's cost of creating products. Both oil and natural gas prices were skyrocketing at the time, putting pressure on margins. On July 17, however, the company warned that earnings would come in below forecast, blaming high costs and slowing demand. The stock tumbled almost six points, or 17%.

A 17% one-day decline is not exactly dead-cat bounce territory (usually a decline between 30% and 70%), but it comes close. You can see how the market took the news. The stock gapped downward, found some footing at the event low, bounced upward, then made a lower low in October before recovering.

As I look at this picture, I am pleased with the trade. Sure, I took a loss, but I sidestepped a massive decline. I even predicted the dead-cat bounce. If you run the scoring system on the symmetrical triangle, you will find it has a −1 score. That means the system incorrectly suggested the decline would be minor. Instead, with changing fundamentals, the stock tumbled 30%, almost double the median 17.81% decline.

18

Triple Bottoms

As I searched for triple bottoms, I felt like a big game hunter hot on the trail of unusual prey. Although that metaphor conflicts with the nature center I am making out of my small backyard, triple bottoms are well known even though seldom seen in the wild. Triple bottoms are rare, but well-shaped triple bottoms are even more scarce. Still, I used all the patterns that I could find, whether or not I would consider investing in them. I included a few that had well-defined bottoms just days apart after a long downtrend; others occurred as part of a retrace in an uptrend. I included them all, but discovered only 226.

THE TYPICAL PATTERN

Figure 18.1 shows an example of a triple bottom. Three bottoms, all near the same price level, appear with well defined, separated, and distinct minor lows. A triple bottom is just that, a bottom that forms after a downward price trend. Usually the downtrend is short, especially for those bottoms that form as part of a price retrace in an uptrend. Think of the triple bottom as occurring as part of the corrective phase of a measured move up (that is, the step portion of a stair-step rise).

The three bottoms can each appear as wide, rounded turns but spikes predominate. The rise between the bottoms is usually gentle, rounded, but need not be. In Figure 18.1, you can see that the three bottoms appear pointed with a generally rounded climb between the first and second bottoms, but a pointed rise between bottoms two and three.

Volume usually trends downward, but do not let an upward trend scare you away. Volume usually peaks on the first bottom with the third bottom

Augat Inc. (Electronics, NYSE, AUG)

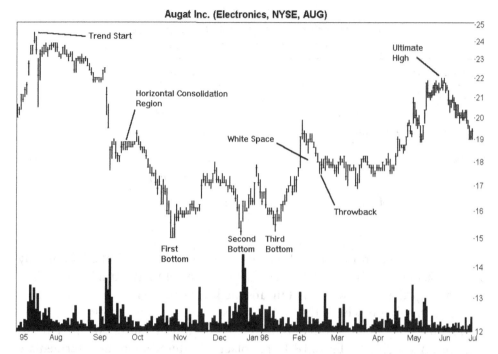

Figure 18.1   A triple bottom. Three minor lows at about the same price level form the basis of this chart pattern. A small ascending triangle doubles as a horizontal consolidation region.

showing the lowest volume level of the three. As Figure 18.1 shows, there is wide variation.

Before I move on to the statistics, let me issue this caution: *Wait for confirmation!* Confirmation occurs when prices close above the highest high in the chart pattern. Only then should you buy the stock. Most times, the stock will never make it up to the confirmation price; instead, prices tumble and post a new low or perhaps even form another bottom. *Always* wait for confirmation. *By definition, a three-bottom pattern is not a triple bottom unless prices close above the confirmation point*, which is why you should not see a triple bottom with a downward breakout.

TREND START AND FLAT BASE

Table 18.1 shows the price performance of triple bottoms after sorting by the price trend leading to the pattern. Where does the trend start? Begin with the first bottom and work backward, following the price trend upward, until you find a *high* price before prices *close* 20% lower. The high price marks the trend start.

Table 18.1
Average Performance of Triple Bottoms Sorted
by Price Trend Leading to the Pattern

Trend Start to Formation Start	Result	Score
Short term (0 to 3 months)	33% (103)	−1
Intermediate term (3 to 6 months)	29% (47)	−1
Long term (over 6 months)	41% (33)	+1
Flat base	39% (35)	+1
No flat base	33% (161)	−1

Note: The number of samples appears in parentheses.

For example, in Figure 18.1, you can see that prices peak at 24.50 on July 17. A 20% decline from this price would be a close below 19.60, a level reached the prior April (not shown). That means the July peak is where the trend starts.

Having found where the trend starts, measure the duration from the trend start to the first bottom of the triple bottom. It measures 105 days in this example. According to Table 18.1, that places the duration in the intermediate term. Those chart patterns with an intermediate-term downtrend leading to the pattern have rises averaging 29%, well below the 41% gain from those with long-term downtrends.

Table 18.1 also mentions a flat base configuration, and Figure 18.2 shows what a flat base looks like. Performance improves when prices spring from a flat base. Look for prices that near or touch the same price level before the triple bottom. The time between the formation and the flat base is not critical, but it should be reasonably close, say, within 3 or 4 months.

Think of the flat base as part of a diving board—the end anchored to the side of the pool—whereas the triple bottom is the end that launches the diver into the air. Picture the flat base in the moment when the board bends toward the water. Prices in the flat base area are near the same price, but the triple bottom is slightly below the price level of the flat base. In the 35 chart patterns with flat bases that I looked at, the rise averaged 39% compared to a 33% rise when no flat base appeared.

I discuss how to use the scoring system in the Scores section of this chapter, but for now, just ignore the scores.

HORIZONTAL CONSOLIDATION REGIONS

Table 18.2 lists statistics related to a horizontal consolidation region (HCR); Figure 18.1 shows a good example of a small one. Although most consolidation regions do not have such a nice, flat top, they all share a common trait: The top

Table 18.2
Average Performance of Triple Bottoms with and Without a Consolidation Region

Description	Result	Score
Consolidation region	31% (106)	−1
No consolidation region	38% (90)	+1
Average length (days)	46	
Prices stop within region ±5%	44%	
Prices push through region	47%	
Prices do not reach region	10%	

Note: The number of samples appear in parentheses.

is flat or the bottom is flat or both are flat. There can be spikes inside the region that puncture the top or bottom, so an irregular appearance is not unusual. In Figure 18.1, the HCR forms the top of a small ascending triangle.

Look for an HCR between the trend start (spanning allowed) and the top of the triple bottom, which is the region, after a breakout, that is both nearby and in the price path. Usually, an HCR blocks an upward price rise, as the

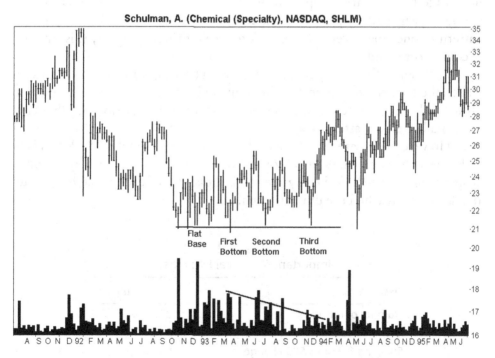

Figure 18.2 A flat base. The average price rise after a flat base is 39%, above the 33% rise from those formations not showing a flat base. Prices appear on the weekly scale.

statistics in Table 18.2 show. When a consolidation region gets in the way of upward price travel, the average rise is 31%, compared to a 38% rise when no resistance zone appears.

For reference, I measured the average length of a consolidation region and found it to be 46 days long—about a month and a half. This result means that you are not looking for a few days of horizontal price action, but a region that is like meeting a muscle-bound bully in a dark alley: clearly intimidating.

How effective is the consolidation region in stopping the upward price movement? Less than half the time (44%), prices stop within the consolidation region including a 5% buffer. I added the buffer to capture those prices that either fall short or poke their heads through the top but fade. Another 10% of the time, prices do not even climb to the bottom of the consolidation region. The remaining 47% of the time, prices eventually push on through.

Figure 18.1 shows one such example. Although the HCR repels prices in February and causes a throwback, prices soon recover and try again, this time punching through to a new minor high.

INSIDE THE PATTERN

Table 18.3 shows important statistics for triple bottoms. As I mentioned earlier, triple bottoms are comparatively rare. I searched over 700 stocks using nearly 10 years of daily price data and found only 226, which is like seeing one pattern in one stock every 30 years. After seeing three patterns, it is time to become worm food.

I measured the average rise from the highest high in the chart pattern (called the confirmation point) to the ultimate high, the highest high before a 20% trend change. The average rise turned out to be 34%, below the 38% rise many bullish chart patterns show.

However, compare the average 34% rise with the Standard & Poor's 500 Index over the same time—a rise of just 6%. I measured this rise by taking a snapshot of the S&P on the day the stock broke out of each triple bottom to the day prices reached the ultimate high.

Table 18.3
Important Statistical Findings

Description	Result
Number of formations	226
Average rise	34%
Standard & Poor's 500 change	6%
Median rise	26%
Rises more than 50%	46/196 or 23%

Sometimes a few large returns can skew the average, so I show the median rise. The median is a number found by sorting the results and choosing the middle number such that half the samples are above the median and half below. The median rise was 26%. I consider this the value that experienced investors trading triple bottoms should be able to achieve, but it does not include commissions, slippage, or other trading costs.

As a measure of how profitable a chart pattern can be, I tallied the number of chart patterns with rises of more than 50%. For triple bottoms, 46 or 23% showed large gains.

FAILURE RATES

Table 18.4 is the first of two tables that list failure rates. To get the results, I measured the rise from the breakout price to the ultimate high and created a frequency distribution of the results. If that sounds confusing, an example makes it clear. Thirty-three, or 17%, of the triple bottoms I looked at showed gains of less than 10%.

Let me give you another example. Suppose that your trading cost (commissions, slippage, and so forth) is 10% and you want to net 15%. How many triple bottoms will meet your minimum? The price needs to rise at least 25% (10% + 15%) to meet your goal. At that rate, nearly half (49%) of the triple bottoms will make the grade but half will not.

Table 18.5 shows another way of looking at the failure rate, this one called the horizon failure rate. With this method, we take an arbitrary time in the

Table 18.4
Maximum Price Rise Versus Failure Rate

Maximum Price Rise (%)	Failure Rate
5	12 or 6%
10	33 or 17%
15	59 or 30%
20	78 or 40%
25	96 or 49%
30	107 or 55%
35	120 or 61%
50	150 or 77%
75	169 or 86%
100	182 or 93%

Note: The sample count is 196 for each row.

Table 18.5
Horizon Failure Rates and Average Rise

Time Since Breakout	Failure Rate (%)	Average Rise (%)
1 week	30	3
2 weeks	32	4
3 weeks	33	5
1 month	30	6
2 months	31	8
3 months	31	9
6 months	34	7

future and count how many stocks are still trading above the breakout price. For example, at the end of the first week after the breakout, 30% of the triple bottoms closed below the breakout price. By definition, the horizontal failure rate at the end of the first day is 0%, so the 1-week failure rate is alarming.

The table shows how the failure rate climbs quickly to 33%, eases down to 30%, and eventually moves to 34% after 6 months. During that time, the average gain rises from 3% to 9%, then drops to 7%. What this result suggests is that you should be ready to take profits after month 3, but no later than month 6, if your chart pattern works as does the average.

BOTTOM PERFORMANCE

Table 18.6 shows an interesting result I found when writing *Encyclopedia of Chart Patterns* (Wiley, 2000). When the right bottom (bottom 3) has a higher low price compared to the center bottom (bottom 2), the formation tends to outperform by 41% to 29%. That difference is startling and statistically significant. When bottom 2 and bottom 3 are the same price, the average price rise after the breakout is just 26%.

Confused? Look at Figure 18.3. The right bottom, labeled as point 3, is above the price of bottom 2. I am comparing the low prices of the two points,

Table 18.6
Performance for Higher Right Bottoms

Description	Results	Score
Average rise when bottom 3 is above bottom 2	41% (88)	+1
Average rise when bottom 3 is equal to bottom 2	26% (22)	−1
Average rise when bottom 3 is below bottom 2	29% (86)	−1

Note: The number of samples appears in parentheses.

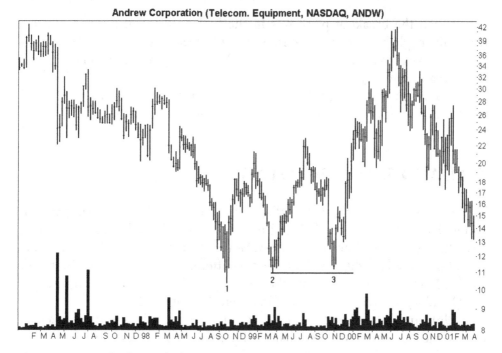

Figure 18.3   A higher right bottom suggests good performance. When the low at bottom 3 is above the low at bottom 2, the chart pattern tends to outperform. Shown on the weekly scale.

shown by the horizontal line. Look how far prices climbed after the breakout. I wish I had a pound of fifties to invest in stocks like this!

YEARLY PRICE RANGE

Table 18.7 shows the performance after sorting the triple bottoms by the breakout price in the yearly price range. By that I mean I found the highest high and lowest low in the 12 months before the breakout, split the range into thirds, then assigned the breakout price to the appropriate category.

Table 18.7
Average Performance Sorted by Breakout Price
According to Prior 12-Month Range

Yearly Price Range	Result	Score
Highest third	39% (79)	+1
Middle third	27% (52)	−1
Lowest third	32% (48)	−1

Note: The number of samples appears in parentheses.

When the breakout price was in the highest third of the yearly price range, the triple bottoms showed rises after the breakout averaging 39%. This result compares to a rise of just 27% when the breakout was in the middle third of the yearly price range.

The results agree with the belief that shorting a stock making new lows and buying a stock making new highs give the best performance.

TALL AND SHORT PATTERNS

Table 18.8 shows how short and tall patterns perform. Short patterns perform better than tall ones, a result I find unusual. Normally, tall patterns handily beat the short ones. The results are 32% for tall patterns and 36% for short ones. I measured height by computing the difference between the highest high and the lowest low, then dividing the result by the breakout price. The median rise (19.12%) marked the midpoint between short and tall.

Unfortunately, the differences are not statistically significant, and I believe the odd result is due to chance. Therefore, I show no score.

VOLUME TREND

Table 18.9 is the first of two volume tables. This table concerns the volume trend from formation start to end, that is, between the first and third bottom lows. I used linear regression (the trend function in some spreadsheets) to plot a best-fit line of volume, the slope of which gave me the trend. A declining volume trend between the outer bottoms resulted in rises averaging 35% after the breakout, compared to a 32% gain for a rising volume trend.

Many times, you need not use the trend function or linear regression to determine the volume trend. Just look at Figures 18.2 and 18.4 that show declining volume trends, for example.

Table 18.8
Performance of Short and Tall Triple Bottoms

Description	Result
Tall (above the median)	32% (98)
Short (below the median)	36% (98)
Median percentage of breakout price	19.12%

Note: The number of samples appears in parentheses.

Table 18.9
Linear Regression Volume Trend and Performance

Description	Result
Rising volume trend	32% (61)
Falling volume trend	35% (135)

Note: The number of samples appears in parentheses.

BREAKOUT VOLUME

Table 18.10 is another disappointing volume table. By that I mean the differences are not statistically significant, so they may be due to chance. To get the results, I compared the average volume with the breakout volume. When the breakout volume was high or very high, the triple bottoms showed gains averaging 35%. When the volume was average, low, or very low, the gains were 33%.

The results agree with other chart pattern types in that high breakout volume is beneficial to performance. Unfortunately, the results do not contain enough octane to use as part of the scoring system.

THROWBACKS

Table 18.11 lists the results of a study of throwbacks. A throwback occurs when prices return to the breakout price within 30 days, and there is clear visibility between the curling action of the throwback and the breakout price. Figure 18.1 shows an example of a throwback. Prices shoot above the breakout price, curl around, and drop to the breakout price within a month. The distance between the curling of the throwback and the breakout price is such that there is plenty of white space between the two areas.

Throwbacks occur half the time and they are something you should anticipate. The case studies at the end of this chapter discuss how to predict them,

Table 18.10
Breakout Volume and Performance

Description	Result
Average rise on above-average breakout volume	35% (71)
Average rise on average or below-average breakout volume	33% (125)

Note: The number of samples appears in parentheses.

but look at Figure 18.1 again. When rising prices bump against overhead resistance—in this case it takes the shape of an HCR—then there is a good chance that prices will throw back to the breakout price. As we see in a moment, performance suffers after a throwback.

I found the ultimate high by looking for the highest high before a 20% decline ensued. How often does the ultimate high occur during the throwback process? Nine percent of the time. That may sound low, and it is, but it is not zero. Keep that in mind the next time you get stopped out on a throwback.

The next four lines (average rise) of Table 18.11 show how performance suffers after a throwback. When volume is above average and a throwback occurs, the average rise is 27% compared to a gain of 41% when no throwback occurs. The same pattern applies to average or below-average breakout volume and throwbacks: rises of 28% compared to 37%, respectively. Thus, throwbacks hurt performance.

Table 18.11
Throwback Statistics

Description	Result
Throwbacks	113/226 or 50%
Score if throwback predicted	−1
Score if throwback not predicted	+1
Ultimate high before throwback	20/226 or 9%
Average rise on above average-breakout volume with throwbacks	27%
Average rise on above-average breakout volume with no throwbacks	41%
Average rise on average or below-average breakout volume with throwbacks	28%
Average rise on average or below-average breakout volume with no throwbacks	37%
Number of throwbacks after a high or very high volume breakout	41/80 or 51%
Number of throwbacks after an average, low, or very low volume breakout	72/146 or 49%
Number of throwbacks that stopped ±5% from the breakout price	70 or 62%
Number of throwbacks that stopped between breakout and formation low	40 or 35%
Number of throwbacks that stopped below the formation low	3 or 3%

With some chart pattern types, a throwback occurs more often after a high volume breakout, which is also the case with triple bottoms, but not by much. After an above-average volume breakout, a throwback occurs 51% of the time, compared to a 49% throwback rate after an average or below-average volume breakout.

When a throwback occurs, where do prices stop? I measured the decline from the breakout price downward and stopped at the *first* minor low. The vast majority of the time—62%—prices stopped within 5% of the breakout price. Another 35% of the time, prices moved lower, but remained above the lowest of the three bottoms. The remaining 3% of the time, prices dropped below the formation low and investors got their clocks cleaned. In all cases, the regions did not overlap.

BULL TRAPS

Table 18.12 shows the frequency of bull traps. They do not happen very often, just 12% of the time. What is a bull trap? A bull trap is when prices rise by less than 10% above the breakout price then tumble and drop below the formation low. When that situation happens, it confirms a bull trap. Those investors expecting a gain have been taken for a ride—in the losing direction—and trapped, you might say.

Figure 18.4 shows an example and how to avoid a trap. The numbers 1, 2, and 3 denote the three bottoms of the triple bottom. Prices staged an upward breakout after they closed above the highest high in the formation before meeting overhead resistance. The stock dropped, and when prices moved below the formation low, a bull trap confirmed.

How can you avoid a bull trap? Look for overhead resistance. In this case, there are two HCRs (shown by the horizontal lines) that pose a clear and present danger to upward price movement. If prices succeed in pushing through the first resistance layer, they would soon meet the second one.

Table 18.12
Bull Traps

Description	Result
Bull trap frequency	24/196 or 12%
Score if trap predicted	−1
Score if trap not predicted	+1

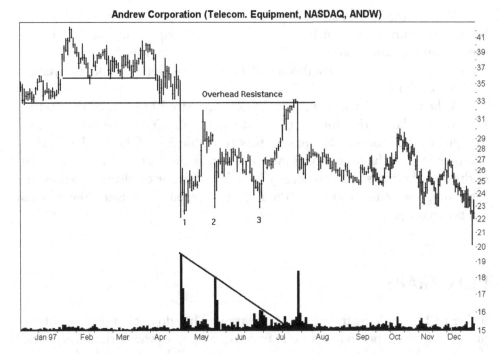

Figure 18.4   A bull trap. Prices stop rising after meeting overhead resistance then tumble, eventually dropping below the formation low and confirming a bull trap. The numbers refer to the triple bottom.

GAPS

A price gap after a triple bottom is unusual, occurring just 20% of the time. When gaps do occur, they add no benefit to performance as Table 18.13 shows. For other chart pattern types, gaps provide an added boost, helping to power prices upward. The dismal results may be due to the small sample size—just 40 gaps appeared.

Table 18.13
Gaps and Performance.

Description	Result
Average rise after price gap on breakout	34% (40)
Average rise with no price gap on breakout	34% (156)

Note: The number of samples appears in parentheses.

Table 18.14
Average Price Performance of Triple Bottoms
During a Rising and Falling Market

Market Trend	FS to FE	FE to UH
Rising S&P 500	35% (141)	34% (174)
Falling S&P 500	31% (55)	30% (22)

Note: FS = formation start, FE = formation end, UH = ultimate
high. The number of samples appears in parentheses.

MARKET TREND

Table 18.14 shows the performance of triple bottoms after sorting by the market trend. In a rising market when the formation was under construction, that is, from formation start to end, prices climbed an average of 35% after the breakout. This results compares to a rise of 31% when the general market, as measured by the Standard & Poor's 500 Index, declined over the same period.

The differences are not statistically significant (so no scores appear), and the results are unusual because with other chart pattern types, a V-shaped market trend works best. In other words, the best performance occurs when the general market declines while the formation is under construction (FS to FE), then rises on the way to the ultimate high.

MARKET CAPITALIZATION

Table 18.15 shows the performance results after sorting triple bottoms by market capitalization. Market capitalization is the number of shares outstanding multiplied by the breakout price. Usually, small caps perform best and large caps perform worst, but Table 18.15 shows mid caps doing worst. It is possible that the addition of more samples could change the performance order.

Table 18.15
Average Price Performance of Triple Bottoms by
Market Capitalization

Capitalization	Result	Score
Small cap (up to $1 billion)	36% (87)	+1
Mid cap ($1 to $5 billion)	30% (67)	−1
Large cap (over $5 billion)	36% (42)	+1

Note: The number of samples appears in parentheses.

SCORES

Table 18.16 shows the performance after evaluating each triple bottom by the scoring system. To use the system, look at each table showing a score, and evaluate your chart pattern according to the table guidelines. Then add the scores together. Scores above zero mean the chart pattern is likely to perform better than the median; scores below zero mean you should avoid an investment. The case studies at the end of this chapter show how to score your chart pattern.

There are no guarantees that your chart pattern will perform as expected. Even if your chart pattern has a perfect score, you could still lose money by buying too late, selling prematurely, or because the chart pattern turns out to be a dud. It has been my experience that this system adds value and helps you make wise investment decisions, but it is not perfect. Consider the scoring system as just one more tool in your toolbox of investment indicators.

Those triple bottoms with final scores above zero had gains averaging 49%. This compares to a rise of just 25% when the scores were below zero. Although you might think that performance is better than sex, the last few lines in the table may chill you out.

I compared the rise for triple bottoms with scores above and below zero to the median rise (26.65%). The median rise includes only those triple bottoms for which all table scores appeared. For example, if the ultimate high has not been found yet because the breakout occurred last week, I excluded the formation from the tally.

Those triple bottoms with scores above zero beat the median rise 67% of the time. These are the correct buy signals. When the score was below zero, the chart patterns said avoid a purchase and correctly performed worse than the median 62% of the time. Anything above 50% means the system adds value.

Table 18.16
Formation Performance by Score

Score	Result
Average rise of chart patterns with scores above zero	49%
Average rise of chart patterns with scores below zero	25%
Median rise used	26.65%
Percentage with scores above zero beating median rise	37/55 or 67%
Percentage with scores below zero doing worse than median rise	51/82 or 62%

CASE STUDY 1

How do you use the scoring system? Consider Figure 18.5, which illustrates the first case study for triple bottoms. The bottoms are somewhat uneven, with the first one above the other two, but they are close enough in price to be worth considering.

Let us step through the tables showing scores, beginning with Table 18.1. Where does the trend start? From bottom 1, work backward, upward, and look for a 20% price decline. The highest high before that decline will mark the trend start. Following the price trend upward, we find that it peaked in mid-November at a high price of 17.31. A 20% decline from that price would be a *close* below 13.85, and that occurred in early September. Thus, the November high marks the trend start.

From the trend start, what is the duration to the formation start? Clearly it is brief, 15 calendar days if you care to count. According to Table 18.1, that places the decline into the short-term category, for a –1 score.

Is there a flat base before the chart pattern, at about the same price level as the three bottoms? No. The table scores no flat base as –1 for a running total of –2.

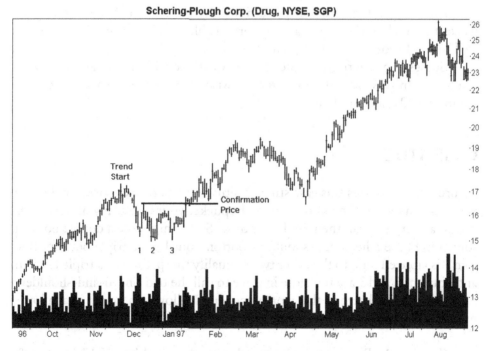

Figure 18.5 A positive score suggests good gains. This chart does not show the ultimate high at 59.21, for a rise of 261%.

Is there a horizontal consolidation region between the trend start and the breakout? No. If you extend the confirmation line to the left, just below the trend start, you can see that there is not much room for prices to climb before they rise above the trend start price. There is no long, flat region posing a threat to upward price travel. Table 18.2 says that a missing consolidation region scores +1 for a running total of –1.

Skip to Table 18.6, the next table listing scores. Is the right bottom above the center bottom? Yes. Bottom 2 has a low price of 14.97, whereas bottom 3 has a low of 15.41, so bottom 3 is above bottom 2, for a +1 score. Running total: 0.

Table 18.7 discusses performance sorted by the yearly price range. Starting from the day before the breakout to a year earlier, we find that the high was at 17.31 and the low was at 11.69, with a breakout at 16.42. Splitting the yearly price range into thirds places the breakout price in the highest third for a +1 score. Running total: +1.

Will a throwback occur? As I mentioned during the discussion of the HCR, my guess is that it would not. There is no overhead resistance to impede upward price travel. Table 18.11 says that when a throwback is not predicted, score that a +1. Running total: +2.

Will a bull trap happen? Unlikely. Again, overhead resistance is the key to a bull trap and with just a 12% trap frequency, my guess is that it would not occur. Table 18.12 scores that a +1 for a running total of +3.

Multiplying the breakout price times the number of shares outstanding places the stock in the large cap category. Table 18.15 says that large caps do well for a +1 score and a final total of +4.

Scores above zero mean the stock is worth considering as an investment candidate. In this case, that would be a wise choice as the stock went on to climb to 59.21, a gain of 261%.

CASE STUDY 2

Figure 18.6 illustrates this case study, a situation where the scores total below zero. As you look at the figure, you might pucker your face as if you were sucking on a sour gum ball then hold your nose. Some might see a double bottom, some might see a head-and-shoulders bottom, but I see a triple bottom. Bottom 1 is close enough to the other two to qualify this pattern as a triple bottom, and bottoms 2 and 3 are too close in price to call the trio a head-and-shoulders. As for the double bottom, that works, too, and it allows you to get in at a lower price. Running briefly through the tables, we find the following.

Table 18.1: Trend start. The trend starts from a high of 17.31. A 20% decline from this price would be a close below 13.85, a level reached in late

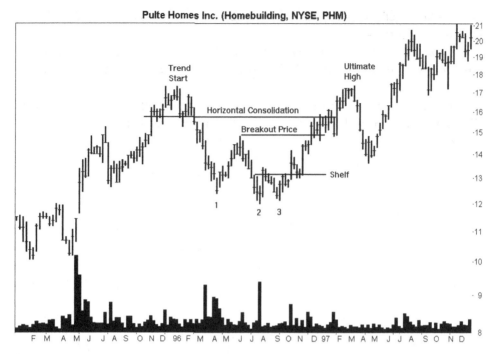

Figure 18.6 A negative score suggests underperformance. Prices rise just 17% before suffering a 22% downturn. Shown on the weekly scale.

September 1995. From the trend start to the first bottom, where the formation begins, is 98 days for an intermediate-term duration. Score: –1.

Table 18.1: Flat base? No. Score: –1. Running total: –2.

Table 18.2: Horizontal consolidation region. There is an HCR straddling the trend start and it appears as the base of a dual (complex) head-and-shoulders top. Score: –1. Running total: –3.

Table 18.6: Higher right bottom. You can see that bottom 3 is above bottom 2. Score +1. Running total: –2.

Table 18.7: Yearly price range. The 12-month high is at 17.31, the low is at 12, and the breakout is at 14.81. Thus, the breakout is in the middle of the price range. Score: –1. Running total: –3.

Table 18.11: Throwback. Is a throwback predicted? Yes. There is overhead resistance set up by the HCR, making a throwback likely. Score: –1. Running total: –4.

Table 18.12: Bull trap. Since a bull trap occurs just 12% of the time, the odds are against a trap. Still, with overhead resistance, there is a better chance of a trap. For a trap to occur, prices would also have to decline below the formation low of 12, a decline of 19% from the breakout price. Also, a flat shelf appears above the three bottoms, providing extra price support. You can score the trap however you wish, but I do not believe a trap is likely to occur. Score: +1. Running total: –3.

   Table 18.15: Market capitalization. The stock is a small cap for a +1 score. Final total: –2. If you score the bull trap as likely, it would send the score to –4.

Scores below zero mean you should avoid the stock. In this case, prices climbed to a high of 17.38 for a gain of just 17%, well below the 26.65% median rise.

19

Triple Tops

To my surprise, triple tops are slightly more common than triple bottoms, but that does not suggest that they are like streetlights, appearing on every corner. I found as many as I could to assure that the results were based on solid statistical research.

THE TYPICAL PATTERN

You can think of a triple top as a double top with an extra hump, or the last three humps in a multiple hump top. Figure 19.1 shows a good example of a triple top. Three distinct minor highs, usually appearing as sharp price peaks contrasting with more rounded looking valleys, appear on the daily or even the weekly scale. In the figure, a rounded-looking valley appears between peaks 2 and 3.

The three peaks should top out at nearly the same price; in the example, prices are all within 6 cents of each other. The volume trend usually slopes downward like that shown in Figure 19.1. Any three-bump formation confirms as a triple top when prices close below the lowest low in the formation, called the confirmation price. That statement is worth repeating: *Prices must close below the confirmation price or else the pattern is not a triple top.*

TREND START

Much can be learned from examining the trend leading to a chart pattern. First, we must determine where the trend starts. Since triple tops occur after a

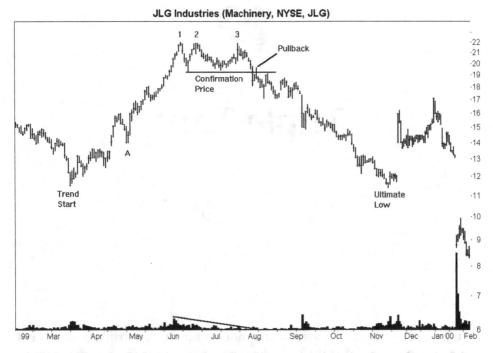

Figure 19.1   A triple top. Numbers 1, 2, and 3 mark the three tops of a triple top. The confirmation price is the lowest price between the tops, and a close below the confirmation price confirms the validity of the formation. Without confirmation, this pattern is not a triple top.

price uptrend, we will be following prices lower until we find a low point from which prices rise by at least 20%. Why 20%? Because it is a commonly accepted determinant of bull and bear markets. Why not apply it to individual stocks too?

Using Figure 19.1 as an example, hop on board as we ride prices lower, beginning from the formation start (point 1), working backward in time. As you can see, prices decline, leading away from the pattern, so we will be looking for a 20% price rise that signals a trend change. The first real test comes in late April (point A) when prices reach a minor low before climbing (remember, we are looking backward). From the *low* at 14, a 20% rise means a daily *closing* price above 16.80. The highest closing price is only 15.88, not high enough to signal a trend change, so we keep looking.

As we work our way downward, we finally come to the low point marked as the trend start in Figure 19.1. The low is at 11.50, so a 20% rise would mean a closing price above 13.80, and prices pierced that about a week earlier. Thus, the low point is where the trend changes from a downward trend to an upward trend, leading to the chart pattern; the low point marks the trend start.

Table 19.1
Average Performance of Triple Tops Sorted by Price Trend Leading to the Pattern

Trend Start to Formation Start	Result	Score
Short term (0 to 3 months)	–20% (146)	0
Intermediate term (3 to 6 months)	–22% (54)	+1
Long term (over 6 months)	–15% (44)	–1

Note: The number of samples appears in parentheses.

From the trend start, how long is the time period to the formation? In Figure 19.1, the duration is 85 days, barely squeezing into the short-term category as defined in Table 19.1. According to the table, those triple tops appearing after a short-term rise have declines averaging 20% after the breakout. That result is better than the long-term category but below the intermediate term.

I discuss scoring in the Scores section of this chapter, so do not concern yourself with scores now.

HORIZONTAL CONSOLIDATION REGIONS

Table 19.2 shows price performance after a triple top with and without a horizontal consolidation region (HCR). What is an HCR? The consolidation region is an area where prices appear with flat tops, flat bottoms, or both, and usually lasts several weeks. Price spikes can puncture the tops or bottoms, so we are looking for a somewhat solid-looking block of horizontal, or nearly horizontal, price movement.

Table 19.2
Average Performance of Triple Tops with and Without a Consolidation Region

Description	Result	Score
Consolidation region	–18% (139)	–1
No consolidation region	–21% (115)	+1
Average length (days)	40	
Prices stop within region ±5%	56%	
Prices push through region	37%	
Prices do not reach region	7%	

Note: The number of samples appears in parentheses.

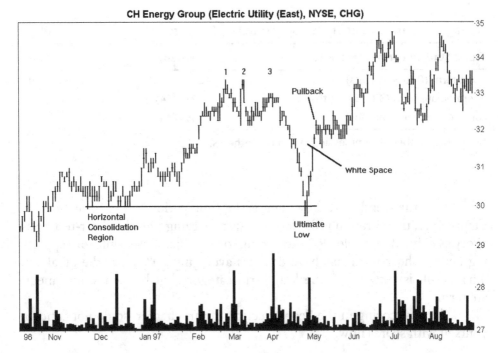

Figure 19.2 An HCR. The consolidation region supports falling prices and stops the decline.

Figure 19.2 shows an example of an HCR. The trend start is off the chart to the left. The consolidation region must appear between the trend start (spanning allowed) and the formation bottom so that the region is both nearby and in the predicted price path. Once prices drop to the consolidation region, you can see that prices stop near that level, then rebound.

Table 19.2 shows that when a consolidation region gets in the way, prices decline by an average of 18%, but decline by 21% when no support region exists.

How long should the HCR be? The length of time varies, but is usually longer than a week. The average length is 40 days, or just over a month, so it should be readily visible on the daily price chart.

When prices drop, how often do they stop within the consolidation region? In 7% of the cases I looked at, prices never made it down to the region. Another 56% of the time, prices stopped within the region after adding a 5% buffer to capture those that stopped nearby. Figure 19.2 shows an example of this overshoot when prices dropped below 30, and below the base of the HCR. The remainder of the time (37%), prices entered the HCR and eventually continued down. Clearly, a consolidation region does not always stop a price decline, but, for trading purposes, assume that it will.

Table 19.3
Important Statistical Findings

Description	Result
Number of formations	260
Average decline	20%
Standard and Poor's 500 change	–2%
Median decline	17%
Declines more than 50%	6/254 or 2%

INSIDE THE PATTERN

Table 19.3 shows general findings for triple tops. By digging through a decade of daily price data, I uncovered 260 triple tops, encompassing over 700 stocks. I consider finding a triple top the same as seeing a robin in the middle of winter: If it happens, click your heels three times because you are probably not in Kansas anymore! The chart pattern you are looking at will probably fail to confirm, so it is not a triple top. I review only confirmed triple tops.

The average decline turned out to be 20%, nearly pegging the 21% decline for all bearish chart patterns. I measured the decline from the lowest low in the formation to the ultimate low, which is the lowest low before prices climbed by at least 20%.

While prices after triple tops were declining by 20%, what was the general market doing? It dropped also, but by just 2%. I measured the decline in the S&P 500 Index from the day each chart pattern broke out to the day each pattern reached its ultimate low.

The median, or midrange, decline is 17%. This decline is what I believe experienced investors—if they trade triple tops often enough—could achieve. It does not include trading costs of any sort. I found the median decline by sorting the performance numbers and selecting the middle value such that the number of samples above the median is the same as the number below.

To measure the maximum performance of chart patterns, I tallied the number of patterns in which the decline was more than 50%. For triple tops, just 6 or 2% showed a massive loss. This is not unusual for bearish chart patterns.

FAILURE RATES

Table 19.4 shows the failure rate for a given price decline. I measured the decline from the breakout price to the ultimate low, then created a frequency distribution of the results. This is not as confusing as it sounds, so let me give

Table 19.4
Maximum Price Decline Versus Failure Rate

Maximum Price Decline (%)	Failure Rate
5	23 or 9%
10	66 or 26%
15	114 or 45%
20	153 or 60%
25	184 or 72%
30	206 or 81%
35	225 or 89%
50	248 or 98%
75	254 or 100%
100	254 or 100%

Note: The sample count is 254 for each row.

you an example. Almost half the formations, or 114, showed declines that stopped less than 15% below the breakout price. Another example: How many triple tops decline less than 25%? Answer: 184 or 72%.

Think of the table as a gauge of how well you can expect to do after taking into account trading costs and other factors. Say commissions, fees, slippage, and other trading costs amount to 5% and you want to make at least 10% on each trade, what are the chances that prices will decline by at least 15% (5% + 10%)? Answer: 45%. Nearly half the triple tops you trade will likely end in failure if you hold out for a 15% average decline.

Table 19.5 shows another way of measuring the failure rate, this one called the horizon failure rate. To compute the rate, count the number of triple tops that have prices closing above the breakout price over time. For example, after the first week, a third (33%) of the triple tops had prices above the breakout price, and all triple tops showed declines averaging 3%. At the end of 2 months, 40% were above the breakout price and the average decline measured 5%.

You can see in the table that the failure rate holds steady for the first month, then starts climbing to 45% after 3 months before receding to 43%. The average decline shows the best performance between 1 and 2 months.

Since the horizon failure rate at the end of the first day is 0%, by definition, you can see how dreadful the results are. The numbers suggest that you should look to close out your short position within the first month while

Table 19.5
Horizon Failure Rates and Average Decline

Time Since Breakout	Failure Rate (%)	Average Decline (%)
1 week	33	3
2 weeks	33	4
3 weeks	33	4
1 month	33	5
2 months	40	5
3 months	45	4
6 months	43	4

the average decline is strongest, and the horizon failure rate is still comparatively low.

YEARLY PRICE RANGE

Table 19.6 shows the performance of triple tops after sorting by the breakout price according to its position in the prior 12-month price range. For example, when the breakout occurred in the highest third of the yearly price range, the 41 chart patterns showed declines averaging 22%. This result compares to a 19% decline when the breakout occurred in the lower two thirds.

Most bearish chart patterns show the largest decline when the breakout occurs near the yearly low, not the yearly high. Perhaps the comparatively low sample count has something to do with these results.

Table 19.6
Average Performance Sorted by Breakout Price
According to Prior 12-Month Range

Yearly Price Range	Result	Score
Highest third	–22% (41)	+1
Middle third	–19% (101)	–1
Lowest third	–19% (92)	–1

Note: The number of samples appears in parentheses.

Table 19.7
Performance of Short and Tall Triple Tops

Description	Result	Score
Tall (above the median)	−22% (127)	+1
Short (below the median)	−18% (127)	−1
Median percentage of breakout price	20.18%	

Note: The number of samples appears in parentheses.

TALL AND SHORT PATTERNS

Table 19.7 shows the performance of triple tops after sorting them by height. The results match most other chart patterns in that tall formations perform better than short ones. I measured the formation height from the highest high of the three tops to the breakout price (the lowest low in the formation), then divided by the breakout price to get the height as a percentage of the breakout price. After sorting the results, I categorized short patterns as those with heights below the median, 20.18%, height; tall triple tops were those with heights above the median.

You can see that tall patterns show declines averaging 22%, whereas short ones have declines of 18%. The results suggest that you should select tall chart patterns and ignore the vertically challenged.

TOP VOLUME

Table 19.8 shows performance when the center top has a volume total above or below the last top. Since volume varies considerably, I totaled the volume from 2 days before to 2 days after each top. For the 5-day period, when the center top showed volume higher than the last top, the decline averaged 21%, but only 18% with the reverse volume trend. The differences are statistically significant, meaning that they are not likely due to chance. When you look at a chart, watch for high volume surrounding the center top and lower volume on the last top for the best average performance.

Table 19.8
Top Volume and Performance

Description	Results	Score
Average decline when top 2 volume is above top 3	21% (140)	+1
Average decline when top 2 volume is below top 3	18% (114)	−1

Note: The number of samples appears in parentheses.

Table 19.9
Linear Regression Volume Trend and Performance

Description	Result	Score
Rising volume trend	−21% (102)	+1
Falling volume trend	−19% (152)	−1

Note: The number of samples appears in parentheses.

VOLUME TREND

Table 19.9 shows performance after sorting by the volume trend from formation start to end, that is, from the top of the first peak to the top of the last peak. I used linear regression to find the slope of a line connecting the volume points, but you can use the trend function if your spreadsheet supports it.

When volume was trending upward, prices declined by an average 21% after the breakout. This result compares to a 19% decline for a falling volume trend. From the sample counts listed in Table 19.9, you can see that a rising volume trend occurs 40% of the time, so it should be easy to find a triple top with a rising volume trend, that is, if triple tops were easy to find in the first place. They are not.

BREAKOUT VOLUME

Breakout volume can be a key to triple top performance. Consider Table 19.10 that compares the performance after high and low volume breakouts. To get the results, I compared the breakout day volume with the average volume of the prior 90 days and sorted the results into one of five volume categories: very high, high, average, low, or very low. I grouped the results into those above average (high and very high) and those average or below (average, low, and very low).

Table 19.10
Breakout Volume and Performance

Description	Result	Score
Average decline on above-average breakout volume	22% (85)	+1
Average decline on average or below-average breakout volume	18% (169)	−1

Note: The number of samples appears in parentheses.

The table illustrates that those breakouts showing above-average break-out volume posted losses of 22% compared to an 18% drop when breakout volume was average or below average. The rumors you heard are true: High breakout volume helps performance!

PULLBACKS

Table 19.11 shows various statistics related to pullbacks. First, what is a pull-back? A pullback is just like a throwback, only it occurs from the bottom instead of the top. That description, of course, is really no help at all unless you know what a throwback looks like. For a good example of a pullback, look at Figure 19.2. A pullback occurs within 30 days of a breakout when prices move lower but quickly return to the breakout price. I also added a white space rule, that is, prices must drop far enough away from the breakout price to show white space as prices curl around. The figure makes this price movement clear. A pullback occurs about half the time (49%).

Table 19.11
Pullback Statistics

Description	Result
Pullbacks	127 or 49%
Score if pullback predicted	−1
Score if pullback not predicted	+1
Ultimate low before pullback	43 or 17%
Average decline on above-average breakout volume with pullbacks	19%
Average decline on above-average breakout volume and no pullbacks	26%
Average decline on average or below-average breakout volume and pullbacks	17%
Average decline on average or below-average breakout volume and no pullbacks	19%
Number of pullbacks after a high or very high volume breakout	42/85 or 49%
Number of pullbacks after an average, low, or very low volume breakout	85/175 or 49%
Number of pullbacks that stopped less than 5% from the breakout price	78 or 61%
Number of pullbacks that stopped between the breakout price and triple top high	42 or 33%
Number of pullbacks that climbed above the triple top high	7 or 6%

I define the ultimate low as the lowest low before prices rise by at least 20%. How often do prices reach the ultimate low during a pullback? About 17% of the time or one in six.

A pullback is detrimental to performance, regardless of the breakout volume. Why? Because prices decline 26% when no pullback occurs, but only 19% when a pullback occurs, after a high volume breakout. Low volume breakouts—those with breakout volumes in the average or below-average categories—have declines averaging 19% when a pullback does not occur and 17% otherwise.

With some chart patterns, a low volume breakout increases the likelihood of a pullback, but not with triple tops. Regardless of the breakout volume level, the pullback rate is 49%.

When a pullback occurs, where do prices stop rising? Most of the time (61%) prices stop within 5% of the breakout price. Another 33% of the time, prices stop between the breakout price (the lowest low in the formation) and the highest of the three tops. The remaining 6% of the time, prices continue moving higher. To get these results, I searched for a pullback and followed prices higher until it was clear that prices had formed a minor high. When that occurred, I assumed that the pullback was over. In Figure 19.2, for example, the day prices climbed to the breakout price is the day the pullback ended (shown as "Pullback" in Figure 19.2).

The results indicate that a stop placed just above the breakout price will usually protect your short position from an adverse rise, but placing the stop slightly above the highest top will work the vast majority of the time. Of course, with the stop placed so far from the breakout price, if the stop gets hit, your loss could be large. To keep your losses reasonable, place the stop as close to the breakout price as you can, but always close out your position if prices rise above the triple top high. Anything that rises that far is likely to continue climbing. Should prices trend downward, lower your stop as prices drop.

BEAR TRAPS

Table 19.12 shows how often a bear trap occurs. A bear trap happens after a downward breakout when prices drop less than 10%, then pull back and continue rising above the formation high. I impose no time limit on this action.

Table 19.12
Bear Traps

Description	Result
Bear trap frequency	57/254 or 22%
Score if trap predicted	−1
Score if trap not predicted	+1

Figure 19.2 shows a bear trap. Prices broke out downward and dropped by 7%, then climbed, working their way higher until rising above the formation high and confirming a bear trap. Those shorting the stock would likely be trapped in a losing position. The good news is that a bear trap occurs only 22% of the time.

Watch for the possibility of a bear trap by looking for a consolidation region, minor lows or minor highs, the impending intersection of a moving average (such as the often used 200-day moving average) with prices, or anything else that you know of that might support falling prices. A rising general market coupled with an HCR might, for instance, be enough to halt a declining price trend, then help power prices upward in a rising-tide-lifts-all-boats scenario.

GAPS

Table 19.13 lists gap statistics. A price gap occurs in a downward breakout when the day's high price is below the prior day's low price. For the 44 triple tops showing a gap on the day prices closed below the formation low, prices scored declines averaging 24%. When no breakout gap occurred, prices declined by just 18%. Thus, gaps help performance and many traders try to take advantage of them when they appear.

MARKET TREND

Table 19.14 shows the influence of the general market, as measured by the Standard & Poor's 500 Index, on the performance of triple tops. I took snapshots of the S&P when the triple top started, ended, and on the day prices reached the ultimate low. When the S&P, while the formation was under construction—from formation start to formation end—was declining, triple tops showed declines averaging 21%, compared to declines of 19% in a rising market. Measuring in a similar manner from the formation end to the ultimate low,

Table 19.13
Gaps and Performance

Description	Result	Score
Average decline after price gap on breakout	24% (44)	+1
Average decline with no price gap on breakout	18% (210)	−1

Note: The number of samples appears in parentheses.

Table 19.14

Average Price Performance of Triple Tops During a Rising and Falling Market

Market Trend	FS to FE	Score	FE to UL
Rising S&P 500	–19% (177)	–1	–18% (89)
Falling S&P 500	–21% (77)	+1	–20% (165)

Note: FS = formation start, FE = formation end, UL = ultimate low. The number of samples appears in parentheses.

the trend was the same with a falling market helping triple tops to show larger losses by 20% to 18%. In this case, a receding tide lowers all boats. Incidentally, I base the scores on when the formation is under construction, not on the results from the formation end to the ultimate low, because you cannot predict how the market will perform on the way to the ultimate low.

MARKET CAPITALIZATION

Table 19.15 shows how performance fared after sorting by market capitalization. I define market capitalization as the number of shares outstanding multiplied by the breakout price. You can see that small caps decline most (21%). If you own stocks in a declining market, pray that they are large caps because they decline least (that is, if you are too chicken to go into cash). Short the small caps.

SCORES

Many of the tables accompanying this chapter show scores. For each table, follow the discussion for evaluating your chart pattern and assign a score. Total the scores. A triple top scoring above zero means it is an investment candidate (since triple tops are bearish, consider shorting the stock or selling your long

Table 19.15

Average Price Performance of Triple Tops by Market Capitalization

Capitalization	Result	Score
Small cap (up to $1 billion)	–21% (104)	+1
Mid cap ($1 to $5 billion)	–20% (90)	0
Large cap (over $5 billion)	–18% (60)	–1

Note: The number of samples appears in parentheses.

Table 19.16
Formation Performance by Score

Score	Result
Average decline of chart patterns with scores above zero	27%
Average decline of chart patterns with scores below zero	15%
Median decline used	16.25%
Number with scores above zero beating median decline	51/71 or 72%
Number with scores below zero doing worse than median decline	84/136 or 62%

holding). Scores below zero suggest the formation will perform worse than the median 16.25% decline, that is, a smaller percentage decline.

Just because a triple top shows a positive score is no guarantee that it will beat the median. It could perform well, and you could make a trading mistake, or it could be a bust even though expertly traded. Do any further research needed to make yourself feel comfortable with your investment decision.

Table 19.16 shows the performance of triple tops arranged by score. I measured the score for each chart pattern and separated the results into two main groups: scores above and below zero. Those chart patterns with scores above zero showed losses averaging 27%. This result compares to a loss of just 15% when the score was less than zero.

To evaluate the scoring system, I compared performance to the 16.25% median decline. The percentage comes from those chart patterns having a score for each table. In other words, I excluded some triple tops because they did not have a complete set of data (the ultimate high was usually missing).

Those triple tops with scores above zero beat the median decline 72% of the time. This result represents the correct "sell short," "avoid buying long," or "sell your long holding" score. Those triple tops with scores less than zero, correctly underperformed the median decline 62% of the time. These triple tops represent the "avoid short selling" or "keep long holdings" signals. A value above 50% means the system adds value.

CASE STUDY 1

Figure 19.3 illustrates this case study, an examination of a stock with a positive score. Let us evaluate the stock using the tables with scores, beginning with Table 19.1. Where does the trend start? Following prices downward from the formation start (the first top high), backward in time, we come to the low marked on the figure as the trend start. This occurs at a low price of 43.91. A 20% rise from this price would be a *close* above 52.69, a level reached about a

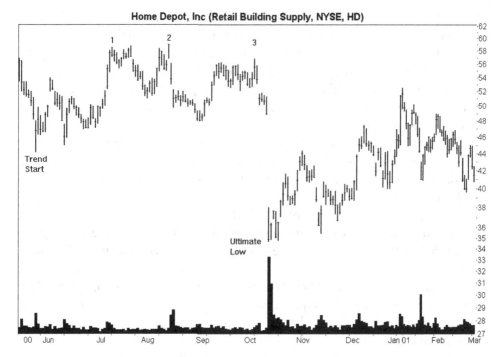

Figure 19.3 A triple top with a positive score. Scores above zero suggest good performance and this stock showed a loss of 28%. An earnings warning started a dead-cat bounce pattern.

week earlier. So, the trend start, as marked, is correct, and it signals the start of a new trend.

From the trend start to the formation start is 48 days, a short-term rise. Table 19.1 scores a short-term rise as neutral.

Table 19.2 lists the performance when a consolidation region interferes with the downward price movement. Is there an HCR between the trend start and the formation start (top 1)? No. Although there are flat bottoms in late June, they are not long enough to suggest a significant support area. The table says that no consolidation region scores +1 for a running total of +1.

Skip to Table 19.6 (the next table having scores), which lists performance of triple tops sorted by the breakout price within the yearly price range. The yearly high was 69.66, reached in mid-April 2000. The low was 43.91, reached about a month later and it appears as the trend start in Figure 19.3. The breakout price, which is the lowest low in the formation, is priced at 47.87, very near the yearly low. Table 19.6 says that a breakout price in the lowest third of the yearly price range scores –1. Running total: 0.

Is the triple top short or tall? The formation height is the highest high, at 59.79, minus the lowest low, at 47.87, giving a height of 11.92. As a percentage of the breakout price, the result is 11.92/47.87 or 25%. That result is above the 20.18% cutoff for short triple tops, so the formation is a tall one. Tall formations, according to Table 19.7, score +1 for a running total of +1.

Volume surrounding the middle and last top is the next topic. Comparing the 5 days surrounding the center peak (2 days before to 2 days after the top) with the last peak indicates that the center peak has higher volume than the last one. Table 19.8 says that when top 2 volume is above top 3 volume, the score is +1. Running total: +2.

The volume trend from the first top to the last top is hard to see in Figure 19.3. I would guess volume is trending upward, and linear regression on the volume series confirms this. Table 19.9 says a rising volume trend scores +1. Running total: +3.

While we are looking at volume, is the breakout volume above average? Clearly the answer is yes as my computer places it in the highest category: very high. Table 19.10 scores above-average breakout volume as +1. Running total: +4.

Is a pullback predicted? No. Usually a large HCR will support prices, but there is scant evidence of a support zone between the formation low and the trend start. Table 19.11 says the likely absence of a pullback scores +1 for a running total of +5.

What about bear traps? Again, no support below the formation makes it comparatively easy for prices to decline. This decline coupled with a declining general market further suggests a bear trap is unlikely (a bear trap requires prices to decline less than 10%, then soar above the formation high. With lumber prices falling and a weak retailing environment, having prices climb above the triple top would be a cute trick). Table 19.12 says that no predicted bear trap scores +1. Running total: +6.

Is there a breakout gap? Sure, and it is huge, measuring nearly $11. Table 19.13 says a gap scores +1. Running total: +7.

What is the market doing from the formation start to the formation end? On the day the formation started, July 11, 2000, (top 1), the S&P 500 closed at 1480.88. The formation ended with the top of peak 3, on October 4. On that date, the S&P closed at 1434.32. Comparing the two, we find that the general market ended lower over that time. Table 19.14 says a falling market scores +1 for a running total of +8.

Finally, the market capitalization is the number of shares outstanding multiplied by the breakout price. Doing the math places the stock in the large cap category. Large caps, according to Table 19.15, score –1 for a final total of +7.

How did the stock do? From the breakout price of 47.87, the stock plunged to 34.59 in 1 day, a decline of 28%. The company issued an earnings warning and that news sent the stock down, forming a dead-cat bounce. The 28% decline is well above the median 16.25% decline, as the score predicted.

If you followed my advice about waiting for confirmation before shorting a stock, you probably would have taken a loss (since you would have shorted at the ultimate low or the day after—a bad move). When trading a dead-cat bounce, wait for the event high before shorting a stock. If that means nothing to you, consult my previous book, *Encyclopedia of Chart Patterns* (Wiley, 2000). It dissects a dead-cat bounce and tells you how to trade it.

CASE STUDY 2

This second case study is illustrated by Figure 19.4. Briefly going through the tables, we find the following.

Table 19.1: Trend start. The trend begins at the October low and climbs into the formation 189 days later. That places the trend duration in the long-term category for a –1 score.

Table 19.2: Horizontal consolidation region. An HCR is the key to the success or failure of most chart patterns. Here, an HCR appears between the trend start and the formation bottom. It has flat tops that touch the same price and, in March, prices dip to the top of the support zone before climbing away. The early January peak supports the bottom of the congestion area. Together, the narrow but long price range suggests a support zone that would at least

Figure 19.4 A triple top with a negative score. Scores below zero suggest performance worse than the median 16.25% decline. This stock dropped just 7%.

cause prices to pause if not repel the decline entirely. Score: –1. Running total: –2.

Table 19.6: Yearly price range. The yearly high was at 22.50, the low was at 11.50, and the breakout was 18.75. If you subtract the low from the high and divide the range into thirds, you will find that the breakout price was in the middle third of the yearly price range. Score: –1. Running total: –3.

Table 19.7: Short or tall. The formation height as a percentage of the breakout price is 20.00%, placing it in the short category, barely, for a –1 score. Running total: –4.

Table 19.8: Top volume. If you compare the 5 days of volume around top 2 with top 3 (see Figure 19.4), you find that top 2 volume is below that shown surrounding top 3. Score: –1. Running total: –5.

Table 19.9: Linear regression volume trend. The volume below peak 1 to peak 3 trends downward, but you may not be able to see it on Figure 19.4, which is why I use linear regression to avoid confusion. Score: –1. Running total: –6.

Table 19.10: Breakout volume. A breakout occurs when prices close below the lowest price in the formation. That situation occurred the day prices reached the ultimate low. Volume on that day spiked upward, placing it in the high category. Score: +1. Running total: –5.

Table 19.11: Pullbacks. Is a pullback predicted? Yes. You can reasonably assume that the HCR will repel prices; at least, that is the way to trade this stock. Score: –1. Running total: –6.

Table 19.12: Bear trap. For the reasons a pullback can be expected, a bear trap is also likely. In a moment, we see that the market was rising while the formation was being created. Coupling that fact with what looks to be a retrace in a long-term uptrend suggests a small decline followed by a resumption of the upward price trend. In short, a bear trap. If you are skeptical of the analysis, then you can score it as you see fit. A +1 score will not change the outcome. Score: –1. Running total: –7.

Table 19.13: Gaps. Is there a price gap on the breakout day? No. Score: –1. Running total: –8.

Table 19.14: Market trend. The market was rising from the first top (the formation start) to the last top (the formation end). Score: –1. Running total: –9.

Table 19.15: Market capitalization. The stock is a mid cap for a zero score. Final total: –9.

As you can see, removing the bear trap or even the pullback predictions would not send the score above zero. Scores below zero mean that you should either hold onto a long position or avoid selling short. In this case, that is good advice as the stock declined just 7% before climbing above the formation top and trapping the bears.

Statistics Summary and Analysis

BULLISH CHART PATTERNS

The following table shows the average rise after a breakout according to the price trend leading to the chart pattern. Usually, a short-term price trend works best.

Price Trend Leading to the Chart Pattern and Resulting
Performance Sorted by Average Rise

Description	Best Performing Trend Term	Average Rise (%)
Triangles, descending, up breakouts	Short	49
Rectangles, up breakouts	Intermediate	42
Triple bottoms	Long	41
Double bottoms, Adam & Eve	Long	41
Broadening tops, up breakouts	Long	41
Double bottoms, Eve & Adam	Short	39
Triangles, ascending, up breakouts	Short	38
Triangles, symmetrical, up breakouts	Short	38
Head-and-shoulders bottoms	Short	38
Double bottoms, Eve & Eve	Short	38
Scallops, ascending, up breakouts	Short	31
Double bottoms, Adam & Adam	Short or Intermediate	27
Scallops, descending, up breakouts	Long	20

The following table shows the general performance of chart patterns measured from the breakout price to the ultimate high along with the change in the Standard & Poor's 500 Index over the same time. Consider the change of the S&P as the return (without dividends) that an investor in an index fund would receive. Compare how much better the average chart pattern performs. Of course, the chart patterns assume you buy at the breakout price and sell at the ultimate high, so the values represent a *best-case* scenario.

Average Rise Performance Sorted by the Average Rise

Description	Average Rise (%)	S&P Change (%)
Triangles, descending, up breakouts	42	5
Double bottoms, Eve & Eve	37	5
Rectangles, up breakouts	37	6
Triangles, symmetrical, up breakouts	35	3
Broadening tops, up breakouts	34	4
Head-and-shoulders bottoms	34	6
Triangles, ascending, up breakouts	34	6
Triple bottoms	34	6
Double bottoms, Adam & Eve	31	5
Double bottoms, Eve & Adam	30	4
Double bottoms, Adam & Adam	27	4
Scallops, ascending, up breakouts	26	4
Scallops, descending, up breakouts	17	4

The next table shows the median rise of chart patterns from the breakout price to the ultimate high. Usually, the median value is below the average rise, so consider it the return experienced investors could make if they traded chart patterns often enough. However, the values do not include any trading costs or dividends.

Median Rise Performance Sorted by the Median Rise

Description	Median Rise (%)
Triangles, descending, up breakouts	34
Head-and-shoulders bottoms	31
Rectangles, up breakouts	29
Double bottoms, Eve & Eve	28

Median Rise Performance Sorted by the Median Rise (*continued*)

Description	Median Rise (%)
Triangles, symmetrical, up breakouts	28
Triangles, ascending, up breakouts	27
Triple bottoms	26
Broadening tops, up breakouts	25
Double bottoms, Eve & Adam	25
Double bottoms, Adam & Eve	24
Double bottoms, Adam & Adam	23
Scallops, ascending, up breakouts	21
Scallops, descending, up breakouts	13

The percentage of chart patterns rising more than 50% appears in the accompanying table. Clearly, you want to select a chart pattern that presents the most bang for the buck, so select those near the top of the list, and avoid trading those near the bottom of the list.

Percentage of Rises over 50% Sorted by Rises Above 50%

Description	Rises over 50% (%)
Triangles, descending, up breakouts	34
Rectangles, up breakouts	29
Triangles, symmetrical, up breakouts	28
Double bottoms, Eve & Eve	27
Head-and-shoulders bottoms	26
Triangles, ascending, up breakouts	25
Double bottoms, Adam & Eve	24
Triple bottoms	23
Broadening tops, up breakouts	21
Double bottoms, Eve & Adam	21
Scallops, ascending, up breakouts	17
Double bottoms, Adam & Adam	16
Scallops, descending, up breakouts	13

The following table shows the failure rate for a given price rise, sorted by the 15% column. For example, 20% of the descending triangles with upward breakouts had prices that failed to climb more than 15% after the breakout.

Determine what your trading costs are, then add how much you want to make. Select a chart pattern that has the fewest failures for your return. For example, say your trading costs amount to 5%, and you want to make at least 20% on average. Which chart patterns show the lowest failure rates for a 25% (5% + 20%) rise? Select the answers from the values in the table.

Maximum Price Rise Versus Failure Rate Sorted by the 15% Column

Description	5% (%)	10% (%)	15% (%)	20% (%)	25% (%)	30% (%)	35% (%)	50% (%)	75% (%)
Triangles, descending, up breakouts	3	9	20	28	39	46	51	66	79
Head-and-shoulders bottoms	3	12	25	33	41	50	58	73	86
Triangles, ascending, up breakouts	6	17	25	38	48	54	61	75	85
Triangles, symmetrical, up breakouts	5	15	27	39	45	52	56	72	85
Broadening tops, up breakouts	8	19	28	43	51	58	64	79	88
Rectangles, up breakouts	10	19	28	37	43	52	58	71	83
Double bottoms, Adam & Eve	6	15	29	39	51	58	64	76	91
Double bottoms, Eve & Adam	4	17	30	37	50	59	64	79	88
Double bottoms, Eve & Eve	4	18	30	35	46	56	60	72	83
Triple bottoms	6	17	30	40	49	55	61	77	86
Scallops, ascending, up breakouts	11	22	32	44	55	64	70	83	92
Double bottoms, Adam & Adam	6	18	34	47	53	59	66	84	91
Scallops, descending, up breakouts	31	43	55	62	69	72	79	87	94

The next table shows the horizon failure rate, sorted by the 2-months' column. The horizon failure rate is a count of the number of formations that have prices below the breakout price at the end of the selected period. For example, at the end of 2 months, 13% of the descending triangles with upward breakouts had closing prices below the breakout price. A common use for the table is to determine which chart pattern *signal* is strongest, that is, has the lowest failure rate over time and to determine when the strength weakens (the failure rate rises). Descending triangles with upward breakouts seem to be the best performers because their horizon failure rate remains the lowest over time. After 3 weeks, however, the failure rate nearly doubles (rising from 6% to 11%), suggesting the signals weaken, and it might be wise to sell before month's end.

Horizon Failure Rate Sorted by the 2-Months' Column

Description	1 Week (%)	2 Weeks (%)	3 Weeks (%)	1 Month (%)	2 Months (%)	3 Months (%)	6 Months (%)
Triangles, descending, up breakouts	4	6	6	11	13	17	20
Rectangles, up breakouts	19	21	23	22	27	31	31
Triangles, ascending, up breakouts	10	15	20	22	27	30	30
Head-and-shoulders bottoms	17	23	21	22	28	25	33
Double bottoms, Eve & Eve	30	26	28	31	30	31	39
Triple bottoms	30	32	33	30	31	31	34
Double bottoms, Adam & Eve	37	32	27	31	32	33	36
Triangles, symmetrical, up breakouts	8	16	20	24	32	33	31
Double bottoms, Adam & Adam	34	28	29	30	33	45	38
Double bottoms, Eve & Adam	27	25	35	34	34	38	41
Scallops, ascending, up breakouts	30	34	32	33	35	37	41
Broadening tops, up breakouts	23	29	28	28	37	40	41
Scallops, descending, up breakouts	42	48	49	54	55	59	57

The following table shows the performance after a breakout from a chart pattern according to the breakout price within the yearly high—low range (split into thirds). Those chart patterns with the breakout near the yearly low are the most numerous, thus, the best performing.

Yearly Price Range Performance Sorted by the Average Rise

Description	Best Performing	Average Rise (%)
Scallops, ascending, up breakouts	Lowest third	52
Triangles, descending, up breakouts	Lowest third	44
Rectangles, up breakouts	Lowest third	42
Double bottoms, Eve & Eve	Lowest third	41
Triangles, symmetrical, up breakouts	Lowest third	40
Triple bottoms	Highest third	39
Double bottoms, Adam & Eve	Lowest third	38
Broadening tops, up breakouts	Highest third	37
Triangles, ascending, up breakouts	Highest third	37
Head-and-shoulders bottoms	Highest third	36
Double bottoms, Eve & Adam	Middle third	35
Double bottoms, Adam & Adam	Lowest third	32
Scallops, descending, up breakouts	Lowest third	23

The performance from chart patterns according to the formation height as a percentage of the breakout price appears in the next table. Tall chart patterns outperform short ones most of the time.

Formation Height Performance Sorted by the Average Rise

Description	Best Performing	Average Rise (%)
Triangles, descending, up breakouts	Tall	53
Triangles, ascending, up breakouts	Tall	51
Rectangles, up breakouts	Tall	50
Triangles, symmetrical, up breakouts	Tall	48
Broadening tops, up breakouts	Tall	42
Head-and-shoulders bottoms	Tall	39
Double bottoms, Eve & Eve	Short	38
Double bottoms, Adam & Eve	Tall	36
Triple bottoms	Short	36
Double bottoms, Adam & Adam	Tall	33
Double bottoms, Eve & Adam	Tall	33
Scallops, ascending, up breakouts	Tall	31
Scallops, descending, up breakouts	Tall	23

The following table shows the average rise after the breakout, according to the volume trend measured from the formation start to the formation end.

Performance nearly splits between a rising volume trend and a falling one, but the falling volume trend wins by a count of 7 to 6.

Volume Trend Performance Sorted by the Average Rise

Description	Best Performing Volume Trend	Average Rise (%)
Triangles, descending, up breakouts	Rising	48
Double bottoms, Eve & Eve	Rising	39
Triangles, ascending, up breakouts	Rising	39
Rectangles, up breakouts	Rising	37
Triangles, symmetrical, up breakouts	Rising	37
Broadening tops, up breakouts	Falling	36
Double bottoms, Adam & Eve	Falling	35
Head-and-shoulders bottoms	Falling	35
Triple bottoms	Falling	35
Double bottoms, Eve & Adam	Falling	31
Double bottoms, Adam & Adam	Falling	29
Scallops, ascending, up breakouts	Rising	27
Scallops, descending, up breakouts	Falling	17

The next table shows the average rise according to the breakout volume. Heavy (above-average) breakout volume seems to propel prices higher than light (average or below-average) breakout volume.

Breakout Volume Performance Sorted by the Average Rise

Description	Best Performing Volume	Average Rise (%)
Rectangles, up breakouts	Heavy	47
Triangles, ascending, up breakouts	Heavy	46
Double bottoms, Eve & Eve	Heavy	44
Triangles, descending, up breakouts	Light	42
Triangles, symmetrical, up breakouts	Heavy	41
Head-and-shoulders bottoms	Heavy	39
Broadening tops, up breakouts	Heavy	38
Double bottoms, Adam & Adam	Heavy	36
Triple bottoms	Heavy	35
Double bottoms, Adam & Eve	Heavy	34
Double bottoms, Eve & Adam	Light	33
Scallops, ascending, up breakouts	Heavy	31
Scallops, descending, up breakouts	Heavy	23

The throwback frequency for each chart pattern appears in the following table. Since a throwback often impedes performance, select a chart pattern with a low throwback rate. For those patterns showing a high throwback rate, consider waiting for the throwback to complete and prices to start rising again before buying.

Throwback Frequency Sorted by Frequency

Description	Throwback Frequency (%)
Triangles, descending, up breakouts	29
Head-and-shoulders bottoms	40
Triple bottoms	50
Rectangles, up breakouts	51
Triangles, symmetrical, up breakouts	51
Triangles, ascending, up breakouts	52
Double bottoms, Eve & Eve	55
Double bottoms, Adam & Eve	59
Double bottoms, Eve & Adam	59
Double bottoms, Adam & Adam	65
Broadening tops, up breakouts	Not measured
Scallops, ascending, up breakouts	Not measured
Scallops, descending, up breakouts	Not measured

The following table shows how often a bull trap occurs. Since a bull trap means a rise of less than 10% before a trend change, select chart patterns that have a low bull trap frequency, then pray.

Bull Trap Frequency Sorted by Frequency

Description	Bull Trap Frequency (%)
Head-and-shoulders bottoms	9
Triangles, descending, up breakouts	9
Double bottoms, Adam & Eve	11
Triple bottoms	12
Double bottoms, Eve & Adam	13
Broadening tops, up breakouts	14
Double bottoms, Eve & Eve	14
Double bottoms, Adam & Adam	15
Triangles, symmetrical, up breakouts	15
Triangles, ascending, up breakouts	17
Scallops, ascending, up breakouts	19
Rectangles, up breakouts	20
Scallops, descending, up breakouts	43

The following table shows whether performance improves after a price gap or no price gap according to the resulting average rise after the breakout, sorted by the average rise with gaps column. For several chart patterns, the performance after a gap is close to the no gap performance.

Performance after a Price Gap Sorted by the Average Rise with Gaps

Description	Best Performing	Average Rise with Gaps (%)	Average Rise Without Gaps (%)
Triangles, descending, up breakouts	Gap	52	40
Rectangles, up breakouts	Gap	42	35
Double bottoms, Eve & Eve	Gap	41	35
Head-and-shoulders bottoms	No difference	34	34
Triple bottoms	No difference	34	34
Triangles, symmetrical, up breakouts	No gap	33	36
Double bottoms, Eve & Adam	No difference	30	30
Double bottoms, Adam & Adam	Gap	29	27
Double bottoms, Adam & Eve	No Gap	26	33
Scallops, ascending, up breakouts	No gap	25	26
Scallops, descending, up breakouts	Gap	19	16
Broadening tops, up breakouts	Not measured	Not measured	Not measured
Triangles, ascending, up breakouts	Not measured	Not measured	Not measured

The average performance of chart patterns when the Standard & Poor's 500 Index was rising or falling between the day the chart pattern started and the day the pattern ended appears in the next table. The statistics in this book suggest that a falling market while the chart pattern is under construction, followed by a rising market trend thereafter, results in the best chart pattern performance.

Market Direction Performance Sorted by the Average Rise

Description	Best Performing	Average Rise (%)
Rectangles, up breakouts	Falling market	48
Triangles, descending, up breakouts	Falling market	42
Triangles, symmetrical, up breakouts	Falling market	39
Double bottoms, Eve & Eve	Rising market	38
Broadening tops, up breakouts	Rising market	36
Head-and-shoulders bottoms	Rising market	35
Triangles, ascending, up breakouts	Falling market	35
Triple bottoms	Rising market	35
Double bottoms, Adam & Eve	Falling market	32
Double bottoms, Eve & Adam	Falling market	31
Double bottoms, Adam & Adam	Rising market	29
Scallops, ascending, up breakouts	Rising market	26
Scallops, descending, up breakouts	Falling market	18

The market capitalization with the highest average percentage rise for each chart pattern appears in the following table. Size matters, and the small ones win; they dominate the list.

Market Capitalization Performance Sorted by the Average Rise

Description	Best Performing Market Cap	Average Rise (%)
Triangles, descending, up breakouts	Small	49
Rectangles, up breakouts	Small	45
Head-and-shoulders bottoms	Small	42
Triangles, ascending, up breakouts	Small	41
Double bottoms, Eve & Eve	Small	39
Triangles, symmetrical, up breakouts	Small	38
Broadening tops, up breakouts	Small or large	36
Triple bottoms	Small or large	36
Double bottoms, Adam & Eve	Mid	34
Double bottoms, Eve & Adam	Small	32
Double bottoms, Adam & Adam	Mid	31
Scallops, ascending, up breakouts	Small	31
Scallops, descending, up breakouts	Small	21

This next table shows the average rise according to the scores for each chart pattern. Note how wide the differences are between scores above zero compared to those below zero.

Score Performance Sorted by the Average Rise of Scores Above Zero

Description	Scores above Zero (%)	Scores below Zero (%)
Rectangles, up breakouts	55	22
Triangles, descending, up breakouts	53	27
Triangles, ascending, up breakouts	50	21
Triple bottoms	49	25
Head-and-shoulders bottoms	48	24
Double bottoms, Eve & Eve	47	25
Triangles, symmetrical, up breakouts	46	19
Double bottoms, Eve & Adam	45	24
Double bottoms, Adam & Adam	45	18
Double bottoms, Adam & Eve	44	19
Broadening tops, up breakouts	38	21
Scallops, ascending, up breakouts	35	18
Scallops, descending, up breakouts	34	10

BEARISH CHART PATTERNS

The following table shows the average decline after a breakout according to the price trend leading to the chart pattern. For many chart patterns, a short-term trend leading to the pattern results in the best performance after the breakout.

Price Trend Leading to the Chart Pattern and Resulting
Performance Sorted by the Average Decline

Description	Best Performing Trend Term	Average Decline (%)
Diamonds, down breakouts	Short	25
Head-and-shoulders tops	Short	24
Triangles, symmetrical, down breakouts	Short	23
Double tops, Eve & Eve	Short	22
Triple tops	Intermediate	22
Triangles, ascending, down breakouts	Short	21
Double tops, Adam & Adam	Intermediate	20
Triangles, descending, down breakouts	Short	20
Double tops, Eve & Adam	Intermediate	18
Scallops, descending, down breakouts	Short	18
Broadening tops, down breakouts	Intermediate	17
Double tops, Adam & Eve	Short	17
Scallops, ascending, down breakouts	Short	16

The next table shows the general performance of chart patterns measured from the breakout price to the ultimate low along with the change in the Standard & Poor's 500 Index over the same time. After factoring trading costs and dividend payments into the results, shorting a stock does not appear worth undertaking the unlimited risk of a short position. Have a very good reason for shorting a stock.

Average Decline Performance Sorted by the Average Decline

Description	Average Decline (%)	S&P Change (%)
Diamonds, down breakouts	22	+3
Head-and-shoulders tops	21	+1
Triangles, symmetrical, down breakouts	20	−2
Triple tops	20	−2
Triangles, ascending, down breakouts	19	0
Double tops, Adam & Adam	18	+1
Double tops, Eve & Eve	18	+2
Triangles, descending, down breakouts	18	−1
Broadening tops, down breakouts	16	−2
Double tops, Eve & Adam	16	+1
Scallops, descending, down breakouts	16	−1
Double tops, Adam & Eve	15	+1
Scallops, ascending, down breakouts	12	0

The median decline of chart patterns from the breakout price to the ultimate low appears in the next table.

Median Decline Performance Sorted by the Median Decline

Description	Median Decline (%)
Diamonds, down breakouts	21
Triangles, ascending, down breakouts	19
Head-and-shoulders tops	18
Triangles, symmetrical, down breakouts	18
Triangles, descending, down breakouts	17
Triple tops	17
Double tops, Eve & Eve	15
Scallops, descending, down breakouts	15
Broadening tops, down breakouts	14
Double tops, Adam & Adam	14
Double tops, Eve & Adam	14
Double tops, Adam & Eve	13
Scallops, ascending, down breakouts	11

The following table shows the percentage of chart patterns declining more than 50%. Perhaps the 50% benchmark for downward breakouts is too steep, as few stocks decline that far. Again, these data emphasize the inherent risk of shorting a stock—the potential gains are limited.

Percentage of Declines Above 50% Sorted by Declines Above 50%

Description	Declines More Than 50% (%)
Triangles, symmetrical, down breakouts	4
Broadening tops, down breakouts	3
Diamonds, down breakouts	3
Triangles, ascending, down breakouts	3
Double tops, Adam & Adam	2
Double tops, Eve & Adam	2
Double tops, Eve & Eve	2
Head-and-shoulders tops	2
Triangles, descending, down breakouts	2
Triple tops	2
Double tops, Adam & Eve	1
Scallops, ascending, down breakouts	1
Scallops, descending, down breakouts	1

Shown in the next table is the failure rate for a given price decline, sorted by the 15% column. For example, 28% of the diamonds with downward breakouts had prices that failed to drop more than 15% after the breakout.

Maximum Price Decline Versus Failure Rate Sorted by the 15% Column

Description	5% (%)	10% (%)	15% (%)	20% (%)	25% (%)	30% (%)	35% (%)	50% (%)
Diamonds, down breakouts	4	16	28	47	65	75	83	96
Head-and-shoulders tops	6	18	39	57	69	78	86	98
Triangles, ascending, down breakouts	6	24	40	55	70	79	90	97
Triangles, symmetrical, down breakouts	5	24	42	59	74	83	89	96
Triangles, descending, down breakouts	7	27	43	62	75	84	90	98
Triple tops	9	26	45	60	72	81	89	98
Double tops, Eve & Eve	13	32	49	67	77	82	88	98
Scallops, descending, down breakouts	13	31	50	67	80	87	92	99
Broadening tops, down breakouts	13	33	54	70	80	86	91	97
Double tops, Adam & Adam	11	33	56	62	71	81	90	98

Maximum Price Decline Versus Failure Rate Sorted
by the 15% Column (*continued*)

Description	5% (%)	10% (%)	15% (%)	20% (%)	25% (%)	30% (%)	35% (%)	50% (%)
Double tops, Adam & Eve	15	35	56	68	79	87	93	98
Double tops, Eve & Adam	12	36	56	69	80	89	92	98
Scallops, ascending, down breakouts	27	45	63	76	84	91	96	99

The following table shows the horizon failure rate, sorted by the 2 months' column. The horizon failure rate is a count of the number of formations that have closing prices above the breakout price at the end of the selected period. For example, at the end of 2 months, 15% of the descending triangles with downward breakouts had closing prices above the breakout price.

Horizon Failure Rate Sorted by the 2-Months' Column

Description	1 Week (%)	2 Weeks (%)	3 Weeks (%)	1 Month (%)	2 Months (%)	3 Months (%)	6 Months (%)
Triangles, descending, down breakouts	7	9	11	12	15	14	20
Diamonds, down breakouts	8	8	12	15	24	30	36
Triangles, ascending, down breakouts	6	7	12	16	28	36	44
Head-and-shoulders tops	18	21	20	23	34	38	43
Triangles, symmetrical, down breakouts	12	15	21	25	35	40	44
Scallops, descending, down breakouts	25	29	32	36	38	41	46
Triple tops	33	33	33	33	40	45	43
Double tops, Eve & Adam	35	35	34	40	44	51	51
Double tops, Eve & Eve	32	38	40	45	44	49	57
Double tops, Adam & Eve	41	41	46	44	52	54	61
Double tops, Adam & Adam	40	44	40	47	53	56	50
Broadening tops, down breakouts	34	35	36	44	55	46	47
Scallops, ascending, down breakouts	49	48	49	51	61	62	59

The next table shows the performance after a breakout from a chart pattern according to the breakout price within the yearly high–low range (split into thirds). Depending on how you count, either the lowest third or the highest third of the yearly price range appears most often in the table.

Yearly Price Range Performance Sorted by the Average Decline

Description	Best Performing Third	Average Decline (%)
Diamonds, down breakouts	Lowest	29
Triangles, symmetrical, down breakouts	Lowest	24
Scallops, descending, down breakouts	Highest	23
Triple tops	Highest	22
Head-and-shoulders tops	Middle	21
Double tops, Eve & Eve	Highest	20
Triangles, ascending, down breakouts	Lowest	20
Broadening tops, down breakouts	Lowest	19
Triangles, descending, down breakouts	Lowest	19
Double tops, Adam & Adam	Highest	18
Double tops, Eve & Adam	Highest	18
Double tops, Adam & Eve	Middle or highest	16
Scallops, ascending, down breakouts	Lowest or highest	14

The performance from chart patterns according to the formation height as a percentage of the breakout price appears in the following table. Clearly, tall chart patterns surpass the performance of short ones.

Formation Height Performance Sorted by the Average Decline

Description	Best Performing	Average Decline (%)
Diamonds, down breakouts	Tall	27
Head-and-shoulders tops	Tall	24
Triangles, symmetrical, down breakouts	Tall	24
Triangles, ascending, down breakouts	Tall	22
Triangles, descending, down breakouts	Tall	22
Triple tops	Tall	22
Double tops, Eve & Eve	Tall	20
Double tops, Adam & Adam	Tall	19
Double tops, Eve & Adam	Tall	19
Broadening tops, down breakouts	Tall	17
Scallops, descending, down breakouts	Tall	17
Double tops, Adam & Eve	Tall	16
Scallops, ascending, down breakouts	Tall	16

The following table shows the average decline after the breakout, according to the volume trend measured from the formation start to the formation end. A rising volume trend appears most often in the table.

Volume Trend Performance Sorted by the Average Decline

Description	Best Performing	Average Decline (%)
Diamonds, down breakouts	Rising	23
Triangles, symmetrical, down breakouts	Rising	22
Triple tops	Rising	21
Double tops, Eve & Eve	Falling	20
Head-and-shoulders tops	Rising	20
Triangles, ascending, down breakouts	Falling	20
Double tops, Adam & Adam	Rising	18
Triangles, descending, down breakouts	Falling	18
Double tops, Eve & Adam	Falling	17
Broadening tops, down breakouts	None	16
Double tops, Adam & Eve	Rising	16
Scallops, descending, down breakouts	No difference	16
Scallops, ascending, down breakouts	Rising	13

The next table shows the average decline according to the breakout volume. Clearly, a heavy volume breakout (above average) propels prices further. A light volume breakout is one that appears average or below average.

Breakout Volume Performance Sorted by the Average Decline

Description	Best Performing Breakout Volume	Average Decline (%)
Triangles, symmetrical, down breakouts	Heavy	28
Diamonds, down breakouts	Light	22
Triple tops	Heavy	22
Head-and-shoulders tops	No difference	21
Double tops, Eve & Eve	Heavy	20
Double tops, Adam & Adam	Heavy	19
Scallops, descending, down breakouts	Heavy	19
Triangles, ascending, down breakouts	Light	19
Triangles, descending, down breakouts	Heavy	19
Double tops, Adam & Eve	Heavy	18
Broadening tops, down breakouts	Heavy	17
Double tops, Eve & Adam	Heavy	17
Scallops, ascending, down breakouts	Heavy	14

The pullback frequency for each chart pattern appears in the following table. Since a pullback takes energy away from prices moving in the original breakout direction, a low pullback frequency is best.

Pullback Frequency (%)

Description	Frequency (%)
Triangles, ascending, down breakouts	43
Head-and-shoulders tops	47
Triple tops	49
Triangles, symmetrical, down breakouts	51
Diamonds, down breakouts	54
Triangles, descending, down breakouts	55
Double tops, Adam & Adam	57
Double tops, Adam & Eve	58
Double tops, Eve & Adam	59
Double tops, Eve & Eve	61
Broadening tops, down breakouts	Not measured
Scallops, ascending, down breakouts	Not measured
Scallops, descending, down breakouts	Not measured

The following table shows how often a bear trap occurs. A bear trap happens when prices drop by less than 10%, then change trend and climb. A low bear trap rate is best.

Bear Trap Frequency Sorted by Frequency

Description	Bear Trap Frequency (%)
Diamonds, down breakouts	16
Head-and-shoulders tops	17
Scallops, descending, down breakouts	21
Triple tops	22
Triangles, ascending, down breakouts	24
Triangles, symmetrical, down breakouts	24
Triangles, descending, down breakouts	26
Double tops, Adam & Adam	28
Broadening tops, down breakouts	29
Double tops, Eve & Eve	30
Double tops, Eve & Adam	32
Double tops, Adam & Eve	34
Scallops, ascending, down breakouts	43

424   Statistics Summary and Analysis

The next table shows whether performance improves after a price gap or no price gap according to the resulting average decline after the breakout, sorted by the average decline with gaps column. Gaps improve performance but often by a small amount.

Performance after a Price Gap Sorted by the Average Decline with Gaps

Description	Best Performing	Average Decline with Gaps (%)	Average Decline Without Gaps (%)
Triple tops	Gap	24	18
Triangles, symmetrical, down breakouts	Gap	23	19
Head-and-shoulders tops	Gap	22	20
Double tops, Adam & Adam	Gap	21	17
Scallops, descending, down breakouts	Gap	21	15
Double tops, Eve & Eve	Gap	19	18
Double tops, Adam & Eve	Gap	18	15
Triangles, descending, down breakouts	Gap	18	17
Diamonds, down breakouts	No gap	18	23
Double tops, Eve & Adam	No gap	15	16
Scallops, ascending, down breakouts	No gap	12	13
Broadening tops, down breakouts	Not measured	Not measured	Not measured
Triangles, ascending, down breakouts	Not measured	Not measured	Not measured

The next table shows the average performance of chart patterns when the Standard & Poor's 500 Index was rising or falling between the day the chart pattern started and the day the pattern ended. A falling market trend appears most often in the table.

Market Direction Performance Sorted by the Average Decline

Description	Best Performing	Average Decline (%)
Diamond tops, down breakouts	Rising market	24
Head-and-shoulders tops	No difference	21
Triple tops	Falling market	21
Double tops, Eve & Eve	Falling market	20
Triangles, ascending, down breakouts	Falling market	20
Triangles, symmetrical, down breakouts	No difference	20
Double tops, Adam & Adam	Falling market	18
Triangles, descending, down breakouts	Falling market	18
Double tops, Adam & Eve	Falling market	17
Double tops, Eve & Adam	Falling market	17
Broadening tops, down breakouts	Rising market	16
Scallops, descending, down breakouts	No difference	16
Scallops, ascending, down breakouts	Rising market	14

The market capitalization with the highest average percentage decline for each chart pattern appears in the following table. For downward breakouts, small caps usually show the largest declines, with large caps retaining most of their value in a falling market.

Market Capitalization Performance Sorted by the Average Decline

Description	Best Performing Market Cap	Average Decline (%)
Diamond tops, down breakouts	Small	27
Head-and-shoulders tops	Small	22
Broadening tops, down breakouts	Small	21
Double tops, Adam & Adam	Small	21
Triangles, symmetrical, down breakouts	Large	21
Triple tops	Small	21
Triangles, ascending, down breakouts	Mid	20
Double tops, Eve & Eve	Mid	19
Triangles, descending, down breakouts	Mid	19
Double tops, Adam & Eve	Small	18
Double tops, Eve & Adam	Small	18
Scallops, descending, down breakouts	Small	18
Scallops, ascending, down breakouts	Mid	15

The final table shows the average decline according to the scores for each chart pattern. Even though declines for bearish chart patterns are meager, the scoring system improves performance as the table shows.

Score Performance Sorted by Scores Above Zero

Description	Scores above Zero (%)	Scores below Zero (%)
Triangles, symmetrical, down breakouts	–29	–16
Diamond tops, down breakouts	–28	–13
Triple tops	–27	–15
Head-and-shoulders tops	–25	–16
Double tops, Adam & Adam	–24	–15
Double tops, Eve & Eve	–24	–17
Broadening tops, down breakouts	–23	–11
Triangles, ascending, down breakouts	–23	–12
Double tops, Adam & Eve	–22	–12
Triangles, descending, down breakouts	–22	–12
Double tops, Eve & Adam	–21	–11
Scallops, descending, down breakouts	–21	–10
Scallops, ascending, down breakouts	–18	–9

Glossary and
Methodology

Since several people have tried to reproduce the statistics in my previous book, *Encyclopedia of Chart Patterns* (Wiley, 2000), I thought it would be a good idea to detail exactly how I came up with the numbers for this book. Much of the methodology changed between books. Thus, *statistical comparisons between the two books may not be valid.* Below is the methodology masquerading as a glossary of terms.

Average rise or decline (ARD).   I measure the rise from the breakout price to the ultimate high or the decline from the breakout price to the ultimate low for each stock, then compute the average. Although the result is an *average* rise or decline, you might consider it a *best-case* result since it assumes an investor opened a position at the breakout price and closed it at the highest daily high or lowest daily low.

The *average rise or decline of successful formations* cited in *Encyclopedia of Chart Patterns* is not directly comparable to the ARD mentioned in this book. When I wrote the *Encyclopedia*, I thought it a good idea at the time to base the ARD on *successful* chart patterns. After all, if you wanted to buy a stock showing an upward breakout from an ascending triangle, you would ignore those breaking out downward. Since I considered gains of less than 5% as failures, they were also excluded from the ARD calculation. This method tended to boost the ARD values; the severity of the effect would depend on the number of 5% failures. In this book, I include *all* rises or declines from any chart pattern breaking out in the selected direction.

Breakout, breakout price.   A breakout occurs when the price *closes* above the highest price (upward breakouts) or below the lowest price (downward breakouts) in the chart pattern, or outside the trendline boundaries. Since breakouts vary for each chart pattern, refer to the associated chapter.

I programmed my computer to find the breakout point when it involved the chart pattern high or low, but I handled trendline breakouts manually. Ascending triangles are an example of when the highest price in the formation represents the breakout price. When prices *close* above the horizontal trendline, a breakout occurs. The price of the horizontal trendline (which is also the highest high in the chart pattern) becomes the breakout price.

When an *upward breakout* occurs at a trendline (at a price other than the formation high), such as in the case of a symmetrical triangle with an upward breakout, I use the *daily low price* on the day of the breakout for measurement purposes. Sometimes, prices gap upward, so the daily low will be the closest price to the trendline.

Downward breakouts follow the same pattern. I use the formation low as the breakout price unless a trendline pierce represents the breakout point. The formation low would be the horizontal trendline in a descending triangle, for example. A trendline breakout would be a downward breakout from a diamond top. In such a case, the daily high price on the day the price closes outside the chart pattern becomes the breakout price. This price is often the closest price to the trendline.

I ignore false or premature breakouts in any computations.

Breakout gap.   This term is what I call a gap that occurs on the breakout day. Usually it is a breakaway gap, one that shows high volume after leaving a consolidation area. For upward price trends, a gap is when today's low price is above yesterday's high. For downward price trends, a gap occurs when today's high price is below yesterday's low.

Breakout volume.   To gauge the breakout volume level, I started a *cumulative total* (not a moving average) beginning 91 days (that is, 3 months, arbitrarily chosen) *before the formation end* and stopped the day *before* the breakout (so more than 91 days may be used if the time between the formation end and breakout is more than a day). I used the running total to determine the average volume over that span. I then computed the volume levels representing very high, high, average, low, and very low volume levels according to the following multipliers.

It is important to note that the testing order is significant.

Volume Level	Multiplier
Very high	More than 5 times the average
High	More than 2 times the average
Very low	Less than or equal to 0.3 times the average
Low	Less than or equal to 0.75 times the average
Average	Everything else

Since I used a computer to make the determination automatic, I arranged the list of multipliers just as in the program. Once the breakout volume passed a particular test, the associated volume level was assigned, beginning with the very high volume test. For example, if the breakout volume was 3.1 times the average volume leading to the breakout, it would flunk the "very high" test but pass the "high" test. Thus, the breakout volume would rank as high.

Since the results from this approach did not always agree with visual inspection, I used the results in groupings, such as "above-average volume" (high or very high volume) compared to "average or below-average volume" (average, low, and very low) both to counter low sample counts and to remove any inspection discrepancy.

Bear trap.   Bear traps occur when prices break out downward but quickly recover. To quantify how often this event occurs, I added the following stipulations. The breakout must be downward. Prices must drop less than 10%, and prices must then rise above the chart pattern top (the highest high in the formation). Only after satisfying those criteria has a bear trap occurred.

How long it takes for a bear trap to occur is usually irrelevant, but tempered by answering the question, "Would the investor be upset with the result?" If prices remained pegged at 7% below the chart pattern for several months, I might conclude that a bear trap did not occur because there was plenty of time to close out the short position with a small gain. This scenario did occur, but very rarely.

Bull trap.   A bull trap occurs when prices break out upward, then reverse course. To investigate how often this occurs, I defined a bull trap as follows: The breakout must be upward. Prices must rise less than 10%, and prices must then decline below the lowest formation low. After meeting those conditions, a bull trap has occurred.

Usually, the time for prices to drop below the chart pattern low was not significant unless it took an unusually long time. For example, if prices climbed by 8% and stayed there for 5 months before declining, I might conclude that there was plenty of opportunity for an investor to sell with a small profit and would not call it a bull trap. This scenario rarely occurred.

Confirmation point, price, or level.   The confirmation point is a price or location that validates a chart pattern. Double bottoms, for example, have a confirmation price equal to the highest high between the two bottoms. If prices fail to rise above the confirmation price before closing below the lowest bottom, then the twin bottom pattern is not a double bottom at all. Waiting for confirmation significantly increases your chances of a profitable trade. You should always wait for confirmation.

Failure rate.   In *Encyclopedia of Chart Patterns*, the failure rate was the number of chart patterns breaking out in an *unexpected* direction plus those breaking out in the *expected* direction but moving less than 5%. In this book, the failure rate includes *all* chart patterns of the selected type breaking out in the selected direction. I measure the percentage change from the breakout price to the ultimate high or ultimate low, then show a frequency distribution of the results in a table called Maximum Price Rise [Decline] Versus Failure Rate.

Failure rate, 5%.   This is the failure rate for stocks breaking out in the expected direction but failing to move more than 5% before reversing course. In the *Encyclopedia of Chart Patterns*, I used the 5% rate to compensate for commissions, SEC fees, slippage, and other trading costs. In this book, I show a range of failure rates. Often, the 5% failure rate is deceptively small as the 10% failure rate is usually double or triple (or more) the 5% rate.

Flat base.   Flat base is a consolidation region in which prices touch or near the same price level multiple times over several weeks or months, and identification is usually easiest on the weekly scale. The bottom of this region appears flat and sometimes forms the base of an impending up move, hence, the name "flat base." Some chart patterns reviewed in this book form after a flat base; the bottom of the chart pattern will usually reside slightly below the flat base level.

Unlike a horizontal consolidation region, a flat base can begin well before the trend start.

Frequency distribution.   This is an easy method to group data to find patterns. For example, if I wanted to create a frequency distribution of the average price rise, I would find the range that the data spanned. Say the results ranged from 1% to 100%. I would label each of 10 bins (10 being a common bin count) with a range. The first bin would count stocks that climbed between 1% and 10%, the second bin would hold results between 11% and 20%, and so forth. Then I would sort the average price rise into the appropriate bin. When finished, I would count the *number* of entries in each bin, thereby giving a frequency distribution—measuring how popular a certain value was. The table labeled Maximum Price Rise [Decline] Versus Failure Rate shows a frequency distribution.

Horizontal consolidation region.   A horizontal, or almost horizontal, congestion area where prices share a common value for an extended time (usually weeks to months). Flat price tops or flat bottoms are the preferred appearance. I allow price spikes and gaps in time as well as the region spanning or crossing the trend start. Occasionally, a small consolidation region (of a week or so) is actually stronger than it appears because prior minor highs, minor lows, or additional consolidation areas appeared before the trend start. In such a situation, I included the small consolidation region as a valid support or resistance zone due to its apparent strength.

To be significant, the region must appear between the confirmation point (but sometimes I use the formation high or low instead) and the trend start, and must be in the price path. The region acts as a resistance or support zone to further price movement. The first valid consolidation region closest to the chart pattern is the only one considered, not ones further away, nor more than one in a single chart pattern.

Horizon failure rate. Coined by David Ipperciel, the horizon failure rate measures the rate of failure over time. For example, suppose I looked at 10 double bottoms. At the *end* of the first week, 3 of the patterns had prices that closed below the breakout price. As such, they qualify as failures. The horizon failure rate would be 30% (3 out of 10) for week 1. After the second week, say only 2 were below the breakout price (any 2 of the 10). The horizon failure rate would be 20%.

By definition, the horizon failure rate at the end of the first day is 0% since all chart patterns must close above the breakout point or else a breakout has not occurred. I measure the percentage rise or decline from the breakout price to the *closing price at the end* of the chosen period, that is, at the end of week 1, week 2, and so forth.

Internal partial decline. An internal partial decline is the same as a partial decline only the breakout fails to occur and the chart pattern continues developing. In other words, two consecutive trendline touches occur on the same side with a *minor low* between them. The minor low should *not* come close to or touch the opposite trendline.

An internal partial decline only occurs *after* the chart pattern is valid. For example, a rectangle is valid after prices touch each trendline twice. That way, an investor would first recognize a *valid* rectangle pattern, see the partial decline form, then place a trade. When prices failed to break out and crossed to the opposite trendline, the partial decline would become an internal partial decline.

Internal partial rise. An internal partial rise occurs *within* a chart pattern after prices touch a lower trendline, rise, then return to the lower trendline without coming close to or touching the opposite trendline. In other words, two consecutive trendline touches occur on the same side with a minor high between them. An internal partial rise is the same as a partial rise only a breakout does not follow and the chart pattern continues developing.

An internal partial rise occurs only *after* the chart pattern is valid. For example, a rectangle is valid after prices touch each trendline twice. With that method, an investor would first recognize a *valid* rectangle pattern, see the partial rise form, and place a trade. When prices failed to break out and crossed to the opposite trendline, the partial rise would become an internal partial rise.

Linear regression. Used to find whether volume is trending upward or downward over the course of the formation, from formation start to its end, not to the breakout (in some chart patterns, the formation end is also the breakout). Simply put, linear regression fits a straight line to a series of points; the slope of the resulting line gives the trend. The actual linear regression equation (also called least squares) is beyond the scope of this book, and good math texts usually explain its use. Some spreadsheets call linear regression the trend function.

Market trend. For a definition, see **Standard & Poor's 500 change.** I base the score values on the FS to FE period, that is, from formation start to formation end (not the breakout).

Market capitalization. Market capitalization is the number of shares outstanding multiplied by the current price. The number of shares outstanding commonly appears in financial reports, at the company's Web site, and in financial periodicals and publications.

Instead of the current price, I used the breakout price to put each chart pattern on an equal footing. For example, say ZYX Corp. had 1 million shares outstanding and a $10 breakout price from a triple bottom. The market cap would be $10 million.

I created three categories: small cap (up to $1 billion), mid cap ($1 billion to $5 billion), and large cap (over $5 billion). Thus, ZYX would fit into the small cap category. The dollar categories are commonly recognized divisions.

Median rise or decline. The median rise or median decline is the midrange value such that half the values are above the median and half below. To find the median, first sort the results then select the midrange value.

The median rise or decline value shown in the section titled Inside the Pattern differs from the median rise or decline listed in the Scores section. The Inside the Pattern value uses chart patterns that have an ultimate high or low price. The scoring system requires not only the ultimate high or low price, but the number of shares outstanding, a yearly high or low, and other items used by each table with a score. Only those chart patterns for which all the score data are present are used to compute the median rise or decline listed in the Scores section.

Minor high. A price peak usually separated from other peaks by at least 1 week.

Minor low. A price trough or valley usually separated from other troughs by at least 1 week.

Partial decline. After prices touch a top trendline, they decline but do not touch (or come that close to) a lower trendline before forming a distinct minor low and usually staging an immediate upward breakout. The partial decline must be close enough to the end of the chart pattern so that if prices were to continue downward, one could reasonably argue that the decline would be part of the formation. Partial declines must begin before the actual breakout and form after a valid chart pattern appears (in other words, after the minimum number of trendline touches).

Partial decline failure. A partial decline failure is when a partial decline occurs but the breakout is downward.

Partial rise.   After prices touch a lower trendline, they rise but do not touch (or come that close to) the upper trendline before forming a distinct minor high and usually staging an immediate downward breakout. The partial rise must form close enough to the end of the formation so that if prices were to continue upward, one could reasonably argue that it would be part of the formation. The partial rise must begin before the breakout and form near the end of a valid chart pattern (in other words, after the minimum number of trendline touches).

Partial rise failure.   A partial rise failure is when a partial rise occurs but the breakout is upward.

Preformation rise.   A preformation rise is when the long-term or intermediate-term price trend is down and there is a sharp, quick rise leading to the formation, usually lasting less than 1 week.

Premature breakout.   A premature breakout occurs when prices close outside the formation trendline boundary but quickly return. A premature breakout cannot be distinguished from a valid breakout when it occurs. In this book, I use the actual breakout and ignore any premature breakouts.

Pullback.   A pullback occurs after a *downward* breakout when prices return to, or come very close to, the breakout price or trendline. I compare the daily high price during the pullback with the breakout price or trendline boundary to determine whether a pullback occurred. Also, there must be white space between the breakout point and the pullback low. This rule prevents the pullback term from being applied to prices clustering near the breakout price.

   To determine how high prices climb after a pullback, I use the first minor high formed at or above the breakout price as the trend end. Although this may not actually be the trend end, to an investor it would appear that the pullback has ended.

Scores.   To determine a score, I use a comparison with the average rise or decline for all chart patterns of a particular type and breakout direction (such as all ascending triangles with upward breakouts) with the result in each table. If the result is above the average, then it scores +1; below average scores –1, and ties or values close to the average score zero.

   For example, the following table shows the average performance of a chart pattern sorted by the price trend leading to the pattern. Suppose the average of 200 patterns is 33.2%. The short-term trend would score zero because the result is very close to the average; intermediate-term scores –1 because the result is below the average, and long-term scores +1 since the result is above the average.

Trend Start to Formation Start	Result	Score
Short term (0 to 3 months)	33%	0
Intermediate term (3 to 6 months)	29%	−1
Long term (over 6 months)	41%	+1

The performance of ascending scallops with upward breakouts ranked by individual score appears in the following table. I show this example to make a few points about the scoring system. Only odd number scores appear because the seven tables in Chapter 13 count +1 or −1 scores. Thus, for this chart pattern, even number scores do not occur.

Scores above zero perform much better than scores below zero. As the score value declines, so does the percentage rise. *The higher the score, the better the performance; the lower the score, the worse the performance.* The average rise for all ascending scallops is 26%, about where the zero score would be.

Score	Rise (%)	Samples
+7	38	6
+5	43	49
+3	35	85
+1	33	97
−1	22	82
−3	20	73
−5	13	37
−7	4	6
Average	26	

The performance shown in the table is not unique to ascending scallops. All the chart patterns reviewed in this book show a similar performance trend.

Sample size.   In many cases, the sample size varies from the total formation count because of unavailable data. For example, if a stock confirmed a triple bottom a week ago, there is a good chance that it has not climbed to the ultimate high. In such a case, I exclude the chart pattern from some statistics because of the missing information.

Standard & Poor's 500 change.   I take snapshots of the S&P 500 Index at various dates, usually when the chart pattern starts, the chart pattern ends, and when the *stock* (not the S&P) price reaches the ultimate high or ultimate low after a chart pattern. If the S&P shows a positive change over any two dates, I conclude that the index was rising over the measurement period. The same applies when a negative change occurs: I assume the index was falling.

In the computation, I use the closing price of the S&P on the day the chart pattern started, ended, and use the daily *high* of the S&P on the day stock prices reached their ultimate high, and the S&P daily *low* price on the day stock prices reached their ultimate low.

Statistically significant.   Most of the performance differences listed in the various tables of this book are statistically significant to within 5%. This means the results are probably not due to chance. However, the performance and scoring of chart patterns showing low sample counts may change if more samples become available.

Tall or short patterns.   I measure the formation height by taking the difference between the highest high and the lowest low in the chart pattern. Then, I divide the difference by the breakout price to get a percentage of height to price. After sorting the results, I use the median (midrange) value as the difference between short (values below the median) or tall (values above the median).

Term, short, intermediate, or long.   I define a short-term trend as one that lasts up to 3 months. Intermediate-term trends last between 3 and 6 months. Long-term trends are those that last more than 6 months.

Throwback.   A throwback occurs after an *upward* breakout when prices decline to, or come very close to, the breakout price or the formation trendline. I use the daily low price of the throwback compared with the breakout price or the trendline boundary to make the determination.

To judge where the throwback stops, I use the closest minor low on or below the breakout price. Although the actual trend may not end at this point, an investor holding the stock could correctly assume that the throwback has ended.

Trend Start.   Where does the price trend start? To find the start, I begin at the formation start and move backward in time. If prices *climb* leading away from the formation (remember, working backward in time), I find the *highest high* before prices *close* 20% or more below the highest high. When this occurs, the highest high marks the trend start. I use the highest high to closing price measure because in a few cases, it more accurately marks the trend start.

If prices *drop* leading away from the chart pattern (working backward in time), I find the lowest low before prices *close* 20% or more above the lowest low. When that occurs, the lowest low marks the trend start.

When the trend start could not be determined because the data I used did not go back far enough in time, the chart pattern was excluded from any computation requiring the trend start.

Ultimate high.   I determine the ultimate high by looking after the breakout for the highest high before prices decline by 20% or more. The 20% decline measures from the highest high to the *close*. I use the closing price instead of the low price because, on rare occasions, the low prematurely signals the end of a trend.

I stop looking if prices *close* below the formation low, assuming that a stop-loss order would be placed at that location. Only rarely did the formation low cut off the search for the ultimate high.

If the chart pattern had not suffered a 20% decline before the end of the data, I excluded it. This is different from *Encyclopedia of Chart Patterns*, where I used the highest high before the data ended as the proxy. Why? At the time, I felt excluding samples unduly penalized performance (because it excluded long-term star performers). With this book, I believe that performance either suffers or gains, depending on the location of the chart pattern. Since the scoring system results may change depending on which samples are included, it is best to go with what you know. So, I exclude samples in which the ultimate high is unknown.

Ultimate low.   I determine the ultimate low by looking after the breakout for the lowest low before a minimum 20% price rise, measured from the lowest low to the *close*. I use the close instead of the high because, on rare occasions, the high prematurely signals the end of a trend.

I stop looking when prices close above the formation high, assuming that an investor would have placed a stop-loss order at that price. Only rarely did the search get cut off because prices climbed above the formation high.

If I ran out of data before prices climbed by 20%, I excluded the sample. This method is different from *Encyclopedia of Chart Patterns*. There, I used the lowest low price to that point as the proxy. At the time, I felt excluding samples unduly penalized performance (because it excluded long-term star performers). With this book, I believe that performance either suffers or gains, depending on the location of the chart pattern. Since the scoring system values may change depending on which samples are included, it is best to go with what you know. So, I exclude samples in which the ultimate low is not known.

Volume trend.   I use linear regression on the volume data to determine the slope of the line. A rising volume trend means volume generally increases over time; a falling volume trend is one that recedes over time.

Yearly price range.   To determine the yearly price range, I start from the *day before the breakout* and find the highest high and lowest low over the prior 12 months. The yearly price range is the difference between the yearly high and low price. In this book, I divided the yearly price range into thirds and compared the breakout price with each third.

Index

Numbers in **bold** type refer to chapters; numbers in *italic* type refer to illustrations.